MIRACLES
of the —
NEW
TESTAMENT

MIRACLES
of the
NEW
TESTAMENT

A GUIDE TO THE SYMBOLIC MESSAGES

ALONZO L. GASKILL

CFI
An imprint of Cedar Fort, Inc.
Springville, Utah

ISBN 13: 978-1-4621-1464-1

Published by CFI, an imprint of Cedar Fort, Inc.
2373 W. 700 S., Springville, UT 84663
Distributed by Cedar Fort, Inc., www.cedarfort.com

LIBRARY OF CONGRESS CATALOGING-IN-PUBLICATION DATA

Gaskill, Alonzo L., author.
Miracles of the New Testament : a guide to the symbolic messages / Alonzo L. Gaskill.
    pages cm
Includes bibliographical references and index.
Summary: Examines the miracles in the New Testament and what we can learn from each one.
ISBN 978-1-4621-1464-1 (alk. paper)
1. Jesus Christ--Miracles. 2. Bible. New Testament--Criticism, interpretation, etc. I. Title.

BX8643.J4G36 2014
226.7'06--dc23

                    2014027744

Cover design by Shawnda T. Craig
Cover design © 2014 Lyle Mortimer
Edited and typeset by Jessica B. Ellingson

Printed in the United States of America

10 9 8 7 6 5 4 3 2 1

Printed on acid-free paper

In memory of Dr. Joseph Fielding McConkie
(1941–2013), who first encouraged us to
think symbolically.

OTHER BOOKS by ALONZO L. GASKILL

LOVE AT HOME:
INSIGHTS FROM THE LIVES OF LATTER-DAY PROPHETS

THE TRUTH ABOUT EDEN:
UNDERSTANDING THE FALL AND OUR TEMPLE EXPERIENCE

SACRED SYMBOLS:
FINDING MEANING IN RITES, RITUALS & ORDINANCES

THE LOST LANGUAGE OF SYMBOLISM—AN ESSENTIAL GUIDE FOR RECOGNIZING AND INTERPRETING SYMBOLS OF THE GOSPEL

ODDS ARE YOU'RE GOING TO BE EXALTED— EVIDENCE THAT THE PLAN OF SALVATION WORKS!

KNOW YOUR RELIGIONS, VOLUME 1—A COMPARATIVE LOOK AT MORMONISM AND CATHOLICISM

CONTENTS

CONTENTS

ACKNOWLEDGMENTS

I express my sincere appreciation to the numerous individuals who reviewed this manuscript and made helpful suggestions. Chief among them are Paul E. Damron, Professor Gerald Hansen Jr., Dr. Richard G. Moore, Lani Moore, Lisa Spice, and Dr. Charles L. Swift, in addition to those who performed the "blind reviews" of the text. I have earnestly sought to incorporate all of their suggestions or, at the very least, to clarify what I have written based on the comments and recommendations of those who were kind enough to offer their time and expertise. Their suggestions and insights have greatly improved the manuscript.

INTRODUCTION

A good, universal definition of what constitutes a "miracle" is difficult to come by. By that I mean, most will acknowledge that miracles are those events that are largely unexplainable by *known* natural laws, yet what falls into that category is not always agreed upon. Should we, for example, include visions in a list of scriptural miracles? Surely they are miraculous events. Or what about the manifestation of any of the gifts of the Spirit, such as speaking in tongues or prophesying? Those are also quite miraculous. If we speak technically, must we not acknowledge that events largely taken for granted—such as the birth of a human being—are miracles also? Thus, the definition of what constitutes a miracle is not always cut and dry, and the ability to create a complete list of New Testament miracles is therefore difficult.

That being the case, the list of miracles we will examine here largely ignore traditional life events, such as giving birth or using the human brain to think and reason—even though most readers will feel a measure of awe at God's handiwork manifest through such events. Instead, our focus will be on that which most would acknowledge as extraordinary, on those events in the New Testament that confront us with a sense that God's power is absolutely incomprehensible and unexplainable to finite humans. We will look at stories where Jesus and the Apostles employ the powers of heaven to change lives, heal the hopeless, and cast out demons. We will examine miracles that evidence that God is in charge and what He wills certainly comes to pass.

One of the difficulties in a study like this has to do with the approach we should take. Is there a place for a systematic look at the miracles? Surely there is. But which approach or system should we employ? It is no secret, for example, that John's approach to the life, teachings, and miracles of Jesus is quite different from that of Matthew, Mark, and Luke (whom we typically refer to as "the synoptics"). Even within John, where scholars consistently see an "orderly framework" of symbolism, not all interpreters agree on what exactly his intended "system" or "orderly approach" is. In their *Dictionary of Biblical Imagery*, Leland Ryken, James Wilhoit, and Tremper Longman highlight a few of the various approaches to John's symbolism common among scholars today. They point out that some commentators see John as presenting an event (or sign), which he then interprets by a discourse that follows the miracle or sign. (For example, Jesus's request for a drink from the Samaritan woman is followed by His discourse on His being the Water of Life.) Other scholars see John instead linking a discourse with two surrounding events. (Christ's discourse on the Light of the World is bookended by the Feast of Tabernacles and its enormous candelabras prior to the discourse, and by giving sight and light to the blind man following the discourse.) An additional approach to John's symbolism is to assume he intended his reader to see a single event or miracle as sandwiched in between two discourses. (He gave a discourse about the Light of the World, then healed a blind man, and then the healed man was expelled from the synagogue, which led Jesus to the discourse on good and bad shepherds.[1])

Which of these approaches is right? Which is the one intended by John? Who's to say? Johannine scholar Raymond E. Brown spoke of the "endless arguments about how to place such scenes in a division of the Gospel" of John, and how the lack of clarity on this matter is evidenced "by the many disputes between scholars about how this book should be divided."[2] It seems that the same may be said of other books of scripture, particularly those most laden with symbolism. Because it is not always evident what is the most accurate or appropriate way to look at the symbolism of a given author or book, our approach here will be to examine each of the miracles individually, and aside from any overarching structure that one scholar or another has proposed. While we acknowledge the value of those structured approaches, it will be best to look at the smaller picture rather than the bigger one for what we are seeking to do here.

The reader should be aware that we are taking the position here that the miracles described in the New Testament actually happened—that they are historical events. And we acknowledge with those who have believing blood that each miracle testifies of Christ and His divine power. Those miracles brought to pass by Jesus's Apostles also testify of His power, but additionally, they remind us that His mantle fell upon those whom He appointed to succeed Him after His Resurrection and Ascension. Though we will examine these for their symbolic value—for their application—we take the position of Augustine (AD 354–430), who said, "We do not, because we allegorize facts, however, lose our belief in them as facts."[3]

While all scriptural miracles *are* testaments of Jesus as the Son of God, the plethora of miracles in the Bible—particularly in the New Testament—seems to suggest that something is intended by them (in addition to witnessing that Jesus is divine). In other words, they certainly testify of Jesus's divinity, but what else might they testify of? What else might they communicate to the reader? As we study the various miracles of the New Testament, it becomes evident that they serve well as great teaching devices, which can help us understand gospel truths buried within the miraculous events. One commentator, Herbert Lockyer, penned this explanation,

> Bible miracles were designed to symbolize the spiritual blessings that God is able and willing to bestow upon our needy hearts. The majority of miracles were acts of mercy and are conspicuous as emblems of redemption. . . . The miracles Christ performed, for example, were parabolical illustrations of the great salvation which He preached.[4]

In other words, Jesus preformed many mighty miracles in the lives of the *ancients*, but each of those can symbolize blessings He has in store for you and me *today*! One of my colleagues here at BYU put it this way,

> It is interesting that while people are concerned about the historicity of symbols, rarely do they concern themselves with the symbolism of history. Just as symbols can correspond to actual events, actual events can be symbolic. I am not just referring to ritual and ceremony, such as the sacrament or temple worship, which are by definition symbolic actions. I am referring to events in everyday life that . . . actually point to meaning outside of themselves.[5]

The trick is seeing the miracles symbolically so that we might draw out of the historic miracle application to our lives today.

It is well-known that in antiquity there were a variety of approaches to reading and applying scripture. For example, the exegetical[6] school of Antioch tended to look for the "literal" or "historic" sense of scripture, whereas the Alexandrian school very much fostered an allegorical approach to the Bible.[7] Which approach was right? I suppose that largely depends on your school of thought and what it is you feel you need from scripture. As one scholar pointed out,

> Every text is capable of different levels of apprehension. At the most elementary level, early Rabbis made a distinction between what was "written" (*kitab*) and what was "read" (*qere*) in the text of Torah; more elaborate distinctions between *peshat* ("literal meaning"), *darash* ("applied or extended meaning"), and *sod* ("mystical meaning") were to follow. Christianity would develop similar distinctions between literal, moral, and allegorical readings of its texts.[8]

Contingent upon what we are using scripture for, or what we need personally from the text, there are a variety of ways to approach the reading and applying of scripture. For example, a word study (of the Greek and Hebrew terms employed) attempts to do something entirely different than drawing a homily out of one of the New Testament narratives. Neither is necessarily wrong, but each has a different purpose and different "rules of engagement," per se. Elder Dallin H. Oaks made this point:

> For us, the scriptures are not the ultimate source of knowledge, but what precedes the ultimate source. The ultimate knowledge comes by revelation. . . .
>
> The word of the Lord in the scriptures is like a lamp to guide our feet (see Psalm 119:105), and revelation is like a mighty force that increases the lamp's illumination many-fold. We encourage everyone to make careful study of the scriptures and . . . to prayerfully seek personal revelation to know their meaning for themselves. . . .
>
> Such revelations are necessary because, as Elder Bruce R. McConkie of the Quorum of the Twelve observed, "Each pronouncement in the holy scriptures . . . is so written as to reveal little or much, depending on the spiritual capacity of the student."

Elder Bruce R. McConkie [also] said, "I sometimes think that one of the best-kept secrets of the kingdom is that the scriptures open the door to the receipt of revelation." This happens because scripture reading puts us in tune with the Spirit of the Lord. . . .

Many of the prophecies and doctrinal passages in the scriptures have multiple meanings. The Savior affirmed that fact when he told his disciples that the reason he taught the multitude in parables was that this permitted him to teach them "the mysteries of the kingdom of heaven" (Matthew 13:11) while not revealing those mysteries to the multitude. His parables had multiple meanings or applications according to the spiritual maturity of the listener. They had a message for both children and gospel scholars. . . .

Those who believe the scriptural canon is closed typically approach the reading of scriptures by focusing on what was meant at the time the scriptural words were spoken or written. In this approach, a passage of scripture may appear to have a single meaning and the reader typically relies on scholarship and historical methods to determine it.

The Latter-day Saint approach is different.

"In the wise words of St. Hilary, . . . 'Scripture consists not in what one reads, but in what one understands.' "[9]

One trouble with commentaries is that their authors sometimes focus on only one meaning, to the exclusion of others. As a result, commentaries, if not used with great care, may illuminate the author's chosen and correct meaning but close our eyes and restrict our horizons to other possible meanings. Sometimes those other, less obvious meanings can be the ones most valuable and useful to us as we seek to understand our own dispensation and to obtain answers to our own questions. This is why the teaching of the Holy Ghost is a better guide to scriptural interpretation than even the best commentary.[10]

Elder Oaks added that "scripture is not limited to what it meant when it was written but may also include what that scripture means to a reader today."[11] We could not agree more with Elder Oaks's point. While there is value in scholarly commentaries (and we shall draw upon many in this text), there is also great value in openness to applications beyond "what was meant at the time the scriptural words were spoken or written."[12] Thus, our purpose here will be to find meaning and personal application in the stories of the miracles preserved for us on the pages of the New Testament. We will *not* seek a singular dogmatic interpretation or application, *nor* will it be our intention to suggest to the reader what the ancients necessarily saw in or meant by a given miracle. Rather, we will look at various potential applications of the miracles and their surrounding storyline to the lives of those of us living in "the dispensation of the fulness of times" (D&C 124:41). Our target audience is the laity of the Church, not the scholars. And instead of a scholarly or academic treatment of these miracle narratives, what we offer here is a series of homilies—ways to apply the passages to the life of the reader—fodder for the teacher and preacher. We acknowledge this is but one approach to these miraculous events, but it is one that many have personally found meaning and benefit from.

We remind the reader of the prophet Nephi's familiar declaration: "I did liken all scriptures unto us, that [they] might be for our profit and learning" (1 Nephi 19:23). This is the task in which we seek to engage. Thus, the following should be understood and kept in mind as the reader digests the concepts presented on the pages of this book:

- What we are offering here is modern applications of ancient stories. In other words, while the original author may not have intended us to see symbolism in a given miracle story, there are some interesting and thought-provoking analogies that can be drawn from these miracles. Thus, what this book seeks to present is not necessarily what the ancients saw in these stories but instead what you and I can draw from them by way of modern applications. This is important for the readers to understand, both as they read this book, but also as they look for applications themselves.[13]

- In addition, as Elder Oaks suggested, the commentary from various authors that I have offered herein should not be seen as the *only* way to apply these miracles, nor necessarily as the best or most correct way. But what others have said about these miracles and their application serve the purpose of getting you and me to think about these stories and what they might potentially offer by way of application to the lives of those of us living some two thousand years after these stories were initially penned.

- As to sources, I've relied on a number of types of sources. I have drawn freely from scholarly commentaries for insights into the historical and linguistic portions of the miracles. I've relied on modern homiletic commentators for their applications of these events to our day.[14] And I've often pulled from the writings of the fathers of the early Church because of their tendency to see symbolic applications in the miracles of the Bible. While I do not hold any of these texts as necessarily authoritative, I offer them here because of the profundity of their insights and applications. I have not drawn on non-LDS sources for doctrine, nor do I present their views regarding the symbolism and application of these miracles as dogmatic interpretations, only as insights worthy of consideration.

- A distinction should be made between the historical meaning of an event, what that event symbolizes, and analogies or allegories that might be drawn from the event under consideration. The *historical* meaning is what the event meant for those of the first century who actually witnessed the miracle. (This is not so much our focus herein.) The *symbolic* meaning would be what the author who penned the story was trying to teach his audience. (We have occasionally pointed these out, particularly as other commentators have highlighted such meanings.) *Analogies* and *allegories* are those things you and I may draw from these stories as personal applications. (These are the primary focus of this text.) Our modern analogies and allegories may be such that they would be completely foreign to those living in the first century. To say that they are what was meant by the original author would, in some circumstances, be inaccurate at best and dishonest (or misrepresentative) at worst. Thus, we are careful to emphasize here that the analogies and allegories presented in this book are simply modern applications. This book is largely *not* about how the ancients saw these events, nor about what they meant for those living in the first century. We are simply asking the questions, "How can a given miracle apply to my life today?" and "How can it teach me principles for the twenty-first century?" But the reader should be careful to distinguish between the historical event, the ancient symbolic connotation, and the modern application and allegorization offered herein.

INTRODUCTION

- Our commentary on each miracle follows a consistent pattern. In order, we will look at the following things for each of the narratives we examine:

SCRIPTURAL CITATIONS: We have offered the scriptural references wherein the miracle is recorded in the New Testament. Many of the miracles of Jesus are recorded in multiple places and by more than one author. Thus, each of these is listed at the beginning of each section.

SUMMARY OF THE MIRACLE: Rather than citing the actual scriptural text, we have summarized each miracle. This became necessary for two reasons. First, many of the miracles appear in more than one Gospel—and not all Gospel authors give all of the details. Thus, it seemed important to offer a harmony or summary of each miracle that included the insights of each of those who recorded it. Second, a summary seemed helpful in the case of those miracles where the King James Version of the Bible (commonly used by Latter-day Saints) was not very clear. Thus, we summarized the text and, in so doing, sought to present the more difficult sections in clearer language.

BACKGROUND ON THE MIRACLE: This section deals less with the symbolism and more with historic, geographic, cultural, or linguistic insights into the miracle. This is offered by way of clarification and less with the intent of seeking application.

STANDARD SYMBOLS: In this section, we list various common symbols employed in the miracle under examination, symbols that appear in the story but have familiar or well-known meanings aside from the miracle being discussed.

APPLICATION AND ALLEGORIZATION: This portion of the commentary offers insights into what ancient, medieval, and modern commentators have seen by way of personal application in these miracles. These are offered non-dogmatically. They are intended only as springboards to encourage the readers to think about ways they might apply these miracles to their personal life, or to the life of those whom they teach.

Now, before we begin our foray into a study of the symbolic meaning of the miracles, I need to impress upon the reader my personal witness that the greatest of all miracles is the Atonement of the Lord Jesus Christ. Unfathomable as God's love is, and as incomprehensible as Christ's passion was, they encompass all other miracles and supersede them all. In many ways, we will discuss the Atonement on the pages of this book and in the context of the other miracles we will discuss. But unlike so many of the miracle stories of the New Testament, the application of Jesus's Atonement—wrought on our behalf—is not metaphorical. It is real, necessary, and salvific, and because of its sacred nature, we will make no attempt to allegorize or spiritualize it here. But it is our hope that our discussion of the many other miracles Jesus and His Apostles brought to pass will bring a greater sense of appreciation for that Ultimate Miracle in the lives of all who read this work.

NOTES

1. See Ryken, Wilhoit, and Longman, *Dictionary of Biblical Imagery*, 455–56.

2. Brown, *The Anchor Bible*, cxliii & cxxxix.

3. Augustine, "On Eighty-Three Varied Questions," 25.

4. Lockyer, *All the Miracles of the Bible*, 15. Lockyer also noted that the miracles were visible emblems of what Jesus is and what He came to do for each of us; see Lockyer (1965), 15.

5. Swift, "Typological Images," 115n33.

6. *Exegesis* means to "draw out" of a text its meaning. An "exegetical" approach, therefore, is one that seeks to "draw out" of a text the meaning or application intended by the original author who penned the text.

7. See Cross and Livingstone, *Oxford Dictionary*, s.v., "Exegesis"; Bowden, *Encyclopedia of Christianity*, 552; Trigg, *Encyclopedia of Early Christianity*, s.v. "Allegory," 23–26; Norris, *Encyclopedia of Early Christianity*, s.v. "Antioch," 54.

8. Johnson, *Sacra Pagina*, 155. While I acknowledge that a fifth- or sixth-century source does not tell us how the first-century Church read scripture, it does seem quite clear that the New Testament Church read the Old Testament—which was their "scripture"—in very symbolic and Christocentric ways, thus giving us some sense of their tendency to see scripture as symbolic and typological. That being said,

INTRODUCTION

we are not here arguing for an ancient interpretation. What we are saying is that, just as many ancients read the scriptures symbolically—as the New Testament often does of the Old, the rabbis did of the Hebrew Bible, and the early post-New Testament Christians did of the Bible generally—we too will look for messages of application which can be drawn from the texts generally, and from their symbols specifically.

9. Elder Oaks was quoting Hugh Nibley here.

10. Oaks, "Scripture Reading and Revelation," 7–9. See also Swift, "Three Stories," 125–46.

11. Oaks, "Scripture Reading and Revelation," 8.

12. Regarding sources, we have largely drawn upon two types of commentaries for the writing of this text: homiletic and scholarly. Some of our homiletic commentators are ancient or medieval, and some are modern. (Authors from very early on in the history of the Christian Church saw the value in a homiletic and symbolic reading of these miracle stories.) While academicians sometimes don't like—or don't see as legitimate—homiletic commentaries, because of our stated purpose in this book, those really are the most appropriate for engaging in a discussion about modern applications. We have also employed a handful of scholarly commentaries, in part because of their historical, cultural, or linguistic insights into the text, but also because they too sometimes offer symbolic insights into the text. Hence our mixture of sources, which to some, no doubt, seem like rather strange bedfellows.

13. While we will offer occasional points of clarification as it relates to language, culture, or history surrounding these miracles, this work is not intended as a historical analysis of the facts nor as a scholarly examination of the miracles. To read what we've done here as such would be to entirely miss the point of this work. We acknowledge that for some academics, such an approach will be frustrating. Nevertheless, we personally see value in asking, "How does this speak to me personally, owing to the circumstances in my life today?" And so, rather than asking, "What did this mean for the first-century Church?" our question will be, "What can I see in this for my life today?"

14. A number of the scholarly commentaries I used also interpreted these miracle stories in symbolic ways, occasionally finding modern application in the ancient accounts and with an intent of promoting application among readers of the scriptural texts.

WATER *to* WINE

JOHN 2:1–11

THE MIRACLE

Some three days after beginning His formal ministry,[1] Jesus, His mother, and some of His disciples attended a wedding in the town of Cana, near Nazareth, in the district of Galilee, which was in the northernmost part of Palestine.

Partway through this wedding celebration, the refreshments for the guests had run out. Jesus's mother, concerned that the bride and groom's celebration might turn into an embarrassment rather than an occasion for joy, requested that Jesus do something about the dilemma.

As was common for the time, water pots used by Jews for purifying themselves, as required by the law of Moses, were present at the home of the host. According to the social and religious rules of the day, individuals would be expected to wash their hands prior to eating.

When Jesus's mother urged Him to intervene, He commanded six pots to be filled to their brims with water. He immediately directed those fulfilling His instructions to take a cup of the new wine to the master of ceremonies, who, we are told, was shocked at the wine's quality. Indeed, he was so shocked that he approached the bridegroom and informed him of what appeared to be a mistake. Traditionally, those sponsoring celebrations (such as the one Jesus was here attending) would serve the best wine at the beginning of the party. However, after the guests had enjoyed a fair amount to drink and their palates were slightly less sensitive to the taste, the host would then introduce poorer quality refreshments because the guests would be none the wiser. However, at this wedding feast, it appeared the exact opposite had taken place. To the master of ceremonies, it looked as if the man being married had given out the weaker wine first and saved the best drink for the end of the party.

John informs us that "the governor of the feast . . . knew not whence" the wine had come (John 2:9). Unbeknownst to most of those present, Jesus had miraculously turned dozens of gallons of water into wine of the finest kind. While a number of things transpired before Jesus actually performed the requested service, what seems most pertinent is that Jesus *did* intervene, thereby saving the celebration and introducing His disciples and a few others present to the miraculous powers the Father had endowed Him with.

BACKGROUND

The presence of Jesus and His mother and the fact that she sought to intercede when provisions became scarce have caused some to assume that the person getting married must have been a close relative of Mary.[2] However, while such an assumption is commonplace, the text is silent on this issue.

Much has been made of Jesus's initial response to His mother, which sounds rude to modern ears. The reader must keep in mind that John has not recorded for us the complete dialogue between Mary and her Son, and thus it would be easy to misread the tone and intent of Jesus's words if that fact is not kept in mind.[3] Jesus said to His mother, "Woman, what have I to do with thee? mine hour is not yet come" (John 2:4). It will be recalled that Jesus also refers to His mother as "woman" when He is hanging on the cross (John 19:26), and He calls Mary Magdalene "woman" after His Resurrection (John 20:15). In antiquity, the title *woman* was not seen as disrespectful. One text states, "In Jesus's day . . . the word *woman* was a title of respect much the same as the term *ma'am* is a courteous address in the southern part of the United States."[4]

Christ's rhetorical question, "What have I to do with thee?" can be translated in a number of ways, but it carries the basic sense that He and His mother have (at that moment) different concerns. One commentator translated Jesus's words as saying, "That is your business: how am I involved?"[5] While Mary, as His earthly parent, was seeking to direct Jesus in this matter that she felt was important, He makes it quite clear that He must now follow the directions of His Heavenly Parent—God.

That being said, the Joseph Smith Translation seems to resolve the question of Jesus's tone in speaking to His mother. In the Joseph Smith Translation for John 2:4, Jesus states, "Woman, what wilt thou have me to do for thee? that will I do" (footnote a). Thus, Jesus appears to have been compliant rather than condescending.

Jesus's comment that His "hour is not yet come" has been interpreted to mean that it is not time for Him to perform the miracle. There is still wine left. One text notes, "Not till the wine was wholly exhausted would his hour have arrived. All other help must fail, before the hour of the great Helper will have struck. Then will be time to act, when by the entire failure of the wine, manifest to all, the miracle shall be above all suspicion."[6] Some commentators also take His words to mean that it is not time for Him to fully reveal His messianic role and powers and that His Father, not His mother, must determine the timing of His "full manifestation."[7] One fifth-century source states: "His mother mentioned to him . . . the lack of earthly wine, when he had come to offer the peoples of the whole world the new chalice of eternal salvation."[8] Elsewhere we read, "By his reply, 'My hour has not yet come,' he was foretelling the most glorious hour of his passion and the wine of our redemption, which would obtain life for all."[9] The Joseph Smith Translation implies that Jesus's words simply mean He will follow His mother's request, as it is not His time to take charge. That day was yet in His future.

Turning the water to wine was no small miracle! Owing to the large number of guests typically attending such a social function, the amount of water needed for this requisite ritual washing would have been considerable. According to John's account of the event, the pots had a capacity of some "two or three firkins apiece" (John 2:6), which translates to somewhere between twenty and thirty gallons of water per pot.[10] Thus, the total amount of water turned to wine in this miracle was somewhere between 120 and 180 gallons.

These water pots were not earthen containers made of dried clay, but rather they were made of hewn stone. This was necessary because, according to the Jewish interpretation of the law, earthen vessels were subject to corruption through absorption, but stone jars were not.[11] Therefore, John makes it clear to his readers that these pots had one purpose: ritual washings as part of the law of Moses. They were not jars for holding drinking water or wine.[12] Thus, no one need assume that Jesus's miracle happened because remnants of wine—the *lees*, as they are called—were present in the bottom of the pots, mixing with the water to make wine. Prior to this miracle, these jars would have *never* been used as receptacles for holding wine.[13]

John explains to the reader why this first recorded miracle was performed. He says that it "manifested forth [Jesus's] glory" to those present with the effect that "His disciples believed on Him" (John 2:11). In other words, it was a testament that God was with Jesus and that He had endowed Him with power from on high. It highlighted to those who witnessed it the fact that the messianic kingdom had arrived.

SYMBOLIC ELEMENTS

Weddings are typical symbols for the covenant relationship that exists between God and His people. The scriptures abound in references to the "groom" (Christ) and His "bride" (the Church).[14]

In antiquity, wine symbolized a variety of related ideas, including truth, life, covenant blessings promised by God to the faithful, and the joys accessible to God's children through the gospel of Jesus Christ.[15]

While jars like those referenced in this miracle do not have a standard symbolic meaning in the ancient Church, in this narrative they may be symbolic of the law and the covenant people—and of Christ's ability and desire to change them from the inside out.

APPLICATION AND ALLEGORIZATION

In this miracle story, John's focus on the jars used for purification can teach us that the law of Moses, potentially symbolized by those jars, is under scrutiny. The jars held water—useful, but not necessarily palatable. Jesus would replace that water with wine, which, among other things, stood as a symbol for joy, truth, atonement, transformation, and union with God.[16] One commentator noted:

> In the ancient Near East, with its scarcity of water, wine was a necessity rather than a luxury. It therefore easily became an image of sustenance and life. . . . Due to its close relationship to the ongoing life of the community, wine becomes . . . a technical term for the covenant blessings promised by God to Israel for obedience and withheld by God for disobedience. . . . Wine becomes an important image of joy, celebration and festivity, often expressive of the abundant blessing of God.[17]

The act of changing the water to wine is sometimes seen by commentators on this miracle as a symbolic statement regarding how the law of Moses, though useful, did not have the power and ability to bring us the eternal joy and life that Christ's gospel, ministry, and Atonement would. Jesus had come to fulfill the law—to turn it into something better, per se.[18]

The fact that this wedding was being held in Galilee (Gentile territory) instead of Jerusalem (the land of the covenant people) can serve as a symbol for the reality that the Jews (symbolized by the Holy City) would reject Jesus as their Messiah, but the "church of the Gentiles" (symbolized by Galilee) would accept Him.[19] Thus, again, the focus of the miracle is on replacement—Judaism being replaced by Christianity, the law of Moses being replaced by Christ's teachings, the lesser law being replaced by the higher law. As one commentator pointed out:

> In introducing Cana as the first in a series of signs to follow, the evangelist [John] intends to call attention to the replacement of the water prescribed for Jewish purification by the choicest of wines. The replacement is a sign of who Jesus is, namely, the one sent by the Father who is now the only way to the Father. All previous religious institutions, customs and feasts [that were required by the law of Moses] lose meaning in his presence.[20]

The basic message we are offered through this miracle seems to be that Christ has come. The law of Moses has been fulfilled, and thus something much better, more helpful, more palatable, more valuable, and more meaningful has been given through God's Son, the Savior of the World. As the nineteenth-century British exegete, Charles Spurgeon, wrote,

> All the wine they ever had under the Old Testament dispensation was far behind that of which we drink. He that is least in the kingdom of heaven is more highly favoured [sic] than he who is chief under the Old Testament dispensation. Our fathers did eat manna, but we do eat the bread that came down from heaven; they did drink of water in the wilderness, but we drink of that living water whereof if a man drink he shall never thirst. . . . We must remember that we are drinking to-day [sic] of that wine which prophets and kings desired to drink of, but died without a taste thereof.[21]

It is fitting that this miracle took place at a wedding, where a man and woman were being united, as Jesus and His prophets were wont to use the imagery of a wedding to symbolize the Messiah's covenant relationship with the Church.[22] A number of early Church fathers saw the wedding at Cana, and its miracle of turning water to wine, as a symbol for the fact that Jesus had come to marry His bride (the Church).[23] As we have already noted, the wine has a number of potential symbols. While some see it as an obvious representation of joy and the new or better kingdom Jesus had come to establish, others see it as a symbol of Christ's blood, which was shed as a gift to His bride.[24]

There seems to be an interesting symbol present in the idea that—contrary to the popular practice of the day—at the wedding at Cana, the best wine was saved until last. Of course, there is the parallel with the law of Moses and the fulness of the gospel of Jesus Christ. As one text notes, "The headwaiter's statement at the end of the scene, 'You have kept the choice wine until now,' can be understood as the proclamation of the coming of the messianic days."[25] The lesser law, the weaker wine, preceded the giving of the higher law or better "wine of joy." Israel lived under this lesser law until Christ came and fulfilled it.[26] But once it was fulfilled, God's gospel of grace offered meaning, joy, and confidence unmatched by the Mosaic message.

Having said that, there appears to be another symbolic parallel that might be drawn from the act of saving the best for last. Satan always offers his best first, and then the "weaker wine" last. Just as the master of ceremonies at the wedding at Cana indicated, that tradition would have the best wine up front to get the guests drunk before the weaker, less satisfying wine was substituted—so also Satan plays the "bait and switch" game with us:

> The world does indeed give its best and choicest, it's *good wine*, first, but has only poorer substitutes at the last. *When men have well drunk,* when their spiritual palate is blunted, when they have lost the discernment between moral good and evil, then it palms on them that which is worse; what it would not have dared to offer at the first,—coarser pleasures, viler enjoyments, the drink of a more deadly wine.[27]

Such is evident in the "new morality" of our day, and in the constant message of "tolerance" for that which Jesus and the Father have labeled as "sin." Satan and his followers seek to get us "drunk" on the many temptations he offers at his smorgasbord of sin, all in the hope that we will not accurately see that which matters most. Then, once we are "drunk" with the "wine of the wrath of [his] fornication" (Revelation 14:8), Satan offers us a steady diet of misery, addiction, loss, and heartache.[28]

It is curious how different Christ's approach is from that of Satan and the world. Satan gives the "best" (his most enticing) first, in the hopes of ensnaring us, and then he strips away what he has offered. Jesus does the exact opposite—He offers the "lesser wine" (the beginning of blessings) at first, but then He gives the "best" (the fulness of blessings—even exaltation) once we have proven ourselves. As Spurgeon states,

> [Christ] does not feast his children after the fashion of the prince of darkness: for the first cup that Christ brings to them is very often a cup of bitterness. . . . Jesus brings the cup of poverty and affliction, and he makes his own children drink of it. . . . This is the way Christ begins. The worst wine first. . . . He seeks to have no disciples who are dazzled with first appearances. . . . After the cup of affliction, comes the cup of consolation, and, oh, how sweet is that! . . . If thou wouldst come to the table of communion with Christ, thou must first of all drink of the wine of Calvary. Christian thy head must be crowned with thorns. Thy hands must be pierced, I mean not with nails, but, spiritually thou must be crucified with Christ. We must suffer with him, or else we can not [sic] reign with him; we must labor with him first; we must sup of the wine which his Father gave him to drink, or else we can not [sic] expect to come to the better part of the feast. . . . The best wine is to come at last.[29]

While Spurgeon speaks in hyperbole when he refers to Jesus offering us the "cup of bitterness" first, nevertheless, in this life that *does* offer us much peace and joy, there is some validity to Spurgeon's point. If we wish to partake of the "better wine," we must be *willing* to drink of the "bitter cup," should it come our way. If we are willing to endure today, we will have cause to rejoice tomorrow. As the Psalmist wrote, "Weeping may endure for a night, but joy cometh in the morning" (Psalm 30:5). Christ held back the fulness of the gospel until the time was right. He also holds back the fulness of blessings from us until the time is right. But one of the applications that can be drawn from this miracle is that they *will* come. And the surest way we can guarantee that we receive them is to place ourselves in a covenant relationship with Him, to become His bride and accept Him as our bridegroom.[30]

The reader will recall that prior to His performing the miracle of turning water to wine, Jesus's mother had approached Him to express her concern that He do something about the fact that the original cache of refreshments had been consumed and the party was about to come to an abrupt end. Mary directs those serving at the feast, "Whatsoever he saith unto you, do it." This too may be a message for you and I—His bride. As a Church and as individuals, we must not rely on our own understanding but rather trust in Him with all of our hearts and obey Him in all that He asks us to do. Then He will be able to bless us richly with the joys symbolized by the wine.[31]

Some have assumed that the number of jars highlighted by John in his record of the miracle are significant.[32] Six is the Hebrew number for deficit, imperfection, or failure to attain completeness.[33] One text on the symbolic meaning of numbers argued that since six falls short of the numerical perfection found in the number seven, it symbolizes incompleteness in the sense of representing man without Christ.[34] Thus, the fact that the jars are associated with the law of Moses and there are six of them could indeed be a subtle hint that the law was incomplete because Christ had yet to come, thereby fulfilling it and giving it both meaning and efficacy. In that vein, it may be significant that there were initially six containers. However, once the water was turned into wine, Jesus commanded that a vessel be used to draw out some wine that it might be given to the host, thereby making seven vessels containing the wine Jesus offered (John 2:8). Seven, the number of perfection, wholeness, and completion, is a perfect symbol for the gospel Christ was restoring.[35]

Through inaugurating His ministry, Jesus was beginning His fulfillment and replacement of the law of Moses. Just as He changed simple water into the best of wines, Christ took the "schoolmaster law" (Galatians 3:24) and transformed it in to the glorious gospel. Similarly, just as He miraculously transformed the unnoteworthy contents of the jars[36] into the highly valued "blood" of the grape (Deuteronomy 32:14), He can also transform our unnoteworthy lives into something significant and precious through the application of His shed blood and through our efforts to do whatever He commands us to do (John 2:5).[37]

Christ seeks a covenant relationship with His bride, us.[38] The wedding at Cana foreshadowed that relationship, and it invites us to be changed *by* Him that we might be one *with* Him.[39] As McQuade stated,

> The water that became wine is symbolic on a number of levels. First it represents the difference between the old and new covenants. But it also stands for the change in a new believer. The old spirit is gone, and the new one that replaces it has an unusual power, directly from God. . . . What of our lives? Are they water or wine? Has God's Spirit filled us with the new life that enlivens like wine, or are we dull, ordinary water that lacks joy? Even if we've come to know Jesus, if sin obstructs the Spirit's work in our lives, we may feel more like water than wine. Even the most faithful of us have dull days that are filled with obedience, but if every day seems dull, perhaps we need a little more of the Spirit's wine in our lives. If we cast aside anger, resentment, and bitterness, confessing our failures, the sparkle may come back. We don't have to live on a constant high, but the idea that God will use us for His purposes should cause within us a burst of joy, not a sigh of despair. Today, are we water or wine?[40]

NOTES

1. Theodore of Mopsuestia (circa AD 350–428) says that this took place three days after Jesus was baptized (see Mopsuestia, "Commentary on John," 89. See also Heraclea, "Fragments of John 12," 89). Though this is a possible interpretation of the Greek, most modern commentators assume this miracle took place three days after Jesus called Philip and Nathanael to be His disciples. See Brown, *Anchor Bible*, 97; Trench, *Miracles of the Lord*, 63. The Joseph Smith Translation offers an entirely different take, saying it was the "third day of the week," rather than the third day after some event (see John 2:1, footnote a; from Joseph Smith Translation).

2. See, for example, McQuade (2008), 150; Trench, *Miracles of the Lord*, 65; Kistemaker (2006), 13; Lockyer (1965), 160; Farrar, *Life of Christ*, 142; Talmage, *Jesus the Christ*, 144; McConkie, *Doctrinal New Testament Commentary*, 1:448–49, 451; *Wilford Woodruff Journal*, 8:187; Hyde, "Marriage Relations," 2:82; Hyde, "Man the Head of Women," 4:259; Matthews, *Miracles of Jesus*, 22.

3. See Brown (1966), 103.

4. Kistemaker, *Miracles*, 14. See also Brown (1966), 102; McQuade, *Top 100 Miracles*, 151; Trench (1962), 66; Tenney, *Expositor's Bible Commentary*, 9:42.

5. See Brown (1966), 99.

6. Trench (1962), 67.

7. Ibid.

8. Ibid.

9. Maximus of Turin, "Sermon 23," cited in Elowsky (2006), 92.

10. See McQuade (2008), 151; Kistemaker (2006), 15; Tasker, Tyndale New Testament Commentaries, 60; Tenney, 9:42; Trench (1962), 71n8; Matthews (1969), 22. See also Brown (1966), 100.

11. See Leviticus 11:29–38, which is likely the source for the Jewish prohibition; Brown (1966), 100; Sloyan (1988), 35.

12. "There was a reason why the Evangelist says, 'After the manner of the purifying of the Jews.' He said this so that none of the unbelievers might suspect that lees had been left in the vessel and then water was poured upon them and mixed with them in order to make . . . wine. . . . Those vessels were never receptacles for wine. . . . They used to fill water pots with water so that they . . . could have the means of purification readily at hand." Chrysostom, "Gospel of John," 22:2, 95.

13. Chrysostom, "Gospel of John," 22:2, 95.

14. See Ryken, Wilhoit, and Longman (1998), 938–39; Conner, *Symbols and Types*, 110–11.

15. See Cooper, *Encyclopaedia of Traditional Symbols*, 192–93; Wilson (1999), 464; Ryken, Wilhoit, and Longman (1998), 953–54; Conner (1992), 181.

16. See Wilson, *Dictionary of Bible Types*, 464; Cooper (1982), 192–93; Fontana, *Secret Language of Symbols*, 106; Tresidder, *Symbols and Their Meanings*, 86; Brown (1966), 105; Habershon, *Study of the Miracles*, 113, 172.

17. Ryken, Wilhoit, and Longman (1998), 953–54, s.v., "Wine."

18. This miracle has undertones present in the parable of the new wine in old wine skins. See Matthew 9:14–17; Mark 2:18–22; Luke 5:33–38. Regarding Jesus's "fulfilling" of the law, Ogden and Skinner wrote, "Jesus was not destroying or canceling out all those sacred writings any more than a university professor is destroying basic arithmetic by teaching integral calculus. He came not to abolish but to complete. As the Latter-day Saints would say to other Christians—or to Jews, Muslims, or anyone else—we do not come to erase any truth you already have but to fulfill, to complete, to add to what you have with the fullness of the everlasting gospel. We would say, as the Lord said, 'I do not bring it to destroy that which 'you' have received, but to build it up.' And Joseph Smith added, 'We don't ask any people to throw away any good they have got; we long ask them to come and get more'" (Ogden and Skinner, *Verse By Verse*, 186–87). Many Latter-day Saints perceive Christ's fulfilling of the law to mean the law foreshadowed Jesus and what He would do during His mortal sojourn. Thus, when Jesus came and did what the law foreshadowed, it was "fulfilled" by Him and through His passion.

19. Cyril, "Gospel of John," 2:1, 88–89.

20. Brown (1966), 104. See also Lockyer, (1965), 161.

21. *Spurgeon's Sermons*, 5:290.

22. See Isaiah 54:1–6; Jeremiah 31:32; Ezekiel 16:8; Hosea 2; Romans 7:1–6; 2 Corinthians 11:2; Ephesians 5:21–33; Revelation 19:7; 21:2, 9.

23. See, for example, Theodore, "Fragments of John 12," 89; Caesarius, "Sermon 167.1," 89; Maximus, "Sermon 23," 90.

24. See, for example, Caesarius, "Sermon 167.1," 89; Augustine, "Tractates on the

Gospel of John," 8.4.1–3, 89–90; Eusebius, "Proof of the Gospel," 9.8.8, 89. By way of application, one commentator noted, "We may contrast this his readiness to aid others with his stern refusal to minister by the same almighty power to his own exremest [sic] necessities. He who turned water into wine might have made bread out of stones (Matt. iv:4); but spreading a table for others, He is content to hunger and to thirst Himself" (Trench [1962], 68). There may be a message in this about what Christians are to do and be—they serve others and neglect themselves. This wedding at Cana is a reminder that brides and grooms are invited to serve their partner and worry not about their own personal needs. The reader will recall the words of President Gordon B. Hinckley, who stated, "I have long felt that happiness in marriage is not so much a matter of romance as it is an anxious concern for the comfort and well-being of one's companion. That involves a willingness to overlook weaknesses and mistakes" (*Teachings of Gordon B. Hinckley*, 325).

25. Brown (1966), 105.

26. While Adam certainly had the fulness of the gospel, throughout most of the Old Testament the law of Moses, not the gospel in its fulness, was what God's people had access to.

27. Trench (1962), 71–72.

28. One text puts it this way: "The world presents us with fair language, promising hopes, convenient fortunes, [and] pompous honors; . . . but when it is swallowed, these dissolve in an instant, and there remains bitterness and the malignity of colo-quintida. Every sin smiles in the first address, and carries light in the face, and honey in the lip; but when we have well drunk, then comes that which is worse, a whip with six strings, fears and terrors of conscience, and shame and displeasure, and a caitiff disposition, and diffidence in the day of death. But when after the manner of puri-fying of the Christians, we fill our waterpots with water, watering our couch with our teas, and moistening our cheeks with the perpetual distillations of repentance, then Christ turns our water into wine, first penitents and then communicants—first waters of sorrow and then the wine of the chalice; . . . for Jesus keeps the best wine to the last, not only because of the direct reservations of the highest joys till the nearer approaches of glory, but also because our relishes are higher after a long frui-tion than at the first essays, such being the nature of grace, that it increases in relish as it does in fruition, every part of grace being new duty and new reward" (Taylor, *Life of Christ*, 72). Elsewhere we read, "O Christian, trust not thou in men; rely not thou upon the things of this present time, for this is evermore the rule with men and with the world—'the good wine first, and when ye have well drunken, then that which is worse.' . . . The devil's house . . . is true to this rule; he brings from first the good wine, and when men have well drunk, and their brains are muddled therewith, then he bringeth forth that which is worse." But of Jesus, our "Lord and Master," it may be said, "thy feasts grow better, and not worse, thy wines grow richer, . . . and thy gifts more precious than before. 'Thou has kept the good wine until now'" (Spurgeon [2007], 5:271–72).

29. Spurgeon (2007), 5:284, 287. This same source also states, "Again: if we have the best things to come dear friends, do not let us be discontented. Let us put up

with a few of the bad things now, for they only seem to be so. A traveller who is on a journey in a hurry, if he has to stay for a night at an inn, he may grumble a little at the want of accommodation, but he does not say very much, because he is off to-morrow [*sic*], he is only stopping a short time at the inn; he says, 'I shall get home to-morrow night,' and then he thinks of the joys of home, and does not care about the discomforts of his hard journey. You and I are travellers. It will soon be over. We may have had but a very few shillings a week compared with our neighbour [*sic*], but we shall be equal with him when we get there. He may have had a large house, with a great many rooms, while we had, it may be only one upper room; ah! we shall have as large a mansion as he in Paradise. We shall soon be at the journey's end, and then the road will not signify, long as we have got there. Come! let us put up with these few inconveniences on the road, for the best wine is coming; let us pour away all the vinegar of murmuring, for the best wine shall come" (Spurgeon [2007], 5:300–01). See also Lockyer, (1965), 161–62.

30. "Jesus' presence at the wedding in Cana points to the celestial wedding banquet at the end of time. Then Jesus will be the bridegroom and God's people the bride" (Kistemaker [2006], 17).

31. See Kistemaker (2006), 18.

32. "Is their being six a detail of significance? It is attractive to say that the fact that they are short of the sacred number seven is important to John. We cannot know. We need to be on the alert, however, for symbolism everywhere" (Sloyan (1988), 35). "Those jars were for the purification of the Jews, but our Lord poured his teaching into them, so that he might make it known that he was coming through the path of the Law and the Prophets to transform all things by his teaching, just as he had transformed water into wine" (Ephrem, "Commentary on Tatian's Diatessaron," 5:6–7, 95).

33. Draper, *Opening the Seven Seals*, 121; Bullinger, *Number in Scripture*, 123, 150; Smith, *Book of Revelation*, 288; Johnston, *Numbers in the Bible*, 67.

34. Johnston, *Numbers in the Bible*, 67.

35. *Seven* symbolizes fulness, completion, entirety or totality, and spiritual perfection. See McConkie (1985), 199; Davis, Biblical Numerology, 118, 122, 123; Drinkard, "Numbers," 711; Cooper (1982), 117; Cirlot, *Dictionary of Symbols*, 233, 295; Julien, *Mammoth Dictionary of Symbols*, 373; McConkie and Parry, *Guide to Scriptural Symbols*, 99; Parry and Parry, *Understanding the Book of Revelation*, 14, 27; Draper (1991), 24, 138; Bullinger (1967), 23, 107; Johnston (1990), 40; Rest, *Our Christian Symbols*, 61; Todeschi, *Encyclopedia of Symbolism*, 186; Smith (1998), 288. Etymologically, seven is connected with the Hebrew words full, satisfied, or complete (Farbridge, *Biblical and Semitic Symbolism*, 136–138). According to one text, "The root of the Hebrew word for seven (*sheva*) is identical to the Hebrew verb that means 'to take an oath,' thus connecting the word *seven* to covenants and covenant making" (McConkie and Parry, *Guide to Scriptural Symbols*, 99. See also Davis (1968), 122; McKenzie, *Dictionary of the Bible*, 621). We cannot say with certainty whether John intended the number of jars to be symbolic. Some argue that he did

not. (See, for example, Brown [1966], 100.) Whether he did or not, the numerology of the passage is intriguing.

36. Augustine noted, "Our Lord, Jesus Christ, changed water into wine; and what was tasteless acquires taste. . . . Scripture . . . is indeed from the Lord. But it has not taste if Christ is not understood in it" (Augustine, "Tractates on the Gospel of John," 9.5:1–3, 96). Thus, we must see Christ in the scriptures if they are to become alive and palatable to us.

37. "As those water pots fulfilled the Lord's purpose, so He can use the poorest means. We are but poor earthen vessels, and somewhat cracked, yet he can use weak things to confound the mighty" (Lockyer [1965], 162).

38. The marriage at Cana foreshadowed that "marriage of Christ and the church." See Bede, "Homilies on the Gospels," 1:14, 98.

39. "He who turned . . . the water into wine, should turn in a like manner the poorer dispensation, the thin and watery elements of the Jewish religion, into richer and nobler, into the gladdening wine of a higher faith. Nor less do we behold symbolized here, that whole work which the Son of God is evermore accomplishing in the world,—ennobling all that He touches, making saints out of sinners, angels out of men, and in the end heaven out of earth. . . . For the prophecy of . . . the day in which his disciples shall drink of the fruit of the vine new in his kingdom is here. In this humble supper we have the rudiments of the glorious festival, at the arrival of which his hour shall have indeed come, who is Himself the true Bridegroom, even as his Church is the Bride" (Trench [1962], 74).

40. McQuade (2008), 151–52.

HEALING *the* NOBLEMAN'S SON

JOHN 4:46–54[1]

THE MIRACLE

While visiting Cana, Jesus was approached by a man who, though not yet a follower of Christ, had heard of His teachings and healing powers.[2] He informed Jesus that his son was at the point of death back in Capernaum and begged Him to come with him back to his hometown so that Jesus might bless and heal the child.

Jesus responds to the man's request by saying, "Except ye [Galileans] see signs and wonders, ye will not believe" (John 4:48). The man's reply to Jesus's rebuke of the crowd was to simply repeat his request: "Sir, come down ere my child die" (verse 49).

Having heard the man's second request, Jesus instructed him to go home, for his son had been healed. John tells us that the man believed Jesus's words and immediately headed back to Capernaum. On his way home, some of his servants met him, informing him that his son had fully recovered. The father inquired as to what time the boy had gotten better and he learned that it was at the "seventh hour" (verse 52) or 1:00 p.m.—the very hour that Jesus had pronounced him healed. At that point, the man's faith was confirmed and he, for the first time, *truly* believed, as did all those in his household.

BACKGROUND

Sometime after turning water to wine at Cana, Jesus returned to the region. It may have been only a few weeks later, or perhaps it was as long as six to nine months after preforming His first miracles there.[3]

The scene of this miracle is technically both Cana (where the father of the sick boy met Jesus) and Capernaum (where the child lay ill, and where he would miraculously recover). Cana is located some twenty miles across the Galilean hills from Capernaum. Therefore, it would be a two-day journey for the father, whose fairly long trek to meet Jesus is itself a symbolic manifestation of his faith, however weak that faith may have been.[4]

The man who approached Jesus requesting a blessing for his son is said to be a "nobleman" (verse 49) or, as the Greek implies, a "royal official." He was most likely a servant of Herod, the tetrarch of Galilee.[5] The fact that his "servants" (plural) came out to meet him upon his return is an indication that he was a man of rank and influence in his community, as a commoner would likely not have such a household staff.[6]

Jesus had come to Galilee from Samaria. In the latter place, He was well received; in the former, he was not. One commentator noted, "After healing a sin-sick soul in Samaria, where Jesus spent two happy, profitable days among those Samaritans who believed in Him and were deeply eager to hear His word, He found His way to Cana to heal the fever-stricken body of a nobleman's son. From 'sympathetic Samaria He journeyed to unsympathetic Galilee.'"[7] This lack of "sympathy" or belief explains the tone of the exchange between Jesus and the royal official.

Jesus's reply to the nobleman's request may seem somewhat shocking to the reader. In what appears to be a spirit of rebuke, He said to the crowd and, by default, to the man, "Except you Galileans see signs, you never believe."[8] This declaration, though it seems out of place and contrary to the man's seemingly faith-filled request, certainly had application to the mass of Galileans (as a whole), and it may say something about the nobleman—as it was his request that appears to have provoked Jesus's general rebuke. Though the man appears to have had faith, some commentators see in Jesus's comments evidence that his faith was, at best, weak. He will believe in a sign if Jesus will show him one, but that is seen by some as evidence of doubt, not faith. And what sign does the man request? Namely that Jesus *go with him* to his home to heal the dying child. Time and again commentators, ancient and modern, note that the man clearly had a "germ of faith," or at least a willingness to exercise "some faith," in Christ. But others point out that his imperfect faith may have limited his access to Christ's power. As Lockyer states,

> While the nobleman's sorrow was the birth-pang of faith, he revealed the *limit* of that faith when he limited the power of Christ to His local presence. . . . He had faith to believe that where Jesus was present, disease would flee. He must "come down," if the son is to be cured. The desperate father was not prepared to believe the word of the psalmist, "He *sent* His word, and He healed them." [Psalm 107:20] Yet although the nobleman's faith was limited and feeble, it was nevertheless real. Our Lord detected with unerring accuracy the weak point of the anxious father's faith and nurtured it.[9]

Whether the man caught the personal application of Jesus's instructive rebuke is unclear. It is possible that, in his pain and worry, he did not hear the words or did not understand what Jesus was seeking to teach. If he did hear, he was clearly undaunted by the declaration and condemnation of the Galileans' faithlessness, as he simply proceeded to repeat his plea: "Sir (or "Lord," as the Greek has it), please come down to Capernaum before my little boy dies."

At the conclusion of their exchange, Jesus told the man to return home, for his son had been healed. The man, trusting in—or hoping for the fulfillment of—Jesus's words, started for home, but because of the distance, he did not arrive until the next day.[10]

SYMBOLIC ELEMENTS

There are two primary symbols in this miracle story: the nobleman who approached Jesus and his dying son back home in Capernaum. The nobleman can be seen as representative of those who have weak faith (as were all of the Galileans chastised in this episode), of those who struggle to trust in God and His powers and promises. The boy who is dying, on the other hand, seems to be a common symbol in the various Gospel narratives for one spiritually ailing because of sin.

APPLICATION AND ALLEGORIZATION

While this miracle is more doctrinal than symbolic in its content, the narrative certainly offers a number of messages to its readers through the actions of its central characters. As we noted, the nobleman can be seen as a symbol of weak faith. In two significant ways, he can be used as a symbol for all those who doubt God.

First of all, we are informed that the "royal official" felt Jesus needed to be present in order to heal his son. Some will assume he approached Jesus with the attitude "What do I have to lose? I've heard much about this guy. If he can do something miraculous, great! If not, my son is no worse off for my having tried." Perhaps, but it seems more appropriate that he serve as a symbol not of those who are only able to muster intellectual curiosity but rather of those who limit God by their lack of faith. Some, no matter how much they wish to believe, place limits on God's power. They doubt that He is powerful enough to solve *their* current conflict or trial. They profess a belief in Him, but they despair in their hour of need. Just as the nobleman showed signs that he did not believe that Jesus could heal without coming with him to his home, so some of us place limitations on what God can do in *our* lives. We profess a belief, but by our actions, we really testify of how little faith we have.

Second, we learn that while the nobleman sought to trust Jesus's claim that the boy was healed, he only *fully* believed Jesus's promise when his servants informed him that the boy had been cured at the very same hour Jesus claimed he had been made whole. It was only at that point the man's faith in Christ solidified.[11] Thus, the nobleman stands as a potential symbol for those who lack faith without proof. He well represents those who desire to believe but ever struggle to *truly* trust if overwhelming proof is not first provided. He is a good example of some who, while feeling the confirming Spirit when first taught the gospel, still hesitate to join the Church because they have not seen an angel, have not been shown incontrovertible evidence, or do not know "for sure." Jesus's rebuke (at the man's expressed desire for a sign) can be seen as a challenge to his claim to believe in Christ's power.[12] One commentator on the passage noted, "A faith so weak must be strengthened, and can only be strengthened through being proved."[13] Thus, Jesus's refusal to go with the man to his home was not evidence that

He did not wish to help the royal official. On the contrary, His refusal can be seen as a sign that He desired to teach the man and increase his faith. By not following the man to his home, but rather only promising to heal his child, Jesus gave the man an opportunity to increase his faith and reliance upon God.[14] Similarly, by not always answering our prayers the way we wish God to, He also gives us opportunities to learn, and He offers us experiences that will strengthen our faith in Him and in His plan for our individual lives.

Thus, the nobleman is a good symbol for each of us with our attempts to believe and our damaging, doubting ways. As Lockyer said, "How prone man is to crave for the outward and physical manifestations of divine power!"[15] The miracle can be seen as symbolically highlighting the limitations we place upon God when we assume that our trial is simply too great for Him to resolve. The story can teach us that we must remember that God knows best what we need and His ways are not our ways (Isaiah 55:8–9). In addition, the miracle narrative symbolically mirrors the tendency of some of us to only *fully* believe—only *fully* trust God—when proof is provided, or when the promptings of our prayers are irrefutable. Such an attitude is the antitheses of faith.

This miracle can teach us that we do not need to see signs and wonders to have faith in Christ or to have a testimony of His gospel.[16] We must remember the Lord's words to Thomas: "Because thou hast seen me, thou hast believed: blessed are they that have not seen, and yet have believed" (John 20:29).[17]

The story also reminds us that Jesus healed people from a distance because of their faith, or (as is the case in this account) to increase their faith. Similarly, He answers our prayers from a distance.[18] Just as the miracle required the nobleman to believe in the distant power of Christ to meet the needs of his son, so the story can remind us that we must believe in the power of God, who seems distant, to address our *ever-present* needs. As Gregory the Great (circa AD 540–604) once noted, the nobleman "asked Jesus earnestly to come down and heal his son. He was asking for the physical presence of the Lord, who is nowhere absent in his spirit. . . . If he had believed completely, he would have known that there was no place where God was not present."[19] The miracle can be viewed as an invitation to truly believe that the Father hears *each* of our prayers and is attentive to *all* of our needs. We must not, with the nobleman, think it best for the Lord to answer *all* of our petitions in *our* chosen way. Indeed, as with the nobleman, God clearly knows what's best for us and what manner of answering our petitions would most benefit our faith and our lives. The story of this miracle can teach us to trust in that, and to exercise faith in the difficult experiences God allows us to have, knowing that "all these things shall give [us] experience, and shall be for [our] good" (D&C 122:7).

Though unmentioned in this story, the symbol of the swine or pig seems germane to this miracle. Anciently, swine or pigs were symbols for individuals who only called upon (or remembered) their God in times of need, but when their life was going well they would forget their Maker. Many professing to be devout Christians act as *swine*, calling out to God when in need, but forgetting Him in their actions, words, and thoughts when all in their personal lives is going as they wish.

Of the nobleman in this miracle story, one commentator wrote, "This petitioner was one *driven* to Jesus by the strong constraint of an outward need . . . rather than one *drawn* by the inner necessities and desires of his soul. . . . Signs and wonders might compel him to a belief, but nothing else. . . . This one, in the poverty of his present faith, straitened and limited the power of the Lord."[20] In other words, the commentator suggests that the man in the miracle may be less an example of a faith-filled follower and more an illustration of the symbolic swine—not going to Jesus out of belief in Him but out of personal desperation. Hence, John Chrysostom (circa AD 344–407) taught that the lesson of the miracle is that we must believe when there is no sign of help, no evidence of a miracle. It is easy to believe when hope is visible on the horizon. However, it is more important to believe when there is nothing more than the counsel to "trust in the Lord" (Proverbs 3:5).[21]

Numerous commentators on this story note that the miracle told therein is really a double-miracle—"on the body of the absent child, on the heart of the present father; one cured of his sickness, the other of his unbelief."[22]

NOTES

1. Since as early as the days of Irenaeus (circa AD 135–202), some have held that this miracle is nothing more than a Johannine repackaging of a miracle reported in Matthew 8:5–13 and Luke 7:1–10 and another miracle reported in Mark 7:24–30 and Matthew 15:21–28. It is not the purpose of this book to examine such

arguments. Thus, it will be left to the readers to draw their own conclusions. A helpful summary of the arguments for and against such a theory can be found in Brown (1966), 192–94. Curiously, there are some strong parallels between this miracle and the turning of water to wine (in John 2:1–11). In both stories Jesus has just returned to Galilee, someone approaches Him with a request, He appears to refuse the request (though not explicitly), the person requesting the miracle persists, Jesus grants the initial request, and in consequence of the miracle, a group of people are said to believe on Him.

2. Though this miracle is called "the second miracle that Jesus did" (John 4:54), the text may only mean that it was the second one He performed in that region. Support for such an interpretation is found in the fact that the father of the ill boy traveled two days to request a blessing of a man he has never met but who has become legendary for His abilities as a healer. As one text notes, "He hears a rumor that a celebrated prophet and preacher is continually going through the cities of Galilee and Judea, and is given to understand that this mighty preacher does not merely charm every hearer by his eloquence, but wins the hearts of men by singularly benevolent miracles which he works as a confirmation of his missions" (Spurgeon [2007], 7:142. See also Lockyer [1965], 163; Kistemaker [2006], 75). The miracle of turning water to wine some six or nine months earlier would not imply Jesus had healing powers. Additionally, it seems likely that this was insufficient to provoke a rumor as widely circulated as this appears to be. One commentator wrote, "The Galilaeans had been impressed by the account of what some of their members had seen when they had been up in Jerusalem at the recent Passover. News moreover of what had happened at the recent wedding at Cana would almost certainly have circulated in the district" (Tasker [1997], 81).

3. See, for example, Matthews (1969), 24.

4. See Brown (1966), 191.

5. See Brown (1966), 190; Matthews (1969), 24.

6. See Origen, "Commentary on the Gospel of John," 13:396, 176.

7. Lockyer (1965), 163.

8. See Brown (1966), 191; Lockyer (1965), 163.

9. Lockyer (1965), 164. Lockyer is not alone in claiming that the problem was the man's inability to believe Jesus could heal the boy only if He were present. The majority of commentators offer this interpretation of the passage and this same explanation for Jesus's rebuke. See, for example, Trench (1962), 76; Tenney, 9:60; Gregory, "Forty Gospel Homilies," 28, 174–75; Cyril, "Commentary on the Gospel of John," 2:5, 175. It is worth noting that a number of individuals since the latter-day Restoration have had the gift to heal from a distance, including the Prophet Joseph Smith, President Lorenzo Snow, and Elder George Halliday. See Smith, *History of the Church*, 4:4–5, footnote ✱; *Biography of Lorenzo Snow*, 263–65; Jenson, *LDS Biographical Encyclopedia*, 3:389, s.v., "Halliday, George."

10. Theodore of Mopsuestia (circa AD 350–428) indicated that when John wrote the man "believed" Jesus when the Lord told him his son was healed, John did not intend for us to understand that the man "believed completely and perfectly." Rather, John

meant "he accepted the word . . . and hoped from something excellent." Theodore points out that there is evidence of the man's "imperfect faith" in that when he learns his son has been healed, "he did not come back to give thanks for the miracle but asked [instead] what time the child had recovered. When he had ascertained that it was the same hour in which the Lord had promised him the healing of the child, 'Then he himself believed'" (Theodore, "Commentary on John," 2.4:46-48, 176). Likewise, Cyril of Alexandria (AD 375–444) noted, "When the official learned that the sick child's recovery coincided exactly with Jesus' command, he is . . . brought to a firmer faith" (Cyril, "Commentary on the Gospel of John," 2:5, 175).

11. Comments like the following are commonplace: "As they learned [that the boy had been healed at the very hour Jesus pronounced him well], the official and his entire household believed" (McQuade [2008], 154). "The grieving father did well to trust as he walked home, but it was not until he learned the reality of his son's healing that the whole truth became apparent" (Ibid., 154).

12. Certainly the man in this episode had faith. His choice to travel the distance, his decision to approach Jesus, his willingness to turn and head home when Jesus told him to are all evidence of faith—no matter how shallow it may have been. We remind the reader here that we are simply drawing a homily from the story, finding application in our own lives. We are not making a claim about the historical centurion and his faith (or lack thereof).

13. Trench (1962), 76.

14. Ibid., 77.

15. Lockyer (1965), 164.

16. See Kistemaker (2006), 78.

17. "The lesson from . . . the miracle is that faith helps faith" (Lockyer [1965], 164).

18. Kistemaker (2006), 78.

19. Gregory, "Forty Gospel Homilies," 28, 175.

20. Trench (1962), 75, 76.

21. Chrysostom, "Homilies on the Gospel of John," 35:3, 174.

22. Trench (1962), 76. See also Lockyer (1965), 164; Cyril, "Commentary on the Gospel of John," 2:5, 176; Chrysostom, "Homilies on the Gospel of John," 35:2, 174.

HAUL *of* FISH

LUKE 5:1–11[1]

THE MIRACLE

Jesus climbed in Peter's boat, and then the chief Apostle and one other disciple (probably Andrew) pushed the vessel slightly offshore so that Christ could teach the gathered people without being physically crowded by them. Thus, there on the banks of the Sea of Galilee, their small ship became a temporary pulpit for the Master Teacher.

Once Jesus was done with His discourse, He suggested that Peter take the boat out into the deeper waters and drop his nets so that he could catch a "haul" of fish. Peter informed Jesus that he and his partners (James, John, and Andrew) had been fishing all night and caught nothing. They were obviously tired and not terribly interested in going back out to sea. However, Peter told Jesus that if He would like for them to return out to sea, they would follow His instructions.

The disciples made their way to the deeper waters and Peter let down a single net.[2] So many fish filled the net that it began to break. Peter beckoned his business partners, James and John—the sons of Zebedee—who were in a nearby boat, to help him. They did so, and between the four of them, they gathered in so many fish that both boats were full and each began to sink because of the added weight.

Peter sensed what had happened was a miracle, and he knew the source of it. He thus fell down at the feet of Jesus and, filled with a sense of unworthiness, begged the Lord to depart from him.[3] However, rather than withdrawing as Peter had requested, Jesus encouraged him to not fear but accept his new call as a "fisher of men."

From that time forward, Luke tells us, they forsook their temporal occupations, and Peter, James, John, and Andrew followed Jesus instead.

BACKGROUND

This miracle took place on the Sea of Galilee immediately after Jesus had concluded speaking with a group of people who had "pressed upon Him" to teach them the "word of God" (Luke 5:1).

The purpose of the miracle was to teach Peter and the other disciple-fishermen of their divine mission: "Follow me, and I will make you fishers of men" (Matthew 4:19). As one commentator noted, "The miracle had its desired effect, for upon reaching the shore, Peter, Andrew, James and John left their fishing nets for the gospel net, and became fishers of men. They were to 'catch' others as Jesus 'caught' them."[4]

The miracle was *not* that Christ knew where fish were hiding in the sea. Rather, the miracle was that He had the ability to make them come where He needed them. As one text puts it, "It was not merely that Christ by his omniscience knew that now there were fishes in that spot. Rather we behold in Him here the Lord of nature, able, by the secret yet mighty magic of his will, to guide and draw the unconscious creatures, and make them minister to the higher interests of his kingdom."[5]

This miracle quite literally fulfills the prophetic words of Jeremiah and the Psalms. For Jeremiah promised, "Behold, I will send for many fishers, saith the Lord, and they shall fish them" (Jeremiah 16:16). And so the Lord has! In the Psalms, we read, "Thou madest him to have dominion over the works of thy hands; thou hast put all things under his feet. . . . The . . . fish of the sea, and whatsoever passeth through the paths of the seas" (Psalm 8:6, 8). And so the Lord does! The fish did not happen to be near the net. Jesus did not see where they were. The Lord of all mankind is also the Lord of all creation. All symbolism aside, the fish rushed to the net because Christ willed that they so do.[6]

SYMBOLIC ELEMENTS

In this narrative, the Sea of Galilee can symbolize the world into which the Apostles would be sent to "gather together his elect from the four winds, from the uttermost part of the earth" (Mark 13:27).

The boat in this story may remind us of the Church—the kingdom of God on the earth. Perhaps it is not coincidental that just before this miracle, Jesus used the small vessel as His pulpit.

The disciples were (and are) symbols of missionaries. Our English word *apostles* comes from a Greek word meaning "one who is sent." Christ was sending out the Apostles to gather the elect, just as His missionaries are sent out today for that same purpose.

The fish can symbolize the souls of men whom we are seeking to gather. Those brought in the boat may be seen as representative of the elect who hear His voice and harden not their hearts (D&C 29:7). Those that fall out of the nets can symbolize those who are not receptive to the gospel message and therefore reject it when His authorized servants approach them.

The nets in this miracle may be seen as representative of the process of conversion. They potentially denote the things that members, missionaries, and apostles do to bring about faith in the Lord Jesus Christ and a testimony of His restored gospel.[7] To His disciples, Jesus said, "Follow me, and I will make you fishers of men" (Matthew 4:19; see also Jeremiah 16:16).

APPLICATION AND ALLEGORIZATION

Since fish were ancient symbols for the souls of men,[8] symbolically speaking Peter, James, John, and Andrew were now being called to focus on converting (on "catching" and "hauling into" the "ship"—which anciently symbolized the Church and the safety it provides[9]) those who were willing to hear and embrace the message of Christ's gospel. "Peter, . . . while drawing the multitude of fishes into his net, has himself fallen into the net of Christ."[10] Jesus calls Peter and his associates to spend the rest of their lives drawing others into the "net," drawing them to Christ and His Church.[11]

Just as fish were used in the early Church as symbols of those who converted to Christ's gospel, the fish was also the earliest symbol used to represent Christ.[12] "The letters of the Greek word for 'fish', *ichthus*, form an acronym for 'Jesus Christ, Son of God, Saviour' (*Iesous Christos Theou hUios* [sic] *Soter*)."[13] Thus, those who follow Christ become "fish," or Christians, taking upon them the name, image, and behavior of their Master. For this reason, the baptismal font in Latin is called *piscina*, which means "the fishpond," and Christian converts in Latin are referred to as *pisciculi*, meaning "little fishes."[14]

Jesus's use of the image of fisherman has a number of additional potential symbolic messages. For example, these former fishermen would no longer seek to catch live fish that would shortly die. Rather, now they were called to "catch" those who are spiritually "dead" that Peter and the Brethren might bring them "eternal life."[15] Also, one commentator noted, "The fisher more often takes his prey alive; he draws it *to* him, does not drive it *from* him."[16] The metaphor of "hunter" would be less appropriate than "fisher" in light of the fact that Christ called Peter and his associates to build the kingdom as much by who they were as by what they taught.[17] As the Lord instructed His Nephite disciples, so also He would instruct all leaders in His kingdom: "What manner of men ought ye to be? Verily I say unto you, even as I am" (3 Nephi 27:27). Peter and his associates in the First Presidency and Twelve were to be fishers. They were to draw men unto them by both the unique things they taught and the unique way they lived.[18]

An additional component of their calling was to be found in Christ's commissioning of them to be fishermen rather than hunters or planters:

> Jesus . . . did not say, "I will make you sowers of the Word of God." And he did not say, "I will make you shepherds of sheep." Farmers who sow seed can assume with relative certainty that they will harvest a crop sometime later in the season. They may not always have a bumper crop, but seldom do they face a complete crop failure. And shepherds can be sure that lambs will be born in springtime. Although there is the probability that they will lose one or two lambs, they are confident that nearly all of them will live and reach maturity. But when fishermen are out on the water, they are unable to predict with any degree of certainty whether they will return with fish. Hence, Jesus called his disciples to be fishers of people, that is, they would have to rely on God to perform the miracle of a catch.[19]

Their work would not be easy. It would require a great deal of faith on their part, just as it required a degree of submission and faith for Peter to return to the sea when he was confident that there were no fish to be caught. But, as with this miracle of abundance performed for Peter and his associates, Jesus promises all His apostles and prophets that the "catch" will be great as they trust in and faithfully follow the Lord's directions.

The fact that Peter and Andrew were not able to bring the net into the ship themselves seems symbolically significant. Of this facet of the miracle, Cyril of Alexandria (AD 375–444) once penned this:

> Note that neither Simon [Peter] nor his companions could draw the net to land. . . . They beckoned to their partners, to those who shared their labors in fishing, to come and help them in securing their prey. For many have taken part with the holy apostles in their labors, and still do so: . . . the pastors and teachers and rulers of the people, who are skilled in the doctrines of the truth. For the net is still being drawn, while Christ fills it, and calls to conversion those who . . . are in the depths of the sea, that is to say, those who live in the surge and waves of worldly things.[20]

Thus, we learn that it is not the duty of the presiding Brethren alone to do the "fishing." They need the help of others—the general membership of the Church—to accomplish such a great and over-whelming task. The miracle highlights the fact that the work was too big for them then and will be too large for those who preside in our day. Thus others must heed their call and help hoist the nets.

One of the overarching messages of the miracle is that Jesus sought to refocus Peter and the others on what their ministry was ultimately to be about, namely the building of the Lord's kingdom upon the earth. He used their personal occupations—something they knew a great deal about—in order to draw an analogy they would understand and thereby to teach them about what He needed them to do on behalf of His kingdom. The most central application of the miracle was simply this: *preach my gospel!*

Having said that, there are a number of other potential messages for us in this miraculous event, things taught to Peter and his brethren that are equally applicable to our lives as disciples of Christ.

First and foremost, we must make the work of the ministry a priority in our lives. We must all serve the Lord and Father's children as "fishers of men." No one who accepts the appellation of Christian can neglect this work. On a related note, we see how Peter fell down, acknowledging the source of his miracle. We too must acknowledge Christ in *all* things and trust in Him at *all* times. While Jesus was the source of Peter's innumerable fish, He immediately thereafter called the soon-to-be chief Apostle to be a "fisher of men." In this is a message about where the success of any missionary or minister comes from (John 15:5). The elder and sister, the bishop and Relief Society president, the Young Men and Young Women leader must all rely on Christ, as He knows where the "fish" are and He can bring the "fish" to the nets of His fishers. "Where the Holy Spirit is free to work, men and women develop into personal workers who are successful in catching men and women for Christ."[21] Likewise, just as Peter (astonished at the catch) fell down at the feet of the Miracle Worker, acknowledging Him as the source of all that is good, we too see Jesus do astonishing things in our lives and in the Church. How do we react? Are we often found at His feet acknowledging Him as the source and expressing gratitude for all that He has done?[22]

Second, there is a potential message that can be drawn from this miracle with regards to faithfulness to commands. Peter was told to cast his "nets" (plural), but (in the King James Version) he only cast out one "net," and negative consequences followed.[23] The net broke, additional work was required, additional people needed to get involved to save the day and repair the damage, and some of the fish were lost. From how the King James Version renders the miracle, an application may be drawn regarding how we must sufficiently trust in Christ so that we are always *fully* obedient to His dictates, regardless of whether we understand why He wishes us to do what He has commanded us to do. The Prophet Joseph taught, "Whatever God requires is right, no matter what it is, although we may not see the reason thereof till long after the events transpire."[24] The story of this miracle (as told in the King James Version) can teach us that being fully obedient brings blessings. Partial obedience, however, will bring consequences.

As a third point, just as Peter and the brethren were to be fishers instead of hunters, you and I are called to be peculiar people (1 Peter 2:9) whose lives draw others to the gospel. Can we honestly say that our lives are such that those who know or interact with us are drawn to the gospel, rather than repelled from it? If we are truly Christian in the way we live, we will not *need* to be hunters.

A fourth point is also worth mentioning. Peter and the brethren were struggling to meet their family's temporal needs. The hours of fishing that night had been a total failure. Nothing had been caught.

Jesus, with no more than a word, provided for them in a dramatic and bountiful way. The miracle of the fish not only shows that Jesus will meet our individual, temporal needs but also that He will meet all of the needs of the Church too. "When the Lord calls us to do something for him . . . he also supplies our physical and spiritual needs. He never fails us. Similarly we ought not [to] fail him either."[25]

As a final point, one commentator noted that, "The miracle had taught [Peter and his associates] to have large expectations in Christ."[26] If we are attentive to all Christ is doing in the world, in our lives, and in the Church, we cannot help but have "large expectations" of Him and a desire to be a part of bringing to pass His great work in the world.

NOTES

1. Some have assumed that this is a retelling (with variation) of the same miracle recorded in John 21. However, the differences are too numerous and too significant to unhesitatingly support that theory. For a good review of the similarities and differences between the two miracles, see Fitzmyer, *Anchor Bible*, 560–62; Leon Morris, *Tyndale New Testament Commentaries*, 123–24.

2. One commentator noted, "After such a night of exhausting toil, Peter might have answered Jesus, 'Now, Master, I am a fisherman and know all about the ways of fish. You are a carpenter. Night is the time to fish, not the morning hour when the sun is shining upon and piercing the water.' But somehow the command of Jesus arrested Peter, who immediately replied, 'Nevertheless at Thy word I will let down the net.' You will note the passage from the plural to the singular. Jesus said nets. Peter replied net. It was as if he said to himself, 'I'll obey His command, although I know the result will be as futile as the past night. I'll let down one net anyhow.' Was this a matter of partial obedience?" (Lockyer [1965], 167). Elsewhere we read, "If they had let down their 'nets' as He told them, instead of the 'net' which was the limit of their faith [Luke 5:4–5], the strain would have been divided and probably none of the fish would have escaped" (Habershon [1975], 168). In other words, whether they doubted Him or not, they certainly did not fully follow His instructions and, consequently, other problems arose. (See also Morris [1999], 125; Trench [1962], 84.)

3. "In the presence of someone with supernatural power, he considered himself sinful and unworthy. The closer he came to Jesus's holiness, the more he saw his own shamefulness because of sin. He now realized the predicament of Isaiah, who saw the Lord . . . and said, 'I am a man of unclean lips.' In Peter's case the focus was squarely on Jesus's divinity and Peter's sinfulness" (Kistemaker [2006], 48).

4. Matthews (1969), 27. See also Kistemaker (2006), 50.

5. Trench (1962), 84. See also Lockyer (1965), 168.

6. In other words, while theologically speaking Jesus does not force us into the kingdom in the way He drove the fish into the nets, He does have power over all creations—as suggested by this event, or the calming of the sea, or the multiplying of

the fish and loaves. The point made in this "Background" section has nothing to do with the symbolism. We only wish to point out that Jesus is quite literally the "Lord of all creation."

7. Wilson (1999), 294.

8. See Conner (1992), 41, 142; Tresidder (2000), 66; Cooper (1995), 68; Hall, *Subjects & Symbols in Art*, 122.

9. See Cooper (1982), 152; Fontana (1994), 112; Hall, *Subjects & Symbols*, 281; Conner (1992), 127; Wilson (1999), 18; Ryken, Wilhoit, and Longman (1998), 101–02; Maximus, "Sermon," 49:1–3, 88; 110:2, 89. In Luke 5:7, we are told that so many were brought into the boats that they began to sink. This reminds us of the challenge the Church faces today in parts of the world wherein conversions are high. So many come into the faith that administering to their needs—and having adequate facilities in which they may worship—is difficult. Such is reminiscent of Helaman 3:25, wherein we are told, "And so great was the prosperity of the church, and so many the blessings which were poured out upon the people, that even the high priests and the teachers were themselves astonished beyond measure."

10. Trench (1962), 85.

11. Augustine (AD 354–430) taught, "They received from him the nets of the Word of God, they cast them into the world as into a deep sea, and they caught the vast multitude of Christians that we can see and marvel at" today (Augustine, "Sermon" 248:2, 87). Similarly, Maximus of Turin (died circa 408–423) wrote, "When Peter lets down the nets at the word [or command of Christ] . . . he is in fact letting down the teachings of Christ. When he unfolds the tightly woven and well-ordered nets at the command of the Master, he is really laying out words in the name of the Savior in a fitting and clear fashion. By these words he is able to save not creatures but souls" (Maximus, "Sermon" 110:2, 88–89).

12. See Hall (1974), 122, 281; Tresidder (2000), 66. See also Fontana (1994), 88.

13. Tresidder (2000), 66. See also Ryken, Wilhoit, and Longman (1998), 290–91; Cooper (1982), 68; Hall (1974), 122; Fontana (1994), 88.

14. See Tresidder (2000), 66; Ryken, Wilhoit, and Longman (1998), 290; Cooper (1982), 68; Hall (1974), 122.

15. See Kistemaker (2006), 50; Trench (1962), 86.

16. Trench (1962), 86. See also 86n4.

17. The language of Jeremiah 16:16 includes hunters as well as fishers: "Behold, I will send for many fishers, saith the Lord, and they shall fish them; and after will I send for many hunters, and they shall hunt them from every mountain, and from every hill, and out of the holes of the rocks."

18. One commentator on the miracle notes, "When the fishing party got to land they left everything. They left the greatest catch they had seen in all their lives. That catch was not as important as what it showed them about Jesus, so they followed him. They became disciples in the fullest sense" (Morris [1999], 126). As a testament to their apostolic calling, we see modern Apostles doing the very same thing when their call to serve comes. Some have walked away from prominent positions in government, industry, or education to embrace a higher calling, just as Peter and

his associates did.

19. Kistemaker (2006), 49.

20. Cyril, "Commentary on Luke," 88.

21. Wilson (1999), 165.

22. McQuade (2008), 143.

23. This distinction between "nets" and "net" only appears in the King James Version of the Bible. In the Greek (and most English translations), Jesus commands Peter to lower his "nets" and Peter does lower "nets" (in the plural). As we've noted above, we are simply drawing a homily here from how the King James Version words the miracle. Historically speaking, Peter appears to have done exactly as the Lord commanded him.

24. *Teachings of the Prophet Joseph Smith*, 256.

25. Kistemaker (2006), 50.

26. Lockyer (1965), 168.

Casting Out *an* Unclean Spirit

MARK 1:21–28
LUKE 4:31–37

THE MIRACLE

One Sabbath day, Jesus was visiting a synagogue in Capernaum. When He arose to speak, He taught with such power that those who heard Him were astonished by both the content of His words and the power with which He delivered them.

While Jesus was teaching, a possessed man began to shout, "Let us alone; what have we to do with thee, thou Jesus of Nazareth? Art thou come to destroy us? I know thee who thou art, the Holy One of God" (Mark 1:24; Luke 4:34).[1] The multiple evil spirits possessing the man recognized Jesus as the Christ and also bore testimony to that reality.[2]

In response to the declaration of the evil spirits, Jesus rebuked them, commanding them to be silent[3] and to depart out of the man whom they were possessing. Though they obeyed Jesus's bidding, before doing so, the evil spirits screamed loudly and physically afflicted the possessed man by "tearing" him and "throwing" him to the ground. From the scriptural description, it appears that they brought upon him something akin to a convulsive seizure, though he was apparently not physically harmed by it.

Those who witnessed this scene were amazed at how evil spirits seemed obligated to obey Jesus's command. Consequently, Jesus became "famous" in Galilee and the surrounding region.

BACKGROUND

Capernaum was a small town on the northwestern shore of the Sea of Galilee. It was the home of Peter and thus had become a sort of "base of operations" for Jesus during His Galilean ministry.[4] Like Paul (Acts 13:15), Jesus may have used the Jewish custom, which permitted recognized visiting teachers to preach a sermon in the synagogue as a means of bringing the message of the gospel to those with "ears to hear" (Matthew 11:15), or He may have simply offered something in response to the teaching of that day (which, too, was customary practice).

Regarding the strange fact that the demons in this miracle boldly testified *of* Christ and *before* Christ, one source mused,

> It is strange that the evil spirit should, without compulsion, proclaim to the world the presence in its midst of the Holy One of God, of Him who should thus bring all the unholy to an end. It remains either . . . to understand this as the cry of abject and servile fear, that with fawning and flatteries would fain avert from itself the doom which with Christ's presence in the world must evidently be near; . . . or else to regard this testimony as intended only to injure in the world's estimation Him in whose favour [*sic*] it is rendered. There was hope that the truth itself might be brought into suspicion and discredit, thus receiving attestation from the spirit of lies; and these confessions of Jesus as the Christ may have been meant to traverse and mar his work.[5]

SYMBOLIC ELEMENTS

There are a number of elements mentioned in this miracle that might have symbolic significance. The central symbol is the man who was possessed. The Prophet Joseph is said to have taught, "The devil has no power over us only as we permit him. The moment we revolt at anything which comes from God, the devil takes power."[6] The possessed man in this miracle is a potential symbol of the consequences of sin. He may represent in a dramatic way the potential danger to all who choose to ignore God's counsels and commands.[7]

The freeing of the man from his demonic captors can be seen as a symbol of the power Christ has to free each of us from *all* that binds us. The painful way in which the evil spirits leave the man—causing him to "convulse" like an epileptic (according to the Greek)—are a testament to how difficult it can be to overcome the power of the devil once we have allowed it to gain footing in our lives.[8] While the miracle makes it clear that Jesus is the source of the miracle, it also strongly suggests that the transition from bound to free is a painful one, hence we are told in vivid and descriptive language that the devils "tore" and "threw" the man before letting him out of their grasp.

The synagogue-attending onlookers—before and after the miracle took place—are good symbols for those whose receptivity to the Spirit allow them to recognize God and His agents when they encounter them. As the Book of Mormon records, "The Lord did pour out his Spirit . . . to prepare the minds of the children of men, or to prepare their hearts to receive the word which should be taught among them" (Alma 16:16).

APPLICATION AND ALLEGORIZATION

Bede the Venerable (circa AD 672–735) wisely noted, "The presence of the Savior is the torment of the devils."[9] One of the major messages that can be drawn from this miracle is that Jesus is stronger than, and serves as a grave threat to, Satan's kingdom. In this miracle, there is an undeniable focus on power—not simply the power to cast out evil spirits but also the power of Jesus's word. Notice that the people who heard Jesus preach were "astonished at his doctrine" (Mark 1:22; Luke 4:32). Similarly, it appears that the demons possessing the man were also astonished at His doctrine, as that appears to be what provoked the outburst during Jesus's discourse. Finally, we learn that those who witnessed the miracle similarly expressed astonishment at the power of Jesus's word to force evil spirits to obey Him.

Thus, a major focus in the symbolism of this miracle is the fact that Jesus's word has power, and none—whether man or demon—can be indifferent once they have been influenced by it. That influence can be sanctifying if we embrace it or damning if we reject it, but none shall escape the miraculous power of Jesus's word! As one commentator recorded:

> The exorcism itself is framed on either side by statements about the authority and power of Jesus' word. Primary attention is not on the exorcism; no rituals or incantations are described. Luke is saying that Jesus is a teacher of the word of God and that word has power. It is that

which the world of demons must now face; it is that which amazes the crowd; it is that which the church after him proclaims.[10]

Truman G. Madsen once noted, "Light always stirs up darkness. That is an eternal law."[11] Through this miracle, it becomes evident that Jesus's "word" provokes Satan's wrath. "The immediate result of the preaching of Jesus was not harmony, but division and strife."[12] So it is in the world today. Like Jesus and His disciples of old, we should expect opposition to the message and opposition to our attempts to propagate personal righteousness in the world. Satan and his followers will ever respond in a violent and loud manner when the Lord and His servants spread the "good news" or build another temple.[13] And why would such be the case? Because Jesus, His kingdom, and His followers pose a significant threat to what Satan is trying to accomplish in this telestial world.

This story is the first of some twenty-one miracles in Luke's Gospel. It seems significant that Jesus's first public confrontation and defeat of the powers of evil should take place "in the place of worship of the people of God."[14] Symbolically depicted but literally intended, we learn from our story that the church or the temple is the place most prone to give us power over Satan. Perhaps Luke records the miracle in the synagogue so that we will remember that Satan has no home there, and so that we will constantly recall that those who regularly visit the Lord's house will find freedom from the things that Satan has used to bind and control us. Like the man possessed, we may find the initial freeing somewhat painful, but we have the promise that if we make our way to the house of God, Satan's power over us can be thwarted.

On a related note, it has been suggested that we may be symbolized by the demoniac discussed in the story. Just as he was freed from Satan's influence shortly after bearing testimony that Jesus is the Christ, so also you and I, through bearing witness of Christ's divine mission, gain a degree of freedom from the adversary and his temptations. Spirit-born testimony not only chases the devil away, it also demands the withdrawal of sins previously committed (D&C 62:3; 84:61).

On the flip side, another commentator on this verse suggested that, just as the demoniac had a conviction of Christ, even people who are still struggling with Satan's influence in their lives can receive a testimony of the gospel. People with ugly pasts—and those in great need of repentance—can still have faith in God, His plan, and His Church. When their testimony is acted upon, forgiveness can come and a freeing from Satan's grasp can be had.

When looking upon the miracle from the perspective of those with limited faith, a secular view—or a corrupt Christology—another possible symbolic message can be seen. As one author pointed out, "Those who reject the deity of Christ show an appalling ignorance that even demons in Jesus's day did not share, for the evil spirits confessed that Jesus is indeed the Son of the Most High God."[15] Even the devils have stronger testimonies than do some who profess to be Christians! Though true, it is a truth that is a travesty. Sadly, so many of God's children do not recognize their Father, nor do they recognize Jesus as their Savior (though His fame and name are so commonly known). Elsewhere, one recognized expert on the miracles rhetorically asked,

> Have we anything today [comparable to] the demon in the synagogue? Has history repeated itself? We think it has. When, in buildings erected for the preaching of the inspired . . . scriptures, preachers discredit the reliability of the Bible, repudiate the miracles, flout the virgin birth, the atoning blood, and the physical resurrection of Christ, what are they with all their education and polish but demons in the synagogue? As they do not represent the Spirit of truth, some other spirit must possess them.[16]

We would do well to regularly ask ourselves: Do we recognize Jesus's authority, power, divinity, and Spirit, as did those who were said to be astonished by His doctrine? Or do our spirits shout against Him, as did the demons residing in the man possessed?

NOTES

1. One commentator wrote, "Apparently it was Jesus' authoritative teaching that stirred the demon in a man who was present in the synagogue. The unclean spirit in the man recognized that the word of God could destroy not only him but 'us,' that is, the whole realm of demons" (Craddock, *Interpretation*, 66–67. See also Liefeld, "Luke," 8:871; McQuade [2008], 133). The plural "us" does not refer to the man and the evil spirit possessing him but rather has reference to the various evil spirits that oppose Jesus and His work. Both Mark and Luke say the man was possessed by "an unclean spirit" (Mark 1:23) or the "spirit of an unclean devil" (Luke 4:33), but the plural "us" in Mark 1:24 and Luke 4:34 suggest that either the man was possessed

with several evil spirits, or the evil spirit in him was asking Jesus—on behalf of all evil spirits in the world—"have you come to destroy us?" The former of these two interpretations seem the most likely. (See Wessel, 8:627; Kistemaker [2006], 119–20. See also Fitzmyer [1970], 545–46; Craddock [1990], 66–67.)

2. Morris (1999), 120. See also Liefeld (1976–1992), 8:872.

3. The Greek is literally "be muzzled" and is the ancient slang equivalent of "shut up!" Clearly, Jesus's dictate is no mild rebuke. (See Cole, *Tyndale New Testament Commentaries*, 114; Fitzmyer [1970], 546; Mann, *Anchor Bible*, 213.) One early Christian source noted, "He would not permit the unclean demons to confess him. It was not right for them to usurp the glory of the apostolic office" (Cyril, "Commentary on Luke," 85).

4. See Wessel, "Mark," 8:626.

5. Trench (1962), 144.

6. Smith (1976), 181.

7. This is not to say that disobedience always results in demonic possession. Only that the figure represented in the story potentially symbolizes the reality that rebellion against God opens us up to the influence of the adversary.

8. See Nicoll, *Expositor's Greek Testament*, 1:346; *Thayer's Greek-English Lexicon*, 582.

9. Bede, "Homilies on the Gospels," 1:13, 21.

10. Craddock (1990), 67.

11. Madsen, *Joseph Smith the Prophet*, 56.

12. Cole (1997), 113.

13. Brigham Young noted, "Some say, 'We never began to build a temple without the bells of hell beginning to ring.' I want to hear them ring" (*Discourses of Brigham Young*, 410).

14. Williamson, *Interpretation*, 50. One text states, "The 'good news of the kingdom of God' Jesus was proclaiming signaled an attack on the forces of evil. . . . A holy war is being launched and, as v. 34 [of Luke 4] suggests, the demons know it. This war will be carried on by Jesus' disciples ([Luke] 9:1–2; 10:8–9, 17)" (Liefeld, 8:872).

15. Kistemaker (2006), 122.

16. Lockyer (1965), 169.

Peter's Mother-in-Law *Is* Healed

MATTHEW 8:14–15
MARK 1:29–31
LUKE 4:38–39

The Miracle

Only moments before this miracle was performed, Jesus had been a few doors down from Peter's home, casting evil spirits out of a man in the neighborhood synagogue. When He had performed that miracle, He, along with His disciples—Andrew, James, and John—immediately left the synagogue and entered Peter's home where He was told of the woman's rather serious sickness.[1]

Jesus stood next to her bed, took her by the hand,[2] and "rebuked" the fever, which then immediately left her. Peter's wife's mother was instantaneously completely healed and straightway began to serve Jesus and His disciples.

Background

It has been said that Capernaum was somewhat noted for its fevers, perhaps because of the marsh-like surroundings, which increased the likelihood of diseases such as malaria.[3] Regardless, Mark says that Peter's mother-in-law was lying in bed "sick of a fever" (Mark 1:30). However, in the Greek Luke says she was "seized" or "tormented" with a "great fever" (Luke 4:38).[4] Thus, Luke (the physician) informs us that this was no mild sickness.

Mark states that "forthwith," or immediately, after Jesus cast out the unclean spirit at the synagogue, He "entered into the house of Simon" Peter (Mark 1:29). Excavations in the area have led scholars to believe that Peter's mother-in-law lived literally a few yards from the Capernaum synagogue where Jesus performed His previous miracle.[5] So, quite literally, He walked out one door and into the next.

SYMBOLIC ELEMENTS

While the story of this miracle is short, one commentator noted, "Even this bare-bones narrative . . . would have symbolic significance for [its] readers."[6] While not all scriptural miracles highlight Jesus's role in the miraculous, this story certainly does. Jesus is depicted as the great physician of body *and* soul. Thus, the miracle emphasizes God's power to cure *all* ills.

One dictionary of biblical types and symbols suggested that the fever of Peter's mother-in-law "is a type of the worries and difficulties which bother many hearts and hinder their usefulness."[7] Perhaps. Thus, while no specific sin is suggested by the fever, it could stand as a general representation of all sins, worries, or difficulties that might prevent us from feeling God's Spirit, from serving in His kingdom, or from returning to His presence.

The manner in which Jesus healed Peter's mother-in-law—both by touch and by word—mirrors how healings take place in the Church today. The physically sick are typically healed through touch, or a priesthood blessing, and the spiritually sick through verbal instruction, whether that comes in the form of counseling with one's priesthood leader or through being "nourished by the good word of God" (Jacob 6:7).

The woman who is taken ill can mirror the bride of Christ (or Church) who while residing in this "lone and dreary world" is potentially susceptible to many spiritual afflictions. In other words, as Peter's mother-in-law falls prey to a sickness common in her day, we (in the Church) can also find ourselves spiritually sickened by the "diseases" of our day and culture—diseases that sicken the soul as much as the body.

Certain symbolic elements present in the Greek do not appear in some English language translations of this story. For example, the Greek verb for "raised up" used in Mark's account (and translated "lifted her up" in the King James Version) is the exact same verb used to describe the resurrection of all people (Mark 12:26), including the Resurrection of Christ (see Mark 6:14, 16; 14:28; 16:7). Thus, Greek-reading students of Mark's account would be struck with how the healing of Peter's mother-in-law seems to foreshadow resurrection from the dead. "Mark probably wishes to imply, therefore, that the 'raising' power that was manifested in Jesus' healing miracles was the same . . . power by which God later resurrected him from death."[8]

APPLICATION AND ALLEGORIZATION

This miracle offers us a number of potential insights into the gospel and Christ's work in our lives. It highlights His power to heal or change with immediacy. Thus, it can remind us of the importance of gratitude for our blessings and His intervention. It cautions us about being unaware of the debilitating spiritual afflictions that spread like a pandemic throughout the world. And it invites us to visit and bless those who have need of our presence and gifts.

In the early fifth century, Jerome (circa AD 347–420) frequently spoke of this miracle as a standard symbol for how Christ heals the spiritually sick. Among other things, Jerome wrote,

> Jesus . . . entered Peter's house, where a woman was lying stretched upon a bed, exhausted with a violent fever. . . . He touched her hand. "Immediately," it says, "the fever left her." Let us therefore also receive Jesus. When he has entered into us and we have received him into mind and heart, then he will quench the fever of unbefitting pleasures. He will raise us up and make us strong, even in spiritual things, so that we might serve him by performing those things that please him. . . . I ask, how great is the usefulness of the touch of his holy [hand]. For it both drives away diseases of various kinds, and a crowd of demons, and overthrows the power of the devil. . . . Let it then take hold of us, or rather let us take hold of it. . . . May we do this so that it might free us from the sickness of the soul, and from the assault and violence of demons.[9]

Elsewhere Jerome wrote,

> May Christ come to our house and enter in and by his command cure the fever of our sins. Each one of us is sick with a fever. When ever [*sic*] I give way to anger, I have a fever. There are as many fevers as there are

faults and vices. Let . . . Jesus . . . come to us and touch our hand. If he does so, at once our fever is gone. He is an excellent physician and truly the chief Physician. Moses is a physician. Isaiah is a physician. All the [prophets] are physicians, but he is the chief Physician.[10]

Part of the mortal experience is to labor under a veil, which constitutes a form of spiritual death. We are all cut off from God's literal presence. Consequently, we are more prone to the enticing of the adversary and the sicknesses of our sinful society. We have "the fever," per se, and must reach out to Christ so that He may heal us, no matter what our moral malady or spiritual sickness.

The reaction of Peter's mother-in-law to her healing—namely that she immediately got up and served Christ and those with Him—not only shows that Jesus's healing of her was complete and instantaneous, but, more particularly, that it can be seen as evidence of her implicit gratitude for the blessing that had come into her life, and for the source of that blessing: Christ.[11] One author suggests,

> This text . . . makes the role of women the model of discipleship. Here the mother-in-law's response to the healing of Jesus is the discipleship of lowly service, a model to which Jesus will repeatedly call his followers . . . and which he supremely embodies in his own service [Mark 8:34; 9:35; 10:43–45]. . . . This is the first of a series of incidents in which a woman represents the right response (the poor widow, [Mark] 12:41–44; the woman with the ointment, [Mark] 14:3–9; the women at the cross, [Mark] 15:40–41; the women at the tomb, [Mark] 16:1).[12]

Peter's mother-in-law is an example to us all. We should each express our gratitude for our blessings and for He from whom all blessings come by serving Christ and serving God's children (Mosiah 2:17; Matthew 25:40).[13]

Some commentators on the miracle have seen in it a message about how Christ is not just focused on lifting sins from us but also on lifting our sicknesses and burdens. In Isaiah 53:4, we read, "Surely he hath borne our griefs, and carried our sorrows." Alma informs us that Christ would "take upon him [the] infirmities [of His people], that his bowels may be filled with mercy, according to the flesh, that he may know according to the flesh how to succor his people according to their infirmities" (Alma 7:12). As Hilary of Arles (circa AD 401–449) put it, Christ absorbed "into the suffering of his body the infirmities of human weakness."[14] Jesus did not just suffer for our sins but also for each and every trial and burden we are called to endure or carry during this mortal experience. He cares as much for the suffering caused by cancer as He does for the sorrow caused by sin. And His Atonement addressed all such trials, be they spiritual, physical, emotional, or otherwise.[15]

One author offered the following rather intriguing insight:

> It is fitting to observe that [this healing miracle] took place in a home. . . . How many homes of the sick and diseased do those modern "faith healers," who exploit the suffering for their own financial gain, visit? Home visitation to receive the needy would be too humdrum for them. They require the tent, with all the paraphernalia of mass psychology to stage their so-called "miracles."[16]

Perhaps this miracle calls us to ask whether we are prone to visit the sick and afflicted in our congregation and community as Christ would. Do we serve at public gatherings where our "sacrifice" will be noticed but regularly neglect our home or visiting teaching? Do we "visit the fatherless and widows in their affliction" (James 1:27)? Do we "go to the poor, like our Captain of old, And visit the weary, the hungry, and cold"?[17] To do so is, as the Apostle James called it, "Pure religion . . . undefiled before God" (James 1:27).

NOTES

1. Whether Peter had been with them at the synagogue or had been home attending to the needs of his sick mother-in-law is unclear from the text. He was certainly in attendance at the healing, but we do not know if he witnessed the miracle at the synagogue, which had taken place only minutes earlier.

2. One commentator reminds us, "Jewish Halakah [or law] forbade touching persons with many kinds of fever. . . . But Jesus healed with a touch. . . . The touch did not defile the healer but healed the defiled" (Carson, "Matthew," 8:204. See also France, *Tyndale New Testament Commentaries*, 157).

3. See, for example, Lockyer (1965), 171.

4. Fitzmyer (1970), 550.

5. The *Anchor Bible Dictionary* states that that north side of Simon Peter's home lay under the balcony of the synagogue (Corbo, "Capernaum," 1:867. See also Marcus, *Anchor Bible*, 196, 198). The remains of the Capernaum synagogue that now stands in that location is from the fourth or fifth century AD (some think as late as the

sixth) but is believed to be built on the remains of a first-century synagogue, "presumably the one in this story" (Marcus [2000], 186. See also Corbo [1992], 868; Wessell, 8:628).

6. Marcus (2000), 199.

7. Wilson (1999), 152.

8. Marcus (2000), 199. It seems curious that Jesus takes the woman by the hand and talks with her in order to heal her. Knowing that some commentators have seen her healing as a foreshadowing of the resurrection and our return to God's presence, there may be a parallel between this miracle and our own overcoming of the perils of mortality. It is noteworthy that the temple endowment has it participants symbolically act out their return to God's presence through a similar interaction with the Father at the veil of the temple.

9. Cyril, "Commentary on Luke," 86. In the spirit of Jerome's teaching, J. H. Newman penned the familiar prayer, "O Lord preserve us all the day long . . . until the fever of life is over, and our work is done" (cited in Williamson [1983], 55).

10. Jerome, "Homilies on the Gospel of Mark," 85. Jerome also wrote, "If we are unable to seize his hand, let us prostrate ourselves at his feet. If we are unable to reach his head, let us wash his feet with our tears. . . . Let us ask the Lord to grasp our hand. 'And at once,' he says, 'the fever left her.' Immediately as her hand is grasped, the fever flees" ("Tractate on Mark's Gospel," 25). So it is with us!

11. Fitzmyer (1970), 549. See also Marcus (2000), 196; Carson (1976–1992), 8:204; Cole (1997), 115; Kistemaker (2006), 60.

12. Williamson (1983), 55. See also Cole (1997), 115.

13. One commentator suggested that the example of Peter's mother-in-law is applicable "to all restored to spiritual health. . . . They should use this strength in ministering to Christ and to his people" (Trench [1962], 148).

14. Cited in Trench (1962), 149n2.

15. One source accurately notes, "The first miracle that Jesus performed in [Luke's] Gospel benefits a man, whereas the second helps a woman" (Fitzmyer (1970), 549). This suggests Jesus's universal concern. He cares about the women as well as the men, the child as well as the adult, the believer as well as the non-believer.

16. Lockyer (1965), 171.

17. Wheelock and Bayly, "Ye Elders of Israel," Hymn no. 319.

A MULTITUDE *Is* HEALED

MATTHEW 8:16–17
MARK 1:32–34
LUKE 4:40–41

THE MIRACLE

Perhaps only hours after Jesus had healed Peter's mother-in-law, sunset arrived and, consequently, the Sabbath day drew to a close. There, still at Peter's house—perhaps in a state of relaxation from the day's labors—Jesus, Peter, and others noticed a multitude of possessed and ill people gathering near the door. Before long, they began to spill into the house itself.

Through the laying on of hands and by direct command, Jesus healed everyone brought to Him that night. "Tired though He must have been because of the limitations of His humanity, Jesus began His healing mission afresh [that evening], continuing far into the night His toilsome work, until He had 'healed them all.' His sympathy was individual, for Luke tells us that 'He laid His hand on *every one* of them.'"[1]

In the process of this powerful and lengthy miracle, some of the evil spirits possessing those Jesus would heal loudly proclaimed that "Jesus is the Christ, the Son of God." When they so spoke, Jesus immediately forbade them from bearing their testimony.[2]

BACKGROUND

Jesus performed this miracle in Capernaum, where He had been staying and where He had labored much of the day. Earlier that afternoon, He had healed the man at the synagogue who was possessed by demons. When He arrived at Peter's home, He found His host's mother-in-law seriously ill and bedridden. He immediately healed her too. Then, as Jesus, Peter, James, John, and Andrew sat down to a meal prepared by Peter's just-healed mother-in-law, people began to gather in droves outside the home. In the words of one commentator, "at sunset it was like a hospital at the door of Peter's home."[3] The possessed and the sick came in hordes to be healed by Jesus. Perhaps the miracle at the synagogue provoked the arrival of those laboring under Satan's influence and the healing of Peter's in-law prompted the appearance of those beset with illness.

It has been suggested that Peter must have had a fairly large home, as it is generally held that Peter's place was where Jesus lived during His Galilean ministry, and Mark suggests Andrew and his family were living there also (Mark 1:29), as was Peter's mother-in-law. Thus, perhaps Peter was somewhat affluent at the time of this miracle.[4] Owing to the number of unplanned guests that arrived that evening hoping to be blessed by Jesus, the spacious home (when compared to those common for that day) would have been a boon.

SYMBOLIC ELEMENTS

The timing of the miracles recorded in this narrative seems significant. It was twilight or sunset and the Jewish Sabbath was wrapping up. While darkness can have ominous implications (including symbolizing sin and death), sunset or twilight typically carries a slightly different connotation. One commentator noted that "twilight possesses a sacral significance."[5] Symbolically speaking, it is the end of one phase and the beginning of another.[6] Such may be implied in this account.

Peter's home in this story can potentially be seen as representative of the place of gathering, of healing. It is, in its usage here, a good type for the church or temple, which offer healing to those who regularly congregate there.

The laying on of hands accompanied by the verbal word are standard symbols for the authorized conveyance of power or blessings.[7]

APPLICATION AND ALLEGORIZATION

All three synoptic authors record this miracle, and all three highlight that this set of miracles happened at night after sunset, once the evening had begun.[8] Near the end of the fourth century, Ambrose of Milan (circa AD 333–397) offered an explanation as to why this fact was so important in understanding the symbolic message of this miracle. He pointed out that the original or first Sabbath came at the end of the creation of this world, and the weekly Sabbaths that have followed are each symbols of the end of God's original cycle of creation. According to Ambrose, in this miracle, Jesus healed the multitude at night—or after the Sabbath had officially ended—as a symbolic message that one phase of creation had just ended but a new one was being inaugurated. In other words, Jesus has come not to destroy the law but rather to fulfill it.[9] In Ambrose's words, "The works of divine healing [were] begun on the sabbath day, to show from the outset [of Christ's ministry] that [a] new creation began where the old creation ceased."[10] Jesus was inaugurating a new dispensation—one of healing and miracles. The law may have become dead (Romans 7:4, 6; 2 Nephi 25:25), but revealed religion was not, and Christ's works would prove that.

Related to the idea that Jesus has come to fulfill, replace, and revitalize the religion of ancient Israel—through a restoration of the fulness of the gospel in the meridian of time—is another symbol that may be drawn from the story. Scholars note that during the apostolic period, Peter's home became a house-church for the Christian converts of the area.[11] Because of its size and location—and through renovations over the years—the Saints utilized it as a place of worship. On a much smaller scale, it *may* be that the Saints in Jesus's day met in Peter's home (in addition to the synagogue) for some component of their worship or devotion, and for other potentially Church-related activities.[12]

In Mark 1:21–28 a singular healing took place at the local synagogue only a few yards from Peter's home. Then, however, a plethora of people was healed, not at the synagogue, but at Peter's home (a future Christian church, of sorts). All of this appears to be a potential symbol for the restoration that was taking place under Jesus's direction. Thus, these two episodes, which took place (according to Mark) on the same day and in the same town, could symbolically suggest that the old law (symbolized by the synagogue) has been replaced by the new law (represented by Peter's house-church residence). The former bore *some* fruits, though not much. The latter produced an unreal amount of fruit. So it is with the law of Moses and the gospel of Christ. One had the power to produce *some* fruit, though not much. The other, however, brings forth in abundance.[13]

Matthew's reference to Isaiah 53:4 ("he hath borne our griefs, and carried our sorrows") being fulfilled in Jesus's healing work of that evening shows that the Apostle saw Jesus's works as evidence of His messianic call. The healings being performed that night were for Matthew a foreshadowing of what Jesus would do, through His Atonement, for all of us. He would take away our sins, our pains, our sorrows, and our suffering. "For Matthew, Jesus' healing miracles pointed beyond themselves to the cross."[14]

As has been suggested, the healing at the end of the Sabbath may be designed to highlight the end of an era. The law of Moses was being fulfilled and Jesus was now bringing to those who would accept Him a higher law, a higher way, and a more fruitful faith. This can be suggested by the number of healings performed at the synagogue in contrast to the number brought to pass at the local house-church. Christ had come to begin a new creation, and a large part of that was to make those who accepted Him new creations. In the words of the Apostle Paul, "If any man be in Christ, he is a new creature: old things are passed away; behold, all things are become new" (2 Corinthians 5:17; see also Galatians 6:15). For Matthew, the entire episode highlights, in a typological way, Christ's coming Atonement when He would heal all sickness and cast out all sin.

All three accounts of this miracle state that friends or family "brought unto [Jesus] all" that needed His help. One author reminded us, "The Lord can heal sin-sick souls without our bringing the loved ones to Him; but if we are really longing for their deliverance, it is for us to bring them by prayer and to lead them to the Great Physician."[15]

What are you personally doing to "bring" those whom you know are "sin-sick" to "the Great Physician" so they might be healed? As this miracle suggests, it is not enough for us to simply pray for their well-being. James reminded us, "What doth it profit . . . a man [to] say he hath faith, and [yet he] have not works? . . . If a brother or sister be naked and destitute of daily food, and one of you say unto them, Depart in peace, be ye warmed and filled; notwithstanding ye give them not those things which are needful to the body; what doth it profit?" (James 2:1–16). The miracle of the multitude healed contains a latent message to us that we must do more than pray for our brothers and sisters in need; we must act on their behalf.

From the perspective of the Restoration in these latter days, one other symbolic element may be worth noting. Just as this miracle shows Jesus manifesting His power at the beginning of a new day—a day that started when the sun had set and darkness had covered the land—so Jesus has chosen to manifest His power in these last days at the beginning of a new era, one that began when (in many ways) a measure of spiritual darkness was covering the land as much as it had at any other time in the history of the world. And whereas Judaism (the common faith of the day in that region) had little of a miraculous nature to offer, so also the Lord restored the gospel through the Prophet Joseph at a time when the "faith of the day" was largely no longer looking for the miraculous to happen.[16] The fruits available to followers of Christ in the years leading up to the Restoration seem to parallel those of Judaism leading up to Jesus's ministry. And the plethora of power Jesus restored in the first century seems to mirror that which He restored in the dispensation of the fulness of times. Both periods of miracle working pierced the dark night into which they were born.

NOTES

1. Lockyer (1965), 172.

2. One source notes, "It is interesting that Luke tells us that thus early the demons recognized that [Jesus] was the Christ. It took the disciples a long time to learn this lesson. . . . The Galileans may have thought Jesus no more than a man, but the evil ones did not make that mistake" (Morris [1999], 121). While some assume Jesus forbade them to bear their testimonies primarily because He felt it was not time to announce such a truth, I am personally more drawn to the explanation that an open proclamation of His messiahship by devils might "expose Jesus to charges of Satanic collusion and blasphemy" (Marcus [2000], 201. See also Craddock [1990], 68).

3. Lockyer (1965), 171.

4. See France (1997), 157. The *Anchor Bible Dictionary* describes Peter's abode as a "vast dwelling" for its day and location. See Corbo (1992), 1:867.

5. Ryken, Wilhoit, and Longman (1998), 901.

6. Tresidder (2000), 105; Todeschi (1995), 248.

7. See, for example, Ryken, Wilhoit, and Longman (1998), 362.

8. " 'That evening after sunset' would be, according to Jewish reckoning, the following day, since the Sabbath ends at sundown" (Wessell [1976–92], 8:628). Commentaries generally point out that Jews would have been hesitant to carry the sick or possessed to Jesus while it was still the Sabbath for fear that in so doing

they would break the oral law. While this may explain the thoughts of some who came "at evening," this is certainly not a universally held view (in the mind of many commentators). On a separate note, while the mention of this event by all three synoptic authors could suggest its importance, it could also simply suggest that Matthew and Luke were (as scholars traditionally assume) drawing on Mark's Gospel and the "Q" text. If that is the case, the commonality of the miracle would not be surprising. The name Q comes from the German word *Quelle*, meaning "source." There is a belief among many biblical scholars that Matthew and Luke heavily borrowed from Mark's Gospel in writing their own accounts of the life and teachings of Christ. The "Q" source, however, is believed by many to have been an early Christian compilation of Jesus's teachings that accounts for the common materials in Matthew and Luke that do not appear in Mark. Thus, while Matthew and Luke may have borrowed much of their material from Mark's text, they may also (according to most scholars) have gleaned a significant amount of information from another document (the "Q"), which no longer exists. See Tuckett, "Q (Gospel Source)," 5:567–72.

9. Ambrose is not alone in his assessment of the symbolic message of the ending Sabbath. One scholarly commentary on the passage noted, "The setting of these healings at the conclusion of the Sabbath is significant for a couple of reasons. . . . This period was marked in Jewish homes by the *Havdālāh* service, in which God's creation of the world was celebrated. . . . These associations of the Havdālāh period perhaps provide part of the background for Mark's picture of the divine act of eschatological [or 'end-time'] re-creation whereby Jesus heals and casts out demons in Peter's house at the conclusion of the Sabbath. The eschatological dimension of Jesus' actions is underscored by the repeated emphasis on completeness: all the sick and demon-possessed are brought to the house where Jesus is, and the whole city gathers at its door" (Marcus [2000], 200).

10. Ambrose, "Gospel of Luke," 84. See also 84–85.

11. See, for example, Corbo (1992), 1:867; Marcus (2000), 200.

12. See France (1997), 157. It seems evident that in His lifetime, Jesus, Peter, a number of the disciples, and other followers of Christ gathered in Peter's home for various meetings and instruction.

13. See Marcus (2000), 200, who states, "Mark's readers may even have seen contemporary significance in the scene shift from a synagogue in 1:21–28 to a house (church) in 1:29–34: it is to the latter, not to the former, that the populace throngs."

14. Carson (1976–1992), 8:206. Matthew says Jesus "took" their "infirmities" and "bore" their "sicknesses" (Matthew 8:17). The Greek used in that verse is clearly understood to be a foreshadowing of Christ's act of "taking" our "sins" and "carrying" our "afflictions" during His Atonement. This passage is without question typological, in that Matthew is trying to cause his readers to see Jesus as the "suffering servant" of Isaiah 53:4 who would eventually redeem them from all suffering and sin. (See Albright and Mann, *Anchor Bible*, 94. See also France (1997), 158–59.) Some Jews in the first century no doubt associated sickness with sin—and Matthew's translation of Isaiah 53:4 highlights that belief. However, for our purposes here, it

matters little what those in Capernaum thought caused illness. We are simply looking at the application to the life of the modern reader.

15. Habershon (1975), 125.

16. This is not to say that no one in Joseph's day was looking for the miraculous. But it is to suggest that some—including some of Joseph's contemporaries—found claims of the miraculous (including claims made by Joseph) hard to swallow. For example, Edward King, a near contemporary of the Prophet Joseph Smith, wrote, "The word of Prophesy is sealed forever" (*Signs of the Times*, 28). King, and others, felt claims about revelation, visions, gifts of the Spirit, and so on were simply untenable. Likewise, in a spirit of belittling, another contemporary of the Prophet wrote, "One of the most distinguishing peculiarities of Mormonism, is, its pretensions to inspiration. Its real believers profess to stand on an equal footing with the apostles, and to be as really inspired and empowered to work miracles as they were. We . . . speak here, of that inspiration of God by which he makes known his will, over and above what he has made known by the light of nature; and which imparts such a degree of divine assistance, as enables the person to whom it is given, to communicate to others, religious knowledge without error or mistake" (Sunderland, *Mormonism Exposed and Refuted*, 14).

THE HEALING *of a* LEPER

MATTHEW 8:1–4
MARK 1:40–45
LUKE 5:12–15

THE MIRACLE

After preaching the Sermon on the Mount, Jesus descended the hill and was followed by a large number of people who had listened to His discourse. But suddenly, they began to disperse. A leper, who had likely been listening to Jesus's sermon from a distance, approached Him in an attitude of worship, kneeling before Him (according to Mark), or prostrating himself at Christ's feet (according to Luke).[1] The leper begged Jesus to heal him, saying, "If you will it, you can make me clean." The afflicted man's words made it clear that he had no doubts about Jesus's ability to heal him, though he may have had reservations about Jesus's willingness—particularly in light of how lepers were treated in first-century Judaism.

In response to the man's request, Jesus reached forth His hand, touched the man, and spoke the words, "I will; be cleansed!" And the man was healed. Jesus's purity entered the leper, making him whole.[2]

The scriptural accounts say that the leper was instantly cleansed. The visible nature of this miracle is almost hard to imagine. When the man first approached Jesus, he was likely in an advanced stage of the disease. (Luke speaks of him as "full of leprosy" [Luke 5:12].) While not all believe this to be the case, some commentators hold that fingers and toes would potentially have been missing from the man. His face may have been grossly distorted. The stench of his rotting gangrene-infested flesh would potentially have been notice-able for some distance around him. And yet in an instant, all was gone. His sores were closed and his deformities removed. His once foul flesh no longer smelled but appeared robust and healthy. While some may seek to rationalize away some miracles, this act of healing and cleansing could not be denied Jesus instructed the leper to go to a priest to be officially declared clean, as was required by the law.[3] Then Christ informed the miracle's recipient that he should go to the temple and make the offering required under the law of Moses as a sign of obedience and gratitude to God for the great blessing he just received (Leviticus 14:1–32)[4] and as a testament to the priests of the reality of the miracle and that Jesus had instructed the man to keep the law.

As the leper prepared to depart, Jesus gave him one additional bit of instruction. He strongly charged the leper to tell no one how he had been healed. But the leper did not obey Jesus's instructions.[5] Rather, he told many, and thus Jesus could no longer openly enter the city with-out being mobbed by those seeking not the Messiah, but a faith healer or miracle worker. Consequently, He was relegated to dwelling in the desert for a time. Nevertheless, the people found Him and came from all parts to hear Him teach and to be healed.

BACKGROUND

The Jews of Jesus's day referred to leprosy as "the finger of God."[6] This may in part be because they tended to see it as evidence of God's displeasure with those who developed it. The experiences of Miriam, Gehazi, and Uzziah may have reinforced this belief in the minds of those who knew their stories. But the epitaph "finger of God" also implied their belief that the disease was incurable except in the rare situations where God Himself cured it, as He had in this miracle.

To touch someone with leprosy was to become defiled yourself. Thus, commentators suggest that Jews faithful to the law typically avoided contact with any and all lepers, and also avoided touching anything a leper was known to have touched. The law of Moses was quite strict on this point. Thus we read, "This touching of the unclean by Christ is noteworthy, drawing after it, as according to the ordi-nances of the Law it did, a ceremonial uncleanliness. Another would have defiled *himself* by touching the leper; but He, Himself, remaining undefiled, cleansed him whom He touched; for in Him health overcame sickness,—and purity, defilement,—and life, death."[7]

Symbolic Elements

Leprosy is a common symbol for spiritual sickness.[8] It is particularly well suited as a teaching device since the one suffering from the disease has outward manifestations of his inward sickness. Additionally, the leper slowly rots because of the ailment, just as the spiritually sick slowly progress in their spiritual decline.

Prostration is a symbol of submission or humility, but also of respect and gratitude.[9] It is an acknowledgment by the one lying face down that he is inferior to or dependent upon the person before whom he prostrates himself.

As we have noted elsewhere, touching the individual sickened by the disease represents the conveyance or transference of power and blessings. Touching that which is unclean shows either a disregard for defilement or a power that places one above the defilement (or above the rules that regulate it).

Application and Allegorization

As noted, leprosy is a standard symbol for the sin-sick soul.[10] It represents those who are lost without the intervention of the Lord and His atoning blood. It is a disease that causes the decay and putrefaction of the living body.[11] In scripture, lepers are the living dead (Numbers 12:12; Job 18:13). And according to the law of Moses, lepers were to be somewhat ostracized or cut off from direct fellowship with the rest of the house of Israel.[12]

Consequently, leprosy was seen in ancient times as a symbol of that which happens to those who transgress God's laws. Sin introduces decay and corrupts our spirits. Sin causes us to be cut off from fellowship with the Lord's Spirit and, potentially, with His covenant people. The leper had to avoid those who were clean, as he knew he was a danger to them and knew that he repulsed them. Indeed, the leper typically felt ashamed and uncomfortable around those who were clean. So it is with the unrepentant sinner. He feels to avoid the righteous as he believes they look down upon him and thus, in many cases, he is not comfortable in their presence. The leper is a perfect type or similitude of what King Benjamin called "the natural man" (see Mosiah 3:19). Of this disease and it's symbolic representation, Wilson's *Dictionary of Bible Types* states,

> This disease is a type [or symbol] of sin from the standpoint of its being incurable and defiling. In nearly every case of healing, the leper is said to be "cleansed." One of the outstanding features of this disease was its defiling influence on others. The leper must live a separated life. . . . He must be shut out of the camp. All of this is true about an unsaved man as regards his relationship to heaven. He cannot enter heaven because of his defilement which is hopeless. Only God can remove it, only God has the remedy.[13]

The leper potentially reminds us that we are each filled with spiritual sickness and are dying from the influence of this fallen world. Like the leper who, when he first contracts the disease, is undoubtedly unaware that he is sick, so also many who are spiritually ailing doubt that they are in any way contaminated by the devil's diseases. Similarly, like the leper, who once his disease advances becomes numb, you and I, if we allow our spiritual sicknesses to advance, can get to the point where we too are "past feeling" (Ephesians 4:19; 1 Nephi 17:45; Moroni 9:20).

The kneeling or prostrating of himself before Jesus's feet is a probable symbol of the leper's faith, humility, and submission to Christ. Ambrose put it this way: "He fell on his face because it is a mark of humility and modesty that each [of us should] feel shame for the sins of his life."[14] The act establishes for the reader that this is no sign-seeking cynic. Rather, he was apparently a humble and sincerely trusting soul who desired the Lord's miraculous intervention in his life.

As we noted, Jesus's choice to reach out and touch the leper would, according to the common Jewish interpretation of the law, defile Him—making Christ unclean before God. Yet Jesus touched the ailing man anyway, for "unto the pure all things are pure" (Titus 1:15). Touching the leper suggests the transference of power.[15] "Anything that touches something holy, like the altar [of the temple], becomes holy itself. Jesus performs several miracles by touch, among them is cleansing a man from leprosy," as a symbol that He was transferring His holiness to the faith-filled recipient.[16] Thus, just as a priesthood holder places his hands on the head of one he is blessing, Jesus placed His hands on the leper to transfer to him a blessing. In the most literal sense, the blessing was healing and cleansing. Since the leper potentially symbolized sin, Jesus's act of reaching out and touching the ill man can represent the transference of Jesus's righteousness onto the spiritually ill. As the Apostle Paul declared, "[God] hath made him to be sin for us, who knew no sin; that we might be made the righteousness of God in him" (2 Corinthians 5:21).

The "gift" Jesus commanded the former leper to offer was that which was required by the law of Moses for those who had been cleansed from that most feared of all diseases (see Leviticus 13; 14). One nineteenth-century commentator on this passage noted, "There is . . . one disease, that of leprosy, which seems more full of typical [or symbolic] teaching than any other, for two chapters are given to laws concerning it in the Book of Leviticus."[17] Around that same time, Charles Spurgeon (famously known as the "Prince of Preachers") wrote, "Leprosy is to be considered by us as the type [or symbol] of sin; and as we read the chapters in Leviticus, which concern the . . . leper, we are to understand every sentence as having in it a gospel sermon to us, teaching what is the condition of a sinner in the sight of God, how that sinner is to be cured, and how he can be restored to the privileges from which the leprosy of sin had utterly shut him out."[18] As the chart below shows, the entire ritual used to cleanse a leper was Christocentric in its symbolism.[19]

REQUIREMENT OF THE LAW OF MOSES	CHRISTOCENTRIC MEANING OF THE SYMBOL
The leper must await the arrival of the priest who will make provisions for the diseased to return to the fellowship of the covenant people. The priest is said to come to the leper rather than the leper going to the priest (Leviticus 14:3).	The sinner must await Christ's arrival here upon the earth, where He will make provisions for our return to fellowship with God and the saved. One source notes, "We go not up to heaven, first, till Christ comes down from his Father's glory to the place where we as lepers are shut out from God."[20]
The priest judges the leper's cleanliness (Leviticus 14:3), and only he has the power to pronounce the leper clean or unclean.	Jesus judges the sinner, and only He has the power to pronounce the sinner clean or unclean, worthy or unworthy.[21]

REQUIREMENT OF THE LAW OF MOSES	CHRISTOCENTRIC MEANING OF THE SYMBOL
The coming of the priest to the leper was not enough. There also needed to be a sacrifice (Leviticus 14:5, 10).[22] One bird was to be killed, its blood being spilt, and the other bird was to be released heavenward.	The two birds symbolized the death and Resurrection of Christ. The bird whose life was taken represented the slain Jesus, and the bird that was to be released heavenward symbolized the resurrected Christ.[23]
One of the two birds was to be linked with a piece of cedar wood (Leviticus 14:6).[24]	Because cedar is slow to decay, it is a symbol of preservation and the absence of corruption. One early Christian source noted, "The cedar is a wood not prone to rot. The incorruptible flesh, the body of Christ, 'did not see corruption.'"[25] Likewise, Christ's Atonement has the power to save us from corruption. Thus, cedar reminds the participant in the cleansing ritual of what Christ has done for all.
The bird associated with the wood was also linked with a scarlet or red ribbon or string (Leviticus 14:4; 17:7).[26]	Most often in scripture, the color red or scarlet represents sin or the blood of Christ that had to be shed because of sin.[27] Red is occasionally associated with both life and death—resurrection and evil. However, these are not contradictory images. All of these images are intertwined and associated with Christ's Atonement, making red in every case a negative symbol.[28]
The second bird was also associated with a piece of hyssop (Leviticus 14:4).	In Hebrew Bible times, the herb hyssop symbolized purification (Exodus 12:22; Psalm 51:7; Hebrews 9:19). One ancient source indicated, "Hyssop symbolizes the effervescence [life-bestowing], activity and power of the Spirit."[29]

REQUIREMENT OF THE LAW OF MOSES	CHRISTOCENTRIC MEANING OF THE SYMBOL
One of the birds was to be slain over an "earthen vessel" and his blood allowed to mix with running water. That blood and water mixture would then be placed upon the bird that would be released (Leviticus 14:5).	The water used in this rite was said to need to be running water, or "living water."[30] The water is a symbol of the Holy Spirit (John 7:38–39). When Christ hung on the cross and His side was pierced, out of His body—the earthen vessel—came blood and water mixed. The placement of the blood on the bird that was to be freed reminds us of the resurrected Christ, who, though blood-soaked because of the Atonement, would rise heavenward because of the Resurrection.[31] Thus, we see Christ's death being foreshadowed by this ritual, and we are taught that the Holy Spirit is an integral part of making the Atonement efficacious.
Once the ritual with the two birds was accomplished, the leper was to shave off all of his body hair (Leviticus 14:8–9).	The removal of all body hair gave the participant the appearance of a newborn, implying that the candidate for cleansing had been spiritually reborn. The removing of the hair was an indication that all old things had been rejected, done away with, or given up. Old vices, practices, inclinations, and sins were banished from the life of the cleansed.[32]
The formerly leprous person was to thoroughly wash himself (Leviticus 14:8).	Washing was an obvious symbol of cleansing. "The running water signifies the life-creating gift of baptism. . . . Through this baptism, whoever has become a leper through sin may be cleansed."[33]
On the eighth day of this cleansing rite, a one-year-old ewe lamb that was without blemish was to be slain as a sin offering (Leviticus 14:10–13).	Christ, the Lamb of God (John 1:29), He who was perfect, He who was firstborn, was to be slain as a sin offering for all.

REQUIREMENT OF THE LAW OF MOSES	CHRISTOCENTRIC MEANING OF THE SYMBOL
The blood of the lamb was to be placed on the right earlobe, thumb, and "great toe" of the one being cleansed (Leviticus 14:14).	Our English word *atonement* comes from a Hebrew word that means literally "to cover." Thus, by placing blood on parts of the body, the priest was suggesting that atonement be made for that thing, or for sins committed with that body part. In this case, we find the blood of the lamb sanctifying the organ of hearing or obedience (the ear), the organ of action (the hand), and the organ of following or walking in the proper way (the foot). Thus symbolically, every aspect of the person's life was to be touched or affected by the Atonement of Christ.[34]
After the blood of the slain lamb had been placed on the ear, thumb, and toe of the one being cleansed, consecrated olive oil was to be placed on those same parts of the body (Leviticus 14:15–18).	The oil was a symbol for the Holy Spirit.[35] To touch those organs with oil was to imply that the Spirit would both cleanse and direct them. Thus, the blood of Christ cleansed every aspect of the candidate's life, and then the process was repeated with the oil to show that the Spirit, too, affected everything the candidate did. "That oil is put on his ear, so that his ear hears his Master's voice, and listens to the Word of God. That oil is put upon his hand that he may be a consecrated man to serve his God. That oil is put upon his foot that his feet may run in the way of God's commands, even to the end."[36]

Though the authors of the synoptic Gospels do not give us the aforementioned symbolic details, Jesus's words to the leper, "Offer the gift Moses commanded" (Matthew 8:4), suggest that the Savior likely intended those scriptural symbols to be brought to the mind of the leper He was healing. *The rites and ceremonies which were necessary in order to cleanse this leper . . .* were but representations of the way whereby we too must be cleansed."[37] And, as should be quite evident to the reader, these rites and ceremonies were about the cleansing power of Christ's Atonement. Jesus's emphasis on the leper fulfilling the requirements of the law after he had *already* been healed was likely an attempt to teach the man (through symbolism) that *all* physical and spiritual sickness is ultimately overcome through Christ. "To the pious Jew, conscious of the ritual uncleanness of the leper, the wonder became even more staggering: Jesus was willing to incur defilement (as they saw it), so that the defiled leper might be made clean. The whole of the gospel is here in a nutshell: Christ redeems us from the curse by becoming under a curse for our sake."[38]

The miracle reminds us of the important fact that, just as the ceremony of the cleansing of the leper (Leviticus 14) had the power to remove the guilt and accountability from the one suffering from leprosy, we can turn to Christ and have our guilt and accountability removed. Part of the way we do that is through submitting to the ceremonies, rites, and rituals God has proscribed for our spiritual health. So much of the ritual, though symbolic of Christ's Atonement, teaches us what we must also personally do to be redeemed, as the following chart illustrates.

REQUIREMENT OF THE LAW OF MOSES	PERSONAL APPLICATION OF THE SYMBOL
The leper is considered unclean and he corrupts all that he touches. If he drinks from a cup, the cup is unclean. If he sits on a chair, the chair is unclean. If he touches another human being, that person is unclean. Thus, direct and close personal contact was avoided out of fear of contracting the disease.	So it is with the sinner; so much of what he touches he corrupts. The corrupt businessman taints others through his business dealings. The corrupt politician harms others through his legislation. The morally corrupt man defiles the women he interacts with through his immorality.[39] Interactions with the spiritually sick must be guarded, as their disease can readily be caught.

REQUIREMENT OF THE LAW OF MOSES	PERSONAL APPLICATION OF THE SYMBOL
The leper is required to have an interview with the priest to ascertain his health. The priest gives the leper instructions as to how to make himself clean and acceptable before God.	We all will eventually have an interview with the Great High Priest (Hebrews 4:14), who will ascertain our spiritual health. We meet regularly with mortal priesthood leaders who, as Christ's representatives, are commissioned to help us gauge how we are doing spiritually. Like the priest in Leviticus, our bishop can give us instructions as to how we might best place ourselves in alignment with the Lord, including what things we must do in order to be spiritually clean before God.
Two birds were to be utilized in the cleansing of the leper.	While we have already highlighted the Christocentric nature of this symbol, there may also be a degree of personal application warranted by the symbolism. True repentance requires that the sinful man die,[40] thereby setting free the soul of the repentant sinner from the evil things that had placed him in spiritual bondage. Thus, the two birds can remind us of our need to allow our natural man to die so we might be free from the bondage and death this world offers. One source notes, "The sending of the living bird outside of the city teaches us to abandon this world, as did Christ in his ascension into heaven."[41]
Part of the ritual that cleansed the leper required the utilization of a piece of cedar wood, a scarlet ribbon, and some hyssop.	Cedar is a symbol of preservation. It prevents corruption. As the symbolism relates to us, the cedar is a reminder of our need to *do* those things and *cling to* those things that would prevent our personal corruption. The ribbon of scarlet reminds us of Christ's blood, which is the only truly preserving power available to us in this fallen world. And the hyssop, as a symbol of purification, emphasizes our need to purify our lives from all that is unholy and impure.

REQUIREMENT OF THE LAW OF MOSES	PERSONAL APPLICATION OF THE SYMBOL
As part of the cleansing ceremony, "living water" was to be used.	We must fill our lives with "living water" (the Holy Ghost and the ordinances of God's Holy House)—and must associate closely with He who is the source of all "living water"—if we are to find the power to overcome the world and return to God (John 4:10–14; 7:38–39; D&C 63:23).
The leper was to wash that he might become clean.	We must be baptized and washed that we may "become clean from the blood and sins of this generation."[42]
The leper was to shave off all of his body hair.	While we are not called to shave off our hair, we are called to become as little children (Matthew 18:3; Mosiah 3:18) and reject the wicked ways of our past, which is what is symbolized by the removal of the hair.
A lamb was to be sacrificed in an effort to pay for the sins of the leper.	The Lamb of God was sacrificed in an effort to pay for the sins of you and I, each of us being spiritual lepers.
Blood and oil were to be placed upon the right ear, thumb, and toe of the leper.	We must live in such a way that the Atonement of Christ (symbolized by the blood) can cover all of our sins, and so that the Spirit of God (symbolized by the oil) can direct all of our actions.

Christ seems symbolized by the sacrifice of the two birds. In a dualistic way, the sacrifices God requires of us also appear to be symbolized.

Related to this last aspect of the symbolism is another curious lesson we can draw from the miracle. Jesus instructed the man He had healed to "tell no man" about what had happened and about the miracle that has taken place in his life. While modern commentators offer a number of explanations as to why Jesus did not want the man to tell, the potential application behind this declaration seems worth highlighting. Too often when individuals have found the gospel and turned from a life of sin, they wish to talk about their past transgressions in an effort to illustrate the miraculous change that Christ has wrought in their lives. However, discussions regarding past sins are traditionally discouraged, and rightly so. Such conversations should be allowed to die with the sins themselves. Alma the Younger noted what the Lord did for him once he had truly repented. He stated, "I cried within my heart: O Jesus, thou Son of God, have mercy on me, who am in the gall of bitterness, and am encircled about by the everlasting chains of death. And now, behold, when I thought this, *I could remember my pains no more; yea, I was harrowed up by the memory of my sins no more*" (Alma 36:18–19; emphasis added). The prophet Jeremiah reminds us of the Lord's own words: "I will forgive their iniquity, and I will remember their sin no more" (Jeremiah 31:34). If the Lord forgets our sins, we too should forget the past and move on with our new lives of righteousness.

This miracle of healing depicts a leper who, in excitement about the change Jesus has brought about in his life, goes about telling people that he was a leper, though no more. The story mirrors the behavior of some who, in excitement about the changes Jesus has brought about in their lives, are tempted to go about telling others, "I was a fornicator, drug user, an alcoholic, but not anymore!" Such confessions, even when they do show what great things Christ can do, are seldom wise. And like the leper who disobeyed Jesus by talking about what had taken place, thereby causing bad things to come of the disclosure, you and I, when we speak of the sins in our past, will potentially bring negative consequences too. By way of application, if we have been cleansed as the leper was, then we would be wise to "tell no man" the details of the things we have overcome.

On a separate note, the leper's curious confidence before Jesus offers a meaningful lesson to those who seek God's help and intervention. One scholar wrote, "The leper provided an example. . . . While his words 'If you will' reflect his sense of unworthiness, his behavior is boldly confident. Whereas the law required lepers to remain at a safe distance so as to prevent accidental communication of uncleanness, this man kneels close enough to Jesus to be touched by an outstretched hand. Christians must be as bold in their supplications for cleansing and healing."[43] While it is natural to feel a degree of unworthiness before the Lord when we have sinned, we must remember that Satan exploits those feelings in an effort to keep us from repenting. In actuality, the Spirit gives us feelings of discomfort so we *will* repent. But the devil seeks to cause us to respond to those feelings by turning *from*

Christ instead of turning *toward* Him. Jesus gave two parables about our need to be bold and confident in petitioning the Lord for His help and intervention. The parable of the "Friend at Midnight" (Luke 11:1–13) and that of the "The Unjust Judge and Importuning Widow" (Luke 18:1–8; D&C 101:81–92) each teach us that we must "pray and not faint" (Luke 18:1), or, as Joseph Smith put it, "weary" the Lord until He blesses us.[44] With the Apostle Paul, we should be able to say, "I have confidence . . . through the Lord" (Galatians 5:10). Like the leper, we must not avoid the Lord when we sin but rather prostrate ourselves before Him as the leper did that we might receive the healing and cleansing miracle of the Lord.

Finally, this miracle presents a potential message about what it means to be good Christians, good followers of the example of Christ. Origen of Alexandria (AD 200–254) wrote,

> And why did [Jesus] touch him, since the law forbade the touching of a leper? He touched him to show that "all things are clean to the clean." Because the filth that is in one person does not adhere to others, nor does eternal uncleanliness defile the clean of heart. So he touches him in his untouchability, that he might instruct us in humility; that he might teach us that we should despise no one, or abhor them, or regard them as pitiable, because of some wound of their body or some blemish for which they might be called to render an account.[45]

Symbolically, Christ's touch of the leper can remind you and me to not judge others, to not place ourselves above someone else because of their weaknesses, sins, or shortcomings. It is a call to remember that we are *all* fallen, imperfect creatures—spiritual lepers of the law, *per se*—who need the help, love, and support of our brothers and sisters in Christ if we are to overcome the debilitating diseases of this sacred sojourn we call life. Christ's act reminds us of our baptismal covenant "to bear one another's burdens, that they may be light; yea, and . . . to mourn with those that mourn; yea, and comfort those that stand in need of comfort" (Mosiah 18:8–9). We cannot fulfill that covenant and promise if we shun those who are different or who are struggling. "The touch of Jesus's hand extended to the sick reveals his deep compassion and love. Similarly, a word of comfort from us accompanied by a mere touch expresses our Christian love to those who are hurting and suffering."[46]

NOTES

1. The leper would not have stood among the crowd as Jesus preached because he was defiled. Thus, he may have secreted himself away within earshot of Jesus's words. But he only approached Christ after the crowd had dispersed. (See Chrysostom, "Gospel of Matthew," 159.)

2. Kistemaker (2006), 195.

3. See Chrysostom, "Gospel of Matthew," 159. Chrysostom also noted, "Jesus did not imply that showing the healing to the priest was something he needed. Rather, he temporarily remits him to the law. This stopped every mouth. He did this lest others might claim that Jesus had arrogated to himself the priest's honor. He performed the miracle himself, yet he caused them to sit as judges of his own miracles. He was saying in effect: 'I am so far from struggling against Moses or the priests that even I guide those cleansed to submit themselves to the priests'" (159).

4. The "gift" required was, among other things, the offering of two small birds; the anointing of the right ear, thumb, and toe of the leper with blood and oil; and the shaving and washing of the body—all to be performed in a rather ritualistic and symbol-laden manner. (See Cyril, "Fragments," 160).

5. The man's telling, though he had been commanded not to, has been seen by some as evidence of a heart overflowing with gratitude, unable to contain the truth of his miracle received. (See Trench [1962], 122.) Said one commentator, "This healed one had zeal without discretion! Elated over his new-found health, he disobeyed the Master's request and went out and blazed abroad the miracle" (Lockyer [1965], 173).

6. Lockyer (1965), 172; Trench (1962), 135.

7. Trench (1962), 136–37.

8. See Ryken, Wilhoit, and Longman (1998), 507; Habershon, *Study of the Types*, 79; Cooper (1982), 96.

9. See Ryken, Wilhoit, and Longman (1998), 522.

10. See Cooper (1982), 96; Conner (1992), 152; Spurgeon (1997), 7:311–27; Ryken, Wilhoit, and Longman (1998), 507; Trench (1962), 134, 135. "The biblical word traditionally translated 'leprosy' does not (at least usually) refer to what we call leprosy (Hansen's disease) but rather covers a variety of skin diseases, including the different forms of psoriasis and vitiligo (both of which make the skin white, cf. 2 Kings 5:27). The leprosy in Leviticus that contaminates clothing or a house is mold or mildew" (Ryken, Wilhoit, and Longman [1998], 507. See also Hare, *Interpretation*, 89).

11. "In ancient times, leprosy was the worst sickness among all physical diseases. As the most fearful of all illnesses, it could be called a living death. Gradually and slowly, one's physical body degenerated; the face and extremities of the body were severely affected, decomposed, and fell away. Eventually hands were without fingers, feet without toes, and heads with deformed eyebrows, eyelids, nose, lips, and ears. Nerve endings no longer registered pain, so a patient was not fully aware of the body's gradual destruction. In advanced cases, gangrene caused parts of the body to become misshapen and die. As a result, an unpleasant odor surrounded the unfortunate individual" (Kistemaker [2006], 193. See also Spurgeon [2007], 7:312–13).

12. "These diseases [the various sicknesses referred to as "leprosy"] are associated with uncleanliness and entail segregation from others. But that segregation is not complete isolation; for although Leviticus 13:46 might mean that lepers should live by themselves, in both Testaments lepers have dealings with other people. One nowhere reads of leper colonies. On the contrary, lepers advertise their presence by wearing ragged clothing, looking unkempt, and crying 'Unclean, unclean'" (Ryken, Wilhoit, and Longman [1998], 507).

13. Wilson (1999), 257.

14. Ambrose, "Exposition of the Gospel of Luke," 90.

15. See Ryken, Wilhoit, and Longman (1998), 362.

16. Ryken, Wilhoit, and Longman (1998), 879. It may be worth noting that Jesus would have been considered unclean because of His contact with the leper. Thus, people of the first century would not see in Jesus's act a transference of cleanliness or holiness. If anything, the diseased would be seen as transferring his uncleanliness to Jesus through their contact. But this is not what Christ experienced, as evidenced by the healing.

17. Habershon (1975), 150.

18. Spurgeon (2007), 7:311–12.

19. In her book on the miracles, Habershon presents a rather detailed comparison between the "Law of Leprosy" and Paul's Epistle to the Romans. While space will not allow us to treat the matter here, suffice it to say that her treatment is well worth examining and it highlights how thoroughly the requirements of the cleansing of the leper ceremony teach us about redemption through Christ's blood. (See Habershon [1975], 279–82, Appendix C.)

20. Spurgeon (2007), 7:320.

21. "It is quite evident that the decision concerning the state of any man must come from the High Priest Himself, Jesus Christ. No pope, nor bishop, nor ecclesiastical authority of any kind can decide the spiritual status of any person. Only the High priest, Christ Jesus, has the right, the power and the privilege of doing this. Only he can know the human heart. . . . Every sinner must come to Jesus Christ for cleansing. There is no other way. Christ Jesus must pronounce him clean. No Catholic priest can do it, no bishop can do it, no protestant preacher can do it, no Jewish rabbi can do it. Jesus Christ alone has the final and official word. He Himself is the one who has told us, 'He that believeth on the Son hath everlasting life'" (Wilson [1999], 257).

22. See Spurgeon (2007), 7:320.

23. See Spurgeon (2007), 7:320–21; Cyril, "Fragments," (2001), 160.

24. See Spurgeon (2007), 7:320.

25. Cyril, "Fragments," (2001), 160.

26. See Harris, "Leviticus," 2:582.

27. See Cooper (1982), 41; Cyril, "Fragments," 160. "Some think that . . . scarlet refers to suffering" (Habershon [1974], 95). "To the Christian, it denotes Christ's passion" (Fontana [1993], 66).

28. Even if red is used to imply a positive reality, such as the Resurrection or

Atonement, it remains at its core a negative symbol in that suffering and death had to be encountered by Christ so that we might reap the positive benefits of His pain while avoiding the negative repercussions of our own actions. Hence, in many instances the colors red and scarlet symbolize the blood spilt by the Savior during His atoning sacrifice (Revelation 19:13; D&C 133:48; Isaiah 63:2; Numbers 19:2), and thereby function as constant reminders of our need for Christ's intervention. (See McConkie and Parry [1990], 33, 92. See also McConkie, *Gospel Symbolism*, 102, 106, 257.) Consequently, red can represent life and death since it is the "life of the body" (Genesis 9:4), and to have blood shed is to take life. It serves well as a symbol for evil and sin because it reminds us of Christ's blood that had to be shed because of the evils mankind has committed. "In some respects . . . Christ's shed blood could be seen metaphorically as the shedding of mortality and sin, and his complete victory over them both (see John 16:33; Mosiah 15:8; Mormon 7:5–7)" (Brown and Smith, Symbols in Stone, 30). Thus when Christ overcame sin in Gethsemane, it was blood that was squeezed out of Him (Luke 22:44; Mosiah 3:7), as though sin too had entirely left His being through that most painful means of payment. Finally, blood is associated with resurrection because of its connection with life—resurrection bringing to pass the eternal life of all. Indeed, in some early societies, red was so closely linked to the concept of life that the bodies of the deceased were painted red to ensure their resurrection and eternal life. (See Tresidder [2000], 156.)

29. Cyril, "Fragments," 160.

30. See Spurgeon (2007), 7:320.

31. "The second bird was dipped into the blood until all its feathers were red and dropping with gore. It was doubtless tied round the cedar stick at the end of which was the hyssop . . . and the whole was dipped in the blood of the bird that was slain; and when this had been done seven times, the [scarlet] strings were cut, and the living bird allowed to fly away. This is a picture of Christ. As a living bird he ascends on high, after being slain for us—scattering the red drops of atonement, he rises above the clouds, which receive him out of our sight, and there before his Father's throne, he pleads the full merit of the sacrifice which he offered for us once for all" (Spurgeon [2007], 7:321).

32. See Spurgeon (2007), 7:324.

33. Cyril, "Fragments," 160.

34. "The sin of the ear—when thou used to hear lascivious songs, malignant words, and idle tattle. . . . How many times has the right hand sinned against God! How have your actions defiled you! . . . How have your feet run after wickedness! How greatly you need to be cleansed!" (Spurgeon [2007], 7:325. See also Cyril, "Fragments," 160). Hugh Nibley offered an interesting insight that may have meaning for some readers: "The willingness of the candidate to sacrifice his own life is symbolized by the blood on the right thumb and right earlobe, where the blood would be if the throat had been cut" (Temple and Cosmos, 58).

35. See Wilson (1999), 300–02; Spurgeon (2007), 7:327–28; Conner (1992), 158; Ryken, Wilhoit, and Longman (1998), 604.

36. Spurgeon (2007), 7:328.

37. Spurgeon (2007), 7:312; emphasis in original. "The ugly, festering sores the leper bore in his body were the outward and visible tokens of sin in the soul, and in Christ's miracle of healing we have a symbol of His power to purify and save from sin" (Lockyer [1965], 174).
38. Cole (1997), 118.
39. See Spurgeon (2007), 7:313–14.
40. Paul makes this point when he speaks of the ordinance of baptism: How shall we, that are dead to sin, live any longer therein? Know ye not, that so many of us as were baptized into Jesus Christ were baptized into his death? Therefore we are buried with him by baptism into death: that like as Christ was raised up from the dead by the glory of the Father, even so we also should walk in newness of life. For if we have been planted together in the likeness of his death, we shall be also in the likeness of his resurrection: knowing this, that our old man is crucified with him, that the body of sin might be destroyed, that henceforth we should not serve sin. For he that is dead is freed from sin. Now if we be dead with Christ, we believe that we shall also live with him: knowing that Christ being raised from the dead dieth no more; death hath no more dominion over him. For in that he died, he died unto sin once: but in that he liveth, he liveth unto God. Likewise reckon ye also yourselves to be dead indeed unto sin, but alive unto God through Jesus Christ our Lord." (Romans 6:2–11)
41. Cyril, "Fragments," 160.
42. McConkie, Mormon Doctrine, 147, s.v., "Cleanliness." The *Encyclopedia of Mormonism* states, "Individuals are ritually washed and anointed before endowments can be performed" in the temple (Luschin, "Temples," 4:1447).
43. Hare (1993), 89.
44. See Smith (1976), 36.
45. Origen, "The Healing of the Leper," 25–26.
46. Kistemaker (2006), 197.

HEALING *of the* MAN *with* PALSY

MATTHEW 9:2–8
MARK 2:1–12
LUKE 5:17–26

THE MIRACLE

Jesus was in Capernaum and word quickly spread of His presence. Someone had opened his home up to Him that He might teach the people. The crowd of those who gathered to hear was so great that it filled the entire house, leaving no room for additional guests. Even the door and the windows were blocked with the bodies of the believing and the curious.[1]

According to the testimony of the synoptic Gospels, included among the curious were Pharisees and scribes, two sects who were less than favorable in their opinions of Jesus. Though the text is silent on how many of the Jewish leadership were present, it is not silent on their disdain for the Master.

Four men, hearing that Jesus—the Healer—was present, gathered up their friend who suffered from palsy and carried him to where the Savior was teaching. But because of the crowd gathered, they could not gain entrance to request a blessing for their friend. But so great was their faith that they were undaunted by the challenge. Carrying their friend and his cot, the four climbed up to the top of the house, removed the tiles that constituted the roof, and lowered the man on his cot into the room where Jesus was teaching.

Guests were no doubt surprised by this act and likely shocked by the boldness and social impropriety of the four friends, interrupting the discourse of such a noted teacher. But Jesus did not take offense. On the contrary, so moved was He by the faith of the friends that He said to the man suffering from the palsy, "Be of good cheer; thy sins be forgiven thee" (Matthew 9:2).

Though they did not vocalize their disgust, the scribes and Pharisees present were infuriated at Jesus's pronouncement, thinking within their hearts that He had committed an act of blasphemy. They reasoned that only God could forgive sins. Who is this man to think Himself authorized to make such a declaration? While they did not believe that Christ's declaration of forgiveness accomplished anything on behalf of the man with palsy, nevertheless, the scribes and Pharisees felt that the act of uttering such a promise was the height of sin.

Jesus, knowing their thoughts, rebuked them. Robert J. Matthews explained:

> Jesus could have told the palsied man that his sins were forgiven, and no one would have been able to prove or disprove whether it actually was so. But when he commanded a sick man to rise and walk, the validity of his power was immediately able to be tested. Hence, it is easier to say that sins are forgiven. But that they would know that he had power to do both, Jesus used the healing of the body as evidence of his "forgiving" power.[2]

How could they disprove or reject the healing of one who could not walk? A number of commentators have suggested that what Jesus initially did was what any priest of the day might have done: tell the man, "*God* has forgiven your sins."[3] What Jesus did next—commanding the paralytic to be healed—was something *none of them* would have had the guts to do.[4] He stood as one unlike His detractors, and His miracle proved that!

Those present at the miraculous healing were "all amazed" and "glorified God" (Matthew 9:8; Mark 2:12; Luke 5:26) because of what they had just witnessed. Luke adds that "they"—presumably those who had thought critically of Jesus, but perhaps others too—"were filled with fear" (Luke 5:26) because of what they had seen.

BACKGROUND

The miracle took place in Capernaum, which had become Jesus's adopted hometown. John Chrysostom (circa AD 344–407) wrote, "Bethlehem bare Him, Nazareth nurtured Him, [but] Capernaum had Him continuously as an inhabitant."[5]

It was commonplace in the first century for homes to be rectangular or square in shape and, whether of a single or double story, to have a set of stairs (sometimes in the back) that led to the roof. Thus, the four men who carried their friend to the top likely did so by those stairs.

The paralyzed man is called "son" by Jesus (Matthew 9:2; Mark 2:5). The Greek speaks of him as a "child" rather than a "son"—thus he may have been comparatively young. Jesus's choice to address the youth, who was a sinner, as "child" or "son" suggests a manifest warmth by the Lord toward this creation of God who enjoyed a rather pitiful existence, physically *and* spiritually. As Saint Jerome (circa AD 347–420) noted, "O Wonderful humility! He addresses as 'son' this abject and infirm paralytic with disjointed members whom the priests did not stoop to touch."[6]

Curiously, Jesus indicates that it was the faith of the paralyzed boy's friends that caught His attention and provoked His blessing upon the quadriplegic. This is not to imply that the ailing child had no faith, only that Jesus was impressed by the greatness of the conviction of his friends.

SYMBOLIC ELEMENTS

The palsy, or paralysis, is often seen as a representation of the effects of sin upon the soul and life of each of us.

The symbolic implications of the four friends have been interpreted variously, but they are usually seen as representing individuals who help in the healing of those who are spiritually sick.

The climbing upon the roof and the removal of its tiles could suggest the innate difficulty of turning one from paths of sin to repentance and righteousness.

APPLICATION AND ALLEGORIZATION

Commentators on the miracle almost universally see the man's palsy as a fitting symbol for how "sin paralyzes the life and the activities of a person, and renders him helpless in the things of God."[7] In this regard, the symbol is a bit like that of leprosy. However, whereas leprosy represents sinners slowly dying from their sins, paralysis suggests that sins prevent them from being spiritually active.

A fitting example of "spiritual paralysis" would be the man who has been ordained to the Melchizedek Priesthood but is living a life of sin. He may be active in his ward and perhaps even hold a calling. However, when called upon to give a priesthood blessing, he feels incapable of so doing, paralyzed by his sinful lifestyle and his unworthiness to speak in God's name. His sins paralyze him because he knows he is not worthy of God's aid, support, or intervention, let alone worthy of the priesthood that he bears.

As has been suggested, the aid of the paralytic's four friends has been interpreted variously. For example, since four is the standard scriptural number for "geographic fullness or totality,"[8] the implication could be that this is everyone's story. To one degree or another, spiritual paralysis affects every soul who graces this earth. Similarly, Christ's healing power is also offered to any and all who seek His aid and forgiveness.

One interpreter of the miracle suggested that the four friends were good symbols of the attributes we need to develop if we are to be a blessing and aid to those sickened by sin: (1) a consecrated life, (2) compassionate love, (3) a propensity to intercession, and (4) undaunted faith.[9]

In a rather profound interpretation, one non-LDS source suggested that the four friends symbolize the fact that it usually takes more than one person to save those who are paralyzed by sin.[10] Paraphrasing the old proverb, "it takes a village" to turn one steeped in sin toward Christ. Thus, the four friends well represent bodies like the ward council. When individuals from various quorums and auxiliaries unite together to save an individual or family struggling with sin or complacency, miracles can happen. Just as one person could not have hoisted the paralytic up to the roof, so one person is seldom enough to save a struggling soul. It is the teamwork of concerned Christians that get the job done.

On a related note, the removal of the roof (by the four friends) has been interpreted as a symbol for the reality that we should be willing do anything necessary to save a soul. Spurgeon noted:

If men be called of God's grace to a deep anxiety for any particular soul, there is a way by which that soul may be brought to Jesus; but that way may not suggest itself till after much consideration. In some cases the way to impress the heart may be an out-of-the-way way, an extraordinary way—a way which ordinarily should not be used and would not be successful. . . . If we want to have souls saved, we must not be too squeamish and delicate about conventionalities, rules, and proprieties. . . . We must make up our minds to do this: "Smash or crash, every thing [*sic*] shall go to pieces which stands between the soul and its God; it matters not what tiles are to be taken off, what plaster is to be digged up, or what boards are to be torn away, or what labor, or trouble, or expense we may be at: the soul is too precious. . . . We must never stop at difficulties; however stern the task, it must always be more difficult to us to let a soul perish than to labor in the most self-denying form for its deliverance."[11]

How much emotional and spiritual energy—and how much ingenuity—are we willing to exert in order to save someone who is spiritually sick or paralyzed? This miracle suggests committed Christians will do all within their power.

The fact that the friends had to climb up to the roof and haul their associate up reminds us that saving a spiritually sick brother or sister may require that we elevate our own lives as we seek to elevate our struggling friend. The miracle certainly suggests that as we elevate the one who is sick, we by default find ourselves elevated. This truth is so evident in temple work: we attend to save the dead but in the process find ourselves elevated spiritually.

Hilary of Poitiers (circa AD 315–367) suggested that the four friends were "ministering angels," per se.[12] This brings to mind President Spencer W. Kimball's oft-quoted remark, "God does notice us, and he watches over us. But it is usually through another mortal that he meets our needs. Therefore, it is vital that we serve each other in the kingdom."[13] We too must be ministering angels to those around us, being "willing to mourn with those that mourn . . . and comfort those that stand in need of comfort" (Mosiah 18:9).

This miracle highlights numerous truths, including pointing to the various places each of us are in spiritually. Many who gathered to hear Jesus were already believing disciples. Some were curious but unsure investigators. Some, like the four friends, were hopeful—though likely not yet baptized disciples. And the Pharisees and scribes can represent those who, no matter what they are shown, will doubt the truth when it is presented to them. It is amazing that all these could be gathered in one place and have different responses to the same miraculous scene!

> Who are we? The paralyzed man, who had lost his life to sin? The loving friends, who worked hard to see him healed? Or the litigious teachers, nailing down the theology of the issue before the man can be helped?
> What will most glorify God today? Our personally turning from sin? Helping others come to faith and turn from wrongdoing? Or discussing the theological implications? Having good theology is important. But it does not substitute for the other two. Loving action . . . is more critical than senseless debates. When we know His power, we live in it.[14]

This miracle and each of its participants seem to offer a poignant invitation to the reader to participate in a measure of self-assessment.

The narrative of this healing also teaches an interesting doctrinal truth about the relationship between the forgiveness of sins and being healed from sickness. Elder Bruce R. McConkie taught,

> Whenever faithful saints gain the companionship of the Holy Spirit they are clean and pure before the Lord, for the Spirit will not dwell in an unclean tabernacle. Hence, they thereby receive a remission of those sins committed after baptism. This same eternal verity is illustrated in the ordinance of administering to the sick. A faithful saint who is anointed with oil has the promise that "the prayer of faith shall save the sick, and the Lord shall raise him up; and if he have committed sins, they shall be forgiven him" (James 5:14–15). The reasoning of the ancient apostle James, in this instance, is that since the miracle of healing comes by the power of the Holy Ghost, the sick person is healed not only physically but spiritually, for the Spirit who comes to heal will not dwell in a spiritually unclean tabernacle.[15]

Thus in the miracle, Jesus healed the boy both physically and spiritually. Indeed, Elder McConkie's comment suggests that to heal the boy *only* physically would be impossible. The very fact that a physical healing took place is a testament to the reality that a spiritual healing also took place, for such is how the Lord's Spirit works.[16]

This miracle also reminds us of the importance of putting "first things first." Physical healing is a boon and a blessing. But the spiritually minded know it is hardly the priority.

> Forgiveness came before healing. How astonished the bearers and people alike must have been when they heard Jesus say, as the helpless man rested before Him, "Son, be of good cheer, they sins are forgiven thee." Was that the act and word of healing that the friends and crowd breathlessly expected? What had forgiveness of sins to do with the palsy? But Jesus set the spiritual and temporal in their right relationship. . . . The bodily infirmity was not such an intolerable weight as the sin of the soul. . . . What is the use of all the physical healing in the world if there be no cure of the disease of sin?[17]

Too often we may be guilty of having grave concern for our temporal well-being—our physical health—while ignoring our spiritual infirmities. Such a misplacement of priorities may be spiritually disastrous.

NOTES

1. Given the size of the average home in those days, it would not take many people to fill the house. However, the implication of the story is that there may have been a significant number gathered on this occasion.
2. Matthews (1969), 31. See also Jerome, "Commentary on Matthew," 75; Fitzmyer (1970), 584; Marcus (2000), 217.
3. The *Anchor Bible Commentary* on this passage notes, "'Are forgiven' can be interpreted as a divine passive. . . . If this were the case, the declaration would be very much like that of a priest, who according to Lev 4:26, 31, etc. 'shall make an atonement on his behalf for his sin, and he shall be forgiven'—the implied forgiver being God. Although there is no explicit statement that such atonement rituals were accompanied by the priest's declaration of divine forgiveness, it can be assumed they were. Part of Jesus' offense, then, may be his usurpation of priestly prerogatives, and this makes particularly good sense if scribes were priests" (Marcus [2000], 21; emphasis added. See also Lockyer [1965], 175). Harper's *New Testament Commentary* on Mark makes a similar claim, suggesting the passive form of the Greek used makes it clear that God is the one forgiving the sins, but Jesus presumes to do so without engaging in any of the law's rites or rituals typically associated with forgiveness of sins (like a sin offering or trespass offering). Thus, Jesus is bringing to pass something a priest might, but He is not doing so in accordance with the prescriptions of the law. (See Johnson, *Commentary on the Gospel*, 56–57.) Similarly, the *Expositor's Greek Testament* notes that the phrase "thy sins be forgiven thee" was "most suitable to the case" and was one "which might have been spoken by any man." The text adds, "The words" of the narrative "suggest a gradual intensification of the fault-finding mood:

first a general sense of surprise, then a feeling of impropriety, then a final advance to the thought: why, this is blasphemy! It was nothing of the kind. What Jesus had said did not necessarily amount to more than a declaration of God's willingness to forgive sin to the penitent. They read the blasphemy into it," (Nicoll [1983], 1:351; emphasis added). In the *Expositor's Bible Commentary*, we find this related statement: "It should be noted that Jesus does not say here that he forgives sins but that they are forgiven. The passive . . . probably suggests that God is the source of forgiveness. . . . The premises was correct: only God can forgive sins" (Liefeld, [1976–92], 8:882). While we freely acknowledge that not all scholars agree on this reading of the episode, it should be noted that it is not an isolated interpretation of the passage.

4. See Lockyer (1965), 175.

5. Lockyer (1965), 174.

6. Jerome, "Commentary on Matthew," 173.

7. Wilson (1999), 309. See also Lockyer (1965), 175. While we are not saying that sin was the cause of the paralyzed boy/man's ailment (though that would have been a common belief in Jesus's day), what we are saying is that paralysis generally can be a teaching device that helps us to ponder the debilitating effects of sin on our spirituality.

8. Gaskill, *Lost Language of Symbolism*, 119–20.

9. See Lockyer (1965), 176.

10. Spurgeon (2007), 9:459–62.

11. Spurgeon (2007), 9:463, 465–66.

12. See Hilary, "On Matthew," 174.

13. *Teachings of Spencer W. Kimball*, 252.

14. McQuade (2008), 135.

15. McConkie (1980–1981), 3:41n1. See also Jerome, "Commentary on Matthew," 75.

16. That being said, if a person is not healed physically, this does not mean that the person has not been healed spiritually. Some physical ailments are meant to be part of our personal mortal challenge. Thus, while God may not grant that the illness be removed, the spiritual cleansing would still be valid.

17. Lockyer (1965), 175.

Lame Man Healed *at* *the* Pool *of* Bethesda

John 5:1–16

The Miracle

Jesus was visiting Jerusalem and on the Sabbath was found in a location ofttimes referred to as the "sheep gate" or "pool of the sheep."

Many who suffered from various maladies—blindness, paralysis, conditions incident to old age—were found in this location. It was a popular belief at the time that the pool known as Bethesda had healing properties, but on a limited scale. Infrequently, the pool would bubble. When this happened, some believed that an angel was stirring the waters. The first person who entered after the "troubling" of the waters was believed to receive a blessing of healing from whatever ailment he suffered.

On the occasion of Jesus's visit, there was, near the side of the pool, a man who had for some thirty-eight years suffered from the same sickness—a form of paralysis that made it impossible for him to walk or even move his own body.

In His omniscience, Jesus knew of the longevity of the man's sickness and of his persistent presence at the pool. Christ asked the feeble man, "Wilt thou be made whole?" (John 5:6). The Lord's query was not designed to gather information but rather to provide the paralyzed man an opportunity to exercise his faith. His reply to the Master was evidence of his trust in God's power to heal, but also of his frustration at his inability to lay hold on God's blessings. He said, in effect, "How can I be healed when there is no one to push me into the water?"

Christ asked nothing more of the man. He simply commanded him, "Rise, take up thy bed, and walk" (John 5:8). The man was immediately healed, every whit! He took up his bed and left the location of the pool.

When they realized he had been healed on the Sabbath, the Jewish leadership felt no joy over the suffering man's relief. Rather, they sought to learn the name of the person who cured him that they might punish the healed man's benefactor. The formerly paralyzed man informed them that he had neglected to ask his healer's name and thus could not help them.

Later, Jesus found the cured man in the temple and approached him. Said the Master to His newfound disciple, "Behold, thou art made whole: sin no more, lest a worse thing come unto thee" (John 5:14). The man departed from the holy precincts and gratefully proclaimed aloud to all—including the Jews who had accosted him—the news that he had been healed by Jesus the Christ.[1] From that time forward, the leadership of the Jews persecuted Jesus for healing on the Sabbath.

BACKGROUND

Until recent times, the exact location of the pool of Bethesda, along with its dimensions, was unknown. However, one text notes,

> The pool described in John [chapter 5] has been discovered and excavated in Jerusalem on the property of the [Roman Catholic] White Fathers near St. Anne's Church. . . . The pool was trapezoidal in form, 165–220 feet wide by 315 feet long, divvied by a central partition. There were colonnades on the four sides and on the partition—thus, John's "five porticoes." Stairways in the corners permitted descent into the pools. In this hilly area the water may have come from underground drainage; some of it, perhaps, from the intermittent springs.[2]

Some hold that the place of the pool (northeast of the temple) was where the sheep that would be used for temple sacrifices were kept.[3] Hence the tendency to refer to it as the "sheep gate" or "pool of the sheep."

In the most ancient manuscripts, verse 4 is missing from the text. The verse is believed by many scholars to be an interpolation[4] added later, either to explain the phrase "when the water is troubled" (verse 7) or because there was a popular tradition about the pool that John did not explain to his readers and thus scribes felt the need to add it. The legitimacy of the last clause of verse 3, "waiting for the moving of the water," is also frequently called into question.[5]

The occasional "troubling" of the waters (verse 7), which some attributed to an invisible angel, is believed to have been caused by bubbling, which took place because of the underground springs that fed the pool.[6]

SYMBOLIC ELEMENTS

As with so many of the miracles of the Bible, the ailing man is (at least) a potential symbol for any man or woman who is debilitated by sin. In the case of this man, some see his sins as the cause of his sickness (physical and spiritual). Some, on the other hand, see the fact that he had yet to be converted to Christ as symbolized by his ailment. He may also symbolize the unhealthy condition in which the law found itself in the first century. It's semi-apostate state left it unable to bless others because it could not help itself.

Among other things, the pool can serve as a type for those things that the Jews of Jesus's day perceived as having the power to heal them: those rites and ordinances associated with the law.[7]

APPLICATION AND ALLEGORIZATION

Commentators—LDS and non-LDS, ancient and modern—have seen numerous potential applications in this miracle. The reader will possibly resonate with some and dislike others. However, for the sake being open to various interpretations and applications, I have presented here a number of different readings of this miracle and its potential symbolic likening.

One Latter-day Saint commentator suggested that the pool and its inhabitants likely represent the spiritually impoverished condition of the religion of the day (in part because of how the law was being interpreted and applied). Thus the man and his circumstance mirrored the law's inability (at that time) to functionally save and bless.[8] This particular interpretation was commonplace among those of the early Christian Church. Augustine (AD 354–430), for example, interpreted the waters of the pool to be a symbol of the Jewish people, and the five porticoes that surrounded the water to be the five books of Moses, which fenced in those who were followers of the law. He (along with many of the early Christian fathers) noted the inferiority of the law when compared to the message of Christ: "But those books [that contained the law of Moses] brought forth the sick, not healed them. For the law convicted, not acquitted sinners."⁹ The law could not save, thus—in Augustine's eyes—the man waiting some thirty-eight years for healing was waiting in vain.¹⁰ Only Christ could heal, and upon His arrival that day, He did just that. Augustine wrote,

> What, then, is meant by this, unless it be that there came one, even Christ, to the Jewish people; and by doing great things, by teaching profitable things, [He] troubled sinners, troubled the water [which symbolize the Jewish people] by His presence, and roused [or pointed them] towards His own death? . . . Wherefore, to go down into the troubled water means to believe in the Lord's death. There *only* one was healed.¹¹

For Augustine, this narrative is symbolic of the inability of the law of Moses to save mankind. Nothing saves but Christ. Judaism or its law, aside from Jesus, never had that power—no matter how long its practitioners waited. The man's thirty-eight-year wait is evidence of this truth.

The fact that the man did not recognize Jesus as the Messiah—but only saw Him as a passerby who had potentially taken interest in his plight—may have some symbolic meaning.

> Waiting as he had those many years, the impotent man was undoubtedly watching the water with intensity and may not have even noticed Jesus. His answer indicated his only concern, even though his healer stood before him. "I have no man," he stated, "To put me into the pool." The man, like Israel, was so intent upon a false hope that he did not (or could not) see salvation embodied in Christ's presence. . . . He did not realize that true healing was not to be found in the water of the pool.¹²

Like the Jewish leadership of the day (who looked to the law and their own piety for salvation), the paralyzed man focused on that which could not bring the cure he so desperately desired. He had faith but it was initially misplaced.

John Chrysostom (circa AD 344–407), in a completely different approach to the miracle, suggested that the story was a foreshadowing of the ordinance of baptism, which would be central in conversion to Christ in the ancient Church.[13] The man whom the waters of Judaism could not heal was cured by Christ instead.[14] Chromatius, bishop of Aquileia (flourished AD 400), held a view similar to that of John Chrysostom. He taught that the miracle pointed to the fact that Christianity offered salvation, which the law of Moses could not offer.[15] He compared the two faiths and their power to redeem, as follows.

WATERS OF BETHESDA	WATERS OF CHRISTIAN BAPTISM
The healing offered was physical—for the body only.	The healing offered is spiritual—for the soul. But faith in Christ can also bring physical healing.
The opportunity for healing was available but once a year.	The opportunity to participate in baptism is always available to any who sincerely seek it.
The healing waters only moved in one place—the pools of Bethesda.	The healing waters of baptism are available throughout the entire world.
The invitation to partake came only generally through noticing the bubbling (or troubling) of the waters—something readily missed.	The invitation comes personally, though the inner promptings of the Holy Spirit—not readily missed by those who feel them.
Because of its limited availability, many are left lying sick near the waters, desiring the healing that others have received, but they are unable to receive it for themselves.	All who desire healing and who are willing to come unto Christ *will* be healed. This ordinance offers healing to all who desire it, not just to a fortunate few.

Owing to the consistent connection of this miracle to the ordinance of baptism, it will come as no surprise that the angel "troubling" the waters was understood by some of the ancients as a symbol for the idea that God would send the Holy Ghost to make the ordinance of baptism efficacious.[16] The Prophet Joseph taught that the Spirit is inseparably connected to the ordinance of baptism. He said, "You might as well baptize a bag of sand as a man, if not done in view of the remission of sins and getting of the Holy Ghost. Baptism by water is but half a baptism, and is good for nothing without the other half—that is, the baptism of the Holy Ghost." Joseph added, "The baptism of water, without the baptism of fire and the Holy Ghost attending it, is of no use; they are necessarily and inseparably connected."[17]

This miracle at the pool of Bethesda can also teach us about the importance of endurance in seeking the Lord's intervention and blessings in our lives. John Chrysostom wrote,

> Astonishing was the perseverance of the paralytic, he was of thirty and eight years standing, and each year hoping to be freed from his disease, he continued in attendance, and withdrew not. . . . Let us be ashamed then, beloved, let us be ashamed, and groan over our excessive sloth. "Thirty and eight years" had that man been waiting without obtaining what he desired, and withdrew not. And he had failed not through any carelessness of his own, but through being oppressed and suffering violence from others, and not even thus did he grow dull; while we if we have persisted for ten days to pray for anything and have not obtained it, are too slothful afterwards to employ the same zeal [as he did]. And on men we wait for so long a time, warring and enduring hardships and performing servile ministrations, and often at last failing in our expectation, but on our Master, from whom we are sure to obtain a recompense greater than our labors, . . . on Him we endure not to wait with becoming diligence. What chastisement doth this deserve! For even though we could receive nothing from Him, ought we not to deem the very conversing with Him continually the cause of ten thousand blessings?[18]

Blessings worthy of being desired and petitions worthy of being offered to the Lord are also worthy of our patience and trust. We must learn to say not only "thy will be done, O Lord," but also "Thy timing be done" as well.[19] The miracle can remind us of the importance in "waiting upon the Lord" (Psalm 37:9). God's promises are sure—but His timing is seldom ours. The man in the miracle waited some thirty-eight years for the Lord's blessing—and while he surely felt a degree of despondency, his continued presence at the water's edge suggests that he never gave up hope that God would hear his prayers and intervene on his behalf.

The location of this miracle, Bethesda, is appropriately named, as Jesus quite literally turned that "house of misery" into a "house of mercy" and grace.[20] Omnipotence had overcome impotence. Salvation had come to the Jewish people—it had come to the world!

Some see as a central message in this narrative the connection between sins and physical maladies. In other words, for some commentators it seems evident that this man's sickness was caused by a life of sin. However, it should be pointed out that when Christ's disciples made such an assumption (see John 9), Jesus rejected the suggestion. Robert J. Matthews wrote,

> There is some indication that this man's affliction was the result of sin, for when Jesus met him later, he said: "Behold thou are made whole: sin no more, lest a worse thing come unto thee." This does not necessarily follow, however, and may only have reference to the loss of salvation being a greater tragedy than the loss of health. Jesus said in another place: "Fear not him that can kill the body, but not the soul, but rather fear him that can destroy both body and soul in hell" (Luke 10:28).[21]

Thus, the story is *not* teaching that sins cause physical ailments (though at times they can). Rather, the miracle suggests that individual or spiritual ailments cannot be overcome by a person or even by the law of Moses but only through Christ, who is the chief Physician. The man's declaration, "Sir, I have no man . . . to put me into the pool" (John 5:7), is a testament to the doctrine of grace. His frank acknowledgment that he had not the power to help himself stands as a potential symbol for the eternal truth that even the best of us, without the intervention of Christ, has no hope of life or salvation.

Finally, the response of the Jewish opponents of Christ to such a glorious happening as this is also instructive. We should ever seek to keep the Sabbath day holy. However, we should not be so legalistic in our religion that we are devoted to laws over love. "Be not weary in well doing" (2 Thessalonians 3:13; D&C 84:33; Galatians 6:9) is the oft-repeated command! The Lord reminded those who criticized how He kept the Sabbath, "The sabbath was made for man, and not man for the Sabbath" (Mark 2:27).[22] Disciples of Christ serve each other on the Sabbath. While it is to be a day of rest from the labors of the world, it is not to be a day of rest from doing good.

NOTES

1. Johannine scholar Raymond E. Brown highlighted the personality of the man herein healed, "If the paralytic's malady were not so tragic, one could almost be amused by the man's unimaginative approach to the curative waters. His crotchety

ALONZO L. GASKILL

grumbling about the 'whippersnappers' who outrace him to the water betrays a chronic inability to seize the opportunity, a trait reflected again in his oblique response to Jesus' offer of a cure. The fact that he had let his benefactor slip away without even asking his name is another instance of real dullness. In vs. 4 it is Jesus who takes the initiative in finding the man, and not vice versa. Finally, he repays his benefactor by reporting him to 'the Jews.' This is less an example of treachery . . . than of persistent naïveté" (Brown [1966], 209).

2. Brown (1966), 207.

3. Brown (1966), 206.

4. An "interpolation" is simply something added after the fact, usually to clarify the original.

5. See Brown (1966), 207; Trench (1962), 155–56; Tenney, 9:62, 63n4. Tenney indicates that verse 4 is omitted by all manuscripts dated prior to the fourth century, though he suggests that the interpolation may have happened as early as the late second century.

6. See Brown (1966), 207; Kistemaker (2006), 210.

7. Just as the man's healing ultimately came through Christ, not through the water in the pool, it may be said of our own healing, Jesus is always the source. We may be immersed in the font or drink the water, but Jesus is the one who heals. Those symbolic acts allow us to make or renew covenants, but they are not—in and of themselves—empowered to heal.

8. See Howick, *Miracles of Jesus the Messiah*, 64–66.

9. Augustine, "On the Gospel of John," 7:111.

10. Because of the connection with the law of Moses, some have suggested that the length of the man's illness—thirty-eight years—may also be symbolic, for Deuteronomy 2:14 speaks of ancient Israel as wondering in the wilderness "thirty and eight years; until all the generation of the men of war were wasted out from among the host, as the Lord sware unto them." One commentator wrote, "The impotent man 'had an infirmity thirty and eight years.' This length of time . . . could have symbolized Israel's long standing plight" (Howick [2003], 66). While it is possible John had this in mind, there is nothing in the text to establish that. (See Brown [1966], 207.) This same source states, "This miracle was not a frontal attack on the law. . . . However, it contrasted for the rulers and keepers of the law the purity and charity of the true kingdom of God with their own dead religion" (Ibid. 65–66).

11. Augustine, "On The Gospel of John," 7:112; emphasis added.

12. Howick (2003), 66.

13. Chrysostom, "Homilies on St. John," 14:125–26. Chrysostom's interpretation may bother some readers, as the lame man in this miracle never gets in the pool. However, this ancient association with baptism was a common one and is not moot when taken in the context of the bigger picture, namely that it is Christ that cleanses and heals—even when we personally partake of ordinances (or vicariously receive them at the hands of others). The ordinance is a symbol of Christ's healing work in our lives. But it is not the ordinance itself that heals. It is the work of the Godhead who bring to pass the healing. (See Smith [1976], 314, 360).

86

14. Brown (1966), 211. Brown points out that this was one of three passages used to prepare catechumens for baptism in the early Church. The other two passages were the story of Nicodemus (John 3) and the story of the man born blind (John 9).

15. See Chromatius, "Sermon 14," 179.

16. See Ambrose, "On the Mysteries," 179.

17. Smith (1976), 314, 360.

18. Chrysostom, "Homilies on St. John," 14:126–27.

19. Maxwell, "Plow in Hope," 59.

20. *Bethesda* is of Aramaic origin, coming from two root words meaning "house" and "goodness," or "kindness." Thus, it is traditionally believed to mean "house of mercy" or "house of grace."

21. Matthews (1969), 33.

22. The Joseph Smith Translation offers some meaning into Jesus's words when it renders the passage as follows: "Wherefore the Sabbath was given unto man for a day of rest; and also that man should glorify God, and not that man should not eat; for the Son of man made the Sabbath day, therefore the Son of man is Lord also of the Sabbath" (Joseph Smith Translation, Mark 2:27–26, in Bible appendix).

MAN *with* a WITHERED HAND *Is* HEALED

MATTHEW 12:9–13
MARK 3:1–6
LUKE 6:6–10

THE MIRACLE

On the Sabbath, Jesus entered a synagogue to participate in the worship services being held therein. Some of the scribes and Pharisees present recognized Him and felt contempt because of the things they had heard about Him.

Though they had not yet spoken to Him, Jesus read His antagonists' thoughts and knew that they were watching Him in order to "catch Him" in some act or statement that they could use against Him. They had heard that He had, on several occasions, healed on the Sabbath, and they had hoped that this day would be no different. The presence of a man with an infirmity served as bait for their prey, or so they supposed.

In an effort to challenge their erroneous beliefs about the Sabbath— but perhaps also their false beliefs about Him—Jesus told a man in the congregation who had a withered right hand to stand up and come to the center of the room. One commentator noted, "It is a deliberate provocation of the Scribes and Pharisees by Jesus."[1] Once the subject of the miracle was "front and center," the Lord rhetorically asked the scribes and Pharisees, "Is it against the law to do good on the Sabbath, to save a life on God's holy day?" Without waiting for a response, He commanded the man with the emaciated hand to stretch it out. The man did so and was immediately healed.

In response to this miracle they had just witnessed, the Pharisees and scribes were "filled with madness" (Luke 6:11), or fury, and began to plot Jesus's death.

BACKGROUND

According to Matthew's account, in the hours leading up to this miracle—and in a state of hunger—Jesus and His disciples had passed through a field of grain and had plucked some of the kernels to eat as they traveled to their destination.[2] The Pharisees had seen or learned that they had done this and had accosted Jesus about His choice to "break" the Sabbath (as they supposed). The "bad blood" from the exchange now spilled over into the Sabbath synagogue service.

Whereas Matthew suggests that Jesus was innocently accosted by the Jews who sought to find reason to accuse Him, both Mark and Luke suggest that Jesus picked this fight. He saw the leaders of the synagogue suspiciously watching Him and He knew the thoughts of their hearts. So Jesus decided to challenge their unspoken judgments by asking them if it was appropriate to heal on the Sabbath, thereby forcing them to make a judgment through obliging them witness to a miracle.

There is a popular tradition within the early Christian Church that the man with the withered hand had been a bricklayer or stonecutter and he had been deprived of his livelihood through the incapacitation of his hand.[3] According to the Greek, the man's hand had "dried up," suggesting this was not a birth defect but the cause of disease or an injury.

Mark informs us that after Jesus had performed this healing miracle, "the Pharisees went forth, and straightway took counsel . . . how they might destroy him" (Mark 3:6). Thus, when Jesus asked, "Is it lawful to do good on the sabbath days, or to do evil? to save life, or to kill?" (Mark 3:4), He was not likely just offering an abstract principle. He was actually speaking prophetically, clearly knowing that, in their hearts, they had murderous desires regarding Him. Perhaps this is why, in response to His question, "they held their peace" (Mark 3:6). The Pharisees expressed concern because, on the Sabbath, Jesus sought to bless a life, thereby (in the view of the Pharisees) desecrating the sanctity of that holy day. However, while they openly condemned Him for doing good on that day, in their hearts they were negating their own moral code by seeking His death.

The Pharisees were furious because, according to their interpretation of the law, Jesus had broken the Sabbath. Of course, Jesus notes that the law says that on the Sabbath you're allowed to save an animal that is somehow in distress. How much greater is a man—made in the image of God (Genesis 1:26–27)—than is an animal? If God had given permission for man to bless the animals on the Sabbath, He would have surely allowed man to bless man on that holy day.

Having said that, it is curious that Jesus heals the man with the withered hand in a unique way. Unlike some of His other healings where physical touch was employed, Jesus makes no physical contact with the ailing man in this miracle. He performed no physical labor that might desecrate the Sabbath. He only spoke a word and the man was healed. Thus, He was cautious in His approach to ensure that He kept the Sabbath holy (not only in the spirit of the law, but also in the letter). Consequently, the charges of His opponents were meritless, without basis *in any way*.[4]

SYMBOLIC ELEMENTS

The hand was an ancient symbol for people's actions, or that which they chose to do or pursue.[5] It often symbolized their "inner state" and "attitude of mind."[6] Thus, one scholarly source on biblical symbolism noted, "The hands are the essence of the individual. Hands communicate our attitudes and perform our deeds. They speak more eloquently than our words, since the actions of the hands come from the heart."[7]

APPLICATION AND ALLEGORIZATION

Though this miracle *appears* to be about a man with a withered hand and how that hand was healed, it also says much about those whose hands are theoretically whole or properly functioning. Speaking of this miracle, the fourth-century author Origin of Alexandria (AD

185–254) said of the Pharisees, "They brought to the Savior the barrenness of their hands. For having a withered hand indicated unfruitfulness."[8] In other words, while they looked down upon the man with the physically withered hand and watched to see if Jesus would heal him, they seemed entirely unaware that *they* were the ones who needed healing. *Their* hands were the ones that were truly withered, in that their works were fruitless—as is evidenced by their attitude during this miracle. Though the man healed may have been physically impaired, the Pharisees were spiritually impaired, making them much worse off than was the invalid whom Jesus restored.

Before He performed the healing, Jesus called the man with the withered hand up and had him stand in the middle of the room.

> See the tender bowels of the Lord. "He set him in the midst," that by the sight He might subdue them; that overcome by the spectacle they might cast away their wickedness, and out of a kind of shame towards the man, cease from their savage ways. . . . And He "setteth" the man "in the midst;" not in fear of them, but endeavoring to profit them, and move them to pity.[9]

Christ does all that He does for us in an attempt to bless us, develop us, and save us. He is gracious and merciful in bringing to our attention our weaknesses and sins—not because He wishes to condemn us but because He desperately desires to bless us. In this miracle, the man is brought to the center of the room quite possibly in hopes that the Pharisees, in seeing the miracle, would be jolted back to the reality of their sinful attitude. This was a wonderful opportunity for them—a gift from God. With regularity, we too have the blessing of experiences that bring center stage our sinful and fallen state. We can respond as the Pharisees did, with anger and disdain, or as Christ would have us, with humility and contrition.

Mark records that Jesus felt angry and "grieved" by the Jews attitude (or by their "stupidity," as the *Anchor Bible* renders the noun).[10] They hardened their hearts because of the way He had publically shown them to be misinterpreting the law. Of their hardened hearts, one commentator noted, "Since the heart is a soft muscle and was thought of as the seat of the feelings as well as the intellect, . . . its petrification can signify an inability to respond in an emotionally appropriate manner."[11] These men had become "past feeling" (Ephesians 4:19; 1

Nephi 17:45; Moroni 9:20). Whenever we allow ourselves to marinate in sinful behaviors or thoughts, we too run the risk of losing our sensitivity to spiritual things.

Related to the hardened hearts of the Pharisees, one commentator pointed out what seems an obvious symbolic wordplay in the Greek of Mark's Gospel:

> The most famous biblical exemplar of hard-heartedness is the Pharaoh of the exodus story, and it may well be that Mark intends his readers to link the Pharisees with the Egyptian king, especially since the Greek words "Pharaoh" and "Pharisee" are so close to each other (*Pharaō/Pharisaios*). This would be tremendously ironic linkage, since in Jewish sources from the Bible onward Pharaoh is the prototypical enemy of God's people and representative of ungodliness.[12]

In a clear way, Jesus appears to be implying that though the Pharisees see themselves as the guardians of the Jewish nation and the law, they are actually instruments in the hands of Satan, as was Pharaoh.

There is much in this miracle about the Sabbath and what is, or is not, appropriate on that holy day. Just prior to this healing, Jesus taught, "The sabbath was made for man, and not man for the Sabbath" (Mark 2:27). That holiest day of the week is a gift to help us be spiritually healed from the sickness and wounds of the world. For Jesus's Jewish antagonists, the Sabbath had become a day of testing men with trivial and vexing rules. For most, the day had become one of inconvenience and constraint. Jesus was trying to teach that "the end is not to be sacrificed to the means."[13] The purpose of the Sabbath is to heal, not to punish man. It is to be a day of joy, not a day of suffering.

A significant potential message of the miracle, therefore, appears to be this: "Many of us are suffering from withered hands. Sin so paralyzed us so that we are not able to do much for Christ, whose pierced hands saved us. But withered hands can be healed and empowered to do great things for our Healer in the midst of a burdened and suffering creation."[14] The Sabbath day can play a key role in that spiritual healing, which we each desperately need.[15] As we keep that day holy, the Lord offers miracles in our lives. That which is weak and unusable can be made whole, strong, and healed. We can become His instruments when we allow Him to heal our hands!

One text on the miracles notes that the hard-hearted Pharisees allowed their rigidness to prevent them from making rational, Spirit-directed judgments. "The Pharisees didn't have a theology problem: They had a heart problem. Can we take them as an example of what *not* to do and instead love others as Jesus calls us to? Then neither our hearts nor our spirits will be shriveled."[16] This miracle invites us to introspection. Do we look for the bad rather than the good in others? Do we feel jealously and anger because of their blessings or success?[17] Is our approach to our faith so rigid that we look for the spiritual failings and infractions of others, all the while not noticing the "beam" in our own eye, which obscures our vision of reality (Matthew 7:3–5)? Saint Ambrose (circa AD 333–397) counseled, "You who think that you have a healthy hand beware lest it is withered by greed or by sacrilege. Hold it out often. Hold it out to the poor person who begs you. Hold it out to help your neighbor, to give protection to a widow, to snatch from harm one whom you see subjected to unjust insult. Hold it out to God for your sins."[18] We cannot be like the Pharisees, who, because they were active in their religion, assumed that they were holy in their behaviors. If our hearts are not soft and our hands are not outstretched, we are not spiritually well.

The story of this man's restoration to health also offers us a potential lesson about our own role in spiritual healing. The man is commanded to act, to stand and stretch forth his hand. He is not allowed to be indolent if he wishes a miracle. There is work that must be done by those of us who seek spiritual healing. However, as Nibley was wont to say, "Work we must, but the lunch is free."[19] In other words, while the man performed his small act of obedience, this narrative reminds us that he simply cooperated with Christ's grace. One of the things that makes miracles "miraculous" is that we cannot do them ourselves. Our token gestures are important, but so insignificant are they that they merely testify of God's mercy, grace, and love to us and for us.

NOTES

1. Fitzmyer (1970), 611.
2. While Luke also mentions the episode of picking the grain on the Sabbath, he places it in a previous week. Mark makes no mention of that event in the context of this miracle. Thus, the two Sabbath "infractions" may have happened a week or two apart, though the text is unclear.

3. See Jerome, "Gospel to the Hebrews," 242; Hilary, "Commentary on Matthew," 239; Lockyer (1965), 177.

4. Athanasius of Alexandria (circa AD 295–373) wrote, "I am not touching you so that they may not bring a charge against me. I am speaking with a speech so that they may not think that touching is an act of work. God did not say, 'Do not speak on the sabbath.' But if speech becomes an act of work, let the one who has spoken be an object of amazement. . . . He did not add plasters, he was not tenderizing with lotions. He did not apply medical ointments. He did this work openly, standing in their midst, and not in a hidden way, so that some might retort: 'He applied a plant, he added a plaster'" (Athanasius, "Homilies," 39).

5. Julien (1996), 191; Todeschi (1995), 128.

6. Cirlot (1971), 137.

7. Ryken, Wilhoit, and Longman (1998), 362.

8. Origin, "Fragments" 238.

9. Chrysostom, "Homilies on the Gospel of Matthew," 10:259.

10. See Mann (1986), 240, 242. Neither Matthew nor Luke reports these feelings by Jesus.

11. Marcus (2000), 249,

12. Marcus (2000), 253.

13. Lockyer (1965), 176; Matthews (1969), 34.

14. Lockyer (1965), 177.

15. One commentator pointed out, "If Jesus is 'the Holy one of God,' whose holiness implies the apocalyptic destruction of demons and disease, then his Sabbath-day healing of the man with the paralyzed hand is a fulfillment rather than an infraction of the commandment to 'remember the Sabbath day and keep it holy'" (Marcus [2000], 252–53).

16. McQuade (2008), 113; emphasis added.

17. Cyril of Alexandria (AD 375–444) wrote, "The nature of an envious person is such that he makes the praises of others food for his own disease and is wickedly maddened by their reputation" or success ("Commentary on Luke," 99).

18. Ambrose, "Exposition of the Gospel of Luke," 100.

19. See Nibley, "Work We Must," 202–51.

CENTURION'S SERVANT
HEALED *of the* PALSY

MATTHEW 8:5–13
LUKE 7:2–10

THE MIRACLE

A man of note and power in the Roman army had a servant whom he deeply loved. The slave or attendant was gravely ill—"grievously tormented" (Matthew 8:6). His master desperately sought his recovery and, upon hearing that Jesus was in Capernaum, made a request that He would heal him.

Jesus indicated that He would come to the centurion's home to heal his servant, but the man of means felt unworthy of Christ's presence in his quarters. Instead, he requested that Jesus merely verbally say that the man would be healed, for he had faith that any articulation by Christ to that effect would accomplish the desired outcome. Jesus's reply was that He had "not found so great faith, no, not in [all of] Israel" (Matthew 8:10; Luke 7:9).

Jesus commanded it, and the centurion's servant was healed of his sickness from that hour.

BACKGROUND

Matthew says that the centurion approached Jesus, while Luke says he sent someone else to make the request. It has been suggested that Luke may have been "expanding" on Matthew's account—engaging in a bit of "independent redaction"—thereby giving the story a "slightly different turn."[1] Some scholars hold that Luke's insertion of messengers being sent was made in order to back up the claim that the centurion was powerful and had command over many, and yet felt unworthy to approach Jesus, thereby accentuating Jesus's greatness and power.[2]

While Matthew speaks of the man as having a painful form of palsy (or paralysis), Luke does not state the illness from which the man is suffering, only that he is near death because of the sickness. Luke (the physician) may have known best the man's medical condition, though it matters little for the story.

The centurion is believed to have been a Gentile who had a fondness for the Jewish people but had not converted to Judaism or Christianity. He was a sincere soul not far from the kingdom—a "proselyte at the gate," as it were.[3] Luke records, "He loveth our nation, and he hath built us a synagogue" (Luke 7:5).

SYMBOLIC ELEMENTS

The centurion was a Gentile, a "heathen" or "non-believer," as it were, in the eyes of many Jews of his day. He is, therefore, a fitting symbol of the Gentile world and how it would embrace Christ and accept His gospel, even without having connection to Judaism or being "of Israel" (2 Chronicles 8:7).

As usual, the sick man can be viewed as a representation of the spiritually sick throughout the world. The fact that he was "grievously tormented" reminds us of what sin ultimately does to us, to our lives, and to our relationships with others.

APPLICATION AND ALLEGORIZATION

The centurion has been seen as an ideal symbol of the future of covenant Israel. Whereas the Jews would reject Christ and lose their status as the "chosen people," the Gentile centurion seems to symbolically foreshadow the fact that it would be those of the "heathen" nations who would *en masse* accept Christianity and follow Jesus. As one commentator noted, "The other nations of the world, as seen prototypically in the case of the centurion, would come to hear and believe with great faith."[4] Consequently, after noting the centurion's great faith—and noting that most of His own people rejected Him—Jesus declared that "many shall come from the east and west, and shall sit down with

Abraham, and Isaac, and Jacob, in the kingdom of heaven. But the children of the kingdom shall be cast out into outer darkness: there shall be weeping and gnashing of teeth" (Matthew 8:11–12).

Ambrose (circa AD 333–397) saw in the centurion's "sick servant" a symbol of most of the inhabitants of this world. He wrote,

> The servant of a Gentile centurion is immediately brought to the Lord for healing; this represented the people of the nations who were held in the bonds of worldly slavery, sick with deadly passions, to be cleansed by the Lord's blessing. The Evangelist [Luke] did not err in saying that he was at the point of death, for he would have died if Christ would not have healed him.[5]

And such will be the case for each of us if we do not turn to the Physician of our souls and receive healing from our spiritual maladies. Our world grows progressively sicker, morally and spiritually. There is but one cure for our ailments—Christ the Lord!

One commentary on the miracle states, "Jesus' acknowledgment of the Gentile centurion's faith contains a criticism of Israel's faith in him. . . . The centurion thus becomes in Luke a symbol of Gentile belief over against the general reaction of Israel."[6] Through this pronouncement we are informed that membership is not, in and of itself, salvific. We need faith, and Jesus's declaration suggests that a significant percentage of those who consider themselves "covenant people" are lacking that faith. Christ will save those who *truly* believe and will reject those who are "Saints" in name only.

> On two occasions we read of the Lord marveling: first at the faith of the Roman centurion in Capernaum; and second, at the unbelief of the Jews in His own country. The "great faith" came from the Gentile, the great unbelief from the Jews. There would have been nothing to cause surprise if it had been reversed. It was not to be expected that the Gentile should understand His power, and yet he seemed to realize that the whole authority of heaven was behind the world of the Man of Nazareth; whereas the Jews of His own country, the very ones who ought to have known Him, were full of unbelief. To doubt Him is, alas, but too common amongst those who ought to know Him.[7]

On a related note, this narrative symbolically says something about various types of faith that exist. The famous story of Thomas, the last of the Apostles to see the resurrected Lord, comes to mind. John records:

> But Thomas, one of the twelve, called Didymus, was not with them when Jesus came. The other disciples therefore said unto him, We have seen the Lord. But he said unto them, *Except I shall see in his hands the print of the nails, and put my finger into the print of the nails, and thrust my hand into his side, I will not believe.* And after eight days again his disciples were within, and Thomas with them: then came Jesus, the doors being shut, and stood in the midst, and said, Peace be unto you. Then saith he to Thomas, Reach hither thy finger, and behold my hands; and reach hither thy hand, and thrust [it] into my side: and be not faithless, but believing. And Thomas answered and said unto him, My Lord and my God. Jesus saith unto him, Thomas, because thou hast seen me, thou hast believed: blessed are they that have not seen, and yet have believed. (John 20:24–29; emphasis added)

There are those who believe because they have seen proof. And there are those who believe because they have faith—they have "believing blood." The Gentile centurion believed. He did not need proof or evidence of Christ's power. He trusted fully in it and, consequently, received the blessing he had desperately sought. We must ask ourselves: "Are we like the Israelites, who needed to see everything right before them, or can we trust like the faithful centurion? . . . If we really believe, seeing is not all there is to believing."[8]

This story can serve as a warning to "members"—those who have entered into covenants—to be cautious about looking down upon those of other faiths. It can serve as a strong reminder of the fact that God blesses all who reach out to Him—Jew or Gentile, member or nonmember. Those who have faith, regardless of their particular denomination, have a right to God's blessings. And those who are members of the restored gospel, if they lack the faith necessary, may prevent themselves from receiving the blessings available. "Of a truth . . . God is no respecter of persons" (Acts 10:34).

Augustine (AD 354–430) wrote, "For when the Lord Jesus promised that He would go to the Centurion's house to heal His servant, he answered, 'I am not worthy that Thou shouldest come under my roof: but speak the word only, and he shall be healed.' By calling himself unworthy, he showed himself worthy for Christ to come not [simply] into his house, but into his heart."[9] Christ's power can only come into our lives when we allow Him fully into our hearts. Outward religiosity does not save, only inner conversion. In the words of Elder David A. Bednar, "A testimony is personal knowledge of spiritual truth," but "conversion brings a change in one's beliefs, heart, and life to accept and conform to the will of God and includes a conscious commitment to become a disciple of Christ." Thus "conversion is an offering of self, of love, and of loyalty we give to God in gratitude for the gift of testimony." Having a testimony is important, but being converted to Christ and His gospel is vital. "Knowing that the gospel is true is the essence of a testimony. Consistently being true to the gospel is the essence of conversion."[10]

NOTES

1. See Browning, *Gospel According to Saint Luke*, 84; Johnson, *Sacra Pagina*, 119. See also Fitzmyer (1970), 648–49, who suggests that Matthew may more accurately represent the Q text in this episode.
2. See Fitzmyer (1970), 650; Johnson (1991), 120.
3. See Lockyer (1965), 178.
4. Simonetti (2001), 161.
5. Ambrose, "Exposition on the Gospel of Luke," 115.
6. Fitzmyer (1970), 653.
7. Habershon (1975), 183.
8. McQuade (2008), 105.
9. Augustine, "New Testament Lessons," 6:298.
10. Bednar, "Converted Unto the Lord," 106, 107, 109.

SON *of the* WIDOW *of* NAIN *Is* RAISED *from the* DEAD

LUKE 7:11–17

THE MIRACLE

After healing the servant of the centurion, Jesus headed to a city called Nain,[1] a small walled village south of Nazareth and about twenty-five miles from Capernaum.

As He and His disciples, and a sizable entourage, approached the gate of the city, a deceased young man was carried out. The boy was the only son of his grieving, widowed mother.

Noting the enormity of the woman's grief and loss, Jesus had compassion on her and encouraged her to not weep. He stopped the procession carrying the boy's corpse and commanded the deceased young man: "Arise" (Luke 7:14). The boy immediately sat up and began to speak, to the elation of his mother and the fear and awe of all who witnessed it.

Word of the miracle quickly spread throughout the region.

BACKGROUND

We do not know if the widow had other children, but we do know this was her only son. Consequently, about to be buried was not only one whom she loved but also her primary means of temporal support.

Robert J. Matthews offered an interesting suggestion as to the provocation behind this healing: "Jesus had compassion on the mother. One wonders if he foresaw his own mother, and his own death, and her sorrow. A prophecy had been uttered that when the spear pierced him it would be the wounding of her own soul and Jesus may have been additionally moved on this occasion because of regard for his mother."[2]

SYMBOLIC ELEMENTS

The deceased son in this miracle can represent those who are spiritually dead—those heading down a road that would make repentance difficult indeed (as he was about to be buried). But, as with the story of Lazarus (John 11), even once entombed in the grave, Christ can still raise the dead. Thus, even the worst of sinners can be redeemed through faith in Christ and sincere repentance.

The widow in this miracle story seems an apt type of the bride of Christ—the Church, which weeps at the loss of each sinner. Just as the widow felt she could not survive without the aid of her son, so also the Church feels a great loss when any stray and are no longer able or willing to serve in the kingdom.

APPLICATION AND ALLEGORIZATION

It is commonly pointed out that this healing story has strong parallels with Elijah's raising from the dead the son of the widow of Zarephath (1 Kings 17). Note a few of the similarities:

ELIJAH	JESUS
Elijah meets the woman at the gates of the city (17:10).	Jesus meets the woman at the gates of the city (7:12).
The woman is a widow (17:20).	The woman is a widow (7:12).
The widow's only son is dead (17:17).	The widow's only son is dead (7:12).
The deceased boy is laid out upon a bed (17:19).	The deceased boy is laid out upon a bier (7:14).
Elijah makes physical contact in order to resuscitate the boy (17:21).	Jesus makes physical contact in order to resuscitate the boy (7:14).
Three times Elijah physically touches the boy (17:21)—the number three being the ancient symbol for God or that which comes from God.	Jesus is the divine being Elijah is seeking to typify.
The deceased child is revived (17:22).	The deceased child is revived (7:15).

ELIJAH	JESUS
Elijah "delivered him unto his mother" (17:23).	Jesus "delivered him to his mother" (7:15).
Because of the miracle, it was known that Elijah was a man of God, and the widow bore witness to that fact (17:24).	Because of the miracle, it was known that Jesus was a man of God, and those who saw the sign bore witness to that fact (7:16–17).

The detailed parallels suggest that Luke understood Elijah to be a typological symbol of Jesus. Elijah's miracle of raising the son of the widow of Zarephath from the dead was a prophetic foreshadowing of Jesus's healing ministry—and of His power over life and death.

In this miracle we see the virgin's Son meet the widow's son, and we are reminded of how the Father raised the virgin's Son from the dead (Acts 5:30–31; 1 Peter 1:21) just as Jesus raised the widow's son from the dead. The miracle reminds us of Christ's power over death, decay, and decadence. As Cyril of Alexandria (AD 375–444) hoped, we all hope: "May our Lord Jesus Christ also touch us that delivering us from evil works, even from fleshy lusts, he may unite us to the assemblies of the saints" who dwell with God in heaven.[3]

Augustine (AD 354–430) drew an interesting application of this miracle. He noted that Jesus raised from the dead the daughter of Jairus (Mark 5:21–24, 35–43), the widow of Nain's son (Luke 7:11–17), and Lazarus (John 11:33–44). Each, Augustine pointed out, were in slightly different situations when they received their miracle. Jairus's daughter was raised while at home—in private. The widow's son was raised on the way to the grave. Lazarus, on the other hand, was raised after he was in the tomb. For Augustine, the implications of these three differences are significant. Said he, "Let us see what He would have us learn in those three dead persons whom He raised."[4] In his view, the daughter of Jairus is a symbol of those who sin in their thoughts—privately, as it were. Whereas the widow's son, Augustine held, was a good symbol for those who actually committed the sinful act but then had regrets about it. Finally, Lazarus was, for our commentator, a good symbol of those who have chosen a life of sin and have developed a habit that makes their return to faithfulness rather difficult.[5] In all three cases, the Atonement of Christ is needed, as is intervention by the Lord. However, the closer one gets "to the grave," in Augustine's view, the harder it is to pull away from sin and overcome spiritual death.

In the view of one commentator, this miracle offered a significant message for the Jews of Jesus's day: "Here was not only an awakening of the dead young man, but also an awakening of a dead Israel to its Messiah."[6] Only those with hardened hearts could learn of or witness such miraculous happenings and yet still deny that Jesus is the Christ. Thus for some, this miracle was a test—not of their *ability* but of their *willingness* to recognize and receive their Messiah.

One commentary on the miracle offers the following interpretation of the spiritual value of this narrative: "The spiritual application of the miracle is not hard to make. Having power to raise the physically dead, Christ is well able, in virtue of His own death and resurrection, to raise to newness of life those who are dead in their sins and trespasses."[7]

It will be noted that unlike many of Jesus's miracles (including the preceding one), this healing does *not* come in response to someone's manifest faith. Nor does it come at the request of the dead boy's mother or the friends that accompanied her to her son's grave. Rather, Jesus simply chose to resuscitate the young man out of His compassion—and apparently for the furtherance of His work and ministry. A parallel seems to exist between this miracle and the Lord's intervention in the life of Saul of Tarsus. Certainly Saul had not exercised faith in the Lord nor requested a blessing at His hands. It seems fair to say that as Saul went about persecuting, torturing, and assenting to the death of Christians, he was spiritually dead. But, like the deceased boy heading to his grave, the Lord intervened in the life of Saul, bringing him back to life—and, in so doing, furthering the work of the Lord. At times the Lord intervenes in our lives because we exercise faith and request His aid. At other times, however, He intercedes because we are spiritually dead and speedily heading to our graves—a symbol of permanence. What a blessing it is that out of compassion the Lord does dramatic things in our lives—and all the more miraculous are His intercessions when they happen in the midst of our spiritual sickness or death.

This miracle offers a symbolic foreshadowing of the resurrection. We weep now when a loved one passes. But in that glorious future day, there will be no more tears, no more sorrow, and no more suffering (Revelation 7:17; 21:4; Isaiah 25:8). Just as Jesus gives the saddened mother reason to rejoice, He will offer each of us the same. As the Prophet Joseph noted, "All your losses will be made up to you in the resurrection, provided you continue faithful. By the vision of the Almighty I have seen it."[8]

NOTES

1. *Nain* is Greek for "beauty."
2. Matthews (1969), 37. Matthews is drawing on the Joseph Smith Translation of this passage.
3. Cyril, "Commentary on Luke," 118.
4. Augustine, "New Testament Lessons," 6:414–15.
5. The reader should note, we question Augustine's application in this one sense; we have no reason to believe that Lazarus was one who had "chosen a life of sin." Indeed, the New Testament seems to suggest the exact opposite about Lazarus. Of course, Augustine is simply drawing a homily from these three stories. But it is worth noting the weakness of his metaphor.
6. Howick (2003), 24.
7. Lockyer (1965), 181.
8. Smith (1976), 296.

BLIND, DEAF, *and* DUMB BOY POSSESSED *of the* DEVIL *Is* HEALED

MATTHEW 9:32–35; 12:22–23

THE MIRACLE

On the same day Jesus healed the man with a withered hand (at the synagogue in Capernaum), He also healed a host of others (Matthew 12:15). In the process, there was brought to him a man possessed of the devil. Satan's influence over the man was such that he could not see nor could he hear or speak.

Preserving none of the details, Matthew simply informs us that Jesus "healed him" (Matthew 12:22)—meaning cast the devil out of him—so that he could again both speak and see. As with so many of the other miracles Jesus performed, those who witnessed it were amazed, and some recognized Him as the Messiah, the Son of David.

However, the Pharisees argued that Jesus cast out evil spirits by the power of the devil, to which He retorted, in essence, "Satan can't cast himself out without destroying his own work. If you say I cast the devil out by a demonic power, do not your own sons operate under that same power when they cast Satan out?"

BACKGROUND

Matthew appears to give this same miracle story in two places in his Gospel. The details are so similar—including the reaction of the

Pharisees to the healing—that it is hard to see these as two separate events. Thus, they will be treated as one here.[1]

This miracle is a small part of a larger narrative on a confrontation Jesus has with the Pharisees. We will focus here only on the symbolic message of the miracle, though Jesus's discourse is instructive doctrinally.

This man is not physically ill, though he has physical symptoms. His ailment is caused by the demon that possessed him, and his "cure" is accomplished by the casting out of that devil and by the receipt of God's Spirit.

Because exorcisms were practiced among the Jews, those who had witnessed this miracle apparently found it difficult to deny that Jesus had indeed performed one. So instead they claimed that though the miracle *had* taken place, it had happened through the power of Beelzebub (the prince of evil spirits) rather than through the power of God.

SYMBOLIC ELEMENTS

The man possessed is a seeming archetype not only for the demonically possessed generally but more particularly for those who have *allowed* their lives to be ruled by the influence of Satan. As we noted earlier in this work, the Prophet Joseph taught, "The devil has no power over us only as we permit him. The moment we revolt at anything which comes from God, the devil takes power."[2]

The Pharisees in this passage are possibly representative of all those who "shut their eyes; lest they see with their eyes, and hear with their ears, and understand with their heart, and convert, and be healed" (Isaiah 6:10). As difficult as it is to understand, there will always be some who simply don't want the gospel to be true and who will do all in their power to convince themselves and others that, contrary to all of the evidence, it is not of God.

APPLICATION AND ALLEGORIZATION

After Christ cast out the devil, Matthew records that "Jesus went about all the cities and villages . . . healing every sickness and every disease among the people" (Matthew 9:35). Of this action one text suggests this means "that He healed every variety of need coming His way, as faith on the part of the afflicted was manifested."[3] In other words, Jesus didn't just heal people from physical ailments; He healed spiritual maladies as well.

Jesus did not tend to the deafness or the blindness or the muteness of the man. Rather, He addressed the cause of those symptoms, thereby healing (with permanence) the root problem. "The divine Healer treats our spiritual disorders in the same way as He dealt with the demoniac. Dealing with symptoms will never please any good doctor, nor does it satisfy our Great Physician. A clean heart is what He promises first; then all thoughts, words, and actions will be clean."[4] If we seek to remove sin by changing only the sinful behaviors, we will never affect a *true* cure or *full* repentance. If, for example, our "cure" for pornography addiction is removal of the computer but not a change of the heart and mind, the man afflicted with the addiction may not look at pornography but his sinful desires will remain. Jesus addressed the cause rather than the symptoms of sin—and so must we. As with the man in this story, for each of us the cause of sin is the same: the influence of the adversary.

One ancient source interpreted the miracle as follows: "He was a blind, mute man who neither saw nor spoke. Symbolically he neither recognized his Maker nor gave thanks to Him. What was visibly done in the case of one man therefore could be understood to have significance for everyone."[5] Those who are outside the covenant or (as in the case of the Pharisees) who refuse to live faithful to the commandments are well represented by the man who is deaf, blind, and mute. They "have eyes, and see not; [and] have ears, and hear not" (Jeremiah 5:21). The man's deafness is a fitting symbol for our unwillingness to hear divinely inspired council—from scripture, leaders, or the Spirit. The man's blindness reminds us of our unwillingness to be honest with ourselves and others, our unwillingness to acknowledge our sins, or our tendency to rationalize sinful behavior. The man's muteness can represent the inability of those steeped in sin to communicate the gospel message to others and also the reality that sin keeps us from being a voice for good in the world and from being a powerful testator of truth to others.

NOTES

1. See Howick (2003), 45; Carson, "Matthew," 8:234; Senior, *Abingdon New Testament Commentaries*, 109.
2. Smith (1976), 181.
3. Lockyer (1965), 186.
4. Ibid.
5. See "Incomplete Work on Matthew," 244.

A Storm *Is* Stilled

MATTHEW 8:23–27
MARK 4:35–41
LUKE 8:22–25

THE MIRACLE

One evening, after a rather burdensome day, Jesus and the Twelve boarded a boat and set out to cross the Sea of Galilee. Jesus quickly fell asleep "in the hinder part of the ship . . . on a pillow" (Mark 4:38). Partway into the crossing, a storm of significant magnitude arose, dowsing the boat with waves, tossing it to and fro, and filling it with water. The disciples felt certain that they would sink and drown.

Shocked that Jesus had not been awakened by the storm and puzzled that He did not sense the extent of their plight, one of the Apostles said to Him, "Lord, save us: we perish" (Matthew 8:25). Jesus awoke and rebuked the wind and the waves, and they immediately stopped! But He also rebuked the Apostles, bringing a cessation of their cries of desperation. Rhetorically, He asked, "Why are ye so fearful? how is it that ye have no faith?" (Mark 4:40).

Rather than being offended, the Apostles were in awe at what they had just witnessed. While they had seen many mighty miracles at His hands (including the raising of the dead), this miracle left them dumbfounded. In their shock and stupor they thought to themselves, "What manner of man is this, that even the winds and the sea obey him!" (Matthew 8:27).

BACKGROUND

From east to west the Sea of Galilee measures about eight miles across, and from north to south about thirteen miles. It is surrounded by high hills on the east and west but has a wide, open stretch on the north and south ends. Like any inland lake surrounded by mountains, it is prone to sudden storms brought about by cold air sweeping down upon the water from the surrounding valleys. Thus, what happened here was not uncommon, but nor was it necessarily predictable.[1]

In 1986, the hull of a first-century fishing boat was discovered intact in the Sea of Galilee. It is believed to be the same type of boat Jesus and the Apostles were in the fateful day this miracle took place. This ancient ship measured 26½ feet long, 7½ feet wide, and 4½ feet high. The rear of the boat where Jesus would have lay sleeping would have been decked in, somewhat protecting it from the elements.[2]

SYMBOLIC ELEMENTS

The ancient Church consistently saw the storm depicted in this miracle as a symbol for the trials of life—persecutions, doubts, family struggles, struggles with health, monetary woes, sin. Isaiah wrote, "But the wicked are like the troubled sea, when it cannot rest, whose waters cast up mire and dirt. There is no peace, saith my God, to the wicked" (Isaiah 57:20–21). The Psalmist penned this: "O Lord God of hosts, . . . Thou rulest the raging of the sea: when the waves thereof arise, thou stillest them" (Psalm 89:8–9).

"The sea," *The New Jerome Biblical Commentary* informs us, is "a common symbol for chaos and death."[3] One scholar notes that the sea "is used often in the LXX [as] the symbol of chaos and disorder."[4] Lockyer sees it as a symbol of "the restless and sinful world."[5]

Many of the Church Fathers saw the little group in the boat with Jesus as a symbol of the Church.[6] One commentator on the miracle wrote, "The tempest-driven *boat* is the Church of Christ, and it sails across the ocean of the world's history to the 'other side' of the life beyond the grave."[7]

Jesus is an obvious symbol for "the captain of one's soul, leading to eternal safety and rest on the distant shore."[8]

The calm that comes through Jesus's command reminds us of that which each of us seeks and that only He can provide.

APPLICATION AND ALLEGORIZATION

The most obvious application of this miracle has to do with the storms of life and our feelings of overwhelming desperation as we traverse them. Of these inevitable mortal gales, Elder Howard W. Hunter said,

> All of us have seen some sudden storms in our lives. A few of them, though temporary like these on the Sea of Galilee, can be violent and frightening and potentially destructive. As individuals, as families, as communities, as nations, even as a church, we have had sudden squalls arise which have made us ask one way or another, "Master, carest thou not that we perish?" And one way or another we always hear in the stillness after the storm, "Why are ye so fearful? how is it that ye have no faith?"
>
> None of us would like to think we have *no* faith, but I suppose the Lord's gentle rebuke here is largely deserved. This great Jehovah, in whom we say we trust and whose name we have taken upon us, is he who said, "Let there be a firmament in the midst of the waters, and let it divide the waters from the waters." And he is also the one who said, "Let the waters under the heaven be gathered together unto one place, and let the dry land appear." Furthermore, it was he who parted the Red Sea, allowing the Israelites to pass through on dry ground. Certainly it should be no surprise that he could command a few elements acting up on the Sea of Galilee. And our faith should remind us that he can calm the troubled waters of our lives.[9]

One commentator applied the miracle as follows: "We may never set foot in a boat, but our lives are . . . filled with storms: emotional, physical, and spiritual. Like the disciples, we turn to Jesus for our answers."[10] Elsewhere we read, "For the sinner rocked by the winds of sin and passion, there is hope if only he will cry, 'Lord, save me; I perish.'"[11] Like most commentators, Saint Augustine (AD 354–430) compared the wind and waves of this miracle to the temptations and trials of life. At that moment when we are tossed to and fro by the storms of desire, temptation, anger, revenge, and greed, we must "awaken Christ." Said Augustine, "Christ is asleep in thee. What does this mean, Christ is asleep in thee? [It means] thou hast forgotten Christ. Rouse Him up then, call Christ to mind, let Christ awake in thee, give heed to Him."[12] Tragically, too often it takes the stormy seas of life to remind us of our intimate and daily need for the Lord. John Chrysostom (circa AD 344–407) wrote,

We are also sailing on a voyage, not from one land to another but from earth to heaven. . . . Let us prepare a strong ship, the kind that the buffeting and discouragements of this life will not submerge, or the wind of false pretense raise up, but will be sleek and swift. If we prepare . . . this way, we will sail with a favoring wind and draw to ourselves the Son of God, the true Pilot. He will not permit our ship to be overwhelmed, even if countless winds blow. He will rebuke the winds and the sea and will bring about a great clam in place of the tempest.[13]

Chrysostom saw in the miracle the truth that Christ "puts an end to the tempests of [our] soul."[14] But He can only do so if we call upon Him, and if we build a craft (or life) that has the ability to endure what God requires we withstand. Peter Chrysologus (circa AD 380–450) taught, "Christ gets into the vessel of his church, always ready to calm the waves of the world. He leads *those who believe in him* through safe sailing. . . . Without the heavenly helmsman the vessel of the church is unable to sail over the sea of the world."[15]

A second, but related, potential message in this miracle has to do with the reality that Christ is at the helm. The ship (the Church) we all ride on our journey back to the Father is often in troubled waters. Satan buffets it as much as he is able in a vain attempt to capsize the work of the Father. As one commentator suggested, all discord and disharmony in the world is caused by Satan, the author of disorder in the natural and spiritual world.[16] So it is! But we need not worry! Christ is guiding the ship, and it will not sink. Ephrem the Syrian (born circa AD 306) pointed out that in the miracle, "the ship carried [Jesus's] humanity, but the power of his Godhead carried the ship and all that was in it."[17] He continues to carry the ship (or Church) today. If we remain in the boat, we will not drown in the seas of chaos that churn throughout the world. But those in the ship (Church), when the storms arise—and they *will* arise—must cling to the boat. Some always get too close to the side, or do not cling tightly to the vessel, and when the storms arise, they find themselves overboard, spiritually drowning in the chaos, which is all around us. Christ is at the helm! But that can only bring security to those who remain safely in the boat!

Finally, numerous commentators highlight parallels between this storm at sea and the one experienced by Jonah. Note some of the similarities.

JONAH	JESUS
Jonah was sent to preach repentance (Jonah 1:2).	Jesus was sent to preach repentance (Matthew 9:13).
Jonah boarded a ship (Jonah 1:3).	Jesus boarded a ship (Matthew 8:23; Mark 4:36; Luke 8:22).
A great wind arose upon the sea (Jonah 1:4).	A great wind arose upon the sea (Matthew 8:24; Mark 4:37; Luke 8:23).
The ship was tossed to-and-fro and appeared as though it would sink (Jonah 1:4).	The ship was tossed to-and-fro and appeared as though it would sink (Matthew 8:24; Mark 4:37; Luke 8:23).
Those aboard the ship feared greatly (Jonah 1:5).	Those aboard the ship feared greatly (Matthew 8:25; Mark 4:38; Luke 8:24).
Jonah slept through the violent storm (Jonah 1:6).	Jesus slept through the violent storm (Matthew 8:24; Mark 4:38; Luke 8:23).
Out of desperation, those onboard awoke Jonah (Jonah 1:6).	Out of desperation, those onboard awoke Jesus (Matthew 8:25; Mark 4:38; Luke 8:24).
Those onboard begged Jonah to intervene on their behalf (Jonah 1:6).	Those onboard begged Jesus to intervene on their behalf (Matthew 8:25; Mark 4:38; Luke 8:24).
Jonah knew how to calm the storm (Jonah 1:12).	Jesus knew how to calm the storm (Matthew 8:26; Mark 4:39; Luke 8:24).
The storm immediately ceased (Jonah 1:15).	The storm immediately ceased (Matthew 8:26; Mark 4:39; Luke 8:24).
The men on the ship greatly feared because of the miracle they had witnessed (Jonah 1:16).	The men on the ship greatly feared because of the miracle they had witnessed (Matthew 8:27; Mark 4:41; Luke 8:25).

The parallels between these two miracles are strong and obvious. The Apostles would have been familiar with the story of Jonah and would likely have made these connections themselves. Of course, there was a significant difference between these two calming of the sea stories: "Jonah was the cause of the storm he encountered—Jesus was the Queller of the storm. Jonah was a fugitive from God—Jesus was God's Messenger doing God's work in God's way for God's glory."[18] The storms of life will come to each of us. We can cause them, as Jonah did, or we can turn to Christ and have them calmed, as the Apostles did. The choice is always ours!

NOTES

1. Mann (1986), 275; Fitzmyer (1970), 729.
2. Marcus (2000), 332–333; Mann (1986), 275.
3. Kselman and Barré, "Psalms," 541.
4. Fitzmyer (1970), 739n31.
5. Lockyer (1965), 184. See also Trench (1962), 92. "LXX" is the standard abbreviation for the Septuagint, the Greek version of the Old Testament commonly used in Jesus's day.
6. See Tertullian, "On Baptism," 3:675. See also Origen, "On Matthew," 64; Chrysologus, "Sermons," 169; Marcus (2000), 336.
7. Lockyer (1965), 184.
8. Matthews (1969), 39.
9. Hunter, "Master, the Tempest is Raging," 33.
10. McQuade (208), 109.
11. Lockyer (1965), 184.
12. Augustine, "New Testament," 6:304–305.
13. Chrysostom, "Commentary on St. John 1," 137.
14. Chrysostom, "Gospel of St. Matthew," 10:190.
15. Chrysologus, "Sermons," 169; emphasis added.
16. Trench (1962), 91.
17. Ephrem "Three Homilies," 64.
18. Lockyer (1965), 182.

Gadarene Demoniac
Is Healed

MATTHEW 8:28–34
MARK 5:1–20
LUKE 8:26–39

THE MIRACLE

After calming the storm on the Sea of Galilee, Jesus and those traveling with Him landed on the southeastern side of the sea at Gergesa or Gadara (modern-day El Koursi), a predominately Gentile region. They had just faced a fierce tempest at sea; they will now face a fierce tempest in a cemetery.

As they departed their boat, they were approached by a naked and wounded man who was demonically possessed and who was enraged (perhaps by their presence). He lived in a cemetery among the tombs and constantly cut at his flesh with rocks or other sharp objects. On a number of occasions, members of the community had apparently sought to restrain the man, but so great were the powers that possessed him, he could not be held by chains or fetters.

As he approached Jesus, the man prostrated himself and cried out, "What have I to do with thee?" (Matthew 8:29; Mark 5:7; Luke 8:28). In response to the man's query, Jesus "commanded him saying, Declare thy name" (Joseph Smith Translation, Mark 5:6). The possessed man responded that his name was "Legion," meaning he was possessed with many evil spirits.

Jesus commanded the evil spirits to withdraw from the possessed man, but before they did, one spoke from within the man and implored Jesus to allow them to possess a nearby herd of swine instead. Jesus commanded them to "go" (or "depart" as the Greek says), and they immediately left the man and possessed the swine. Straightaway the pigs, some two thousand in number, rushed down the hill and drowned themselves in the Sea of Galilee.

Those who watched and those who learned of the miracle wondered at what had happened and at the condition of the man once haunted. The formerly possessed man, now a devoted disciple of the Lord, sought to follow Him in His ministry. But Jesus commanded him to stay in Gergesa and the surrounding region and to bear witness to those of that region "how great things God hath done" for him (Luke 8:39). The man accepted his call "and began to publish in Decapolis how great things Jesus had done for him: and all men did marvel" (Mark 5:20).

BACKGROUND

While Mark and Luke speak of just one man as possessed, Matthew says that there were two possessed men who approached Jesus during this miracle. The Joseph Smith Translation changes Matthew, however, so that it harmonizes with Mark and Luke. Thus, according to the Joseph Smith Translation, there was only one possessed man healed during this episode on the coast of the Sea of Galilee. One expert on the miracles suggested that Matthew, who "always wrote with Jewish leaders before his mind," may have spoken metaphorically when he said there were two possessed men healed as it would fulfill the Jewish law of witnesses (see Deuteronomy 17:6; 19:15).[1]

Decapolis was largely Gentile in population and Gergesa was most likely the same. Thus, though Jews traditionally did not tend swine, the large herd of pigs in that region would not be unusual.

When asked his name, the tormented man responded, "Legion." A Roman legion consisted of six thousand soldiers. Was the man possessed by this many demons? The text is silent as to the exact number. However, we *do* learn from Mark that two thousand pigs were each possessed when the spirits left the man and took up residence within the swine. Consequently, logic would suggest that the man had no less than two thousand evil spirits resident within his body, and perhaps more—*a shuddering thought!*

Many are bothered that this miracle of healing required the death of two thousand swine in addition to harming the livelihood of at least one herder. Ancient Christians consistently pointed out that Jesus did *not* command the evil spirits to enter the pigs; He simply commanded them to leave the man they were possessing. Saint Jerome (circa AD 347–420) explained that it "ought [not] to disturb anyone that by the Lord's command two thousand swine were slain by the agency of demons, since those who witnessed the miracle could not have believed that so great a multitude of demons had gone out of the man unless an equally vast number of swine had rushed to ruin, showing that it was a legion that impelled them."[2]

This possessed man would have had no foreknowledge of the Lord or His miraculous works. He lived alone among the tombs and was tormented for an extended period of time by the demons that held him bound. Thus, when Christ approached and the demoniac ran out to meet Him, his declaration—"Jesus, thou Son of God"—came not from the possessed man but rather from the demons within, demons who knew well of Jesus's power (James 2:19).

In speaking of this miracle, the Prophet Joseph Smith taught, "We came to this earth that we might have a body and present it pure before God in the celestial kingdom. The great principle of happiness consists in having a body. The devil has no body, and herein is his punishment. He is pleased when he can obtain the tabernacle of man, and when cast out by the Savior he asked to go into the herd of swine, showing that he would prefer a swine's body to having none. All beings who have bodies have power over those who have not."[3]

SYMBOLIC ELEMENTS

Everything in the description of the demoniac is "unclean." The portrait painted by the Gospel authors is unmistakable. As one scholar noted,

> This healing is in Gentile country. The story is set in the territory of one of the Hellenistic towns of Decapolis on the southeastern shore of Lake Tiberius (the Sea of Galilee). The incident is preceded by a crossing of the sea and followed by a notice of the return crossing. [Notice] the interest of the text in the fact that this is Gentile country, "opposite Galilee," as Luke 8:26 specifies. Nothing about it is kosher; everything is unclean: the spirits, the tombs, the pigs, the territory.[4]

Symbolically speaking, we are to see uncleanliness in the fact that the man is demonically possessed, in his nudity, in his personal filth, in the blood from his cuts, in the town in which he lived, and in the cemetery in which he dwelt. Even the pigs are a statement of symbolic uncleanliness and unacceptability. Saint Ambrose (circa AD 333–397) explained, "A man who has an evil spirit is a figure of the Gentile" or non-believing "people, covered in vices, naked to error, vulnerable to sin."[5] Ephrem the Syrian (born circa AD 306) wrote that "legion" was a symbol of the fallen world and its sins.[6] Thus, the picture here is one of sinfulness and spiritual filth. This episode is so pregnant with symbolic representations of spiritual uncleanliness that it is almost impossible for the reader to miss the point.

Just as the possessed man likely symbolized the results of a sin-filled life, his healing (by Christ) is a symbolic reminder of what the Savior offers each of us. "Jesus went to Gadara and there found a demoniac, but He left behind an evangelist"—a missionary! "What a miracle of power and of grace!"[7] The physical healing of this man testifies of the spiritual healing Jesus offers all, the spiritual healing we each need if we are to dwell in God's presence throughout eternity.

As we noted above, anciently, swine or pigs were sometimes seen as symbols for individuals who only called upon or remembered their God in times of need, but when their life was going well, they would forget their Maker.[8] Chromatius (flourished AD 400) explained, "The swine to which the demons fled symbolize the unfaithful and unclean people who . . . were living according to the sins of the world. . . . Living nearby this worldly sea they are steeped in error and inordinate desire. This made it easy for them to be overcome by the demons."[9] Cyril of Alexandria (AD 375–444) wrote, "It will never happen that those who love Christ will become subject to [demons]. It will never happen to us as long as we walk in his footsteps, avoid negligence in the performance of what is right, desire those things which are honorable, and belong to that virtuous and praiseworthy lifestyle that Christ has marked out for us by precepts of the gospel."[10] Thus, pigs were ancient symbols for "fair-weather friends of God." They typified those of us who are inconsistent in our prayers, scripture study, and devotion to the Most High God. They represent those who pray—and even plead—when hard times come, but when their lives are going well become lackadaisical in their faithfulness to basic gospel practices, including keeping the commandments and living faithfully to those principles that allow us to enjoy the companionship of the Holy Spirit. Many professing to be devout Christians act as *swine*, calling out to God when in want but forgetting Him in their actions, words, and thoughts when all is going as they wish in their personal lives.

As we have also noted, anciently, the sea was a consistent symbol for chaos and death.[11] Here it is potentially representative of the chaos that comes to the life of those who embrace the ways of the adversary. It can symbolize the spiritual death that comes to all who follow Lucifer. In this miracle, the sea reminds us of the very essence and character of evil—which always outwits and defeats itself. Satan and his minions seek power over others and desperately desire a body in which to dwell. And yet, in possessing the bodies of the swine, the demons actually drown themselves in the sea. And so it is with all the devil does. In the words of one commentator, he is "stupid, blind, self-contradicting, and suicidal, [and] can only destroy."[12] Each act that Satan performs and each behavior he inspires is self-defeating for him and for all those who listen to his promptings. Those enticed by his whisperings truly do experience chaos and spiritual death.

It seems clear that the term *legion* in this miracle—whether referential to six thousand, two thousand, or an undetermined number of demonic spirits—symbolically suggests the strong power of the adversary of righteousness, in this man's life and in the lives of all who allow him to reign.

APPLICATION AND ALLEGORIZATION

This miracle is largely a testament to the influences of the world upon our spirituality. It testifies to the fact that those who neglect to do the "gospel basics" open themselves up to the influence of the adversary. And when Satan gets his foot in the door, he is never satisfied with just enticing us to commit a little sin. As symbolically depicted in this miracle, he seeks to wreak havoc in every facet of our lives. Thus, the description of our possessed man seems to speak in symbolic terms of the general consequences of sin's influence upon man:

- Jews avoided tombs because they held dead men's bones—something unclean according to the law of Moses. This man dwelt amid the graves. "To dwell in tombs was deemed a sign of insanity. How sin separates men from their fellow man!"[13] As we give into the temptations of the devil, we make choices that we would never make in our right minds. We become "spiritually insane," as it were, and we begin to separate ourselves from those who are true disciples of the Lord. They are uncomfortable around us, and we become gravely uncomfortable around them. The Spirit, which they carry, is something the sinful find hard to tolerate.

- The possessed man wore no clothes. Sin makes us shameless and often leads to greater and greater immodesty. The farther one goes from God, the less modesty and propriety matter—in dress, speech, actions, and associations.

- The man possessed by "Legion" is described in the Gospels as being "fierce." Sin commonly destroys in a man or woman the finer qualities such as love, gentleness, or compassion. It often makes those who embrace it rude, loud, obnoxious, and even hurtful toward others. What once would have been unthinkable in the righteous man's life now becomes commonplace as the Spirit of the Lord withdraws and the spirit of the devil takes up residence in the heart and mind of his victim.

- Our demoniac cut himself with the sharp rocks strewn about the tombs. Sin is ultimately self-destructive. The misery that always results from sin is as a self-inflicted wound. Those who have lost the companionship of the Holy Ghost make choices that harm themselves and others. They lose their conscience and their rationality, and pain is ever the result!

If we wish to avoid the suffering of the possessed person, we must avoid his practices. Truly, "wickedness never was happiness" (Alma 41:10). Symbolically, our demonized friend reminds us that nothing good ultimately comes from sin—but much bad *always* follows it!

The story of this miracle reinforces the Apostle Paul's counsel to "put on the whole armor of God" (Ephesians 6:13–18). The Lord does not leave us defenseless in a world dominated by the evil one. However, we must proactively use that which the Lord has provided for our protection. The Prophet Joseph Smith indicated that Satan simply can't have power in our lives if we do not permit him to wield it. But, if we live rebellious lives—if we stray from what we know to be right or true—then the adversary can gain power over us.[14] Similarly, Saint Ambrose penned this: "People are the authors of their own tribulation. If someone did not live like a swine, the devil would never have received power over him."[15] Does the way we live insulate us from the adversary, or open us up to enticement and corruption? Saint Augustine indicated that, for the purpose of teaching a hidden truth, Jesus "let the demons go into the swine: to show that the devil hath dominion in them that lead the life of swine."[16] If we are unfaithful to the "little things" the Lord—through His prophets—has commanded us, the devil *will* have dominion. And with that dominion, he will bring chaos and spiritual death to our lives and (if he can) to our marriages and families. The pigs "are delivered up, not at the will of the demons but to show how savage the demons can become against humans. They ardently seek to destroy and dispose all that is, acts, moves and lives. . . . It is by our vices that we empower them to do harm. Similarly, . . . they become subject to us under Christ who is triumphant."[17]

NOTES

1. Lockyer (1965), 186.
2. Jerome, "Life of Saint Hilarion," 6:309.
3. Smith, (1976), 181.
4. Williamson (1983), 104. See also Albright and Mann (1971), 101; Adam Clarke, Holy Bible, 5:303; Fitzmyer (1970), 735, 737; Carson, "Matthew," 8:217; Wessel, "Mark," 8:657–59; Mann (1986), 278n2, 279n11; Morris (1999), 170; Wood, "Mark," 687.
5. Ambrose, "Gospel of Luke," 140.
6. See Ephrem, "Commentary on Titian's Diatessaron," 140.
7. Lockyer (1965), 191.
8. For example, in the Apostolic Fathers we find the following statement regarding the symbolism of the swine: " 'Thou shalt not join thyself to men who resemble swine.' For when they live in pleasure, they forget their Lord; but when they come to want, they acknowledge the Lord. And in like manner the swine, when it has eaten, does not recognize its master; but when hungry is cries out, and on receiving food is quite again" (Roberts and Donaldson [1994], 1:143). More generally, one commentator noted that because of the law of Moses (Leviticus 11; Deuteronomy 14), "to eat swine was to become a Gentile and [to be] outside of the covenant" (Craddock [1973], 187). The Anchor Bible suggests that "pigs = alien and heathen people" in the

parables of Jesus (Albright and Mann (1971), 84).

9. Chromatius, "Tractate on Matthew," 171. Chromatius added, "The [possessed man] who met the Lord in the country of the Gerasenes, that is, the country of the Gentiles, might be understood to . . . [represent] all of those held captive by the devil in the error of idolatry. They are burdened by the chains of their offenses and the fetters of their sins. They were not living in the town, that is, in the covenant community where the law and the divine precepts were in force. Rather, they dwell in the tombs, worshiping idols" and living in such a way as to ensure their spiritual death ("Tractate on Matthew," 170).

10. Cyril, "Commentary on Luke," 140–141.

11. See Kselman and Barré, (1990), 541; Fitzmyer (1970), 739n31; Lockyer (1965), 184. See also Trench (1962), 92.

12. Trench (1962), 103.

13. Lockyer (1965), 188.

14. See Smith, (1976), 181. Tertullian (circa AD 155–250) likewise taught that "the devil has no power over those who belong to the household of God" ("On Flight During Persecution," 4:117). See also Oden and Hall (1998), 69.

15. Ambrose, "Exposition on the Gospel of Luke," 140.

16. Augustine, "First Epistle of John," 7:496.

17. Chrysologus, "Sermons," 171–172.

DAUGHTER *of* JAIRUS *Is* RAISED *from the* DEAD

MATTHEW 9:18–19, 23–26
MARK 5:22–24, 35–43
LUKE 8:41–42, 49–56

THE MIRACLE

Jesus and His disciples were in Capernaum, where He taught a crowd who had gathered to hear the words of one whose fame had begun to spread. While He was teaching, a man named Jairus—one of the rulers of the local synagogue—interrupted and, in a spirit of faith, fell at Jesus's feet and begged Him to come to his home to lay hands upon his daughter, who lay at death's door. Jesus, along with Peter, James, John, and Jairus, immediately departed, initially thronged by the crowd.[1]

Partway to the home, one of Jairus's servants or relatives met them and informed the distraught father that Jesus would not be needed as the twelve-year-old girl had died during her father's absence. Knowing how this would impact Jairus, who had already manifest great faith in the Master, Jesus turned to him and in the spirit of a promise said, "Be not afraid," Jairus, "only believe" (Mark 5:36).[2]

They continued their journey, and upon arrival, Jesus found the house filled with mourners in the attitude of weeping and wailing. Jesus rhetorically asked them why they were weeping, indicating that the girl was not dead but merely "sleeping."[3] His declaration was clearly an invitation to exercise faith, as the girl's father had, though the narrative indicates that most did not believe on His words. Indeed, they "laughed Him to scorn" (Matthew 9:24; Mark 5:40; Luke 8:53). Perhaps because of their lack of faith, Jesus dismissed all of them, only allowing the girl's parents, Peter, James, and John to be present for the miracle.

Upon entering the room, Jesus took the hand of the deceased girl and commanded, "Damsel, . . . arise" (Mark 5:41). Immediately her spirit returned to her body, and she arose and walked about the room. Jesus instructed the parents to feed their daughter and also to tell no one about what had just taken place.

BACKGROUND

Jesus had performed many miracles prior to this one, but so far as scripture records, this is the first time He had brought someone back to life.[4] That makes this miracle all the more significant.

Jairus is referred to as a "ruler of the synagogue" (Luke 8:41). This suggests he had prominence in the community. It also highlights the significance of his act of prostration before Christ. He most likely was a well-respected man in Capernaum, and yet he displayed great humility in throwing himself at the feet of Jesus: an act that might cause some in the community to lose respect for him. Nevertheless, Jairus cared more about his daughter than his reputation, more about the opinions of God than those of man.

Jairus speaks of the girl as "my little daughter" (Mark 5:23). However, the text tells us that she was twelve years of age at the time of her premature death. While twelve years of age is but a child in the modern age, in Christ's day it was the age of womanhood; and this young "damsel" was culturally near betrothal age.[5] Thus, Jairus's term of endearment ("my little daughter") was less a statement about the woman's youthfulness and more about his love for his only daughter, whom he would ever perceive as his "little" girl.

In the King James Version, Matthew's account suggests that the girl was already dead when the father left to find Jesus. Mark and Luke, on the other hand, inform us that she was near death's door but had yet to pass. The Joseph Smith Translation, however, has Matthew in agreement with Mark and Luke.[6]

Professional mourners were often the custom in antiquity.[7] While not everyone used them, those who could afford them often did, as the tears and wailing symbolically suggested the deceased was greatly loved. We have no means of knowing if any of those found by Christ at the home of Jairus were "paid mourners." However, their response to Christ's declaration that the girl was not dead provoked this assessment by one author: "His words caused peals of laughter, for they knew that she was dead. At the same time, their hilarity demonstrated their insincerity and revealed that their sadness was just an outward show."[8] It may well be that had those present really been moved by their love for Jairus's daughter and family, they would have responded in a more reverent and contemplative manner. Thus, it may not be a coincidence that when Mark says they were ejected from the house, he uses the same verb employed throughout his Gospel for the exorcism of demons (see Mark 1:34; 3:15, 23).[9] This is not to imply that Mark thinks these "mourners" are possessed, only that they are harkening to the wrong spirit or they would see Christ for who He is and know that He spoke the truth.

Jesus's command to "tell no one" about what had taken place is left unexplained by all three Gospel authors who record this narrative. While Jesus had given that same counsel elsewhere (see Matthew 8:4; Mark 7:36), in this case it seems particularly puzzling as so many were aware of the girl's death. Thus, her emergence from the house would surely let others know that she had been brought back to life. How the family would keep this a secret seems bewildering. That being said, perhaps Jesus's declaration when He first entered the house (the girl is "not dead, but sleepeth") was calculated to facilitate the parents' ability to keep this miracle private. Some might reason that she actually was not dead but merely in a coma.[10] And why would Jesus not want it known that she had been the recipient of Jesus's most miraculous act yet? Robert J. Matthews suggests that this was a "move by Jesus to protect the girl from 'idle curiosity' by throngs who would come to see her."[11]

The fifth-century archbishop of Ravenna, Peter Chrysologus (AD 380–450), felt that Christ's declaration that the girl was merely sleeping was an attempt by the Master to bolster the faith of those present. It was an attempt to help them believe that what they desired was possible. He wrote, "In order to move faithless hearts to faith, he says that the ruler's daughter is sleeping and is not dead. Ostensibly it is not easier to rise from death than to rise from sleep. So he says, 'The girl is asleep, not dead.' With God, indeed, death is sleep, for God can bring a dead person back to life sooner than a sleeping person can be wakened from sleep."[12]

SYMBOLIC ELEMENTS

The girl brought back in this episode well symbolizes each of us. If we wish to live—if we wish to see a day when we shall be raised from the dead and enjoy eternal life—we must trust in the Source of all life. The girl's father asks Jesus to "heal" his daughter. The Greek verb employed also means to "save."[13] And that is what Jesus seeks to do for each of us, to "save" us from sin and death.

When the girl returns to life—born again, as it were—Christ orders that she be fed. Luke says Jesus "commanded [them] to give her meat" (Luke 8:55). The Greek here does not mean flesh but simply implies food of any kind. Eating is a sign of communion, and communion is symbolically connected to the sacrament of the Lord's Supper. In other words, there is a potential connection between the girl's new life and Christ's order that she be fed. One fourth-century source explained,

> The entire mystery of our salvation is prefigured in this girl [and her return to life]; after she was raised from the dead, as Luke reports, the Lord directs her to eat something. Evidently the order of our faith and salvation is here shown. For when each believer among us is freed in baptism from perpetual death and [thereby] comes back to life upon acceptance of the gift of the Holy Spirit, it is necessary that the person also be directed to eat that heavenly bread about which the Lord says, "Unless you eat the flesh of the Son of Man and drink his blood, you have no life in you."[14]

The act of eating depicted here can symbolically remind us of our need to regularly renew our covenants through partaking of the sacrament, lest we again find ourselves dead to the things of God. Eating food may give us physical life, but the weekly renewal of our covenants offers us access to Christ's Atonement and thus eternal life.

The age of the damsel is significant. We are told that she was twelve years of age at the time of the miracle. The number twelve has been interpreted by Latter-day Saint commentators as the symbolic number for priesthood.[15] Thus, the act of bringing her back to life was a priesthood act performed by one having authority. So also, each of us through that sacred priesthood ordinance of resurrection[16] will one day be raised from the dead. Until then, it is through acts of the priesthood that we enter into covenants with our Father and, through those covenants, enjoy spiritual life here while anticipating eternal life in the world to come.

The disbelieving people in this narrative were said to have laughed at Jesus's suggestion that the girl was merely sleeping. In so doing, they became perfect symbols for a class of people who rob themselves of blessings, including opportunities for spiritual experiences. In 2 Nephi 9:29 we are informed, "To be learned is good if they hearken unto the counsels of God." The natural man is dead to the things of God. He does not see nor can he know God's hand, will, or way. As the Apostle Paul declared, "But the natural man receiveth not the things of the Spirit of God: for they are foolishness unto him: neither can he know them, because they are spiritually discerned" (1 Corinthians 2:14). Among other things, the disbelieving crowd described in this miracle can symbolize the dangers of doubting the pronouncements of God, which so often require faith from us. They are ideal representations of those who believe that they *see* or *know* better than God's chosen seers *see* and *know*. As with the faithless in this story, when we doubt the words of God's authorized servants, we run the risk of missing those sacred experiences God wishes to make available to us.

Jairus's faith in Christ, while he himself was a "ruler of the synagogue," seems symbolically significant. As one commentator noted, "By his recognition of Christ as the Miracle-Worker, Jairus revealed how deeply he felt the powerlessness of all ecclesiastical and legal machinery in the presence of death. The synagogue hierarchy could not help him, hence his request to the omnipotent Son of God."[17] The synagogue as an institution is sometimes seen as a symbol for the weakness of Judaism *aside from* its Messiah. It was but a machine—an organization—apart from the Christ. In that regard, Jairus reminds us that neither the Church nor the synagogue (in and of themselves) has power to save. It is Christ who saves. All other things are vehicles to Him. And where He is rejected, as He was generally by the leadership in Christ's day, the power to be saved is lost.

On a related note, the name "Jairus" is potentially figuratively significant. It means literally him "whom God enlightens."[18] While we are not told if Jairus was a disciple of Jesus prior to this event—and his place in the leadership of the synagogue almost suggests that he was *not*—we do not doubt that he was a devoted disciple *after* his encounter with the Lord. For truly Christ had "enlightened" him as to the source of salvation.

Sleep is but a euphemism for death (See 1 Corinthians 15:6, 18; 1 Thessalonians 4:14; 5:10; D&C 86:3).[19] All who die merely "sleep," as all shall be raised again. And, as the young maiden faced Christ, we too shall face Him and give an accounting of our lives.

APPLICATION AND ALLEGORIZATION

Could there be a message in Jesus's act of dismissing the mourners? Their unbelief certainly stands in contrast to the great faith of Jairus. Aside from their lack of faith, their outward behavior demanded their removal. As President Boyd K. Packer has said, "Reverence invites revelation."[20] Or as another put it, "The boisterous and tumultuous grief gave not promise of the tone and temper of spirit, which became the witnesses of so holy and awful a mystery."[21] This miracle reminds us that if we wish to brush shoulders with the divine, we must cultivate an atmosphere conducive to the presence of divinity. God's Spirit cannot dwell in unclean tabernacles. But nor can it commune with those whose lives are filled with irreverence and noise.

This miraculous story seems to offer a message of hope amid despair. One cannot imagine a more painful scenario than the loss of a child. It seems all other things would pale in comparison. Yet in the miracle at hand, the loss contained a lesson. One commentator penned this:

> Jairus came to Jesus with faith. But when he heard of his daughter's death, how grieved and hopeless he must have felt. Yet Jesus, honoring that first bit of faith, told him not to worry. "Hold onto your faith," was His message in this father's darkest hour.
>
> That's the message Jesus gives to us, too. Nothing is impossible for Him, no situation too bleak for us to trust that His help will . . . change our lives. Let's hold on, no matter what lies before us.[22]

Jesus Himself declared, "If thou canst believe, all things are possible to him that believeth" (Mark 9:23). This miracle gives us reason to believe in that promise.

There may be another application that can be drawn from this episode. Unlike the woman with an issue of blood—which we shall examine shortly—in this miracle it is *not* the faith of the sick that brings healing but the faith of her father.[23] Thus, in this miracle we find support for vicarious acts of holiness: for prayer and fasting on behalf of others. We find backing for the principle of placing the name of one who is in some way afflicted upon the temple rolls. Just as Jairus exercised faith in Christ and on behalf of another, you and I may witness miracles in our own lives as we pray and fast for others who have cause to mourn or who stand in need of God's intervention. Their received blessings may become blessings to us all.

Finally, Chromatius (flourished AD 400)—a leader in the Church of the fourth century—saw in this miracle a message about those who reject Christ. For him, those who "laughed Jesus to scorn" were symbols of all who, when they hear the hope of eternal life available through Christ Jesus, ridicule believers and mock their doctrine. According to Chromatius, when Jesus cast them out of the house, He was teaching us (through the symbolism) that the "incredulous and unbelieving . . . are to be excluded from the promise of eternal life or from God's kingdom" because they have rejected "him who is the Author of life and the Lord of the heavenly kingdom."[24]

NOTES

1. Others of the Twelve may have journeyed to Jairus's home, though we cannot say for certain. Regardless, only Peter, James, and John are highlighted by name in the narrative, and only they are allowed into the chamber of the deceased maiden, wherein they were permitted to witness her return to life.

2. One commentator penned this: "This brings us a glimpse of Jesus as the divine Encourager. . . . Jesus overheard the message brought to the father. . . . He checked the rise of fear in the brokenhearted [parent]. . . . Before the father's hope had a chance to perish, Jesus met the bearer's sad message with the encouraging word, 'Fear not; believe only, and she shall be made whole.' Unbelief did not have time to insinuate itself into the father's mind. Christ preoccupied the father with the word of hope, and with his usual tenderness and compassion He consoled him. His keen appreciation of the hour of greatest trial is revealed in His heartening message" (Lockyer [1965], 192. See also Kistemaker [2006], 154; Trench [1962], 108–109).

3. One commentator clarified: "His words do not mean that the girl was only apparently [or seemingly] dead, but rather that her death, like sleep, is limited in time" (Fitzmyer [1970], 749).

4. See Matthews (1969), 43. Not all are in agreement on this fact. See, for example, Howick (2003), 117.

5. See Fitzmyer (1970), 745. See also McKenzie (1965), 549, s.v. "Marriage"; Jeremias, *Jerusalem in the Time of Jesus*, 368.

6. Mark and Luke also place the timing of this miracle immediately after the Gadarene miracle (which we have just discussed). However, Matthew places it after the curing of the paralytic.

7. See Marcus (2000), 362; Albright and Mann (1971), 111.

8. Kistemaker (2006), 155.

9. See Marcus (2000), 372.

10. Indeed, some modern commentators have done exactly that, downplaying the significance of the miracle, suggesting that Jesus Himself said she was not dead. See Matthews (1969), 43.

11. Matthews (1969), 43. See also Lockyer (1965), 193.

12. Chrysologus, "Sermons," 184.

13. See Albright and Mann (1971), 113; Marcus (2000), 365. C. S. Mann noted that "the Greek word translated by *cured*" or *healed* "is used in contexts elsewhere when it obviously refers to salvation from sin" ([1986], 284).

14. Chromatius, "Tractate on Matthew," 185.

15. See Draper (1991), 24, 46, 56. 83; Smith (1998), 48, 53, 267, 288. See also Parry and Parry, Book of Revelation, 295; Brown and Smith (1997), 146. Non-LDS commentators often also associate this number with the equivalent of the priesthood, referring to it as a symbol for "ruling" power, church "governance," "apostolic government" or "divine governance"—which are equivalent to priesthood (Conner [1992], 176; Johnston [1990], 83–84; Davis [1968], 122; Bullinger [1967], 253). Non-LDS commentators have also described multiples of twelve as a "symbol of priesthood courses and order" (Conner [1992], 176; Ford, *Anchor Bible: Revelation*, 72–73).

16. See Young, "Increase of Saints," 15:139; Kimball, "Conference Issues," 12.

17. See Lockyer (1965), 191.

18. Marcus (2000), 356.

19. See Marcus (2000), 362, 371; Albright and Mann (1971), 111.

20. Packer, *Mine Errand From the Lord*, 192.

21. Trench (1962), 110.

22. McQuade (2008), 111.

23. See Woodward, *Book of Miracles*, 113.

24. See Chromatius, "Tractate on Matthew," 185.

WOMAN *with an* ISSUE *of* BLOOD *Is* HEALED

MATTHEW 9:20–22
MARK 5:25–34
LUKE 8:43–48

THE MIRACLE

On His way to the home of Jairus, Jesus was surrounded by people who were pressing in on Him and His disciples. Many were jostling and maneuvering to get as close as they could to Jesus, perhaps to catch a glimpse of Him or to overhear His words as He walked and talked with Jairus and the members of the Twelve accompanying Him.

At this time in Capernaum, there was a woman[1] who had suffered for some twelve years with an "issue" or "flow of blood" that could not be stopped.[2] She had been treated by many physicians, but to no avail. The bleeding had continued—even grown worse—and in the process, she had impoverished herself seeking a medical cure. This distraught woman, having heard that Jesus was near, thought to herself, "If I may but touch his clothes, I shall be whole" (Mark 5:28). And so she set out to see the Lord.

Obscured by the crowd, she reached out as Jesus passed, touching only the tassel hanging from the corner of His mantle or shawl.[3] The contact was so inconsequential that no one could have felt it, particularly amid the throng. But Jesus did! He knew that He had been touched, and not simply touched, but touched by someone exercising faith in Him.

Jesus immediately stopped and inquired, "Who touched me?" (Luke 8:45). His Apostles, puzzled that He would ask such a question when dozens were pressing in upon them, responded, "Thou seest the multitude thronging thee, and sayest thou, Who touched me?" (Mark 5:31). Jesus's reply was that He felt virtue—or "power," as the Greek says—leave Him when He was touched.[4] Thus, He knew this was not a simple touch but the touch of faith.

Christ surveyed the crowd and as He did so, the woman trembled, fearful that her act of faith might be cause for rebuke. Shaking, she came forward and fell at Christ's feet, telling Him all regarding her years of illness and her failed attempts at healing. Rather than rebuking her, in a spirit of love and compassion, the Lord spoke: "Daughter, be of good comfort; thy faith hath made thee whole" (Matthew 9:22). Indeed it had, for from the moment she touched Jesus's robe, her bleeding stopped.[5]

BACKGROUND

One commentator wrote, "We need to remind ourselves of the enormity of the crime she had committed in coming through the crowd and touching Jesus."[6] In antiquity, blood was believed to make one ritually unclean. In the circumstance of this woman, anything she touched would have been perceived as unclean also. Thus, an attempt to interact with Jesus—or even an endeavor to touch His robe—would have been perceived as inappropriate as it would transfer her defilement to Him.[7] However, instead of uncleanness passing from her to Jesus, healing power flowed from Him to her—a clear symbol for the power of God and the weakness of sin in His presence.[8]

On a related note, people who are sick are traditionally surrounded by caregivers who can daily attend to their needs. However, under the law—because no contact was to be made with her—this woman was relegated to a solitary life. She had no one to tend to her day-to-day physical needs, and she could not attend the temple or synagogue because of her defilement. Thus, spiritually and physically she was alone. After twelve years, her pain must have been unimaginable.

A belief that a physical object could be the source of power or healing was common in the first century. For example, we read of the Apostle Paul that "from his body were brought unto the sick hand-kerchiefs or aprons, and the diseases departed from them, and the evil spirits went out of them" (Acts 19:12).[9] It is likely that the sickly sister who is central to this miracle knew of such manifestations of these divine powers and sought to exercise faith in them as a means of being healed, while avoiding (to the degree possible) defiling others. Yet, it will be noted that Jesus tells her "thy faith hath made thee whole," not "thy act" or touching or the "article which thou touched." In many ways, the faith we exhibit is more important than the acts attached to it. Hence, we can participate in all of the ordinances of the gospel, but if we do not have faith, they will have no power. Healing comes by faith (James 5:15), not simply by an act of touch. Even in the case of a fringe, handkerchief, or apron that seemingly facilitates healing, it is yet faith—not the act of touch or the article touched—that makes the healing possible. Elder Dallin H. Oaks has said,

> Faith is essential for healing by the powers of heaven. The Book of Mormon even teaches that "if there be no faith among the children of men God can do no miracle among them" (Ether 12:12). In a notable talk on administering to the sick, President Spencer W. Kimball said: "The need of faith is often underestimated. The ill one and the family often seem to depend wholly on the power of the priesthood and the gift of healing that they hope the administering brethren may have, whereas the greater responsibility is with him who is blessed. . . . The major element is the faith of the individual when that person is conscious and accountable. 'Thy faith hath made thee whole' was repeated so often by the Master that it almost became a chorus." . . .
>
> Another part of a priesthood blessing is the words of blessing spoken by the elder after he seals the anointing. These words can be very important, but their content is not essential. . . . In some priesthood blessings—like a patriarchal blessing—the words spoken are the essence of the blessing. But in a healing blessing it is the other parts of the blessing—the anointing, the sealing, faith, and the will of the Lord—that are the essential elements. . . .
>
> Fortunately, the words spoken in a healing blessing are not essential to its healing effect. If faith is sufficient and if the Lord wills it, the afflicted person will be healed or blessed whether the officiator speaks those words or not. . . . The words spoken in a healing blessing can edify and energize the faith of those who hear them, but the effect of the blessing is dependent upon faith and the Lord's will, not upon the words spoken by the elder who officiated.[10]

When we receive a blessing, it is imperative that we remember Christ's words: "Thy faith hath made thee whole." As with the sister in this miracle, we might ask ourselves, do we have the faith to be healed? And is our faith placed where it should be?

After healing her, Jesus told the woman to "go in peace" (Mark 5:34; Luke 8:48). One commentator pointed out, "The Hebrew word *shalōm* carries the meaning of wholeness, soundness, rather than the sense of an absence of strife implied by the English translation."[11] Thus, Jesus's commission to "go in peace" really means something like "go, now, being whole and physically sound" after these twelve long years of suffering.

The church historian Eusebius (circa AD 260–340) claimed that after being healed this woman commissioned a statue of the event, which she prominently displayed in front of her house.

> At the gates of her house on an elevated stone, stands a brazen image of a woman on her bended knee with her hands stretched out before her like one entreating. Opposite to this there is another image of a man, erect, . . . stretching out his hands to the woman. . . . This statue, they say, is a statue of Jesus Christ, and it has remained even until our times so that we ourselves saw it while tarrying in that city.[12]

Thus, apparently in gratitude for the miracle received at the hands of her Lord, Veronica (as some ancients called her)[13] had a permanent memorial erected. And, according to Eusebius, it still stood in his day—more than three hundred years after the event.

SYMBOLIC ELEMENTS

As with so many other healing miracles, the woman with an issue of blood herein can represent each of us—having spiritual maladies that Christ can heal.

Blood is a standard symbol for sin. Thus it is that when Christ wrought His Atonement on our behalf—paying for the sins of the world—the blood (or sin) was squeezed out of Him, drop-by-drop and pore-by-pore. Symbolically speaking, as you and I come unto Christ and become perfected in Him (Moroni 10:32), we too must have the sinful things of the world squeezed out of us. (And that process can be painful.) Just as Christ during His Atonement became free of the symbol of sin, we must become free of the reality of sin. Christ is the only means by which we can achieve that.

The number twelve, as highlighted in the previous miracle, has been described as a symbol for priesthood or priesthood power.[14] Thus, the number here employed can remind us that her healing came by the power of the priesthood—as it does for each of us.

The "fringe" or "hem" of Christ's garment is a curious symbol in this miracle. It carries two potential meanings. First of all, the knotted strings on the four corners of Jesus's *tallit* or prayer shawl, which likely were what the woman touched, are symbols for the commandments of God. Therefore, symbolically speaking, the commandments are a source of healing to each of us. Second, the fact that the woman only touched the "hem"—the very edge—of Jesus's clothing, and yet was healed, is a beautiful type for the doctrine of grace. We do so little. Christ does so much! Our meager attempts to reach out to Christ, even if they constitute nothing more than token gestures, are nevertheless accepted by Him. And they allow Him to then pour out His healing, grace-filled influence upon us. As one ancient source suggested, "Her touch on the hem of his garment was the cry of a believing heart."[15] And that is what Christ asks of us in order that we might become recipients of His grace.

APPLICATION AND ALLEGORIZATION

The choice the woman made to come forth and "tell the whole truth"—even though she was filled with fear—has been seen by one commentator as an "encouragement" to all who profess to be followers of Christ to proclaim "their faith in Jesus boldly and not to hold back out of fear of the consequences."[16] Each of us will encounter circumstances when our testimony of Christ or of His restored gospel will be unpopular or will appear to bring rejection or criticism. However, in the spirit of this sickly sister, we too are invited to acknowledge our faith in Him and His Church, and accept what may come. Do we love the Lord more than we love the honors of the world? If so, we will find the faith to do as this woman did, and ultimately, like her, we will find God's blessings flowing to us because of our faith.

Similarly, Christ knew that the woman had been healed even though He had not yet seen her. And her healing certainly came by His consent, as we cannot force God's hand.[17] And yet, though she had been healed, Jesus called her out of the crowd. Why not carry on? Why not continue to make His way to the bedside of Jairus's daughter? One commentator on the miracle suggested that "it was needful that she should be drawn from her hiding-place, and compelled to avouch both what she had sought, and what [she] had found, of help and healing."[18] So it is with us. Just as Jesus expected the woman who had received so great a blessing at His hand to stand forth, surely He must expect you and me to openly acknowledge the goodness of God in our own lives. As the Psalmist wrote, "Come and hear, all ye that fear God, and I will declare what he hath done for my soul" (Psalm 66:16). We too must come out of our places of hiding and testify boldly that there is a God who does hear and answer prayers.

We are told that many in the crowd pressed in upon Jesus, curious to hear His words or perchance see a miracle performed by His hand. Yet, close though they were, they knew Him not. We are left wondering, "How many throng Christ, are near to Him outwardly, yet never seem to touch Him!"[19]

> Many *throng* Christ; his in name; near to Him outwardly; in actual contact with the sacraments and ordinances of his Church; yet not *touching* Him, because [they are] not drawing nigh in faith, not looking for, and therefore not obtaining, life and healing from Him, and through these.[20]

Do we, as the curious crowd, get near but never truly "touch" Him? Are we active in the Church but not really alive in Christ? Or are we more like the faith-filled sister who, aware of her own disease—a symbol for spiritual sickness—reached out to Christ and was healed. I am reminded of the words of Elder Bruce R. McConkie, who penned this:

> A faithful saint who [receives a priesthood blessing] has the promise that "the prayer of faith shall save the sick, and the Lord shall raise him up; and if he have committed sins, they shall be forgiven him." The reasoning of the ancient Apostle James, in this instance, is that since the miracle of healing comes by the power of the Holy Ghost, the sick person is healed not only physically but spiritually, for the Spirit who comes to heal will not dwell in a spiritually unclean tabernacle.[21]

As with the sister in this miracle, Christ can heal us of our maladies—physical and spiritual. But we must "touch" Him or, better put, allow Him to *truly* touch us.

For years the woman turned to the things of this world for her healing. She spent untold wealth on earthly remedies that could not heal her and ultimately made her worse. Yet, Christ was able to heal her instantly. To what "earthly" things are you and I looking in the hope of salving some pain that besets us? The world does not have the cure to our ills, pains, or disappointments. Only Christ does! Will we spend years looking to that which cannot heal before we turn to Christ and find relief from our trials? "God forbid that we should forsake the Lord, to serve other gods" (Joshua 24:16).

When that which is clean comes in contact with that which is unclean, the unsoiled thing traditionally becomes soiled. Symbolically, you and I must remember the warning of Moroni: "And again I would exhort you that ye would come unto Christ, and lay hold upon every good gift, and *touch not the evil gift, nor the unclean thing*" (Moroni 10:30; italics added). Close association with that which is "unclean" is always spiritually dangerous. That being said, one of the beauties of this story is its message that the "unclean" can become "clean" by inter-acting with Christ. Thus, you and I, as we reach out to Him, can have our sin-filled lives cleansed. We need not worry about soiling Christ. He willingly takes that risk. Indeed, as the Apostle Paul has informed us, "For he hath made him to be sin for us, who knew no sin; that we might be made the righteousness of God in him" (2 Corinthians 5:21). If we mingle with that which is defiled, we too will become defiled; but if we associate with that which is holy, we too may become holy.

NOTES

1. One fourth-century Christian text gives the name of the woman with the issue of blood as Veronica (*Gospel of Nicodemus*, 70. See also Lockyer [1965], 194).

2. Scholars believe that this woman suffered from an acute form of vaginal bleeding, which could not be stopped. One commentator pointed out that "the linguistic background for the present phrase"—an issue of blood—"lies in statutes in Leviticus regarding the vaginal discharge outside of her period. . . . Two third-century Christian documents, the Epistle to Basilides of Dionysius of Alexandria (chapter 2) and the Didascalia Apostolorum (chapter 26), confirm this diagnosis. . . . It is impossible to be certain whether the woman's ailment is an abnormally heavy monthly flow (menorrhagia) or a chronic light hemorrhage, . . . but in view of the narrative's emphasis on her immediate knowledge of the cure ([Mark] 5:29), a chronic condition is more likely" (Marcus (2000), 357. See also 366; France (1997), 170). The ancient Church also saw this "issue" and a "continuing menstrual period" (Chrysostom, "Gospel

According to Matthew," 183).

3. While the King James Version reads "hem," the Greek suggests she touched the *tzitzit*, or twisted and knotted wool cords that hung from the mantles Jewish men wore, cords that served as a reminder of the 613 commandments associated with the law of Moses (see Nicoll [1983], 1:154; Albright and Mann [1971], 111; Mann [1986], 285; Fitzmyer [1970], 746).

4. As in this healing miracle, the Prophet Joseph also spoke of feeling strength, power, or "virtue" drawn out of him while giving priesthood blessings (see Smith [1976], 280–281).

5. Matthew records, "Jesus . . . said . . . thy faith hath made thee whole. And the woman was made whole from that hour" (Matthew 9:22), which seems to imply that the healing may have taken place at the instant that Jesus spoke to her. However, Mark records that the moment she touched the tassel of Jesus's cloak, "the fountain of her blood was . . . straightway . . . dried up; and she felt in her body that she was healed of that plague" (Mark 5:29). Similarly, Luke records that she "touched the border of his garment: and immediately her issue of blood stanched" (Luke 8:44).

6. Lockyer (1965), 195. Lockyer may speak in hyperbole here, but his point is generally valid: what the woman did (owing to her issue of blood) would have been inappropriate.

7. See Albright and Mann (1971), 111; Marcus (2000), 357–58.

8. See Marcus (2000), 367.

9. One commentator noted of this verse, "We are to picture small bits of cloth, pressed to Paul's skin, and then applied to the sick" (Johnson [1992], 340).

10. Oaks, "Healing the Sick," 49–50.

11. Mann (1986), 286.

12. Eusebius, Ecclesiastical History, 253.

13. See, for example, the Acts of Pilate, where we read, "And a woman called Bernice (Latin: Veronica) crying out from a distance said: 'I had an issue of blood and I touched the hem of his garment, and the issue of blood, which had lasted twelve years, ceased'" (*Acts of Pilate VII*, 1:511. See also "Gospel of Nicodemus," 8:419, 442; "Avenging of the Saviour," 8:474).

14. See Draper (1991), 24, 46, 56, 83; Smith (1998), 48, 53, 267, 288. See also Parry and Parry, *Understanding the Book of Revelation*, 295; Brown and Smith (1997), 146. Non-LDS commentators often also associate this number with the equivalent of the priesthood, referring to is as a symbol for "ruling" power, church "governance," "apostolic government" or "divine governance"—which are equivalent to priesthood (see Conner [1992], 176; Johnston [1990], 83–84; Davis [1968], 122; Bullinger [1967], 253). Non-LDS commentators have also described multiples of twelve as a "symbol of priesthood courses and order" (Conner [1992], 176; Ford, *Anchor Bible: Revelation*, 72–73).

15. Jerome, "Homily 33," 74.

16. Marcus (2000), 369.

17. See Trench (1962); Howick (2003), 172.

18. Trench (1962), 117.

19. Lockyer (1965), 196.

20. Trench (1962), 117. Augustine put it this way, "Few are they who by faith touch him; multitudes are they who throng about him" ("Sermon 62:4," 75).

21. McConkie, *Mortal Messiah*, 3:40–41n1.

TWO BLIND MEN
Are HEALED

MATTHEW 9:27–31[1]

THE MIRACLE

While yet in Capernaum and as He departed from Jairus's home, Jesus was followed by two blind men who had apparently heard of the twelve-year-old girl's miraculous return from death. As they trailed the entourage, they cried out, "Thou Son of David, have mercy on us" (verse 27).[2]

Jesus stepped into the home of an unnamed person and these two blind men followed Him.[3] Seeing their persistence and manifest faith, the Lord asked them, "Do you believe that I'm able to heal you?" To which they responded (no doubt, with eagerness in their voices), "Yes, Lord! We believe!"

Jesus then reached out and placed His hands upon their eyes while pronouncing the blessing: "According to your faith be it unto you." And they were instantly healed.

As with the miracle of raising Jairus's daughter from the dead, Christ also commissioned these men to "tell no one" what He had done. Nevertheless, Matthew records that these two recipients of a miracle "spread abroad" the news of what Jesus had done to and for them, and "His fame" spread "in all that country."

BACKGROUND

The blind men refer to Jesus as the "Son of David," which was one of the popular Jewish designations for the Messiah during that era (see

Matthew 15:22; 20:30, 31; 21:9; Mark 10:47; Luke 1:32; 18:38, 39). Thus, the implication of their employment of this title is that these men believed that Jesus was the Christ.[4]

Though they cried out to Jesus when He was outside of Jairus's home, He did not respond to their initial pleas. This may have been an effort to "prove" them and their faith in Him.[5] Or it may have been an attempt to remove Himself from the setting of Jairus's house before He performed another miracle, as those whom He had initially found at the home of the deceased girl were less than believing. Thus, He may not have wanted to perform the act of healing in front of these cynical gawkers.

Jesus did not *need* to touch in order to heal. He likely made physical contact in order to increase the faith of the blind men, as they were not physically able to enjoy the full impact of His countenance and presence.[6]

Noting the frequency of blindness in the Bible, one commentator pointed out that blindness was

a far more common calamity in the East than with us. The particular climate, soil, and customs of Eastern countries produce severe forms of ophthalmic inflammation [commonly] resulting in blindness. Smith's *Dictionary* accounts for the prevalence and severity of eye troubles in those days in Palestine "by the quantities of dust and sand, pulverized by the intense heat of the sun; by the perpetual glare of the light; by the contrast between the heat and the cold."[7]

For these, and other reasons, the commonality of this malady confronting Christ (throughout the Gospels) should not surprise us.

In the King James Version of this story, Jesus "charged" the men to tell no one of the miracle (verse 30). However, in the Greek, Jesus "sternly warns" them to tell no man. The seriousness of His charge is increased in the original.[8] While these men clearly disobeyed Christ, their fault was one "which only grateful hearts could have committed."[9]

SYMBOLIC ELEMENTS

One commentator noted, "Blindness had a special, symbolic meaning concerning the spiritual condition of Israel. It symbolized moral and spiritual decay and apostasy."[10] Consequently, in scripture sin is frequently equated with "moral blindness" (see Deuteronomy 28:29; Isaiah 59:10; Job 12:25; Zephaniah 1:17; 1 Nephi 7:8; 13:27; 2 Nephi 9:32; D&C 38:7; Moses 6:27), and thus, freedom from blindness is a symbol of redemption from sin or of being born again. Jesus is the "light of the world" (John 8:12) to those who are in "darkness" (D&C 38:8).

Touch is a significant symbol, not simply in this miracle but generally. The connotation of the act of touch is conveyance. We touch our mate to convey love. We touch an injured person to covey concern or comfort. We touch someone being ordained to convey authority or priesthood. So also in this miracle Christ touches to convey healing. The touch is not the actual healer any more than the touch of a spouse is the actual love. Rather, the touch is the symbol of what one is conveying.

Spreading the word of Christ's miracle against His will can be seen as a symbol of disobedience amid blessings. "To obey is better than sacrifice, and to hearken than the fat of rams" (1 Samuel 15:22). This symbolic gesture is well representative of how humans often receive the gifts of God but then subsequently disobey His words or will.

APPLICATION AND ALLEGORIZATION

Covenant Israel was in apostasy. They could physically see Jesus but perceived Him not as their Messiah (Isaiah 6:9–10). Christ had come as the "Light of the World" so that the blind—physically and spiritually—might see. Those who pursue Him in faith, as did these two men, will receive spiritual sight. Those who perceive Him as passing interest can never truly know Him nor the great blessings that He offers.

One fourth-century source suggested that this miracle teaches us about the order of faith. Hilary, bishop of Poitiers (circa AD 315–367), wrote, "The blind men saw because they believed; they did not believe because they saw. From this we understand that what is requested must be predicated on faith and that faith must not be exercised because of what has been obtained."[11] Hilary's point is simple: true faith requires that we trust when we have not seen. If we are willing to take a step in the dark, then the Lord can intervene and provide. Thus, Ether 12:6 cautions us: "Dispute not because ye see not, for ye receive no witness until after the trial of your faith." If we must see first, it is not faith.

Jesus touched these men because they couldn't see. Each of us has had similar experiences where the Lord has reached down and "touched" us physically, spiritually, intellectually, or emotionally. In our "dark" hours, He will sometimes give us reprieve from our darkness, either by speaking comfort to our souls, enlightening our minds, or freeing us from our maladies. Are we anxiously pursuing Him, as did the blind men, so that we might be within the reach of the Master's touch?

These two men, though blind (perhaps from birth), nevertheless walked in faith. They had never seen Jesus like others who believed in Him had. They had never seen one of His miracles performed and were only recipients of the rumors—yet they believed. And because they believed they followed. I am reminded of the lyrics to John Newton's famed autobiographical hymn, "Amazing Grace."

> Amazing grace! How sweet the sound
> That saved a wretch like me.
> I once was lost, but now am found,
> *Was blind, but now I see.*
>
> 'Twas grace that taught my heart to fear,
> And grace my fears relieved.
> How precious did that grace appear
> The hour I first believed.
>
> Through many dangers, toils and snares
> I have already come;
> 'Tis grace has brought me safe thus far
> And grace will lead me home.
>
> The Lord has promised good to me
> His word my hope secures;
> He will my shield and portion be,
> As long as life endures.
>
> Yea, when this flesh and heart shall fail,
> And mortal life shall cease,
> I shall possess within the veil,
> A life of joy and peace.

When we've been there ten thousand years
Bright shining as the sun,
We've no less days to sing God's praise
Than when we've first begun.

Oh to have faith sufficient to walk in the dark! Oh to experience the change of life John Newton did! Like Newton (who was literally blind), all of us are in some way or measure *blind*, but Christ can bring us sight. And like the sightless in this miraculous healing story, we too can feel so overwhelmed by the gifts God gives that we can hardly refrain from telling the world!

According to the story, the two men are not healed along the way, as one would expect. Instead, their healing comes at the end of the journey—when they complete an interview with the Lord wherein their faith in Him is evidenced by their declaration, "Lord, we believe!" So it is with each of us. Full healing, spiritually and physically, only comes at the end of the journey. When we have that final interview with the Lord (at the Judgment Day)—and when we testify to Him that we know that "salvation comes in and through his atoning blood and in no other way"[12]—then we shall truly and fully be healed. Then we shall truly and fully see. Then, and only then, we will take up permanent residence in the house—or "mansion" (John 4:1–3)—God has prepared for those who love and serve Him. But we too must endure to the end!

NOTES

1. It is believed by many that the miracle recorded in Mark 10:46–52 is the same miracle as here described.

2. The ability to see is one of the great gifts God gives to humankind. When someone loses sight, the other four senses fill in, and even heighten. Nevertheless, to be without vision can be a great trial. In the modern world the blind can work and read and do so many other day-to-day tasks. However, anciently this was not the case. "In Jesus' day the blind were relegated to the rank of beggars, which is still true today in underdeveloped countries. For them, the loss of eyesight means unavoidable poverty and an exclusive dependence on family members" (Kistemaker [2006], 169). Thus, while you or I may not see the plight of these two men as devastating, in their day it was exactly that.

3. Some commentators assume that the house Jesus entered was the house in which He was living in Capernaum (Peter's home). See, for example, Lockyer (1965), 184; Albright and Mann (1971), 112.

4. See Carson, "Matthew," 8:233; Barclay, Gospel of Mathew, 1:349. One LDS commentator suggested this: "It is unlikely that these blind men recognized Jesus as the Messiah. They probably addressed him in this manner as a title of homage" (Howick [2003], 185). Perhaps. We really have no way to tell for certain what their intended meaning was. But the fact that they pursued Him and ultimately received the healing they sought suggests that this was more than a rhetorical device. They appear to have had faith in Jesus—to really believe in His power and person.

5. See Matthews (1969), 46; Kistemaker (2006), 171.

6. See McConkie (1987-1988), 1:320; Matthews (1969), 46; Trench (1962), 122.

7. Lockyer (1965), 184. See also Ryken, Wilhoit, and Longman (1998), 99; Kistemaker (2006), 169–170.

8. See Albright and Mann (1971), 112; Kistemaker (2006), 171.

9. See Trench (1962), 123. It is also possible that they told others because they knew of no other way to explain what had happened in their lives. Clearly they were blind, but now they see. Perhaps the questions of the curious caused them to feel they had no other option but to explain the miracle and its source. It is also possible that they told of the miracle because, like for some in the modern Church, sharing such sacred things (which really should be kept locked within our bosom) makes the recipients of the miracle feel special or chosen above those to whom they share. We should hope the latter explanation is not the cause.

10. Howick (2003), 182. The Dictionary of Biblical Imagery similarly states, "Figuratively, blindness refers to an inability to recognize the truth, usually a culpable condition. As such, it describes judges whose judgment is perverted because of bribed idolaters whose worship is illogical as well as wrong and people who simply do not want to know. Such blindness to the truth and mental confusion could actually be the result of God's judgment on those who did not want to admit the truth and who therefore forfeit the ability to perceive it at their cost. This is true of the Israelites, both leaders and followers. Only God in his mercy can reverse this condition. Paul describes gradual blindness when he writes of those whose 'foolish hearts were darkened.' In another vein he talks of seeing poorly now in contrast to seeing perfectly in the life to come. The imagery of sight and blindness is especially prominent in the account of Jesus' earthly ministry. . . . Jesus performed miracles of giving sight to the blind. . . . Jesus described the religious leaders and teachers of his own generation in terms of blindness. . . . Those who rejected Jesus' words came under a judgment similar to that of Israel—a state of permanent blindness. . . . Although metaphorically blindness may describe mere ignorance, it usually carries the overtones of an unwillingness to face up to the truth. . . . Similarly, Christian believers who revert to their pre-Christian way are described as blind, not perceiving the contradiction expressed in their behavior" (Ryken, Wilhoit, and Longman (1998), 99).

11. Hilary, "On Matthew 9:9," 86.

12. McConkie, A New Witness, xvi.

MUTE MAN POSSESSED *by the* DEVIL *Is* HEALED

MATTHEW 9:32–34

THE MIRACLE

A man unable to speak was brought to Jesus to be healed. The cause of his disability was demonic possession rather than some physical defect.[1] Jesus cast the demon out of the man, and he immediately began to converse with those who had gathered.

It had apparently been many years since miracles were part of the religion of Israel. Since their captivity and exile under the Assyrians, Babylonians, and Persians, miracles had ostensibly ceased.[2] Thus, the Jews who witnessed what Jesus had done for this deaf-mute were absolutely amazed, and a number of them suggested nothing comparable had ever happened in Israel.

The Pharisees, as leaders in Israel, were both disturbed and angered by the miracle Jesus had performed and rationalized their rejection of it by claiming that Jesus accomplished the act by the power of Satan.

BACKGROUND

Jesus performed this miracle while He was visiting Capernaum and apparently after He raised the daughter of Jairus from the dead. How soon thereafter is uncertain.[3]

Though the King James Version of the story only speaks of the man as "mute" or "dumb," the Greek word translated "dumb" here is *kōphos*, which can mean "lame in tongue," mute or "dumb," but also "dull in hearing," or "deaf."[4] Indeed, of the fourteen times the word appears in the New Testament, eight times it is translated as "dumb" (Matthew 9:32–33; 12:22; 15:30–31; Luke 11:14), once as "speechless" (Luke 1:22), and five times as "deaf" (Matthew 11:5; Mark 7:32, 37; 9:25; Luke 7:22). This has led several commentators to suggest that perhaps the man was a deaf-mute rather than simply one who was "dumb," or unable to speak. Thus, one commentator wrote, "The word *kōphos* ('could not talk') in classical, Hellenistic, and biblical Greek means 'deaf' or 'dumb' or 'deaf mute'; the two aliments are commonly linked, especially if deafness is congenital. Perhaps the man here was not only mute but a deaf mute."[5] While we can't say for sure, for the sake of our homily here we'll assume that he could have been both deaf and mute.

Beyond the symbolism inherent in the statement that the man was "bought" to Jesus, his condition could have prevented him from knowing personally about Jesus's powers or from personally asking Jesus for a miracle. However, those who accompanied him likely heard of Christ's power, perhaps conveyed this to him, and accordingly took their friend or family member to meet the Master.

This is not a healing but rather an exercising of an evil spirit. Thus, whatever Jesus did to free the man of his captor—and the text is silent on how He did it[6]—we must assume that it was likely different from how He would have healed a man who was born a deaf-mute. Jesus was not curing physical sickness in this miracle; He was curing spiritual sickness.

SYMBOLIC ELEMENTS

As the early Church Father Hilary suggests, the deaf-mute of this miracle probably represents ignorance of the gospel more than sin or wickedness.[7] While deafness can certainly be a symbol of those who refuse to hear truth, it can also be a symbol of those who simply do not know.[8] Ironically, this man was deaf and yet heard Jesus's words, thereby being healed. But the Pharisees, who could hear just fine, were entirely unable to hear the spirit of Christ's message, and thus they remained spiritually sick and demonically deceived.

The fact that the man needed to be "brought" to Jesus highlights in symbolic terms his ignorance of the truth. In Jesus's day, someone in his condition most likely would not be privy to the stories circulating regarding Jesus or have the education to know how to write to Jesus to communicate a request to be healed. Thus, he stands as an apropos symbol of one who does not know the truth and one who needs to be introduced to it by others who already have a witness.

The way Jesus performs the miracle is also potentially symbolic. One expert on the subject wrote, "This demoniac's condition was not due to functional or organic disorder, so Jesus dealt not with the apparent malady, but with its root or cause by casting out the demon. . . . The divine healer treats our spiritual disorders in the same way as He dealt with the demoniac. 'Dealing with symptoms only will never please any good doctor, nor does it satisfy our Great Physician. A clean heart is what He promises first; then all thoughts, words, and actions will be clean.'"9

APPLICATION AND ALLEGORIZATION

In the Doctrine and Covenants we learn, "For there are many yet on the earth . . . who are only kept from the truth because they know not where to find it" (D&C 123:12). Such seems to be an important message present in the symbolism of this miracle. "The condition was not a natural one but was the scheme of a demon. It is . . . for this reason that the man needs others to lead him to Jesus."10 Satan is alive and well in the world today. He has deafened the ears of many to the truths of the gospel and thus they need to be guided to the truth by those who have heard and embraced the Lord's word and way. Note that the man was not simply deaf but apparently mute also.11 However, once his ears were unstopped he immediately began to speak. So it is with those who have been made deaf by the adversary to the truths of the gospel. Once the Lord is allowed to unstop their ears, so too is their testimony unleashed, that they might proclaim to the world their new-found life-saving truths! Jerome (circa AD 347–420) wrote, "Spiritually, just as the blind men receive light, so too the dumb man's tongue is loosened that he may speak and give glory to him whom he once rejected."12

One of the most important symbolic messages of this miracle has to do with how people embrace or reject truth when they encounter it. "This miracle . . . is reported with the greatest brevity. All emphasis lies on the divergent responses of 'the crowds' and 'the Pharisees.' We are probably intended to see these as reactions not to this miracle only but to the [miracles] as a whole."13 Wherever Jesus went, He seemed to split His audience into those who believed, and those who rejected and fought against His message, calling them a "manifestation of evil (John 7:34; 9:16; 10:19)."[14] So it is with the restored gospel—it splits its audience into those who believe and embrace, and those who reject it and declare it "evil!" Certainly those who testify of the greatness of the miracle well represent those who are prone to accept the truths of the gospel when they encounter them. And the Pharisees, on the other hand, well symbolize those who, with suspicious and doubting hearts, reject truth in so many ways.

> Today there are numerous people with a thorough knowledge of the Scriptures who openly deny and repudiate the Bible's cardinal doctrines. They refuse to accept Jesus's virgin birth, his physical resurrection from the dead, his ascension to heaven, and his promised return. They are like the teachers of the Law and Pharisees in Jesus' day against whom Jesus uttered his woes. He called them blind leaders of the blind. Eventually they would have to face their God and give an account of their words and actions.[15]

This miracle reminds us that some will embrace and some will reject the gospel message. What Jesus gives us is undeniably true, but some will ever seek to rationalize it away. Some will claim to "know," but they are in reality deaf to the truth, and thus their mouths are stopped because they refuse to be witnesses of Christ. Jesus came to free those who believe in Him from Satan's rule and to establish His kingdom upon the earth. At His command, the devils must depart from Christ's kingdom and return to the realm of Satan.[16] It is curious how many humans seem more comfortable with Satan than they do with the Saints!

NOTES

1. Such seems evident by the language employed in the verses. See also Matthews (1969), 47; France (1997), 173.

2. This is not to suggest that no one could have a spiritual encounter with the divine during the era leading up to the birth of Christ. Rather, I only wish to imply that Judaism had been in captivity and had lost its prophets. The faith that was once revelatory and apocalyptic had become legalistic and—generally speaking—spiritually stale. In many ways, this is the point of Klaus Koch, who argues, "After the decline of five hundred years, Jesus of Nazareth . . . picked up the thread of the great prophets" (*Rediscovery of Apocalyptic*, 138n37.

3. See Lockyer (1965), 185. The chronology is a bit difficult, and commentators point out that we cannot be certain of the order of the miracles, or even if this event is a repeat of another story (see Matthew 12:22–24). See, for example, Albright and Mann (1971), 112.

4. See Thayer (1999), 367; Vine, *Expository Dictionary*, 274.

5. Carson, (1976-1992), 8:234. Elsewhere we read, "The word translated *dumb* (κωφός) can also mean 'deaf,' as in 11:5 = Luke 7:22; Mark 7:32. The corresponding Hebrew word is used in rabbinical writings to refer to deaf-mutes" (Buttrick, *Interpreter's Bible*, 7:359. See also Lockyer (1965), 186.

6. Jesus often used some form of touch to heal those who were sick, dead, or dying, but with the demonically possessed, He traditionally simply commanded and the devils departed. "The Gospel writer omits the detail on how Jesus drove out the demon, but similar incidents in the Gospel narratives indicate that demons were expelled simply by Jesus' spoken word. Jesus voiced no magic formulas, did not resort to spells, and uttered no chants. He merely spoke and the demons departed" (Kistemaker [2006], 114). Christ likely simply commanded the demon to depart and he withdrew.

7. Hilary, "On Matthew," (2001), 188.

8. Conner (1992), 138; Wilson (1999), 112.

9. Lockyer (1965), 186.

10. Chrysostom, "Gospel of Matthew," (2001), 188.

11. Being mute can be a symbol of a lack of testimony or the absence of knowledge. See, for example, Conner (1992), 156; Ryken, Wilhoit, and Longman (1998), 575.

12. Jerome, "Commentary on Matthew," (2001), 188.

13. Hare (1993), 108. See also Lockyer (1965), 186.

14. Ibid.

15. Kistemaker (2006), 117.

16. Ibid., 114.

JESUS FEEDS *the* FIVE THOUSAND[1]

MATTHEW 14:14–21
MARK 6:33–44
LUKE 9:11–17
JOHN 6:1–14

THE MIRACLE

Jesus had crossed over the Sea of Galilee, which is called Tiberias, leaving Jerusalem because He was being followed by a group who were curious about His miracles but not sincerely interested in His teachings. Now, somewhere near Bethsaida, a different multitude is with Him. They had followed Him all day, hearing His words and contemplating their meaning.

As the day drew to a close, the Apostles said to Jesus, "We're out in the middle of nowhere. Send the crowd away so that they can purchase for themselves some food and obtain lodging." However, Jesus felt pity on them, as they were sheep without a shepherd (Mark 6:34). So He told the Apostles that they should feed them. Surprised, the Brethren told the Savior that they had nothing to feed them with—only two small fish and five barley loaves of bread that they had gleaned from a small boy in the crowd. And their purse was nearly empty, holding only two hundred pennyworth, which would be hardly enough money to purchase sufficient food for five thousand men, their wives, and as many (if not more) children.

Jesus, having in mind something more, asked the people to sit down upon the grass in groups as He took the meager amount of food available to them and, looking heavenward, said a blessing upon the victuals—at which point He had the Apostles distribute the food to the throng.

The people ate to their content. When the people were filled, the Apostles gathered the leftovers, which filled twelve baskets.

BACKGROUND

This is the one miracle of Christ, aside from His Resurrection, that is recorded in each of the four Gospels. That is suggestive of its significance.

The miracle speaks of the five thousand "men" fed that day. However, the number filled was surely more than fifteen thousand—and perhaps even higher—as the accounts tell us that the families of these men accompanied them also.[2] Thus, Christ's miracle of multiplying the loaves and fishes is multiplied in its scope and significance.

The Apostles suggest that the total amount of money they have with them is approximately two hundred pennyworth. One commentary on the Greeks states, "A denarius," or pennyworth, "represented the wages paid to a laborer for one day's work; hence two hundred denarii means the amount of remuneration which one man receives for two hundred days of work."[3] That amount of money would not have been sufficient to purchase food for five thousand people, let alone a crowd of fifteen or twenty thousand.

"Barley loaves," as the King James Version translates the Greek, may give the wrong impression. These are certainly not "loaves." They are small pancake-looking breads, akin to single-serving pitas.[4]

The description of "fish" may also be misleading. The Greek word *opsarion*, employed by John and here translated as "fish," actually suggests small fish—sometimes dried or pickled, like one today might purchase in a can or jar. In other words, these two fish are the equivalent in size to sardines.[5] That's hardly enough to fill one man's stomach, let alone thousands.

SYMBOLIC ELEMENTS

Eating is generally seen as a symbol of communion. It this case, it is a perfect representation of communion with God both here and in the hereafter.

Immediately after this miracle, Jesus gave His discourse on the Bread of Life, in which He identifies Himself as the "bread" (John 6:22–71). In that discourse, Jesus indicated that unless we "eat" or partake of Him, we cannot have eternal life (John 6:51–58). Thus, the bread in this miracle is a fitting symbol for Christ. And partaking of it is well representative of communion with God and making covenants.

Some commentators (ancient and modern) have seen in the five "loaves" or pitas a reference to what would have constituted scripture in Jesus's day, namely the five books of Moses. Judaism ultimately developed a symbolic connection between bread or manna and the Torah or God's law. This certainly could be part of the symbolism here.[6]

Fish were occasionally used in the New Testament as symbols for those who sought entrance into God's kingdom (see Matthew 4:19; 13:47–48; Mark 1:17). For the early Christians, fish were common symbols for Christ, who was Himself the ultimate model for what it means to be a "member of God's kingdom." As we noted previously, "the fish . . . is the earliest emblem of Christ. . . . Seals and lamps in the catacombs of Rome bore this emblem as a secret sign. Gospel texts reinforced its symbolism through an analogy made by Christ between fishing and converting people. . . . The baptism font was in Latin called *piscina* ('the fishpond'). . . . Fishes represented the true and faithful."[7] Another source states, "While the single fish represents the Savior, several fishes represent faithful Christians."[8] The Greek word for fish, *ichthus*, forms an acronym that typically stood for "Jesus Christ, Son of God, Savior" (*Iesous Christos Theou Huios Soter*).[9] Consequently, offering the faithful followers fish may well represent an invitation for them to take Christ and His teachings into their lives. Just as the food we eat is broken down by our bodies and becomes part of us, we must take into our lives the teachings of Christ and allow them to become part of us.

Matthew, Mark, and Luke each refer to the location of this miracle as a "desert place." The implication of this term is that it was a secluded place—a place away from the world. Symbolically speaking, our most miraculous encounters with Christ will typically come when we are withdrawn from the world, in a place of solitude and seclusion wherein the Spirit can be heard because worldly distractions are gone.

Jesus's choice to have the people sit in groups may be a symbol for the reality that salvation is often pursued in communities, wards, and stakes. Christ's division of His followers here may foreshadow a time when the Church would be large enough to require such divisions so that the needs of individuals were not lost in the crowd but met by the "ward family" instead. Additionally, the Greek implies a transformation. The people go from chaos to order—standing and milling to sitting in organized groups. As one commentator put it, "Human disorder is transformed into organic, paradisiacal order."[10] And this is what Christ can do in and to our lives. He can turn the chaos common to this mortal world into order and peace. Which of us does not need His intervention on that front?

The baskets in which Jesus's Apostles gather the leftover food are curious. The usual words for basket (in Attic Greek and in the Septuagint) would be *kanoun* or *spyris/spuris*. However, these are not the words that are used here. The Greek word translated "basket" here is *kophinos*, which means literally "coffin."[11] While this may be entirely coincidental, commentators suggest that something symbolic *may* be intended.[12]

As we mentioned previously, the number twelve is commonly employed as a symbol for covenant Israel (the Twelve Tribes) and for priesthood (the Twelve Apostles). Its use here may simply be a symbolic reference to the fact that this miracle was enacted through the priesthood. But it also paints Jesus as the new Moses who gives the law or word to God's covenant people.[13]

The fact that there are five loaves and two fish is consistently highlighted by commentators. The number seven is the standard Hebrew number of perfection or completion—something Christ's Atonement offers us. In Jesus's other great feeding miracle—the feeding of the four thousand—the disciples gather "seven baskets" of leftovers (Mark 8:8).[14] Perhaps it's all coincidental, but many commentators seem to think otherwise.

APPLICATION AND ALLEGORIZATION

Jesus satiated the hunger of those who had devotedly followed Him that day. So He does for each of us as we faithfully pursue Him and seek to know His words.

One point worthy of noting in this miracle is the fact that it records that Jesus addressed both the spiritual needs of His followers and also their physical needs. He fed their spirits and then fed their bodies. Christ does this for each of us also. He does not solely answer our prayers regarding spiritual things; He also tends to and cares about our temporal needs. For that, we owe Him thanks. And because of that we must follow His example and care (spiritually and temporally) for those whom He has placed around us.

Jesus has His Apostles distribute the bread and then use baskets to gather in the remains. The Greek word translated "apostle" means "sent one." It has been suggested that "what is symbolized here is the ingathering of Israel."[15] God has His "sent ones" whom He calls to go forth and "gather Israel." The Apostles head this effort, the missionaries support it, but each Saint is expected to fully engage in this activity central to the work of God's kingdom. Luke alone mentions the town Bethsaida as the site of this miracle. Bethsaida is the Greek name for the Aramaic phrase "house of hunting" or "house of fishing"—and Jesus calls each of us to be "fishers of men" (Matthew 4:19; Mark 1:17; Jeremiah 16:16).[16] Missionary work in the Church will increase in its success not by the additional numbers of youthful proselytizers serving, but by members engaging in the conversion process. If the lay members step up to the plate, conversions will increase dramatically, as will the retention of those who join.

The gathering of the excess food is a reminder to each of us that God blesses us, and abundantly so. Just as there was more given than was needed, each of us—if we have attentive and grateful hearts—can attest to the fact that God's blessings in our lives are not merely sufficient but abundant. God gives enough and to spare (D&C 104:17).

We are informed that the meager beginnings of this meal—five pieces of pita bread and two sardine-sized fish—were the offering of a young lad in the crowd. From those teeny items came a meal sufficient to feed thousands.[17] From this we may conclude that our offerings to the Lord—no matter how small they be and no matter how seemingly insignificant our gifts appear—will be sufficient for Him to perform miracles. If we give what little we have, the Lord will be capable of doing great things with us and through us. President Boyd K. Packer once said, "If you will listen spiritually, you will be good enough for all you are called to do."[18] Cyril of Alexandria (AD 375–444) wrote this:

> This teaches us as well, that we, by expending a little for the glory of God, shall receive richer grace according to the saying of Christ,

"a good measure, pressed down, shaken together, running over, will be put into your lap." [Luke 6:38] Therefore, we must not be slothful regarding the communion [or expression] of love toward our brothers and sisters but rather put away from us, as far as possible, the cowardice and fear that lead to inhospitality. Thus we might be confirmed in hope through steadfast faith in the power of God to multiply even our smallest acts of goodness.[19]

The Lord takes what little we can sincerely give and magnifies it so that it is sufficient for the work He needs to accomplish. Our only requirement is to be worthy and willing. The rest is up to Him!

Jesus, the maker of the miracle, offers thanks to God. The Talmud states, "He that enjoys aught without thanksgiving is as though he robbed God."[20] There is a potential lesson to be learned here regarding gratitude and acknowledging the source of all good—even that which we ourselves provoke. We can do nothing aside from God, and thus we own Him thanks in all things, including those wherein we are the chief instrument.

One commentator suggested this application: "What was being enacted before the people was not a simple feeding, but a dress rehearsal for the Messianic Feast."[21] In other words, Jesus was symbolically foreshadowing the Last Supper or institution of the sacrament, the meal of covenant renewal and spiritual rejuvenation. And that meal, which we partake of on a weekly basis, is itself symbolic, not only of Christ's death on our behalf but also of that great eschatological banquet in which those worthy of exaltation shall sit down and eat in the kingdom of God—never to go out of God's presence again. This may explain the use of the word *kophinos*, or coffins. Christ has died for us and we must die as to the things of this world, that we might find ourselves in communion—eternal communion—with God, Christ, and all exalted beings.

Jesus suggested to the Apostles that they do something impossible: feed five thousand people (or more) with basically no supplies. At times, God calls us to do things that seem overwhelming or impossible. On our own, they *should* be overwhelming to us and may actually be impossible—aside from His intervention. But, He can perform miracles with what little we have to offer. We are reminded of the words of the Apostle Paul: "I can do all things through Christ which strengtheneth me" (Philippians 4:13). One commentator on the miracle wrote,

Out of such a meager meal, Jesus fed many, to the surprise of His disciples. Do we too expect so little from our Lord that we doubt His ability to solve our crises? Though we bring our needs before Him, do we feel we also need to describe the solution to Him? Like the disciples, we need to ask ourselves whom we address here: Is He Lord, or simply a person? Does He rule the universe, or everything but the universe of our hearts?

He brings much out of little. He can do that with our hearts, too, if we are willing.[22]

Christ can solve our trials and can make it possible for us to do all that He has called us to do. We must remember that, doubt not, and look to Him for direction.

Jesus blessed the bread and fish, miraculously multiplied them, and then "gave them to His disciples" to distribute among the multitude. Christ is the source of all that is good in our lives. But He administers the gospel and many of its blessings through His chosen leaders—prophets, apostles, the Seventy, stake presidents, and bishops. As He Himself has said, "Whether by mine own voice or by the voice of my servants, it is the same" (D&C 1:38). As the multitude received their blessings through the Twelve, we too should sustain our leaders that we might receive at *their* hands the blessings Christ has in store for us.

NOTES

1. Many commentators think that the miracle of feeding the four thousand (see Matthew 15:29–38; Mark 8:1–9) and the miracle of feeding the five thousand (discussed here) are the same event. The details of the two are almost identical. In both cases Jesus says, "We need to feed them. What food do we have?" In both miracles the Apostles respond with, "There's no way we can feed that many people out here in the middle of nowhere." (In the minds of some, this response would make sense the first time, but should this same scenario come up a second time, it seems the Apostles would simply say, "Lord, we only have a little bread and a couple of fish, but you could multiply them as you have in the past." However, in the miracle of the four thousand, the Apostles are depicted as having any recall of the feeding of the five thousand. Thus, some feel that it makes no sense that these are two separate events.) In both miracles the solution is found in a few "loaves" and a couple of small fish. And in each narrative Jesus has the people sit down, He blesses and breaks the food, the Apostles distribute it, and then there are significant amounts of leftovers—more than what they started with. The differences between the two miracles are much less than the similarities.

2. One commentator on the miracle reasoned, "If we agree that there are just as many

men as there are women, the crowd doubles in size. And if we add children, the total count may well be in excess of twenty-five to thirty thousand people" (Kistemaker [2006], 24. See also Habershon [1975], 167). Some argue that a group of five or ten thousand people at such a gathering would be unheard of in those days. The most we can do is report what the text and its numbers suggest. While the numbers seem great, all four Gospel authors recorded them, suggesting that these numbers did not seem unrealistic to them.

3. Hendricksen, New Testament Commentary, 220. See also Brown (1966), 233; Tenny in Gaebelein (1976–1992), 9:71. 1:747; Marcus (2000), 407; Mann (1986), 302.

4. Hendriksen (1953), 219–20.

5. Lockyer (1965), 198; Kistemaker (2006), 26. They may or may not have been dried or pickled. The fact that the boy was carrying them with him suggests that they likely were. However, the size of the fish is what is significant here. Whether they were dried or pickled is irrelevant.

6. See Marcus (2000), 407.

7. Tresidder (2000), 66. See also Marcus (2000), 420; Fitzmyer (1970), 767.

8. Rest (1987), 9.

9. See Cooper (1982), 68. The use of this acronym may date to as late as the third century, and thus it is not known to have been used in the first century.

10. Marcus (2000), 419.

11. See Nicoll (1983), 1:749. (See also 1:209.) In addition, see *Oxford English Dictionary*, 3:440, s.v., "Coffin." In each of the four Gospel accounts of this miracle, Wycliffe renders (in the middle-English) the word translated "basket" (in the King James) as coffins. Thus, for example, Wycliffe's translation of Mark 6:43 reads, "And thei token the relifs of brokun metis, twelue cofyns ful, and of fischis."

12. Raymond E. Brown, for example, speaks of the "strong Eucharistic motif" found in each of the four Gospel accounts of this miracle (See Brown [1966], 246–249). Perhaps that has something to do with the choice of words here.

13. See Marcus (2000), 421.

14. Ibid., 411.

15. See Mann (1986), 303.

16. Fitzmyer (1970), 765.

17. This is not to say that no one in the crowd could have had any food on them. But the bulk of the meal, the majority of what was eaten, was not from the bags of those attending but from the baskets circulated by the Apostles.

18. Packer (2008), 532.

19. Cyril, "Commentary on the Gospel of John," (2006), 215–16.

20. See Lockyer (1965), 198.

21. Albright and Mann (1971), 179. See also Mann (1986), 300.

22. McQuade (2008), 116.

Jesus Walks on Water

MATTHEW 14:24–33
MARK 6:47–52
JOHN 6:16–21

The Miracle

After the feeding of the five thousand and their families, Jesus sent the Apostles to Capernaum while He remained behind in the region of Bethsaida, perhaps to finish His work among the multitude He had blessed and then fed, or perhaps to have some time alone for prayer and contemplation.

As the Apostles attempted to cross the Sea of Galilee, a strong wind came up, pushing them backward so that they spent some eight or more hours rowing toward the shore but making little headway.[1]

Sometime between 3 a.m. and 6 a.m., Jesus appeared upon the storm-tossed sea, walking toward the boat. The Apostles saw Him but assumed He was a spirit—a ghost of sorts—and they were greatly frightened.

Jesus, now close enough to the boat to be seen, spoke to them, saying, "Be of good cheer; it is I; be not afraid" (Matthew 14:27; Mark 6:50). At this their hearts were settled and their fear abated.

Peter, wanting a confirmation that this was indeed His Lord—but perhaps also wanting to understand the power by which miracles such as this operate—petitioned, "Lord, . . . bid me to come unto thee on the water" (Matthew 14:28). Jesus bade him, and in the midst of the tempestuous sea, Peter climbed over the side of the boat and began to walk toward Christ.

Suddenly, the chief Apostle came to himself and realized the seemingly impossible thing he was doing—amid a dangerous, storm-tossed sea—and abruptly he was overcome with fear. With that fear came doubt, and immediately Peter began to sink into the sea. Again, exercising faith—though of a different kind—he cried out to Jesus, "Lord, save me!" Jesus, reaching His hand out, took Peter's and brought him to the ship. As they entered the boat, the Lord rhetorically inquired of Peter, "O thou of little faith, wherefore didst thou doubt?" (Matthew 14:31).

Immediately, the wind stopped blowing and the boat was suddenly at the Capernaum shore. In awe, the disciples were filled with a spirit of reverence and worship and proclaimed, "Of a truth thou art the Son of God" (Matthew 14:33).

BACKGROUND

When the Apostles feared that what they were seeing was a ghost, Jesus spoke to them in an effort to comfort them—not only by His voice but also through the words He spoke. He bid them to "be of good cheer" and to not be "afraid." But He also said to them, "it is I," or, as the Greek reads, "*I am* He." In other words, Jesus used the familiar Greek phrase *egō eimi*, or "I am," typically meaning, "It is I, Jehovah!"[2] Thus, be of good cheer and fear not.

The fact that this miracle of walking on the water took place at Passover time seems to connect it in a more than coincidental way to the crossing of the Red Sea at Passover many centuries before.[3]

SYMBOLIC ELEMENTS

Peter is a perfect symbol for each of us—filled with faith at one time and then distracted by the world at another.[4] His courage to step out of the boat seems to mirror our faith-filled acts. Such faith gets us to serve a mission or accept a daunting calling. When Peter sank, however, we see our doubtful selves represented. We see in Peter's fear our own fears and the times in which we doubted God or questioned our own abilities to accomplish what He had called us to do or to be.

The boat was seen by the ancients as a symbol of the Church.[5] When the storms of life come, we must stay in the boat. By analogy, there is safety within the Church. If people think to brave the storm alone—by leaving the Church—they place themselves in grave danger.

The storm is a fitting representation of trials. Anciently, the chaotic sea was often seen as a symbol of the abode of the devil and ultimate death. Thus, Jesus's act of walking on the sea is a valuable symbol of His power to conquer death and the devil.[6] The storm reminds us of the trials we each face, but also of the trials that have come to the Church throughout its history.

The time at which the miracle takes place also seems symbolic. As one commentator noted, "The miracle happens in the fourth watch of the night (3 a.m. to 6 a.m.), the time when darkness is beginning to loosen its grip over the earth, in accordance with the common biblical theme of God's help arriving at dawn."[7] As Thomas Fuller famously said, "It is always darkest just before the day dawneth."[8] Which of us has not experienced that eternal verity?

APPLICATION AND ALLEGORIZATION

One of the most obvious applications of this miracle is found in Peter's struggle to stay afloat. He asked for Christ's power, and Jesus granted it to him. But when his faith wavered, the power withdrew. So it is with each of us. Power can be given to humans, but only if they have faith.[9] Each of us has opportunities to draw upon the gifts of the Spirit. As Doctrine and Covenants 46:11 states, "To every man" and woman "is given a gift by the Spirit of God." But those gifts are only operable so long as we have and exercise faith. Christ will at times seem distant, but He never truly is. Doubt and sin distance *us* from Him. But He is ever watching and waiting. He is ever near. He is mighty to save. We, like Peter, must remember to call out to Him.

It seems significant that Jesus is described as being a great distance from the disciples when the storm raged around them. They were in the middle of the Sea of Galilee, and He was on the land, upon a mountain, by Himself. Yet He knew their plight and appeared to them in in their hour of need. This is a good reminder to you and me that just because we cannot see, we should not assume that He is not there. As Moroni counseled us, "Dispute not because ye see not" (Ether 12:6).

Matthew is the only one to record Peter's request to walk upon the water; nevertheless, the chief Apostle is a wonderful symbol in this miracle narrative. President Howard W. Hunter drew this analogy:

It is my firm belief that if as individual people, as families, communities, and nations, we could, like Peter, fix our eyes on Jesus, we too might walk triumphantly over "the swelling waves of disbelief" and remain "unterrified amid the rising winds of doubt." But if we turn away our eyes from him in whom we must believe, as it is so easy to do and the world is so much tempted to do, if we look to the power and fury of those terrible and destructive elements around us rather than to him who can help and save us, then we shall inevitably sink in a sea of conflict and sorrow and despair.

At such times when we feel the floods are threatening to drown us and the deep is going to swallow up the tossed vessel of our faith, I pray we may always hear amid the storm and the darkness that sweet utterance of the Savior of the world: "Be of good cheer; it is I; be not afraid."[10]

We must keep our eyes on the Lord. Like Peter, if we become distracted by the world and its "waves," we will become overwhelmed and sink. We cannot afford even for a moment to cast our gaze elsewhere. *Ever keep your eye on Christ!*

One author pointed out that "Peter was able to walk on the water until he remembered he didn't know how."[11] Expounding on this, Sister Patricia T. Holland taught,

Peter's success hinged on his remembering it was through spiritual laws and not his own that he had power. In the frequently painful path from childhood to godhood, what temptations do we encounter that so divert our direction and cast clouds over our memory?

I have often heard, "When I was a child I believed everything was possible. I believed I could grow up to become anything I imagined. But then I grew up! There was anxiety in my home. I had self-defeating experiences in high school. My mission was more difficult than I expected. Now I'm often confused, depressed, and afraid." Perhaps you've heard those kinds of comments yourselves.

Not only have we forgotten the glorious things we once knew, but we have also forgotten we were asked to endure some trying things— we who are children of Christ through adoption and the crucifixion. We too are to learn obedience by the things which we suffer.[12]

There is a tension between faith and self-reliance. An honest assessment of our self may keep us from trying or doing many things the Lord would have us do. For all of the criticism one sees in print regarding

Peter—here and in other episodes in the New Testament—thankfully that impulsive Apostle often "forgot he couldn't" and therefore tried. We should doubt less, trust more, and try often. Like Peter, we should believe the Lord's promise: "Ask, and it shall be given you; seek, and ye shall find; knock, and it shall be opened unto you" (Luke 11:9). As we forget what we're not "able" to do, we're more prone to experience what we "can" do.

There is in this miracle a latent commission to each of us to be grateful and worshipful. One source notes, "Once . . . all was calm, the disciples . . . worshiped Him, saying, 'Of a truth thou art the Son of God.' This should ever be the attitude of those delivered by Christ's power."[13] May we frequently find ourselves upon our knees gushing with gratitude for the blessings of our day. God is so very good to us. I wonder if we acknowledge that just a little too infrequently.

Drawing on the metaphor that the boat represented the Church, Hilary of Poitiers (circa AD 315–367) saw symbolism in the coming of Jesus to the disciples during the "fourth watch." He wrote,

> But the Lord comes in the fourth watch. For the fourth time, then, he will return to a roving and shipwrecked church. . . . The first watch was that of the law [of Moses], the second of the prophets, the third of the Lord's [mortal] coming in the flesh and the fourth of his return in splendor [at the beginning of the millennium]. But [at the second coming] he will find the church in distress and beleaguered by the spirit of the antichrist and by disturbances throughout the world. He will come to those who are restless and deeply troubled. And since, as we may expect from the antichrist, they [who follow Christ] will be exposed to temptations of every kind, even at the Lord's coming they will be terrified by the false appearances of things and crawling phantasms with eyes. [Revelation 13:11–15] But the good Lord will then speak out and dispel their fear, saying, "It is I." He will dispel the fear of impending shipwreck through their faith in his coming.[14]

Leading up to Christ's Second Advent, things in the world will get bad. (All the more reason to keep our eyes fixed upon the Lord!) Many of the Saints will fear the direction of society and the outcome of its choices. The Church—or boat—will feel the turbulence of the times. Some will "jump ship." Others will desperately cling on, fearing what is ahead. When Jesus returns, the Church will certainly have been navigating difficult waters. And Christ's appearance will bring to the faithful a feeling of relief much like that felt by the Twelve in this miracle.

John Chrysostom (circa AD 344–407) offered this application of the miracle: "This is the way [God] constantly deals with our fears. He does not . . . easily remove the darkness. He did not come quickly to their rescue. He was training them. . . . Accordingly, neither did he present himself to them at once. . . . He was instructing them not too hastily to seek for deliverance from their pressing dangers but to bear all challenges courageously."[15] Mortality is about growth; it is about being stretched. If Jesus rescues us from all pain, all suffering, all difficulty, there can be no growth. Thus at times, God calls us to walk by faith during a faith-trying hour. But we have to trust that though we cannot see Him, He is there. Are you ready to look Jesus straight in the eye and step out of the boat?[16]

Augustine (AD 354–430) suggested that the storms in this miracle could remind us of the very difficult—even dangerous—mortal experience, and the wooden boat in which the Apostles road well symbolized the cross of Christ. He wrote that "there is no way to cross over to the homeland" we call heaven "unless you are carried by the wood" of His cross. So, "let yourselves be carried by the ship, be carried by the wood!"[17] In Augustine's view, this miracle is a wonderful symbol for our dependence upon Christ. Just as the Apostles found themselves rowing for hours into a headwind and making no progress at all, so also you and I, if we rely solely upon our works, will find ourselves unable to change our fallen nature and incapable of getting ourselves into the celestial kingdom. As one Latter-day Saint author put it:

> I see in this experience of Peter an analogy for our mortal lives. We are placed in the midst of a fallen world where we are tossed about by the waves of life. Like Peter, we have been invited by Jesus to come unto Him. Peter learned, as all of us must, that we can't make it without the help of our Savior. Like Peter, we need to remember that our best efforts will fall short, but the Savior is there to save us.[18]

We must rely upon Christ's Atonement, upon His cross and His sacrifice for each of us. That is the only way we can truly make progress during this mortal journey.

NOTES

1. Robert J. Matthews wrote, "The disciples had been on the sea for 8–10 hours, from the previous evening, and had rowed [only] 25–30 furlongs (3½ miles)" (Matthews [1969], 50).

2. See Marcus (2000), 432, 434; Brown (1966), 252, 254–55; Nicoll (1983), 1:750.

3. See Brown (1966), 255. "In John the special emphasis on *egō eimi* . . . does seem to orient this story" of the walking on water "more precisely, that is, the majesty of Jesus is that he can bear the divine name" (Brown [1966], 255. See also 533–38; Marcus [2000], 432).

4. In the book of Matthew, Peter seems representative of "everyman." He is not spiritually dead like many of the Pharisees, nor is he perfect as is Jesus. He well represents us: mortals who love God but must be refined and perfected over time as we seek to keep our covenants.

5. See, for example, Augustine, "Sermon 75:4," 11–12.

6. See Marcus (2000), 432–33.

7. Ibid., 431.

8. Fuller, *Pisgah Sight of Palestine*, 208.

9. See Matthews (1969), 50. See also Howick (2003), 115.

10. Hunter, "Beacon in the Harbor," 19. See also Holland, *Broken Things to Mend*, 8–9.

11. L'Engle, *Walking on Water*, 19.

12. Holland, "Walking on the Water," 1.

13. Lockyer (1965), 202.

14. Hilarly, "On Matthew 14:14," 12. See also Chromatius, "Tractate on Matthew 52.5," 12–13.

15. Chrysostom, "Gospel of Matthew," 13.

16. See McQuade (2008), 119.

17. Augustine, "Tractate 2.4.3 on John," 95.

18. Moore, "Teaching and Being Taught," 36.

PEOPLE *Are* HEALED *by* TOUCHING JESUS'S GARMENT

MATTHEW 14:34–36
MARK 6:53–56

THE MIRACLE

Jesus and His Apostles made their way from Capernaum to Gennesaret. Upon their arrival, people immediately recognize Him and word quickly spread that He was in the region. Soon individuals from throughout the area brought to Him their sick, carrying them on their beds when necessary. In every village and city He entered, the sick were laid in the streets before Him and the people begged Him to just let them touch the fringe on the corners of His garment. As many as made contact were healed.

BACKGROUND

The Gennesaret mentioned here is not the name of a town or village but rather of a 3½-mile-long plain on the western shore of the Sea of Galilee, situated between Tiberias and Capernaum, and comprising numerous small villages and towns.[1]

Some Jews actually believed that the tassels on the *tallit katan*, or prayer shawl, had magical or protective powers.[2] Illustrative of the belief that the garment was endowed with some kind of supernatural strength is the following story from the *Babylonian Talmud*:

There was a man who was very careful in his observance of the *mitzvah* (i.e., the Law). He was ever found wearing the *tallit katan*, as the God of Israel had commanded. One day he heard of a prostitute in a far-off city and determined to make a visit. As the moment of his indiscretion arrived, now wearing nothing but his sacred undergarment, a miracle took place. The four knotted cords of his garment "struck him across the face", thereby awakening him to the sinful choice he was about to make. Stunned by the miraculous occurrence, he and the prostitute dropped to the floor to contemplate what they had just witnessed. As the man explained to the harlot about how his fringes had testified of his evil desires, she was spiritually moved. She left her life of sin, followed him home, earnestly studied the Torah, converted, married him, and they lived happily ever after.[3]

Admittedly, this account dates from the third or fourth century. Thus, we cannot say if those in Gennesaret held such beliefs. But some commentators have suggested that this may be why the sick are asking to touch Jesus's garment rather than asking Him to touch them.[4] Certainly the woman with an issue of blood—who thought she would be healed if she could but touch the hem or tassel on Jesus's *tallit katan*—suggests that such a belief *may* have been common in the first century (Matthew 9:20–22; Mark 5:25–34; Luke 8:43–48).[5]

SYMBOLIC ELEMENTS

As always, the ill in this miracle can represent you and me in our spiritually sickened state. As mortals, we each suffer from the spiritual diseases common to this earthly experience. Some of us are terminal while others merely have the "common cold," which they will shortly fight off.

The tassels on Jesus's shawl are specifically symbolic of the 613 commandments associated with the law of Moses. More particularly, they are a reminder to the wearers of their covenants. In this episode, they may symbolize "faith as a grain of mustard seed" (Matthew 17:21). Being a teeny part of the garment, they remind us of how little the Lord asks of us in order to gain His intervention.

Those who carry the sick to Christ—and noise His presence throughout the region—are potential representations of individuals who keep their baptismal covenant to "bear one another's burdens, that they may be light" and "mourn with those that mourn" while bringing "comfort [to] those that stand in need of comfort" (Mosiah 18:8–9). In the words of the Lord, they "lift up the hands which hang down and strengthen the feeble knees" (D&C 81:5. See also Hebrews 12:12; Isaiah 35:3). These are they that "stand as witnesses of God at all times and in all things, and in all places . . . even until death" (Mosiah 18:9).

APPLICATION AND ALLEGORIZATION

The main application of this miracle seems to be that each of us struggles with spiritual ailments. We need Christ. He has the power to heal us as none else do. If we can exercise the simplest of faith in Him, His power will be sufficient to heal us. *Sometimes* that healing will come in the form of a physical healing, but it will *always* come in the form of a spiritual healing (if we place our faith in Him).

This miracle also reminds us that we need to bring others to Christ. We need to do missionary work and minister to others who are spiritually ill, carrying them along into the presence of the Lord. If our lives are right with God, we who have made covenants will recognize Him (as the people of Gennesaret did). When we do, we must noise abroad the good news that is Jesus Christ and His restored gospel. We must testify of Christ's power to heal, to lift up, and to bring joy to the lives of those who look to Him.

NOTES

1. See Carson, (1976-1992), 8:343; Marcus (2000), 436; Edwards, "Gennesaret," 2:963.
2. Rabbi Nahman of Bratzlav maintains that the garments "are a safeguard against immorality," pointing to examples of drunken Noah and elsewhere in Genesis. Thus, by wearing the pure white *tallit katan*, we mitigate darkness and destruction (Rabinowicz, *Encyclopedia of Hasidism*, 512–13).
3. See Babylonian Talmud, *Tractate Menachot*, 44a.
4. See, for example, Marcus (2000), 437.
5. Elder McConkie emphasized that regardless of what they believed, the garment was not the source of healing. "Healings come by the power of faith" ([1987–88], 2:169).

DAUGHTER *of a* GREEK WOMAN *Is* HEALED

MATTHEW 15:22–28
MARK 7:25–30

THE MIRACLE

Jesus was in the coasts of Tyre and Sidon when He was approached by a woman from Syrophenicia who practiced the Canaanite religion. She was a Gentile, and the daughter of this practicing pagan was possessed of the devil. So the mother requested that Jesus cast the evil spirit out of her young child.

Initially, Jesus ignored the woman. He simply did not acknowledge her or her request. " 'The Word' had no word for her."[1] Then His disciples chimed in, asking Him to send her away as she had apparently asked them to perform the same miracle she was requesting from Jesus.

Finally, Jesus responded to His petitioner, telling her that His mission was not to Gentiles but only to "the lost sheep of the house of Israel." Undaunted by His rebuff she worshiped Him, begging Him for His intervention.

Jesus's response to her continued pleadings was that it was not appropriate to give the food prepared for the children to the pets in the house. This woman, humble but undeterred, responded, "True, Lord! However, the dogs get to eat the crumbs that fall from the table to the floor." Her response to the Master—evidence of her great faith—brought her the blessing she desired. Jesus said, "Great is thy faith: be it unto thee even as thou wilt" (Matthew 15:28). The woman returned to her home and found that her daughter had been healed in the very hour Jesus promised it.

BACKGROUND

Commentators suggest that Mark's reference to the woman being "a Greek" is unclear. It could mean that she was of Greek descent, or that she was *not* Greek but spoke to Jesus in that language, or simply that she was a Gentile—as the term "Greek" had become the functional equivalent of the term "gentile."[2] The text is simply unclear on this matter.[3]

This miracle takes place in Gentile territory—in a land primarily inhabited by Gentiles. That being said, the setting of this miracle serves to remind us that the power and influence of Jesus's message is for all the world, not just for the Jews. Thus, Robert J. Matthews wrote, "The real question is whether Jesus is the Savior of Israel *only* or also of the pagans. From the fact that he healed the daughter, it is evident that salvation was first offered to Israel, but the non-Israelites can become heirs by faith."[4]

This miracle story is unique in that it is the only example in scripture of Jesus having a discussion or "argument" with someone and then Him conceding the point of His "opponent" or foe.[5] This is not to suggest that Jesus "lost" the argument. But it does suggest that, for whatever reason, He challenged the woman with an argument against her request and then allowed her faith and determination to seek to overturn it. Curious!

Whereas the King James Version says that the woman "worshiped" Jesus, the Greek suggests that she prostrated herself before Him.[6] This is clearly an act of worship, reverence, humility, and submission. But the Greek is clearer than the King James Version regarding what exactly her act of "worship" was.

The analogy of "dogs" and "children" may be more loaded than is evident from a cursory reading of the text. One commentator pointed out,

> There was much bad blood between the Tyrians and the Galileans, partly because much of the agricultural produce of Jewish Galilee ended up in Gentile Tyre, the main urban area near Galilee, while the Jewish peasants often went hungry. When Jesus speaks, therefore,

about the unfairness of taking bread out of the mouths of the (Jewish) children and giving it to the (Gentile) dogs, his statement may partially reflect the socio-economic [*sic*] tension between the two communities.[7]

Matthew and Mark use the diminutive *kunaria*, "puppies," instead of the Greek word *kunes*, "dogs."[8] For some commentators, this softens the dialogue, which otherwise seems quite harsh.

SYMBOLIC ELEMENTS

The Greek woman (referred to as a "dog" in the King James Version) seems representative of those outside of the covenant. She well typifies non-Jews who nevertheless exercised faith in the Jewish Messiah. Dogs were typically negative symbols in Bible times. One commentator explained:

> Although it may come as a shock to readers in our canine-loving society, the OT/Jewish tradition generally thinks negatively about dogs. . . . "The biblical writers . . . seem unfamiliar with any kind of warm personal relationship between a dog and its master." . . . To call someone a dog, therefore, was an insult. This negative imagery is related to the fact that the dogs pictured in the Bible and in Jewish tradition are generally the wild, scavenger sort rather than the domesticated variety. . . . Such wild dogs lived outside of cities and ate carrion, including the flesh of unclean animals and even human beings; dogs, therefore, are often associated with uncleanness. . . . [T]he New Testament continues this negative attitude; what is holy should not be thrown to the dogs, who are associated with pigs and are often a symbol for opponents and heretics. In [Revelation] 22:15 the "dog" is an outsider to the community of God's grace, an idolater whose life is based on a lie. Such NT symbolism probably develops a Jewish association between dogs and Gentiles.[9]

Not all commentators believe Jesus is trying to be insulting when He refers to this Gentile woman as a "dog." One interpreter of the Greek suggested that He may actually be referring to her not as a wild, scavenger type of dog but rather as a "household dog" or "pet" that would be acceptable in one's home.[10] This still implies that the Gentiles had a lesser status than the Jews (at that point in history), but nevertheless, they do have their place in God's plan.[11] Confirming this, one text suggests, "Indeed, the Syrophoenicean woman's self-description as a dog that is within the house, but that is in a position inferior to that of the children, corresponds to the way in which Gentile sympathizers with Judaism ("Godfearers" [as they were called]) were regarded by some Jews."[12]

The children (referred to as "eating" at the "table") were symbols for covenant Israel partaking of the blessings God provides.

The crumbs of bread metaphorically discussed are an emblematic reference to the blessings of the gospel offered through Jesus Christ. One commentator added,

> In its reference to the leftovers eaten by the dogs, the woman's response recalls the account of Jesus' feeding of five thousand of his fellow Jews, at the conclusion of which twelve baskets full of bread were collected ([Mark] 6:43). The Jewish "children," then, have *already* been fed by Jesus, and there is plenty of food left over for the Gentile "dogs." . . . They, too, will presently be fed by Jesus ([Mark] 8:1–9).[13]

Another suggested that the woman's request of "crumbs for the dogs" implies that she sees herself in terms of being insignificant, but also that she conceives her request "of the healing asked as only such a crumb for Jesus to give" because of His greatness.[14]

The possessed daughter is a fitting representation of the spiritual sickness that is found in each of us—member or non-member—and the girl's restoration to health reminds us that Christ can heal all who come unto Him. In addition, she may symbolically represent the Gentiles generally, as Epiphanius the Latin (circa late fifth or early sixth century) suggested that she represented the Gentiles who "had been led astray by idolatry and sin" but whom Christ then healed and brought into the fold.[15] Just as the Gentiles believed false doctrine and worshiped false gods, this girl was similarly outside of the covenant and filled with idolatrous beliefs and practices. But just as Jesus healed her, His gospel also brought the Gentiles into light and truth and spiritually healed them.

Jesus's initial lack of response to the woman is a potential symbol of the reality that He was sent first to the Jews and then only after to the Gentiles. Thus, while all will be blessed with their opportunity to hear the gospel, each must do so in turn.

APPLICATION AND ALLEGORIZATION

In the Greek, Matthew suggests that the crumbs of the children accidently fall to the floor and are snatched up by the dogs. In Mark, however, the Greek suggests that the children, out of affection, "intentionally give their leftover bread to them." One commentator pointed out, "Mark's formulation may reflect his view that Jewish Christians, the first people to be 'fed' by Jesus with the bread of the gospel, should then turn around and spread it not only among themselves but also among the Gentiles."[16] As Spurgeon once said, "The brightest jewels are often found in the darkest places." Jesus was largely rejected by His own, but here a Gentile—a pagan—saw Him for what He was. "Never let us speak of any district as too depraved to yield us converts, nor of any class of persons as too fallen to become believers. . . . Our heavenly Father has children everywhere."[17]

Jesus did not immediately give her what she wished for. He didn't say no, but nor did He acquiesce to her request when she first put it to Him. Yet, the woman did not give up. When at first He did not answer her petition, she petitioned again. If the Lord had told her no, certainly she would have accepted that—as her posture and attitude was one of faith. "If she is a Gentile in nationality, she is an Israelite in disposition."[18] But Jesus did not turn down her request, though He did make her wait. She asked, she knocked, and ultimately she received. It has been said, "True prayers never come weeping home." Surely this sister discovered the truth behind those words. This same source suggests, "If her attitude teaches us anything, it is perseverance in prayer."[19] Elsewhere we read,

> He tried her faith by his silence, and by his discouraging replies, that he might see its strength; but he was all the while delighting in it, and secretly sustaining it, and when he had sufficiently tried it, he brought it forth as gold, and set his own royal mark upon it in these memorable words, "O woman, great is thy faith; be it unto thee even as thou wilt."[20]

Such is what He seeks to do *for* and *with* each of us. If our prayers do not seem answered at once, we must know that the Lord is developing us for bigger and greater things. Luke reminded us that "men ought always to pray, and not to faint" (Luke 18:1). Elder Neal A.

Maxwell explained, "Since the Lord wants a people 'tried in all things' (D&C 136:31), how specifically will we be tried? He tells us, I will try the faith and the patience of my people (see Mosiah 23:21). Since faith in the timing of the Lord may be tried, let us learn to say not only, 'Thy will be done,' but patiently also, 'Thy timing be done.'"[21]

On a related note, the story seems to illustrate the verity that we are frequently given tests during our mortal probation (D&C 101:4–5; Abraham 3:25), and our response to these "tests" is of eternal significance. As has been said, "Just as stars shine most brightly in the darkest of nights, so also our faith excels in the severest of circumstances."[22] Christ *seemed* to treat this sister with a measure of disdain or indifference. However, in the end He gave her the blessing she sought. But in the process, her faith was tested and her belief in Him was both developed and proven. The Lord will surely give each of us experiences that will provide reason for doubt or fodder for faith. How we respond will make all the difference, in that circumstance and throughout the rest of our lives.

Jesus calls her a "dog," and yet she disputes it not. Indeed, she embraces the metaphor. Of this, one commentator wrote,

> And, you observe, when she said "Truth, Lord," *she did not go on to suggest that any alteration should be made for her.* "Lord," she said, "Thou hast classed me among the dogs:" she does not say, "Put me among the children," but she only asks to be treated as a dog is. "The dogs eat the crumbs," she says. She does not want a purpose altered nor an ordinance changed, nor a degree removed: "Let it be as it is: if it be thy will, Lord, it is my will"; only she spies a gleam of hope, where, if she had not possessed faith, she would have seen only the blackness of despair. May we have such a faith as hers.[23]

We may learn from the example of the Syrophenician woman to accept what God has made us and the station He has given us. We may rightly petition for His blessings, but we should not seek to change our station or that which He has called us to do and be.

There seems to be a message in this miracle regarding grace. Jesus spoke of the Gentiles as "dogs" and the women did not dispute it. Indeed, she conceded the point by saying, "Truth, Lord." Yet, as one commentator pointed out, "she depended upon the goodness of Christ's heart, not on the goodness of her cause."[24] She was not worthy of the blessing she requested—as none of us are. But she did not allow that to dissuade her. And so each of us must do.

> If thy sense of unworthiness be enough to drive thee to self-destruction, yet I beseech thee, out of the depths, out of the dungeon of self-loathing, still cry unto God; for thy salvation rests in no measure or degree upon thyself, or upon anything that thou art or hast been or canst be. Thou needest to be saved *from* thyself, not *by* thyself.[25]

Satan wants nothing more than for you and me to get caught up in our own unworthiness, in how inconsequential we are. If he can get us thinking about that, he knows we will be discouraged and reluctant to approach God or to turn to God. Yet this woman, unworthy of God's blessings, sought for His grace and, because of her faith, received it. May we learn that lesson!

NOTES

1. Lockyer (1965), 204. See also Trench (1962), 214.

2. Ibid.

3. See Marcus (2000), 462–463; Matthews (1969), 52; Trench (1962), 213.

4. Matthews (1969), 52. See also Howick (2003), 132.

5. See Marcus (2000), 470.

6. See Friedrich, *Theological Dictionary of the New Testament*, 6:758–66; Mann (1986), 320 Marcus (2000), 467.

7. Marcus (2000), 462.

8. See Mann (1986), 321; Wessell, (1976–1992), 8:682; Cole (1997), 188; Harrington, "Gospel According to Mark," 612; Lockyer (1965), 205. While some translate this as "little dog" instead of "puppy," that is not consistently the case. Joel Marcus notes the disagreement (in various sources) as to how to interpret the Greek (see Marcus [2000], 463–64). We have chosen to render the Greek "puppy" as that seems to be a common rendering and seems to agree with the sentiment expressed by Jesus in the passage.

9. Marcus (2000), 463–64. See also Lockyer (1965), 205.

10. See Nicoll (1983), 1:217.

11. Marcus put it this way: "The dog . . . though admittedly in a position inferior to that of the children, is still part of the 'household of faith'" ([2000], 470. See also Trench [1962], 216).

12. Marcus (2000), 464.

13. Ibid., 470.

14. See Nicoll (1983), 1:217. See also Lockyer (1965), 206.

15. See Epihpanius, "Interpretation of the Gospels," 27. See also Hilary, "On Matthew 15:3," 28.

16. See Marcus (2000), 465.
17. Spurgeon (2007), 10:360–61.
18. Lockyer (1965), 206.
19. See Lockyer (1965), 206.
20. Spurgeon (2007), 10:361–62.
21. Maxwell (2001), 59.
22. See Kistemaker (2006), 135.
23. Spurgeon (2007), 10:369.
24. Ibid., 10:366.
25. Ibid.

DEAF MAN *with a* SPEECH IMPEDIMENT *Is* HEALED

MARK 7:32–37

THE MIRACLE

Jesus was in Decapolis when a group of people brought to Him a man who was deaf and had a significant speech impediment, which made communicating difficult. Having heard of and having faith in Jesus's miraculous powers, they asked that He lay His hands on the impaired man that he might be healed.

Rather than doing so in front of the crowd, Jesus took the man aside, and instead of laying His hands on him, Christ put His fingers in the man's ears and then spit and touched the man's tongue with the saliva. As He did so, Jesus looked heavenward and commanded, "Be opened" (Mark 7:34). The man was immediately blessed with the ability to hear, and his speech impediment was taken from him.

As He had done many times before, Jesus charged those who were aware of the miracle that they should tell no one what had happened. However, in their astonishment they published the news of the miracle widely, saying, "He maketh both the deaf to hear, and the dumb to speak" (Mark 7:37).[1]

BACKGROUND

Owing to the fact that they asked Jesus to "lay hands" upon the man, it seems evident that this was a common manner of healing during the time of Christ. Curiously, Jesus instead employs a different, less common means—perhaps in an effort to help the one being healed exercise faith.

While the Greek word translated "impediment" in the King James Version can mean that the man was entirely incapable of speaking, the fact that the healing allowed him to "speak plain" suggests that he probably could speak *some* prior to the miracle, just not clearly.[2]

The man was evidently not born deaf but rather lost his hearing through disease or some accident. Were he born deaf, then he would be incapable of speaking at all. Consequently, his deafness could not have been congenital.[3]

Jesus took the man aside in order to heal him. Certainly this was not to prevent anyone from witnessing the miracle, as the narrative indicates that after the deaf mute was healed, Jesus brought him back before the crowd and charged them not to tell. It may be that Jesus took him aside so that the recipient of this godly gift could focus his faith on Christ and not be distracted by the hysteria that would almost certainly surround him if this healing were done publically.

SYMBOLIC ELEMENTS

The deaf mute is an appropriate symbol of fallen man, unable to see things as they really are and inarticulate in the things of God.[4] Indeed, Jesus indicated that He often spoke in parables "because they seeing see not; and hearing they hear not, neither do they understand" (Matthew 13:13. See also Mark 4:12; Luke 8:10). Jesus's invitation to each of us is: "He that hath ears to hear, let him hear" (Mark 4:9). Even those who are physically deaf can hear God if they listen for Him. Are we listening? The opening of the ears is a symbol in Jewish texts for receiving revelation.[5]

Withdrawing from the crowd is a symbol of withdrawing from the world, with all of its commotions and distractions.

Regarding the symbolism associated with fingers, one source states, "The biblical image of the finger carries with it the general notion of power and influence. . . . The phrase 'the finger of God' is often used in Scripture to indicate God's authority, his signature or trademark, his work or his power. . . . The image of fingers can also convey divine power in action."[6]

Anciently, saliva was believed to have healing properties.[7] Thus, it is "an apt symbol of the supernatural residing within [Christ], and emanating from [Him]."[8] It is a symbol of the antidote against evil.[9]

Looking upward is sometimes a symbol of heavenly dependence, prayer, and communion. In this miracle, Jesus's look heavenward informs the deaf man from whence Christ's power comes.[10]

Sighing or groaning, as Christ did during this miracle (see verse 34), has been seen as a symbol of Jesus's "deep feeling and compassion for the sufferer."[11] It can represent the reality that He cares intensely about our spiritual and physical woes.[12] He feels so much empathy for us that He comprehends our pain (or even our disability) before He heals it. Our pains are not inconsequential to Him, as He has experienced them all (Alma 7:11–13).

Owing to the fact that this miracle took place among Gentiles, many in the ancient Church saw it as a symbol of what was about to take place in the Church, namely that the gospel was about to be taken to the spiritually deaf and inarticulate Gentiles who would embrace it and thereby be healed of their pagan beliefs and practices.[13]

One commentator pointed out that Jesus's "use of spittle ironically foreshadows the way in which his enemies will later spit at *him*. This connection may suggest that Jesus's curative power is somehow related to the salvific effect of his suffering."[14] In other words, He may have used the spittle as a symbol for the reality that the miracle of healing comes *because* of the miracle of His suffering and Atonement.

APPLICATION AND ALLEGORIZATION

Jesus took the man aside in order to heal him. So it is with us. As one commentator put it, "It is only in the hush of God's presence that we learn of our sin and guilt and of our deep need of sovereign grace."[15] Thus, if we are to find Christ—to see His hand manifest and to hear His voice—as this representative man did, we too must withdraw from the noise and distractions of the world where we can focus and follow, where we can feel of His Spirit and recognize the subtle promptings, which come to those who seek Him.

When the man's hearing was restored, so was his speech. And so it is in a spiritual healing. "For the ear must be opened to receive divine instruction *before* the tongue is able to speak forth God's praise."[16] We cannot testify of what we do not know. (This may be an apt warning to missionaries who wait until they enter the mission field to seek a personal testimony.)

That which Jesus touches He heals. That is the great miracle! President Howard W. Hunter put it this way: "Whatever Jesus lays his hands upon, lives. If Jesus lays his hands upon a marriage, it lives. If he is allowed to lay his hands on the family, it lives."[17] Each of us has "parts" that do not work as God designed. We may have broken faith or a broken heart. We may not be able to hear the Spirit or see God's hand in our lives. We may be overcome with sin or troubled by sadness. Regardless, if we will allow Christ to place His hands upon us, He—*and only He*—can heal us, regardless of our affliction.

NOTES

1. Jesus had quite literally fulfilled the words of Isaiah: "The eyes of the blind shall be opened, and the ears of the deaf shall be unstopped" (Isaiah 35:5).
2. See Mann (1986), 323; Matthews (1969), 53; Lockyer (1965), 207.
3. See Lockyer (1965), 207.
4. See Lockyer (1965), 207–8.
5. See Marcus (2000), 479.
6. Ryken, Wilhoit, and Longman (1998), 286.
7. Ibid., 810. See also Marcus (2000), 473–74.
8. Lockyer (1965), 208. See also Trench (1962), 221.
9. See Cooper (1982), 157.
10. See Locker (1965), 208; Trench (1962), 221.
11. Marcus (2000), 474.
12. See Howick (2003), 192.
13. See, for example, Lactantius, "Divine Institutes," 104.
14. Marcus (2000), 478. While we assume Jesus spit into His hand and then transferred the saliva into the mute man's mouth, some scholars believe He actually spit into the man's mouth before placing His fingers therein. This would more fully mirror what Marcus speaks of here.
15. Lockyer (1965), 208.
16. Ibid.; emphasis added.
17. Hunter, "Reading the Scriptures," 65.

JESUS FEEDS *the* FOUR THOUSAND

MATTHEW 15:29–38
MARK 8:1–9

THE MIRACLE

Jesus was in Decapolis, an area largely populated with non-Israelites. He had gone up onto a mountain and sat Himself down when the people began to come to Him. For three days, these "non-members"—consisting of some four thousand men and their families—followed Him, listened to Him, sat at His feet, and contemplated the significance of the Man and His message.

Evidencing their great faith, they brought to Him their lame, blind, dumb, maimed, and others in need of healing, and Jesus restored them. These non-Israelites marveled and wondered because of Jesus's power and holiness.

Concerned that they had been with Him for some three days and many had had little or nothing to eat during that time, Jesus told His Apostles, "We need to feed them or they might faint." His brethren of the Twelve responded, "There is no way we can feed that many people out here in the wilderness. All we have are seven loaves of bread and a few fish."

Taking matters into His own hands, Jesus had the multitude sit on the ground. He took their meager supplies in hand, gave God thanks for them, and then broke them and directed His Apostles to distribute them among the attendees. The food was distributed, the people ate until they were filled, and when the Apostles gathered the leftovers, some seven baskets were filled with the remains of the feast. Jesus then sent the people on their way.

BACKGROUND

Whereas the miracle of the feeding of the five thousand took place among Israelites, this miracle is described as happening among mostly non-Israelites—pagans, as it were.[1]

While some scholars see the miracle of feeding the five thousand and that of feeding the four thousand as one and the same, others feel that there are enough differences to justify believing that these are indeed two separate feedings.[2] The following chart highlights some of the similarities and differences between the two events.

DIFFERENCES
In the first miracle, He feeds five thousand men and their families. In the second miracle, He feeds four thousand men and their families.
In the first miracle, the people were apparently with Jesus all day. In the second miracle, they have been with Him three days.
In the first miracle, they have five loaves and two small fish. In the second miracle, they have seven loaves and a "few" little fish.
SIMILARITIES
Both take place in the same general area.
In both narratives, Jesus goes up onto a mountain.
In both miracles, Jesus begins by healing the sick and afflicted of the crowd.
Both have Jesus multiplying food for a hungry multitude.
Both represent Jesus as concerned for the physical welfare of the attendees.
Both depict Jesus asking the Twelve what He should do.
Both have the Apostles saying to Christ that it is not feasible for them to feed that many people.
Both have Jesus asking the people to sit.
Both depict Jesus as blessing the food before distributing it.
Both have the main staples as a few bits of bread and a few small fish.
Both have the participants eating until they are filled.
Both have the Apostles gathering the remains into baskets.
Both depict there being more food left over than was had in the first place.
In both miracles, Jesus is depicted sending them away after they have been filled.

If one harmonizes the four accounts of the first feeding miracle and also harmonizes the two accounts of the second one, the vast majority of what happens in these two stories is the same. The readers will have to decide for themselves if these are the same story being retold in slightly different ways, or if they are indeed two different narratives with a very similar plot line. There is enough that is different to warrant an examination of these two as separate events.

The Greek word translated "basket" in Mark's account of this miracle is different from the word used in the feeding of the five thousand. According to commentators, the baskets in this version of the story are very large, big enough to place a human being in.[3] This may be designed to highlight the grandness of the miracle, or it may be designed to explain why in the first miracle twelve baskets of leftovers were gathered whereas in this one only seven baskets were gathered.

SYMBOLIC ELEMENTS

Many of the symbolic details of this miracle are nearly identical with those of the miracle of the feeding of the five thousand, and the reader is encouraged to look at our previous discussion of that miracle.

In ancient times, the number seven represented fullness,[4] completion,[5] entirety or totality,[6] and spiritual perfection.[7] Etymologically, the number seven is connected with the Hebrew words *full, satisfied,* or *complete.*[8]

APPLICATION AND ALLEGORIZATION

As noted, many of the particulars of this miracle are virtually indistinguishable from those listed in the miracle of the feeding of the five thousand, and we would suggest to read the applications of that event, which we offered in our discussion of that miracle previously.

One commentator on this miracle pointed out that this story is worded in such a way as to be clearly intending to remind the reader of the ordinance of the sacrament of the Lord's Supper. Even the details of the disciples distributing the bread to the congregation seem to mirror the early Christian practice of the deacons administering the bread and cup to the people after these same deacons had received the emblems from he who presided at the sacrament table.[9] Since the number seven represents wholeness and spiritual perfection, the use of the number here seems a subtle reminder that through partaking of the emblems of the sacrament,[10] you and I become "whole" or "spiritually perfect" again.

One source suggests this application: "The disciples in this story were involved in the act of giving until everyone was supplied. All that Jesus supplied, the disciples gave to others. . . . The lesson his people must learn is to give freely to those in need. Freely you have received, freely give."[11] Similarly, King Benjamin counseled us to administer of our substance to those who stand in need. Never, says he, "suffer that the beggar putteth up his petition to you in vain" (Mosiah 4:16). Some will argue, "It is his own fault that he is poor. If he worked hard, as I do, he would have sufficient for his needs. So why should I give him what *I've* worked for when *he* makes little effort to pull his own weight?" (See Mosiah 4:17). To this, King Benjamin responds, "O man, whosoever doeth" or thinketh "this the same hath great cause to repent; and except he repenteth of that which he hath done he perisheth forever, and hath no interest in the kingdom of God" (Mosiah 4:18). Just as the Apostles in the miracle of the feeding of the four thousand are charged to give freely to others of what Christ has given them, so also you and I are called to bless and give to those around us. According to King Benjamin, my temporal substance simply doesn't belong to me. *My* substance isn't actually *mine*. It belongs to God. He is the source of all (Mosiah 4:22–23), and in these verses He is commanding you and me to freely use the temporal things with which He has endowed us to bless those whom He has placed around us (See D&C 42:30; Galatians 2:10).

In the early fifth century, Theodore (circa AD 350–428), the bishop of Mopsuestia, saw an important welfare principle being taught in this miracle. He wrote, "Note that they partook according to their need. They did not receive food in order to take it away with them. Fragments were left, as a symbol for measuring use according to need, rather than introducing acquisitiveness that goes beyond what is needful."[12] In other words, should you and I ever need welfare assistance from the Church, we should remember to only take what is necessary for our subsistence that the remains might be used for others in need. It is often a forgotten principle that the purpose of Church welfare is to maintain life, not lifestyle.

Origen (AD 185–254), one of the great teachers of the early Christian Church, saw an interesting metaphor in this miracle. He explained:

> Think of this mountain to which Jesus went up and sat as [a symbol for] the church. . . . Look at the crowds who come to this mountain where the Son of God sits. Some of them have become deaf to the things that have been promised. Others have become blind in soul, not looking toward the true light. Others are lame and not able to walk according to reason. Others are maimed and unable to work profitably. Each of these who are suffering in soul from such things go up along with the multitudes into the mountain where Jesus sits. Some who do not draw near to the feet of Jesus are not healed. But those who are brought by the multitude and cast at his feet are being healed. Even those who . . . feel themselves unworthy to obtain such things, are being healed. . . . See the catechumens [or investigators and newly baptized]? . . . They are coming to it with their own deafness and blindness and lameness and crookedness. In time they will be cured according to the Word. . . . And so the multitudes are astonished at beholding the transformations that are taking place. They behold those who are being converted from such great evils to that which is so much better.[13]

The Church is a place of healing and conversion. It is the place where Christ feeds our souls. We, like the multitude, must get ourselves there to be nourished and healed. But we must also bring as many others as we can—the less active, the nonmember, the spiritually sick—that they might be "nourished by the good word of God" (Jacob 6:7) and spiritually healed.

NOTES

1. Mann (1986), 325; Matthews (1969), 54.
2. See, for example, Matthews (1969), 54; Mann (1986), 325, 326. Mann notes, "The perplexity of the disciples [regarding what could be done to provide food for the crowd], in spite of a supposedly previous occasion, is a strong reason for thinking that this account is a duplicate [of the miracle in which Jesus is said to have fed five thousand]. Indeed, given a previous occasion [on which the almost identical situation was placed before them], the question in [Mark 8:4] attributes to the disciples a stupidity which can only be described as awe-inspiring" ([1986], 326).
3. See Mann (1986), 327; Kistemaker (2006), 36.
4. McConkie (1985), 199; Davis (1968), 122–123.
5. Davis (2000), 118, 122–123; Drinkard (1985), 711; Cooper (1982), 117; Cirlot

(1971), 233, 295; Julien (1996), 373; McConkie and Parry (1990), 99; McConkie (1985), 199; Parry and Parry (1998), 14, 27.

6. Draper (1991), 24; Cooper (1982), 117; Julien (1996), 373.

7. Bullinger (1967), 23, 107; Draper (1991), 138; Johnston (1990), 40; Rest (1987), 61; Todeschi (1995), 186; McConkie (1985), 199; Davis (1968), 122; Smith (1998), 288.

8. Farbridge (1923), 136–138.

9. See Mann (1986), 326–327.

10. Both bread and fish are ancient symbols of Christ.

11. Kistemaker (2006), 37.

12. Theodore, "Fragments 86, 87," 36.

13. Origin, "Commentary on Matthew 11:18," 33.

BLIND MAN *Is* HEALED

MARK 8:22–26

THE MIRACLE

On a visit to Bethsaida, Jesus was approached by the friends of a man who was blind. They desired that Jesus heal the man and, therefore, brought him to the Master.

Jesus took the blind man by the hand and walked with him until the two of them were outside of the village, whereupon Jesus anointed the man's eyes with spittle and laid His hands upon him to bless him.

After the blessing, Jesus asked the man if he could now see *anything*. The man acknowledged that he could indeed see *some* things, but they were greatly distorted. He indicated to Jesus that men looked to him like trees.[1]

Jesus again placed His hands upon the blind man—specifically upon his eyes—and then once again asked him to open his eyes and look. This time the man could see clearly all that was before him.

Jesus sent the man home with the instruction that he tell no one in Bethsaida what had brought this miracle into his life.

BACKGROUND

The location of this miracle is uncertain, as there are believed to have been at least two places that bore the name Bethsaida. Thus, this event may have taken place on the east side of the Jordan at a city also called Julias (in honor of the daughter of Augustus Caesar). Or the miracle may have been performed on the northeast bank of the Sea of Galilee, just outside of a town also known by the name *el-Araj*.[2] The

language of the Greek implies a smaller town or village and, therefore, suggests that latter of the two Bethsaidas was the location of the
miracle.[3]

Since Philip, Andrew, and Peter came from Bethsaida (John 1:44),
this may explain Jesus's visit to the city on the occasion of this miracle.

It is not entirely clear why Jesus makes the choice to take the man
outside of the village before performing this miracle. It has been suggested that by so doing, He shows His desire to "avoid publicity" at this
point in His ministry.[4] While His counsel to the healed man (that he
not tell anyone what had taken place) seems to support that supposition,
it should be noted that Jesus performed most of His miracles in Mark
in a public setting—and this is certainly not the first miracle Mark
records Christ performing.[5] Therefore, it is unlikely that His reason for
the private miracle was solely anonymity. At this point in His ministry,
He is clearly already known for His power to perform healings and
other miracles. The feeding of the four thousand earlier in this chapter suggests that Jesus is not at this juncture seeking to "fly under the
radar," so to speak. Perhaps His retreat with the blind man was for the
purpose of avoiding the clamor and excitement of the locals, or because
He desired to establish personal contact with the man without others
crowding, commenting, and curtailing the Spirit.[6] More than likely,
His retreat from the city was because of their famed faithlessness (see
Matthew 11:20–24; Luke 10:13–14). One commentator has pointed
out that while Jesus performed many miracles in Bethsaida, He "saw
no spiritual growth."[7] Thus, His withdrawal from the populace and
His admonition that they not be told about the miracle may have been
entirely because they simply did not deserve to witness or hear of such
sacred things.[8] The fact that the people of Bethsaida generally rejected
Jesus's message makes performing a miracle such as this (the healing of
the blind) fitting for the location.[9]

SYMBOLIC ELEMENTS

Blindness traditionally represents some degree of ignorance: intellectual, spiritual, or otherwise. The taking away of blindness can symbolize enlightenment, conversion, or understanding.

Spittle and water are often equated with the influence of the Holy
Spirit. The fact that the fluid came out of Christ and into the man being
healed reminds us that it is through Jesus that we access God's Spirit.

The element of touch, as we have suggested previously, represents conveyance of power or blessings.

APPLICATION AND ALLEGORIZATION

The Greek account of this miracle indicates that those who brought the blind man to Jesus "begged" or "beseeched" Jesus to heal him.[10] Herein is symbolized the ultimate attribute of a true Christian: loving one's neighbor as one's self (Matthew 19:19). Adam Clarke wrote, "Christ went about doing good, and wherever he came he found some good to be done; and so should we, if we have a proper measure of the same zeal and love for the welfare of the bodies and souls of men."[11]

The application of spittle to the man's eyes "was simply an acted parable, to draw the man's attention to what Jesus was about to do."[12] In other words, Jesus did not apply the spittle because it had healing properties, but that which it symbolized did indeed have the power to heal. It will be recalled that the Savior taught, "He that believeth on me, as the scripture hath said, out of his belly shall flow rivers of living water. But this spake he of the Spirit, which they that believe on him should receive" (John 7:38–39). Here, from Jesus's own "belly," comes the "living waters" that would heal this man. The spittle was a symbol of the Spirit, which is key in any blessing of healing. Indeed, Elder Bruce R. McConkie wrote, "The miracle of healing comes by the power of the Holy Ghost."[13]

The two-stage healing of the man has been taken by some commentators as a symbol of our need to be believing and, when the blessing desired is not immediately received, to increase our faith so that God might bless us according to His divine will. One text suggests that "persistence in prayer" is encouraged by the unique two-staged nature of this healing miracle.[14]

One scholar pointed out that the blind man's obligation to open his eyes and look can be seen as a symbol for our need to "look" more closely in order to perceive the things of God, in scripture and all around us. "We are able to see spiritual truths, which the Holy Spirit makes us see ever more clearly by opening our spiritual eyes."[15] Elsewhere we read, "For a while there is much of their old blindness remaining, much for a season impairing the clearness of their vision. Yet in good time Christ completes the work which He has begun."[16] In other words, there is much of the divine to be understood and "seen"—in people, in ordinances, in experiences, and in talks and lessons. But we must "look" and allow the Spirit to open our "spiritual eyes" that we might truly see. Too often we only see the blurry picture, as the blind man initially did. But there is more to be perceived if we, like him, open our eyes and look.

Several commentators have suggested that this miracle foreshadowed the spiritual sight Jesus would soon give to His disciples.[17] Thus, we read, "The gradual restoration of sight in this case was meant to symbolize the slowness of the Twelve in attaining spiritual insight. They got their eyes opened very gradually like the blind man of Bethsaida."[18]

Jerome (circa AD 347–420) draws an interesting symbolic message from this miracle. Regarding Jesus's command that the formerly blind man return "to his house" but not "go into the town," Jerome explained,

> Note the text exactly. . . . If this blind man is found in Bethsaida and is taken out and cured, and he is commanded: "Return to your own house," certainly, he is bid: "Return to Bethsaida." If, however, he returns there, what is the meaning of the command: "Do not go into the village?" You see, therefore, that the interpretation is symbolic. He is led out from the house of the Jews, from the village, from the law, from the traditions of the Jews. . . . It is said to him, "Return to your own house"—not into the house that you think, the one from which he came out [Judaism], but into the house that was also the house of Abraham, since Abraham is the father of those who believe [in Christ].[19]

Thus, for Jerome, the miracle is about conversion away from the law and to Christ, who has the power (through that conversion) to heal each of us from our spiritual blindness.

Ultimately, this miracle is about the gift of sight and about the state of blindness each of us labor under. As one commentator on Mark queried, "Reader, art thou in this [blind] man's state? Then come to Jesus that he may restore thee."[20] One text on the miracles noted we all have "cataracts . . . over the eyes of the soul, which . . . He is able to remove."[21] The miracle reminds us that the solution to our spiritual blindness is this: "Our daily prayer should be that the Spirit might open the eyes of our understanding to discern more fully the divine will for [our] life."[22] Even those who believe that Jesus is the Christ could see more clearly—in more detail—if they allowed Christ (and His Spirit) to touch their eyes. We would be more inspired, more directed, more enlightened, and more holy if the Spirit of Christ were more operative in our lives. Only those cured from their spiritual blindness become converted to the restored gospel. But it is also the case that only those who receive their "spiritual sight" eventually gain exaltation.

NOTES

1. Sources points out that since the blind man recognized that what looked like trees were really men moving about, he clearly was not born blind. Otherwise he would have recognized neither. See Nicoll (1983), 1:396; Mann (1986), 336–37; Kistemaker (2006), 179; Lockyer (1965), 212.
2. See Strange, (1992), 1:692; Johnson (1960), 126; Nicoll (1983), 1:395.
3. See also McConkie (1980–81), 3:28 for an alternate view of the location.
4. See Hunter, *Gospel According to Saint Mark*, 91.
5. See Wessel in Gaebelein (1976–1992), 8:691.
6. See Wessel in Gaebelein (1976–1992), 8:691.
7. Kistemaker (2006), 178.
8. In support of this explanation, see Matthews (1969), 56. See also Clarke (1846), 5:315.
9. See Strange, (1992), 1:693; Johnson (1960), 145.
10. See Cole (1997), 199.
11. Clarke (1846), 5:315.
12. Cole (1997), 200.
13. McConkie (1980–81), 3:41n1.
14. See, for example, Cole (1997), 200n1. Elder McConkie suggested that the two-stage nature of the healing (rather than healing the man all at once) was "to strengthen the weak but growing faith of the blind man" ([1987–88], 1:379).
15. Kistemaker (2006), 180.
16. Trench (1962), 226.
17. See Johnson (1960), 125. Johnson states, "Since the disciples have not yet learned to see, a miracle is necessary to open blind eyes." Another commentator similarly pointed out, "The disciples had been blinded to spiritual truths by their constant preoccupation with their own immediate bodily needs. It was only fitting therefore that the next miracle should be the opening of the eyes of the physically blind man of Bethsaida, as a picture of what God would yet do for them. It is also fitting that [Mark] 8:29 . . . should contain the account of the opening of the eyes of Peter to the messiahship of Jesus" (Cole [1997], 199. See also Wessel [1976–92], 8:691–92; Lockyer [1965], 213).
18. Nicoll (1983), 1:396.
19. Jerome, "Homily 79," (1998), 109. One LDS author suggested that the man who was healed was not a Jew but rather a heathen (Howick [2003], 194, 195).
20. Clarke (1846), 5:315.
21. Lockyer (1965), 213.
22. Lockyer (1965), 213.

Epileptic *Is* Healed *after* Jesus's Disciples Try *and* Fail

MATTHEW 17:14–21
MARK 9:14–29
LUKE 9:37–42

THE MIRACLE

Coming down from the Mount of Transfiguration (or Mount Hermon), Jesus found His nine Apostles (who had not ascended the mount with Him) in a discussion with the scribes, who were questioning them. A multitude surrounded them, listening to what may have appeared to be a debate.

When the crowd saw Jesus approaching, they immediately left the Apostles and scribes and ran to Christ being "greatly amazed" (Mark 9: 15).

A man in the crowd dropped to his knees and pled with Jesus to heal his son, his only child, who had been possessed by a devil since he was an infant. This demon caused the young man to foam at the mouth and have seizures akin to those of an epileptic, and also caused him to throw himself into fires or into bodies of water. It was as though the demon inside him was trying to kill him. According to the father, he had asked the Apostles to heal his son, but they were unable.[1]

After expressing His disappointment at the faithlessness of the people of His day,[2] Jesus commanded that the young man be brought

———— 201 ————

to Him, whereupon Jesus commanded the devil to leave. The demon's response was a violent one, sending the young man into a seizure and then leaving him motionless as though he were dead. But Jesus reached out, took the boy by the hand, and lifted him up. The young man arose, healed from the infirmity that had held him captive for years.

Once they had removed themselves from the crowd, the Apostles asked Jesus why it was that they could not cast the evil spirit out of the young man though they had tried—and tried in great faith. Jesus's response was simply, "This kind goeth not out but by prayer and fasting" (Matthew 17:21).[3]

BACKGROUND

We are told that when the multitude saw Jesus come down from the Mount of Transfiguration, they were "greatly amazed" and thus ran to Him (Mark 9:15). Some have assumed that Jesus, having only recently had His experience with Moses and Elijah on the Mount, may have been radiating a glory that was noticeable to those who now saw Him.[4]

Commentators suggest that the conversation between Jesus's nine Apostles and the scribes may have centered on their failure to heal the young man who was "possessed" (or ill with epilepsy). "The scribes, delighted with the failure, taunt them with it, and suggest by way of explanation the waning power of the Master, whose name they had vainly attempted to conjure with. The baffled nine make the best defense they can, or perhaps listen in silence."[5]

While the young man *may* well have been possessed by Satan, it is worth noting that his symptoms are all common to epilepsy:[6] he convulses violently, causing him to fall into anything near him (including the fireplace); he foams at the mouth during his seizures; he clenches (or grinds) his teeth; after an attack, he is left listless; and his symptoms are episodic. The young man's father even refers to him as a "lunatic"— a word meaning "moonstruck," as the ancients believed that changes in the moon governed epileptic seizures.[7] Jesus *does* rebuke Satan, causing the boy to be freed of his malady. But that does not necessarily mean the boy was possessed in the sense that we use the term today. Some have suggested that all sickness is ultimately a result of the influence of the devil upon this fallen world, and when he is bound during the Millennium (and throughout the eternities), all sickness, disease, and death will cease.[8] If this is the case, then Jesus rebukes the ultimate source of the young man's ailment, though it is uncertain whether he was actually "possessed" (in the proper sense of the word) or just severely ill (causing him to act in a way that those of Jesus's day would have thought was demonic possession).[9]

SYMBOLIC ELEMENTS

The epileptic boy can be seen as a symbol for the episodic struggle with sin that those who seek a life of holiness will encounter. Each of us throughout our lives will find ourselves tempted here and there. At times we seem strong in the face of temptation, and at other times we are seemingly overcome.

The mountain is a standard symbol for the temple or God's abode. Most commentators highlight the fact that Jesus came down from the Mount of Transfiguration (where He had communed with God and angels) to be confronted by the wicked and the worldly. He left God's presence and was met by the devil. So it is with us. We have havens (like the temple) that can insulate us from the world. Yet, we have to leave those at times and in so doing are greeted by the adversary and his servants.

The father of the sickened youth well symbolizes those who have a stewardship for others. Whether bishops, Relief Society presidents, youth leaders, or home and visiting teachers, all who have a steward-ship should feel the urgency and concern of this father who pled and wept on behalf of his son.

In this miracle, the Apostles remind us of every priesthood holder who seeks to do the will of God and attempts to muster sufficient faith to bring to pass miracles on behalf of others. Flawed, as we all are, the Apostles (in this episode) temporarily faltered and lacked the faith necessary, as each bearer of the holy priesthood does at various times in his life. As one commentator noted, "The use of Jesus' divine author-ity and power, even when properly held, is dependent upon individual faith."[10]

APPLICATION AND ALLEGORIZATION

Origin (AD 185–254) suggested that each disease or weakness listed in the scriptures is a symbol of some spiritual malady, a "symptom in the soul," as it were. The blind are representative of individuals who don't see truth for what it is. The deaf symbolize those who will not harken to the words of God or who fail to hear the subtle promptings of the Spirit. And the epileptic, he suggested, are shadows of those who wax and wane in their faithfulness:

> This disease attacks those who suffer from it at considerable intervals [between attacks], during which time he who suffers from it seems in no way to differ from the man in good health, at the season when the epilepsy is not working on him. You will find some souls that are often considered to be healthy [spiritually speaking, but who are actually] suffering from symptoms like these. . . . But there comes a time when they are attacked by a kind of epilepsy, and then they seem to fall from their solid foundation and are seized by the deceits and other desires of this world.[11]

Episodic sin is not uncommon, particularly among those who are fighting to live the gospel, as the spirit is willing but the flesh is so very weak (Matthew 26:41). Those who struggle are not always evidentially sinful. They may appear to be as spiritually healthy as the next guy, but then Satan tempts and their bad behaviors once again rise to the surface, affecting them and often others. Do you struggle with episodic sin? Christ can heal you.

Jesus informed the Apostles that their failure to heal was the result of the fact that they lacked faith, and that the miracle they were seeking to accomplish could only be brought to pass by prayer and fasting. There seems to be a general message in this for all disciples of Christ: to not pray before performing an ordinance, or even before serving in some gospel capacity, suggests one is self-sufficient for the miracle they are seeking to bring to pass.[12] It implies faith, but not faith placed in God—rather faith in one's own skills and abilities. Such faith is ever misplaced!

On a similar note, Augustine (AD 354–430) said, "If a man prays so that he may throw out someone else's demon, how much more so that he may cast out his own?"[13] Tertullian (circa AD 155–250) spoke of fasting as "the weapon of choice for battling with the more dreadful demons" that attack us in mortality.[14] And Jerome (circa AD 347–420) said that "the more violent devils" of life "cannot be overcome except by prayer and fasting."[15] Fasting and prayer are gifts of God designed to strengthen the practitioner in the hour of weakness. Many Latter-day Saints have yet to discover the power of these tools in the battle against the adversary.

NOTES

1. Some have seen in this not a case of demonic possession but instead a bad case of epilepsy, which was often interpreted by the ancients as demonic possession. However, the language of the account seems to suggest that Jesus and His disciples understood Satan was the cause of the malady (either by possessing the boy or by causing the boy's illness).

2. Not everyone agrees on whom Jesus had in mind when He leveled this criticism. Some think it was the disciples (who failed to successfully heal the boy). Some think it was the scribes who were just debating the Apostles. Some think it was the gawking crowd or the youth's father. And some believe it is a general reference to the generation that Jesus had been sent to. (For a survey of the sources, see Fitzmyer [1970], 809. See also Nicoll [1983], 1:232; and Trench [1962], 229.) One commentator wrote, "His words were a rebuke to them all: to the scribes for contending with the nine and lacking faith in the Son of God; to the father for his wavering faith; to the multitude for their avid interest in seeing miracles performed, and their blindness in recognizing the Messiah; and to the nine Apostles, because they had allowed their faith to weaken even though they had specifically been given the power to heal and cast out devils (see Matthew 10:1, 8)" (Howick [2003], 198).

3. This begs the questions: Is Jesus saying, "This kind goeth not out, but by prayer and fasting (except if you are the Son of God)"? Or is He suggesting, "And I have prayed and I have fasted and thus I have the power and Spirit requisite that I can do this"?

4. See McConkie (1987–88), 1:410; Matthews (1969), 57; Lockyer (1965), 217; Trench (1962), 227–28.

5. Nicoll (1983), 1:401. See also Lockyer (1965), 216; Kistemaker (2006), 139; Trench (1962), 227; Howick (2003), 198.

6. Perhaps the boy both suffered from epilepsy and from an evil spirit. Some assume this is the case because Mark's account refers to the source of the boy's ailment as a "dumb and deaf spirit" (Mark 9:25). Strangely, the other Gospel authors do not mention this. It is possible that the boy was indeed possessed (in addition to his epilepsy), which caused him to be deaf and mute. Or it is possible that during his epileptic seizures, he was incoherent, making him appear temporarily deaf and mute. The text is simply unclear on this point.

7. See Lockyer (1965), 216–17; Nicoll (1983), 1:231–32; Kistemaker (2006), 138.

8. Obviously, sickness and death did not exist before the Fall (which Lucifer provoked), nor—as we noted—will they exist during the Millennium (when the devil will be bound) or throughout the eternities (when he will have been cast out). This is the reasoning behind those who hold that disease is a result of Lucifer's influence upon the earth and its inhabitants. Elder Parley P. Pratt wrote, "Many spirits of the

departed, who are unhappy, linger in lonely wretchedness about the earth. . . . The more wicked of these are the kind spoke of in scripture, as 'foul spirits,' 'unclean spirits,' spirits who afflict persons in the flesh, and engender various diseases in the human system. . . . If permitted, they will often cause death" (*Science of Theology*, 117). President Brigham Young taught,

> You never felt a pain and ache, or felt disagreeable, or uncomfortable in your bodies and minds, but what an evil spirit was present causing it. Do you realize that the ague [a malarial fever characterized by regularly returning paroxysms, marked by successive cold, hot, and sweating fits], the fever, the chills, the severe pain in the head, the pleurisy [sic], or any pain in the system, from the crown of the head to the soles of the feet, is put there by the devil? You do not realize this, do you? I say but little about this matter, because I do not want you to realize it. When you have the rheumatism, do you realize that the devil put that upon you? No, but you say, 'I got wet, caught cold, and thereby got the rheumatism.' The spirits that afflict us and plant disease in our bodies, pain in the system, and finally death, have control over us so far as the flesh is concerned. But when the spirit is unlocked from the body it is free from the power of death and Satan; and when that body comes up again, it also, with the spirit, will gain the victory over death, hell, and the grave. . . . When we have done with the flesh, and have departed to the spirit world, you will find that we are independent of those evil spirits. But while you are in the flesh you will suffer by them, and cannot control them, only by your faith in the name of Jesus Christ and by the keys of the eternal Priesthood. (*Complete Discourses of Brigham Young*, 2:1201)

Elder McConkie wrote, "The devil uses and delights in diseases and afflictions, and in some cases he has power to impose them, as when 'Satan . . . smote Job with sore boils from the sole of his foot unto his crown' (Job 2:7), or when Jesus loosed from her infirmity 'a daughter of Abraham, whom,' he said, 'Satan hath bound, lo, these eighteen years' (Luke 13:11–17; Acts 10:38)" ([1987–88], 2:448). Clement of Alexandria put it this way: "The accursed Satan is the cause of disease to the human bodies" ("Commentary on Luke, Homily 96," 225).
9. See Fitzmyer (1970), 808; Nicoll (1983), 1:231–232, 401; Matthews (1969), 75; Trench (1962), 228–29.
10. Howick (2003), 201.
11. Origin, "Commentary on Matthew 13:4," in Simonetti (2002), 60.
12. As we cannot always fast before giving a blessing, this may imply a need for personal holiness each and every day as much as it does a need to fast or pray prior to giving a priesthood blessing.
13. Augustine, "Sermon 80:3," 61.
14. See Tertullian, "On Fasting 8:8," 125.
15. Jerome, "Against Jovinianus 2:15," 125.

TRIBUTE MONEY APPEARS
in the MOUTH *of a* FISH

MATTHEW 17:24–27

THE MIRACLE

In Capernaum, Peter was approached by a collector of tribute who wanted to know if Jesus was a tribute-paying man. Peter, apparently with no hesitancy, answered in the affirmative. However, when Peter arrived back at the house, Jesus chastised him, saying "What were you thinking, Peter?" Jesus then logically explained to the Apostle the paradox of what he had done: "From whom do kings collect tax? From their children, or from strangers who are citizens of the kingdom?" Peter responded, "From others, but certainly not from the king's children." To which Jesus replied, "Right. Thus, the children of the king are free from taxation."

That being said, in an attempt to not offend the Jewish authorities, Jesus sent Peter (a fisherman by trade) to the sea to catch a fish. He told the senior Apostle, "The first one you catch after you have dropped your line will have a coin in its mouth. Take that out and give it to the tribute collector." Peter did as his Master had commanded him and the tribute was paid.

BACKGROUND

Curiously, Matthew—a former tax collector—is the only one of the four Gospel authors to record this miracle. Perhaps his former profession made this event more meaningful to him than to others of the Twelve.

This "collector" of tribute was not a government agent, nor was it income tax that he was collecting. Rather, it was an "ecclesiastical tax" that he sought, which was to be paid as "an atonement for sins."[1] Elder Bruce R. McConkie explained,

> This was not a civil, but an ecclesiastical tax. It consisted of an annual payment of a half shekel or *didrachma* and was levied upon all males twenty years of age and older for the maintenance of the temple. As originally announced by Moses, it was an offering whereby men made an atonement for their sins; that is, the payment was in the nature of a sacrifice designed to accompany prayers beseeching forgiveness from personal sins. Jesus, of course, was without sin and needed to offer no such supplication. Indeed, in his days, rabbis and priests generally claimed exemption from this tax.[2]

Though some in modern times have misinterpreted Jesus's comments here to imply that He was against paying taxes, such was not at the heart of the Savior's teachings. Jesus's reaction to what Peter had done was solely based on the fact that Christ was sinless and thus needed no atonement to be made on His behalf. Indeed, the very reason Jesus appears to chide Peter was because Peter suggested Jesus would pay a tax levied against sinners. To do so would by default suggest that Jesus sins. Whether concerned that this might be used against Him by His antagonists, or for some other reason, Christ was careful to not give anyone reason to assume that the Great Atoning One needed an atonement made on His behalf.

There were in the various provinces those who received customs who, as soon as they learned of a "new arrival," would approach and demand, coerce, or request tribute. This "collector" appears to be such a man.[3]

The royal family enjoyed the privilege of exemption from taxation, something Peter surely understood.[4]

The value of this coin (according to the Greek, a "stater") is believed by scholars to be equal to four drachmas and thus the equivalent tribute for two men—Peter and Jesus.[5]

SYMBOLIC ELEMENTS

The "king" in Jesus's analogy to Peter ultimately represented God. Indeed, the tribute was collected to maintain God's house.

The "child" of the king exempt from paying taxes can been seen as typifying Jesus. He was excused from the "atonement tax" because he was in all ways sinless. As we make and keep sacred covenants we too become exempt from the tribute tax because Jesus pays it for us—through His Atonement.

The "tribute" or tax sought in this miracle is a symbolic representation of the Atonement. It represents the price that must be paid for sin.

As we have mentioned previously, anciently "fish" were often symbols for Christ. Thus, in this miracle the message seems to be that though Peter got the money for his personal "atonement tax" from a fish, it ultimately still came from Christ.

APPLICATION AND ALLEGORIZATION

One common message seen in this miracle is the truth that God doesn't need your tithing or money. You certainly need to pay it, as doing so develops and blesses you. However, just as Jesus could control the coin, the fish, and Peter's hook, so He can also do the same for His modern prophets and apostles. The Church will have what it needs to move the kingdom forward. You and I are invited to contribute to that, but we ought not to assume that God is in need of our meager "tribute." He has the means if the need arises.

We are told that Jesus sought to not "offend" and thus paid what He did not owe. One commentator wrote, "The moral enforced" by this miracle's narrative "is that greatness in the kingdom is best proved by service and humility. [Jesus's phrase] 'Lest we cause them to stumble' provides a lesson of meekness and wisdom."[6] True Christians are not arrogant or brash, and they do what they can to avoid causing hurt or offense. The Apostle Paul surely learned from the example of Jesus this true principle: "If it be possible, as much as lieth in you, live peaceably with all men" (Romans 12:18).

Peter meant well when he told the tribute collector, "Of course Jesus pays His tributes!" But somehow, perhaps because of all of the time he spent around Him, Peter momentarily forgot who Jesus really was. He was not simply another faithful Jew obedient to the law of Moses and its requirements. He was God's Only Begotten Son—the sinless Son of an exalted Father. He needed no atonement and thus could pay no such tribute! Peter knew that in his heart of hearts. But sometimes the miraculous can become mundane if we are not careful.

It happened with Peter, and it can happen with us. We must focus on the faith and the divine nature of what God has given us, lest it becomes less than a miracle in our minds and in our hearts. Many members have lost their testimonies of the restored gospel because they neglected to remember how miraculous the latter-day kingdom of God is. Are you being more attentive to this than was Peter?

NOTES

1. Matthews (1969), 59; see also McConkie (1987-1988), 1:412.
2. McConkie (1987-1988), 1:412. See also Nicoll (1983), 1:233–34; Albright and Mann (1971), 212; Lockyer (1965), 218; Trench (1962), 235–36.
3. See Nicoll (1983), 1:233.
4. See Nicoll (1983), 1:234.
5. See Albright and Mann (1971), 212; McConkie (1987-1988), 1:412; Matthews (1969), 59; Lockyer (1965), 220.
6. See Lockyer (1965), 219.

JESUS PASSES *through a* CROWD UNSEEN

JOHN 8:59

THE MIRACLE

It was the Feast of the Tabernacles and Jesus was discoursing at the temple. He had subtly condemned the scribes and Pharisees who had brought a woman to Him whom they claimed they had *inadvertently* "caught" in the act of adultery. Of course, the entire thing was a setup and Jesus could see this. On that occasion, the Savior had also proclaimed to His hearers that He was the Light of the World. In this same discourse, He had declared Himself to be Jehovah—the God of the Hebrew Bible. And He had told His antagonists that if God were *really* their God and Father, then they would love His Son, but instead, they actually "do the deeds" of their *real* "father"— the devil! For all of these things, and others that He spoke, those with whom He conversed took "up stones to cast at him." However, John tells us that Jesus "hid himself" and left the temple "through the midst of them," and they could not detect Him.

BACKGROUND

While this episode may not seem miraculous, it is lumped among the miracles of Jesus by some simply because Jesus was spared an attempt on His life in a rather astounding way. He was standing in the midst of the very people who sought to kill Him, most likely surrounded by them. He said things that infuriated them. However, once

He had finished saying what He wished to say, He was gone—imperceptible to those who wished to take His life. As John records, Jesus passed "through the midst of them" and left the temple.[1] He "went out unperceived," as one commentator translates the passage.[2] Or "in all probability he rendered himself *invisible*," as another put it.[3] One can argue that Jesus just blended in with the crowd. However, the ability to be "lost" in such a way seems unlikely and uncharacteristic of Him. Hence, the perception by some commentators that this was a miracle in which the Lord was as incognito as He was during His post-passion appearance on the road to Emmaus (Luke 24:16. See verses 13–35).[4]

SYMBOLIC ELEMENTS

Jesus's imperceptibility in this miracle is a subtle metaphor for the veil and how it conceals sacred things from the unworthy while also revealing holy things to those who are prepared and worthy to received them.

Jesus's exit from the temple has also been seen as a symbol for His turning from His own people (symbolized by the Jews and the temple) to humanity in general (symbolized by the blind man He would heal in the next chapter of John).[5] In other words, for some the exit represents His ultimate rejection of those who rejected Him. It foreshadows the fact that the gospel would be sent to the Gentiles, who would embrace it more readily than had Jesus's own people, the Jews.

APPLICATION AND ALLEGORIZATION

One of the potential messages of this brief miracle is this: Jesus can be lost because of our wickedness. Christ's Jewish antagonists rejected Him and thus could no longer see Him. Theodore of Mopsuestia (circa AD 350–428) explained:

> He passed through them and left the place as if their eyes were closed by divine power so that they might not know how he had left from their midst. . . . Clearly, then, he slipped away from the Jews and, moving on, he performed the work on the blind man [John 9:1–7]. Right after his discourse, then, one miracle was followed by another. This is so since, on the one hand, he was not seen by those who could see (because they were possessed by [spiritual] blindness) while on the other [hand], he gave sight to the one who did not have the natural ability to see.[6]

You and I run the same risk. We too can become spiritually blind so that we cannot see the truth. If we reject Christ—or even refuse to heed His council as given in scripture and through the living prophets—we run the risk of no longer being able to perceive Him and His ways. He and His Spirit will become indiscernible to us, and we will be left to ourselves. Doctrine and Covenants 93:39 wisely warns us, "And that wicked one cometh and taketh away light and truth, through disobedience, from the children of men." We must regularly assess whether we are doing things that cause us to lose "light and truth" and our ability to discern Christ and His will for us.

Another potential application of this miracle is found in the truth that Jesus is ever near the faithful, though we may not physically see Him. Each of us, as we seek to live faithfully to our covenants, become recipients of sacred, spiritual experiences: encounters with the divine that, while usually not visual, are nevertheless real and impactful. As we develop a spiritual sensitivity, we will feel and know that the Father is near and is working in our lives because of His Son and through His Holy Spirit.

NOTES

1. This is the way the Greek reads. Not all commentators think this phrase was in the original. One called it "a late Greek tradition" and a "scribal addition" (Brown (1966), 360). See also Tasker, *Tyndale New Testament Commentaries*, 122). Even if one drops the clause, it is still puzzling how Jesus so readily is "lost" when He was initially surrounded by His antagonists.

2. Nicoll (1983), 1:782.

3. Clarke (1846), 5:583; emphasis in original. Leon Morris suggested that the passive tense in the Greek suggests that the Father may have "hidden" Jesus, making Him imperceptible so that "these evil people could not carry out their plan" (*Reflections on the Gospel of John*, 344). Elsewhere Morris wrote, "'Hid himself' is really a passive, 'was hidden.' John is perhaps hinting that God protected his Son. It is not so much that Jesus by superior cleverness concealed himself from them. It was rather that he was concealed by Another, and so passed out of the Temple" (*New International*, 421. See also Ellis, *Genius of John*, 156; Bruce, *Gospel of John*, 206).

4. See also the events described in Luke 4:29–30.

5. See Morris (1995), 421.

6. Theodore, "Commentary on John," 318.

JESUS CASTS OUT
a MUTE DEVIL

LUKE 11:14–15[1]

THE MIRACLE

Jesus encountered a man who was mute and who was possessed of the devil. The Savior had compassion on the man and thus cast the evil spirit out of him. Upon doing so, the man immediately regained his ability to speak.

When Jesus's antagonists witnessed this, they reasoned that He must have cast this evil spirit out by the power of the devil—or by the power of the chief of the devils, Beelzebub—rather than by the power of God.

BACKGROUND

This miracle sets up the parable or illustration that Jesus gave immediately after it (see Luke 11:16–26). It does not appear that Jesus performed the miracle to set up the parable. Rather, it appears that He performed the miracle and the controversy that followed is what provoked the unplanned parable.[2]

Whereas the King James Version says that the devil was "dumb" or mute, the Joseph Smith Translation changes the passage so that it states that the man was the one who was mute, though likely because of the devil that possessed him.

The name Beelzebub is believed to belong to the Canaanite god Baal. Beelzebub means quite literally "Baal, the Prince"[3]—thus he is referred to here as the "chief" or "prince" of devils.

SYMBOLIC ELEMENTS

The possessed man is a suitable symbol for those who allow the world or the devil to have more influence in their lives than do God and His gospel. Demonic possession is representative of not allowing God to reign but instead allowing Satan to rule in one's life.

The lips and the mouth are often seen as synonyms for the heart, or one's true desires.[4] Thus, Jesus said, "For out of the abundance of the heart the mouth speaketh" (Matthew 12:34). The mouth is often seen as a window to the soul or the inner person.[5] Hence, the words we speak sometimes reveal who we are. One commentary suggested that being mute or silent can symbolize "faithlessness" or "rebellion."[6] To have the voice silenced can imply that someone is unable to connect with others.[7] Since revelation was often associated with the voice of God,[8] to have the voice silenced would potentially suggest that someone is not the source of revelation or a recipient of it.

APPLICATION AND ALLEGORIZATION

Sin robs us of the Spirit of God and of our ability to communicate with Him. When we sin, we prevent the Lord from working with us and through us. When we are guilty of serious sin, our testimony can be silenced. We become mute, as it were, and the devil holds sway in our lives.

Just as a house divided against itself cannot stand, if we are divided in our hearts as to our allegiance, we too will not stand. If sin and sanctity are constantly waging a war within us, can we have God's Spirit to speak to and through us? One or the other must reign. We cannot keep one foot in Zion and one in Babylon and think that God will commune with us.[9] Elder Neal A. Maxwell noted, "Even if we decide to leave Babylon, some of us endeavor to keep a second residence there, or we commute on weekends."[10]

NOTES

1. See Luke 11:14–26. Some commentators think that this miracle is the same as that recorded in Matthew 9:32–35 and 12:22–23.
2. See Matthews (1969), 60.
3. See Fitzmyer, *Anchor Bible*, 920.
4. See Ryken, Wilhoit, and Longmann (1989), 515, s.v. "Lips."
5. Ibid., 575, s.v. "Mouth"; Todeschi (1995), 277.

6. Ibid., 790–91, s.v. "Silence."

7. Ibid., 918, s.v. "Voice"; Todeschi (1995), 277.

8. Ibid., 919, s.v. "Voice."

9. See Asay, "Be Men!" 41.

10. *Neal A. Maxwell Quote Book*, 25.

JESUS HEALS *a* MAN BORN BLIND

JOHN 9:1–7

THE MIRACLE

As Jesus was walking along in Jerusalem, He saw a man who had been born blind. His disciples who were with Him asked if the man's premortal sins or the sins of his parents caused his blindness. Jesus responded that the man's blindness was for the purpose "that the works of God should be made manifest in him."

Having compassion on the man, Jesus approached him, spat on the ground (to make clay), and anointed the man's eyes with the mud. He then told the man to go to the pool of Siloam and wash. The man did so and returned healed.

BACKGROUND

The suggestion from the disciples that sins committed in a premortal state might have caused the man's blindness is significant in suggesting a belief in a premortal existence of the soul.[1]

While anciently saliva was often thought to have healing properties, Jesus's use of it here was likely for the purpose of aiding the faith of the blind man. The afflicted could not see Jesus, but he could feel His fingers upon his eyelids and could feel the mud once it was applied. This would have aided in his ability to have faith in the process he was experiencing.[2]

The pool of Siloam was situated in the southern end of the city near the point where the Kidron and Tyropean valleys merged. It was a holding pool for the waters that were brought in by canal from the spring of Gihon. These waters were used in ceremonies associated with the Feast of the Tabernacles and the pool was known (in rabbinic sources) as a place of purification.[3]

SYMBOLIC ELEMENTS

As noted above, anciently saliva was believed to have healing properties.[4] Thus, it is "an apt symbol of the supernatural residing within [Christ], and emanating from [Him]."[5] It is a perfect symbol of the antidote against evil.[6]

After Jesus told His disciples that the purpose of the man's blindness was for the glorification of God—and before He healed the man—He said to them, "I must work the works of him that sent me, while it is *day*: the *night* cometh, when no man can work. As long as I am in the world, *I am the light of the world*" (John 9:4–5; italics added). Jesus's comment here is related to the Feast of the Tabernacles, which utilized light as one of its themes and symbols—and which had just been commemorated by Jesus and His disciples. At the close of the first day of this eight-day holiday, the temple priests would enter the court of the women where there were four huge candelabra some fifty cubits (or seventy-five feet) in height. They would light these massive lamps, and so great was the illumination that came from them that, according to the Talmud, "there was no courtyard in Jerusalem that was not lit up with the light" (Sukkah 5:3). So with this as the backdrop, Jesus indicates that *He* is the "light of the world." One commentator explained,

> Before narrating the miracle, the evangelist [John] is careful to have Jesus point out the meaning of the sign as an instance of light coming into darkness. This is a story of how a man who sat in darkness was brought to see the light, not only physically but spiritually. On the other hand, it is also a tale of how those who thought they saw (the Pharisees) were blinding themselves to the light and plunging into darkness. The story starts in vs. 1 with a blind man who will gain his sight; it ends in vs. 41 with the Pharisees who have become spiritually blind.[7]

While this miracle comes at the beginning of a much bigger story (John 9:1–41) about how the Pharisees were angered by this healing, nevertheless, the message is one of light. Jesus is the source of the light and He is the One who can bring light into our lives. Rejection of Him robs us of light. Embracing Him brings us healing and light (D&C 93:39).

The anointing of the man with mud was seen by those of the ancient Church as a symbol for the creation and as a testament that Jesus is the Creator of all. Irenaeus, bishop of Lyons (circa AD 135–202), put it this way: "He [healed the man] this way in order to show it was the same hand of God here that had also formed man at the beginning. . . . The work of God is, after all, the forming of man. He did this by an outward action, as Scripture says, 'And the Lord took clay from earth and formed man.' . . . He was making clear to those who can understand, that this was the same hand of God through which man was formed from clay."[8]

Washing in the pool has been interpreted as a symbol of both baptism and obedience: Baptism because the ancient Church connected this narrative of washing with that sacred rite. Obedience because there seemed no reason to send a man born blind to the pool. Jesus could have healed him right there as He had so many people previously. However, the narrative reminds us that blessings are often predicated upon obedience.[9] Hence, the LDS Bible Dictionary states of prayer, "The object of prayer is not to change the will of God, but to secure for ourselves and for others blessings that God is already willing to grant, but that are made conditional on our asking for them. Blessings require some work or effort on our part before we can obtain them. Prayer is a form of work, and is an appointed means for obtaining the highest of all blessings."[10]

APPLICATION AND ALLEGORIZATION

The anger of the Pharisees over this miracle, and the theme of light in the background of the narrative, brings to mind this passage from earlier in the Gospel of John: "And this is the condemnation, that light is come into the world, and men loved darkness rather than light, because their deeds were evil. For every one that doeth evil hateth the light, neither cometh to the light, lest his deeds should be reproved. But he that doeth truth cometh to the light, that his deeds may be made manifest, that they are wrought in God" (John 3:19–21). A primary application of the miracle seems to be the reality that light always triumphs over darkness.[11]

As noted, the early Christians associated this story with the ordinance of baptism. Indeed, this story was traditionally read (prior to baptism) to those who submitted themselves for the saving ordinance.[12] Thus, Ambrose wrote, "Come and be baptized . . . and you too will be able to say, 'I went and washed'; you will be able to say, 'I was blind, and now I can see,' And, as the blind man said when his eyes began to receive the light, you too can say, 'The night is almost over and the day is at hand.' "[13] Just as we associate baptism with cleansing and with spiritual healing, the man in the story is instructed by Jesus to go to the pool and wash. It was only *after* he did so that he was "cleansed" of his infirmity. John interprets the name of the pool as "sent" or "sent one," and Jesus is the "sent one" through whom our sins are remitted. As Augustine put it, we must be "baptized in Christ."[14] Finally, some seven times, John speaks of the fact that the man was "born blind" (see verses 1–2, 13, 18–20, 24). You and I are each born into a world where a veil has been drawn over our minds, causing us to forget our premortal state and also necessitating our need for baptism (because of the sins we commit through our "blindness"). For these reasons and others, the ancients viewed this story as highlighting the healing power of baptism.

In the late fourth century, John Chrysostom (circa AD 344–407) wrote that "it was [Jesus] who saw the blind man, not the blind man who came to him. And so intently did Jesus look at him that even his disciples perceived it."[15] For Chrysostom, this miracle is an invitation for you and me to look for those around us who need us to minister to them. Don't do as the proverbial home teacher does, saying, "If you need anything, let me know." Rather, seek out those in need and ask God to guide you to them.[16] Christians must be proactive in their Christianity, not passively waiting for someone to ask for their help.

Some have seen in the man's trial—which was given by God for His glory—a metaphor about our own trials. One commentator wrote, "We may not be able to read the meaning of our tears on this side of heaven, but once with Him Who never causes any child of His one unnecessary tear, we shall understand His wise and good reasons for [our] permitted trials."[17] Surely there is divine purpose in much of what we suffer. We can turn our trials into the glorification of God, or we can create of them a heap of ashes. Our response will determine which will be the case.

On a similar note, if mud can be seen as a symbol for the creation (as those in the ancient Church perceived it as representative of), then this episode reminds us that Jesus is ever seeking to recreate us in His image. He is giving us experience, as He did this blind man, that will stretch us and grow our faith in Him and His gospel.

One of the things the story subsequent to the miracle highlights is that the young man who was healed was terribly persecuted because he was (through his healing) affiliated with Jesus. One text highlights the significance of this:

> Disowned by his parents and cast out of the synagogue by the Pharisees, the man had the benediction of Him who Himself knew the weariness and pain of excommunication. It is interesting to note the man's progress of knowledge respecting his Healer. He speaks of Him as a Man ([verse] 11), a Prophet ([verse] 17), from God ([verse] 33), Son of God. Is ours an ever-deepening knowledge of Him? Is ours the confession, "Whereas I was blind, now I see?" This man believed, confessed, and worshiped. How commendable are the man's implicit faith, his fearless confession of his healing to his neighbors and the hostile Pharisees, his utter disregard of consequences because of his expulsion from the synagogue, his brave confession, his simplicity in confounding the wise, his belief in, and worship of, the Son of God! May grace be ours to emulate such traits![18]

Faithfulness amid persecution is a trait of the holy. As with this young man, each of us may have circumstances in which we are treated harshly because of our commitment to Christ or because of our faith in His restored gospel. However, like the young man in this miracle, the more he remained faithful to Jesus, the stronger his testimony of Christ grew. And so it can be for each of us.

NOTES

1. Givens, *When Souls Had Wings*, 58.
2. See Matthews (1969), 61; Lockyer (1965), 222; Howick (2003), 81.
3. See Brown (1966), 372; Kistemaker (2006), 184.
4. Ryken, Wilhoit, and Longman (1998), 810. See also Marcus (2000), 473–74.
5. Lockyer (1965), 208. See also Trench (1962), 221.
6. See Cooper (1982), 157.
7. Brown (1966), 376–77.
8. Irenaeus, "Against Heresies," 324. See also Ammonius, "Fragments on John 317,"

324; Ambrose, "Letter 67:4–6," 326; Lockyer (1965), 222; Trench (1962), 184.

9. See Lockyer (1965), 222; Kistemaker (2006), 183.

10. Bible Dictionary, "Prayer."

11. See Brown (1966), 379.

12. See Brown (1966), 380–81.

13. Ambrose, "Letter 67:4-6," 326.

14. See Brown (1969), 381. See also Ambrose, "Letter 67:4-6," 326.

15. Chrysostom, "Homilies on the Gospel of John 56:1," 320.

16. One source commented, "Jesus looked at the blind beggar and asked what he could do for him. The disciples, by contrast, saw the man and questioned what the cause of the man's blindness might have been. In short, Jesus looked forward while his disciples looked backward" (Kistemaker (2006), 183).

17. Lockyer (1965), 221.

18. Lockyer (1965), 223.

WOMAN *with a* LONG-STANDING ILLNESS *Is* HEALED *on the* SABBATH

LUKE 13:10–17

THE MIRACLE

It was the Sabbath and Jesus was teaching in a synagogue when He saw a woman who was severely hunched over, unable to stand up straight. She had suffered from this condition for some eighteen years. Jesus addressed her and, placing His hands on her head, said, "You are rid of your infirmity!" She instantly stood up straight and glorified God for the miracle she had received.

When the leader of the synagogue saw what Jesus had done, he was annoyed and remarked to the crowd gathered there, "There are six days in which men ought to work: in them therefore come and be healed, and not on the sabbath day" (Luke 13:14).

Just as the man had publically rebuked Jesus, the Master publically rebuked the rabbi, pointing out his hypocrisy. Said Jesus, "Do you not unbind your animals on the Sabbath so that they can obtain a drink of water? Just as you unbind your animals on the Sabbath, I have unbound this woman who has had needs for some twenty years. Surely she is as worthy of relief on the Sabbath as any ox or ass."

When he heard these words, the rabbi was embarrassed—not repentant, but shamed. However, the crowd rejoiced at what Jesus had done that day.

BACKGROUND

The Greek is unclear as to whether it was her head that she could not lift up or her torso that she could not straighten.[1]

The phrase "daughter of Abraham" (verse 16) suggests that "she was one of the inner circle of pious Israelites 'waiting for the consolation of Israel' ([Luke] 2:25; 19:9). As a 'daughter of Abraham,' she was possessed of Abraham's faith and such faith [should not have to] tarry for healing because it was the Sabbath day."[2] It is often pointed out that she did not request to be healed as so many others had. However, her presence in the synagogue was itself an inferred plea to God for intervention. It was a symbol of her complete faithfulness and trust in God regardless of whether her secret desires were ever vocalized.

In the Greek, Jesus's reference to "hypocrites" is in the plural, suggesting that He was condemning the view of the rabbi but also probably others in the crowd who as well thought negatively of Him and the good He had done.[3]

The rule the rabbi claimed Jesus was breaking had to do with a physician's right to practice his healing craft six days a week but not on the Sabbath—with the sole exception of life or death emergencies. Chronic diseases, such as the one had by this woman, were certainly not an emergency. Thus, the rabbi claimed justification in criticizing Jesus.[4] While the law may have forbidden a doctor to work on the Sabbath, surely it did not forbid God from showing mercy on *His* holy day. In the words of one author, "When God prescribed the Sabbath for man, forbidding him to work therein, He did not thereby bind His own hands and make it improper for Himself to work, mercifully, on that day. As the Lord of the Sabbath, nothing, not even such a day, can stay Him in His ministry of grace and power."[5]

According to Elder McConkie, Jesus's declaration that "Satan hath bound" her is likely not a suggestion that she was demonically possessed. Rather, it is more likely intended as a frank acknowledgment that sickness and disease are often the result of Lucifer's influence in the world. And when he is bound during the Millennium, all those things shall cease—just as they miraculously ceased for this faithful sister.[6]

The Joseph Smith Translation suggests that it was Jesus's "disciples" (rather than the crowd) that "rejoiced" at the way He handled His critics.

SYMBOLIC ELEMENTS

Some have seen the cured woman as a type for the Church, in contrast to the "barren fig tree" that Jesus cursed (Matthew 21:18–20), which has been seen as a symbol of the synagogue.[7] The one accepted Christ and was healed; the other rejected Him and consequently was barren of fruit.

The woman's infirmity is a fitting symbol of the very disease that the rabbi and those who sided with him were cumbered with. Augustine (AD 354–430) wrote,

> The whole human race, like this woman, was bent over and bowed down to the ground. . . . The devil and his angels have bowed the souls of men and women down to the ground. He has bent them forward to be intent on temporary and earthly things and has stopped them from seeking the things that are above. . . .
>
> Quite unjustly, they criticized [Jesus] for straightening her up. Who were these, except people bent over themselves?[8]

The disease fits the faithless so well because, like the hunched over woman who cannot clearly see what is before her, the rabbi and his sympathizers just witnessed a miracle but could not see it. All they had in view were the legalisms they so stringently clung to. And so they could not see the obvious—that the Son of God stood there before them. Their eyes and hearts were perpetually earthbound, ever looking downward, never looking upward.

APPLICATION AND ALLEGORIZATION

One commentator explained, "Her terrible crippled state could not keep her from the house of God. . . . 'What good cheer is in this story for those who, amid bodily infirmities, mental oppression, or household burdens and afflictions, find their way statedly to God's house.'"[9] Another wrote, "This woman did not use the excuse of her aching back to 'stay home from Church.'"[10] While there may be times (because of afflictions or trials) that getting to Church is difficult for us, this faithful sister is a reminder that we should do what we can to not look for excuses to remain home. No doubt she had reason to feel "too sick to go" that day, and yet she was where she should have been, even though it was probably painful for her to physically get there. And because she was where she should have been, she received a marvelous blessing that absence would have robbed her of. This is a beautiful reminder to all who hesitate on those difficult days to rise up from their bed of affliction and put on a happy countenance, for God has miracles in store. Let us not rob ourselves of the opportunities to receive them.[11]

An additional application has less to do with the Sabbath and more to do with the woman as a symbol of sin, and her healing as a figure representing redemption:

> What is the lesson to be drawn from this miracle? Why, there are many spirits bound with infirmity! Sin has made them crooked, and they look downward to the earth rather than upward to the skies. They are in dire need of the loosening of the fetters of their iniquity, and Christ alone can perform the miracle of majesty and mercy whereby they can walk straight before Him and before man. If the woman's condition appealed to the heart of Jesus, how moved He must be by the countless millions bound by Satan! The question is, Do we share His vision and compassion, and are we striving to bring the sin-bound to Him, whose "truth has still its ancient power?"[12]

The miracle of this woman's loss of her burdens brings to mind the Lord's words: "Come unto me, all ye that labour and are heavy laden, and I will give you rest" (Matthew 11:28). As He did for this sister, so He can for each of us—and so we should seek to do for those whom we perceive could use our comfort and aid.

NOTES

1. See Nicoll (1983), 1:566.
2. Lockyer (1965), 224.
3. See Nicoll (1983), 1:566; Fitzmyer (1985), 1011, 1013.
4. See Lockyer (1965), 225.
5. Ibid.
6. See McConkie (1987–88), 2:448. See also McConkie, *Millennial Messiah*, 641; Kistemaker (2006), 84; Pratt (1965), 117; Young (2009), 2:1201; Clement of Alexandria, in Just (2003), 225.
7. See Fitzmyer (1985), 1010.
8. Augustine, "Sermon 162 B," in Just (2003), 225, 226.
9. Lockyer (1965), 224.
10. Matthews (1969), 63.
11. I fully acknowledge that there are some who simply cannot make their way to Church because of physical or emotional disabilities. No doubt the Lord understands that. My reference here is only to those who can but rationalize in order to not.
12. Lockyer (1965), 225.

MAN *with* DROPSY *Is* HEALED *on the* SABBATH

LUKE 14:1–6

THE MIRACLE

It was the Sabbath day and Jesus was a guest in the home of a Pharisee. Present for the meal were Jesus and His host, but also many other lawyers and Pharisees. In addition, a man with dropsy (or edema) attended the dinner. Of course, Jesus was not naïve. He knew this was in some measure intended as a test. Luke records that those present "watched Him" (Luke 14:1) to see what He would do in the circumstance they intended to put Him in.

Jesus, knowing their hearts and intents, directed their attention to the man with dropsy and asked, "So, is it lawful to heal someone on the Sabbath?" Not expecting that He would know their intent, thereby turning the tables on them, they were speechless.

Jesus took hold of the man, healed him, and sent him on his way. He then said to His tempters, "Suppose a child or an ox of anyone of you falls into a well—would you not immediately pull it up, even on the Sabbath?"[1] Again, they found themselves speechless.

BACKGROUND

As with the miracle we just examined, this one also has at its core the question as to whether it is appropriate to do good on the Sabbath.

"Dropsy," or edema, causes an accumulation of fluid in the connective tissues and cavities of the body, thereby potentially provoking swelling, distention, poor circulation, and probable heart and kidney troubles.[2] Jesus not only healed the man of this but provoked a physical transformation that would have been visibly evident to those present. We read, "The man's kidneys had worked poorly, but now they functioned normally, and the extra water in his body suddenly disappeared. The man's appearance changed completely. Indeed, the people could not help but see the radical transformation in him."[3]

The text is unclear if the man with dropsy was an invited guest, a plant to provoke Jesus to break the Sabbath, or someone who simply wandered in off the street.[4] Regardless of whether he was there in craft, because he was an invited friend of the host, or because he wandered into the domicile, Jesus used the occasion to the shame of His foes.

If the man with dropsy was placed before Jesus for the purpose of baiting Him into breaking the Sabbath, it seems evident that the sickly man did not realize he was a pawn. His ability to be healed would have been greatly reduced if his heart was as corrupt as most of the guests there that day.[5]

SYMBOLIC ELEMENTS

In the previous healing story, Jesus used the analogy of an animal needing to be loosed to symbolize how He can free us from those things that bind us. Here Jesus uses the analogy of an animal that falls into a well and is drowning in its water to mirror a man who is drowning in his own bodily fluids. In both cases, the sick person is a representation of ailments incident to mortality: the first of spiritual sickness, and the second potentially of physical infirmities. Jesus is able to heal both.

The Pharisees and lawyers in this miracle can aptly represent those who profess religiosity but never really experience the "mighty change" of heart (Mosiah 5:2). They didn't let Christ reach out and change them—save them. They were in close proximity to Him, but for all of their show of piety or religiosity, they actually resented Him for the things He required of them. They didn't wish to be holy. Rather, they wished to be left wholly alone, not being commanded or required to do anything more than acknowledged God externally. But a change of heart? Too much to ask of these men who considered themselves members of the "true" faith—the restored religion of their day.

APPLICATION AND ALLEGORIZATION

God expects us to seek to obey His divine laws to the best of our ability. When we do so, we live lives filled with His Spirit and our interactions with our fellow beings are also enhanced. Yet, if we keep the law simply for the sake of the law and do so without love, then we are actually guilty of breaking it.[6] John reminded us, "If a man say, I love God, and hateth his brother, he is a liar: for he that loveth not his brother whom he hath seen, how can he love God whom he hath not seen? And this commandment have we from him, That he who loveth God love his brother also" (1 John 4:20–21). The commandments are important, but if we use them as an excuse to not help or bless others, we are actually sinning, regardless of how faithful to the law we "technically" are.

Jesus physically and noticeably changed the man with dropsy right in front of the eyes of sinners. This was an invitation to each of them to let Him touch them too, to let Him change them as He had changed the man with edema. Just as this disease caused injury to the heart—but Jesus healed the man's heart—He here invited His sinful hosts to allow Him to heal their hearts also. Have we let Jesus touch our lives and our hearts? Just has He cleansed the man of the damaging fluids within His body, He can cleanse you and me of those things in our lives and hearts that daily do us damage.

Being a member of the Church is not sufficient for salvation. If your focus is more on being in the *right Church* and less on living the *right way*, you are as hypocritical as were these Pharisees and lawyers. God stood before them, but they did not love Him, nor did they love their fellow man. They only loved themselves. Their faith played mostly a social role, but they were clearly not converted. In order to dwell *with* God, we will need to seek to become *like* God. This reality had yet to dawn on Jesus's antagonists.

NOTES

1. This rendering of Christ's words are from the Anchor Bible Translation (see Fitzmyer [1985], 1038. See also Nicoll [1983], 1:571; Kistemaker [2006], 91).

2. See Matthews (1969), 64; Fitzmyer (1985), 1041.

3. Kistemaker (2006), 91.

4. Homes in Christ's day did not always have secure front doors such as what we are accustomed to in modernity. In addition, one author pointed out, "Depending on

the weather, the host would serve the Sabbath meal outside in his courtyard rather than in a crowded room inside" (Kistemaker [2006], 89). The man could have even been there as an act of charity (whether feigned or sincere) by the rabbi. Any of these reasons could explain the presence of an uninvited attendee. That being said, many feel his presence was calculated, and in the hope of provoking Jesus.

5. See Trench (1962), 207.

6. See Kistemaker (2006), 92.

Jesus Raises Lazarus
from the Dead

JOHN 11:17–46

The Miracle

Jesus was in Perea (east of Jordan and about a day's journey from Bethany) when He learned that Lazarus, His dear friend, was gravely ill back in Judea. A messenger had brought word to the Lord on behalf of Mary and Martha, Lazarus's sisters.

When Jesus learned of Lazarus's condition, He said to His disciples that this sickness was not permanent but rather "for the glory of God" (John 11:4). Thus, instead of leaving for Bethany immediately, Jesus abode two more days in Perea and then said to His disciples, "Let's now go to Judea" where Mary and Martha are waiting.

As they prepared to leave, Jesus employed a metaphor, saying, "Our friend Lazarus is sleeping, but I am going to wake him up." However, the Apostles did not understand what Jesus was suggesting. Thus, one of them said to Him, "Since he has been so sick, getting some rest is a good thing." Seeing how they had missed His point, Christ frankly declared, "Lazarus is dead! And I'm glad we didn't go to Bethany when he was merely sick, as what is about to happen will help you to believe." And so they departed.

When Jesus arrived, Lazarus had been dead and buried for four days, and many mourners had gathered and were offering comfort to Mary and Martha.

Martha, hearing Jesus was nearly to the house, went out to meet

Him and cried, "If you had been here, Lazarus would not have died. Whatever you ask God, He gives you. Please, Jesus, ask that he be brought back to life!" Jesus's response to Martha's request was simply, "Martha, your brother will rise again."

"I know he'll be resurrected," Martha rejoined—though what she pled for was his return to life *now*! Jesus calmly declared, "I am the resurrection, and the life; he that believeth in me, though he were dead, yet shall he live: and whosoever liveth and believeth in me shall never die. Believest thou this," Martha? (John 11:25–26). "Yea, Lord: I believe" (verse 27). With this Martha turned and headed back to the house where Mary had remained.

When Martha arrived home, she let Mary know that Jesus was nearby and that He had requested to speak with her. Mary quickly arose and went out to meet Him. Many of the mourners at the house, assuming she was going to Lazarus's grave, followed after her.

When Mary arrived at the place where Jesus was, she fell down at His feet and said, "Lord, if only you had been here, Lazarus would not have died." As Jesus looked upon her and upon those who had come with her, and as He saw their weeping for Lazarus, He groaned and was deeply troubled. "Where is Lazarus's grave?" Jesus inquired. And so they beckoned Him to follow them to his tomb.

Jesus wept, and the mourners who had accompanied Mary noticed this and said among themselves, "See how He loved him!" Others inquired, "Could Jesus have not saved Lazarus had He been here?" Overhearing this, and knowing their thoughts, Jesus groaned again within Himself as He followed them to the site of Lazarus's grave.

Lazarus had been buried in a cave that had a stone sealing off its mouth. Jesus commanded some of the men in the party of mourners to remove the stone. However, Martha protested, saying "Lord, he's been dead for four days. He has begun to decompose and will stink horribly." Jesus reminded her, "Martha, didn't I tell you that if you would believe you would be privileged to see the glory of God manifest?" And so the men did as Jesus had asked them, removing the stone from the mouth of the cave.

Once the entrance to the makeshift tomb was unobstructed, Jesus looked heavenward and offered a prayer to the Father, saying, "Father, I thank thee that thou hast heard me. And I know that Thou always hearest me. But for these who stand by listening, I'm saying this that they may believe that Thou has sent me." When He concluded His prayer, Jesus spoke with a loud voice: "Lazarus, come forth" (verse 43). And he did, bound in his grave clothes so that he could barely move. Jesus ordered those witnessing the miracle to "loose him, and let him go" (verse 44), free from those things that bound him.

Many who witnessed this believed in Jesus, knowing that He was indeed sent of God. Some, however, did not believe and went their way, reporting to the Pharisees all that Jesus had done.

BACKGROUND

This miracle, though it should have ended any controversy as to Jesus's divinity, actually provoked some concerted effort by the Pharisees and chief priests to take His life.

Bethany is believed to have been situated just east of Jerusalem and southwest of the region or territory of Perea. Apparently, so famous was this story that today Bethany is known as *El 'Azirîyeh*, a name that comes from the appellation Lazarus.[1]

Jesus's hanging back on the outskirts of town where Martha, and then Mary, met Him has been taken by some as evidence that He wanted to keep His presence in town from being too widely known— perhaps because He knew He was in danger (John 11:8).

There was a belief among the rabbis that the spirit of the deceased hovered near the body for three days after death. After the third day, it was believed to withdraw, and after that any hope of resuscitation was dashed.[2] Because of this common belief, many assume that Jesus waited to go to Bethany until there would not be any doubt that Lazarus had truly been raised from the dead. No one could argue four days after the death that "his spirit was still near, and so it just reentered his body."

Because of the general warmth of the climate, and because embalming was not a common practice among first-century Jews, burial would have taken place on the very day of his death. Mourning for the deceased—which, of necessity, usually took place *after* the burial— traditionally lasted for approximately a month, or slightly more.[3]

It is worth noting that Jesus did not "resurrect" Lazarus. He brought him back to life, but He did not resurrect him. Jesus was the first to be resurrected, and He had yet to do so. Additionally, resurrected beings cannot die a second time, but years after this miracle Lazarus *did* die again.

The tomb of Lazarus would have been on the outskirts of town so that ritual impurity (through contact with the deceased) would not be of any concern. This would most likely have been a vertical shaft tomb, and the stone placed over the mouth of the cave was simply to prevent animals from getting in and desecrating the corpse.[4]

On the way to Lazarus's tomb, Jesus is said to have "wept" and "groaned," being greatly "troubled" (verse 33). This fact has been variously interpreted. Some feel that Jesus was weeping because His dear friend Lazarus had died. That makes little sense owing to the fact that Jesus knows Lazarus is shortly going to be brought back to life. Others think Jesus "groaned" and "wept" because He loved Mary and Martha and they were in such pain at that hour. This too seems problematic in that Jesus is said to "weep" and "groan" because He was greatly "troubled." It seems to some commentators that Jesus is bothered by something that has happened and that is provoking His emotion. Some suggest that He is troubled by the lack of faith of Mary and Martha. Others think it is because there were mourners all about the place loudly wailing and manifesting dramatic expressions (as was customary).[5] What is curious is that the Greek suggests He was feeling not sorrow but a measure of anger, which is completely different from what the King James Version portrays. But what would Jesus be "angry" about? It has been suggested that His anger was because Satan had manifest his temporary power in the lives of three of Jesus's closest and most intimate of friends. This was a personal assault of sorts, and the Lord was not happy with Lucifer.[6] While we cannot say for certain the motivation behind the tears, in light of the Greek, the latter suggestion seems to make the most sense.

SYMBOLIC ELEMENTS

The name Lazarus means "God helps," and this story is one of the great evidences of that fact. Lazarus is referred to as one whom Jesus "lovest" (verse 3). He is in all probability a symbol for those whom Jesus loves and "helps," namely His faithful followers. And, as Jesus gives life to His beloved friend Lazarus, He will also give life to all who become His friends. As He promised in an 1833 revelation, "I will call you friends, for you are my friends, and ye shall have an inheritance with me" (D&C 93:45).

Generally, the grave clothes in this miracle are seen as symbols for those things that bind us to the world and thereby prevent us from being bound to God. They represent vices, weaknesses, fears, addictions, sins of commission, and sins of omission. However, Lazarus's burial clothes also carry an additional curious symbolic suggestion. When Jesus came forth from the tomb, His burial clothes remained behind, perhaps to suggest that He would never need them again as He would never die again. Lazarus, on the other hand, comes out with his burial clothes, almost as a suggestion that he would need these again because he would go through this same experience years later.[7]

The tomb is a potential type both of the grave that shall someday hold each of us and of the influence of Satan that encapsulates us when we choose sin over sanctification.

APPLICATION AND ALLEGORIZATION

The most obvious application of this miracle is the promised reality that Jesus can raise us from death, physical death but also (and more important) spiritual death. "Christ is the Quickener of the dead, spiritually and physically."[8] The fact that Lazarus's "raising" was not a "resurrection" places the fulfillment of this symbolic shadow as much in the mortal sphere as in the postmortal one. "As He brought the body of Lazarus back from corruption, so He is able and willing to deliver men from their loathsome sins."[9]

Jesus commands Lazarus to be "loosed." Through Him each of us can be loosed: loosed from doubt or addiction, loosed from fear or financial struggles, loosed from anger or ill will, or loosed from any ungodly thing that binds us. Even from those sins, weaknesses, or fears that we cannot conquer on our own, Jesus can free us.

Significantly, Jesus had power over death and thus also had power over earthly things. With that power, He could have moved the stone from the front of the cave without employing servants. With that power, He Himself could have removed the grave clothes from Lazarus. But He instead had others do it. In this we find meaning for our own lives. We are free to call upon God to aid us in any cause or need, but we must not forget that God expects us to first do what *we* can. He does not expend His miraculous and intervening powers where they are not needed. What mortal man can do, God expects us to do. What only God can accomplish, we should trust that He will.

We are told that out of love, Jesus did not immediately run to the aid of His ailing friend. Though this caused Mary and Martha a great deal of grief, Jesus knew that He would be a greater blessing to each of them if He allowed this to unfold in His way rather than in their way. For Jesus Himself learned "obedience by the things which he suffered" (Hebrews 5:8). So it is in life. We are periodically called upon to "wade through much affliction" (1 Nephi 17:1) with no end in sight. Jesus could swoop in and save us from our trials, but He knows that not always doing so really is what's best for us. That can be hard, as it was for Mary and Martha, but it can also strengthen our testimonies as it did for many of those who witnessed Christ's miracle at the mouth of Lazarus's tomb. As has been said, "The wisdom of divine love does not always shield its objects from suffering, sorrow, and death."[10] But it does promise strength sufficient to endure the hour, and rich blessings are the reward.

While this application is probably not harmonious with the actual text, nevertheless, Augustine (AD 354–430) offered us the following: "Why did Christ weep except to teach us to weep?"[11] When others are in pain, we can mourn with them. It seems one of the great godly attributes is compassion—to mourn with those that mourn (Mosiah 18:9).

NOTES

1. See Nicoll (1983), 1:795; Brown (1966), 422.
2. See Brown (1966), 424; McConkie (1987-1988), 1:533; Nicoll (1983), 1:802; Locker (1965), 228.
3. See Nicoll (1983), 1:798; Brown (1966), 424; Trench (1962), 251.
4. See Brown (1966), 426; Nicoll (1983), 1:801; Trench (1962), 259.
5. See Brown (1966), 424.
6. See Brown (1966), 435; Locker (1965), 228; Nicoll (1983), 1:800–801; Kistemaker (2006), 162.
7. See Brown (1966), 427; Woodward (2000), 136.
8. Locker (1965), 230.
9. Ibid.
10. Ibid., 227.
11. Augustine, "Tractates on the Gospel of John, 49:19," in Elowsky (2007), 21.

Jesus Heals *the* Ten Lepers

LUKE 17:11–19

The Miracle

Jesus was passing through Galilee and Samaria on His way to Jerusalem when He entered an unnamed Palestinian village wherein resided a number of individuals suffering from leprosy. A group of ten men, each afflicted with this dreaded disease, saw Him but kept their distance (as would have been expected).[1] Nevertheless, learning of who He was, they cried out to Him, "Jesus, Master, have mercy on us."

In response to their pleas, Jesus instructed them to go to the local priest and present themselves before him, as required in the law (see Leviticus 13:49; 14:1–4). And as they made their way to their priest, they were healed.

Upon realizing his cure, one of the ten—a Samaritan—turned around and went back to Jesus, though he had not yet made his way to his priest. He threw himself down at Christ's feet, loudly glorified God, and offered profuse gratitude to his Savior.

Jesus inquired of the man, "Were there not ten of you in that little crowd? Where are the other nine? It appears you are the only one who feels to give glory to God for this miracle." Then Jesus added an additional blessing, not received by the others: "Arise and go thy way. Thy faith hath made thee whole" (presumably) spiritually.[2]

Background

Jews in Jesus's day traditionally avoided Samaria and Samaritans (see John 4:9). Thus, some have questioned Luke's suggestion that

Jesus would pass through the "midst," or middle, of Samaria. Some have interpreted Luke's words to mean that Jesus passed through the middle of the two regions, moving from west to east on the boarders of Samaria and Galilee. Others have thought Jesus traveled south through Galilee and then east along the border of Samaria until He could descend into the Jordan Valley and Jericho.[3] In the end, the text is unclear. We can only guess as to the geography Luke is describing.

Jesus told the one Samaritan leper who thanked Him that his faith had made him whole. Yet all ten were healed. Clearly, Jesus was speaking of spiritual wholeness. In other words, while all ten received a miraculous physical healing at the hands of the Christ, only this man received forgiveness of his sins. In essence, Jesus's words to this appreciative soul were "your faith has brought you salvation,"[4] a blessing the other nine could not lay claim on.[5]

Samaritans were traditionally looked down upon by Jews. There had been "bad blood" between the two peoples for many years.[6] Traditionally, the two avoided mixing, though when people have leprosy, they do not get to choose their company.[7] Jesus called the one who returned a "stranger" (Luke 17:18), or one not of the house of Israel. Luke highlights the fact that the one who returned to praise Jesus and glorify God was a Samaritan *because* "the nine were presumably Jews, members of the house of Israel."[8] The implication of this is significant. Jews looked down on Samaritans for their religious inferiority, but it was *not* the members of the "true" faith that praised God and Christ; it was the religious outcast—the apostate—that truly loved and trusted God. One source notes, "Obedient enough to carry out Jesus' injunction to present themselves to the priests, [the nine Jews] were cured—physically; but their failure to react responsibly (in not glorifying God and thanking Jesus) reveals that they have missed the greatest moment of their lives."[9]

SYMBOLIC ELEMENTS

Leprosy is a common scriptural symbol for sin or spiritual sickness.[10] But it is also a representation of the punishments of God. Hence, the Jews often called it "the finger of God."[11] The general perception by Jews in Jesus's day was that the afflicted was being punished by God.

While Luke speaks of the ten lepers, he divides them up into two groups: the nine and the one. The number one is commonly employed to symbolize unity or cohesion.[12] In this narrative, the suggestion is that the Samaritan leper had, through his faith, become one with God. The number nine, on the other hand, carries the symbolic meaning of judgment, irrevocability, or completion.[13] One commentator wrote,

> Nine is . . . the number of finality or judgment, for judgment is committed unto Jesus as "the Son of Man" (John 5:27; Acts 17:31). It marks the completeness, the end and issue of all things as to man—the judgment of man and all his works. . . . The signification of the number nine is judgment, especially divine judgment, and the conclusion of the whole matter so far as man is concerned.[14]

Luke tells us that Jesus healed ten lepers, but only one came back to acknowledge and thank Him. And of that one, he said, in effect, "Thy faith hath saved your soul."[15] The numerology of this passage suggests the nine are not so fortunate, and they will be judged for their ingratitude.

In a way, this miracle symbolizes the passing of a dispensation and the passing of the old law—the law of Moses—through the coming of a new law—the law of the gospel. When Jesus healed the lepers, they were sent, as the law required, to the priests who did not heal but who were authorized to pronounce them "clean." But the Samaritan ultimately did not make his way to the priest but instead made his way to the Great High Priest. Symbolically speaking, there was a new priest appointed to pronounce us clean—Christ the Lord.[16]

APPLICATION AND ALLEGORIZATION

Jews generally denied the Samaritans the "external and internal religious presuppositions" perceived as necessary "for attaining salvation."[17] Their position was traditionally one of condescension toward the Samaritans, perceiving them as having wrong beliefs and strange practices, and as distant from God and His Spirit. The Jews of Jesus's day perceived themselves as spiritually superior to those of other religions. Yet in this miracle, it was the nonmember (Samaritan) who was more faithful than members (Jews). This should never be, certainly not among those who believe in and live the restored gospel. Nor should we ever look down upon others for their religious beliefs and practices. In many cases (such as this one), their relationship with the Lord might be quite good. We must make certain that our acknowledgment of and devotion to God is more like the nonmember Samaritan than the member Jews. Membership in the Lord's Church is of no significance if it does not change who we are, if it does not make us aware of Him and His mercies toward us.

On a similar note, one commentator on the miracle highlighted the Christian behavior of the Samaritan "stranger": "None returned 'save this stranger'—sometimes we receive more generous treatment from strangers than from our own friends and relatives."[18] A student once said to me, "I attended some non-LDS worship services this weekend. I was treated so warmly and genuinely. It made me assess the degree to which I reach out to those I do not know—to the 'strangers' I encounter." This should be a subtle invitation to us all. Do we look out for the "strangers" around us, at church or at work or at school? Are we humbly living and acting in such a way that it brings glory to the Lord and an awareness to others that we believe in Him and trust in Him? "By failing to return, [the nine] indicated that they thought more of themselves than of their Healer—a fitting type of multitudes [today] who externally profit by the mercies of Christ" but who fail to acknowledge Him.[19]

Leprosy is a curious disease. It can remain largely dormant in a person for a number of years. Individuals have been known to have it for as many as ten years before any symptoms were visibly evident. However, over time it manifests itself and can spread to various parts of the infected person's body. So it is with sin. We may have certain unaddressed issues that are not evident for a number of years: sinful desires or small inappropriate behaviors. While they may be well hidden for a time, eventually they will surface and, if left unchecked, can consume us spiritually. One small sin can lead to another until the disease of our unfaithfulness spiritually consumes us. As with any disease of the body, diseases of the spirit should also be arrested early before they grow to a point that they are terminal.

This miracle highlights the need for gratitude. In our prayers, we constantly beg God for things or blessings. Honest self-assessment would show most of us that we ask more of God than we thank Him for. In this regard, most of us are much more like the nine than the one. Do we think enough upon the daily blessings we receive from the Father? Do we stop and say a silent prayer several times a day because of an awareness of some mercy He has extended, some prayer He has answered, or some unexpected blessing He has poured out? Such blessings are there in each of our lives *every day*. Yet, too often we do not stop what we're doing—as the Samaritan leper did—and gush over God's goodness. He blesses us *every day*! We have reason to thank Him *every hour*! Ingratitude is a dark sin.[20] May we never be like the nine but ever like the one!

NOTES

1. One commentator suggested that the "legal distance" a leper was required to keep from one unaffected was "100 paces." "They dare not approach the clean people with such a measured distance as the law commanded (Leviticus 13:46; Numbers 5:2; II Kings 5:5). The distance was not only necessary because of contagion, it also typified the great separation sin makes" (Lockyer [1965], 230–31).

2. Perhaps each of the ten was healed physically and spiritually, though the text doesn't explicitly state that. Perhaps the additional blessing to the "10th leper" is simply to hear from the lips of the Lord Himself that he is now "whole" or forgiven or accepted. Which of us would not cherish such a promise, articulated by the Lord's own lips to our own ears?

3. See Fitzmyer (1985), 1153; Kistemaker (2006), 198–99.

4. Fitzmyer (1985), 1148; Kistemaker (2006), 201.

5. See Matthews (1969), 66; Lockyer (1965), 232.

6. Lockyer (1965), 230; Kistemaker (2006), 198–99.

7. One commentator on the Greek suggested that according to Luke's described geography, this leper colony was likely in a town right on the boarders of Galilee and Samaria, and that would explain the mixture of Jews and Samaritans in the crowd of lepers (Nicoll [1983], 1:593. See also Kistemaker [2006], 199).

8. Fitzmyer (1985), 1155. See also Lockyer (1965), 230, 232; Kistemaker (2006), 200–201.

9. Fitzmyer (1985), 1155.

10. See Cooper (1982), 96; Conner (1992), 152; Spurgeon (1997), 7:311–27; Ryken, Wilhoit, and Longman (1998), 507; Trench (1962), 134, 135. "The biblical word traditionally translated 'leprosy' does not (at least usually) refer to what we [today] call leprosy (Hansen's disease) but rather covers a variety of skin diseases, including the different forms of psoriasis and vitiligo (both of which make the skin white). The leprosy in Leviticus that contaminates clothing or a house is mold or mildew ([Leviticus] 13:47–59; 14:33–57)" (Ryken, Wilhoit, and Longman [1998], 507. See also Hare [1993], 89).

11. Lockyer (1965), 172; Trench (1962), 135.

12. See Bullinger (1967), 24, 50–51; Cirlot (1971), 232; Julien (1996), 304; Todeschi (1995), 185; Cooper (1982), 113–14; Davis (1968), 122–23.

13. See Bullinger (1967), 207, 213, 235; Davis (1968), 122.

14. Bullinger (1967), 235–236, 242. Another source states, "This is the last of those single numerals known as digits, beyond which we have merely combinations of those previous digits. It, therefore, marks the end. It is the number of finality or judgment" (Johnston [1990], 77).

15. Fitzmyer (1985), 1156.

16. See Habershon (1975), 161–62.

17. Fitzmyer (1985), 1152.

18. Lockyer (1965), 232.

19. See Lockyer (1965), 232.

20. See Lockyer (1965), 232.

BARTIMAEUS *and* ANOTHER BLIND BEGGAR *Have* THEIR SIGHT RESTORED

MATTHEW 20:29–35
MARK 10:46–52
LUKE 18:35–43

THE MIRACLE

Jesus was departing from Jericho with a multitude of disciples. As they walked along the roadside, two blind beggars sensed the commotion and inquired as to what was happening. When they learned that Jesus was passing by, they shouted out, "Jesus, thou Son of David, have mercy on us!" Those in the entourage who heard them shouting chastised the blind beggars, insisting that they keep quiet. But they cried all the more, "Have mercy on us, O Lord, Son of David" (Matthew 20:31).

When Jesus heard their cries, He stopped and asked those in the entourage to bring to Him the persons who were crying out. At least one of the blind men threw off his outer garment as he jumped to his feet. When the two of them approached Christ, He asked, "What will you that I should do unto you?" And they begged, saying, "Lord, open our eyes." Jesus then touched their eyes and said, "Receive thy sight; thy faith has made thee whole. Go thy way."

The two men, beggars because of their blindness, went their way praising God for His goodness to them. In addition, all the people who witnessed the miracle also gave praise to God.

BACKGROUND

Whereas Matthew speaks of two blind beggars being healed, the accounts of this miracle given by Mark and Luke only speak of one person healed. Some have assumed that there were likely two, as "blind men often went about in pairs to help each other," but that one was more enterprising than the other and in effect acted as the spokesman for the other.[1] Others have assumed that the contradiction is the result of an early scribal error that corrupted the text of Matthew's account.[2] Robert J. Matthews rightfully points out, whether there were two men healed or only one is immaterial to the miraculous part of this event.[3]

Another variation we find in the three accounts of this miracle has to do with whether Jesus was coming to or going from Jericho. Matthew and Mark have Him leaving the city, whereas Luke speaks of the miracle taking place as Jesus comes "nigh unto Jericho."

Mark tells us that the name of the one blind beggar was "Bartimaeus, the son of Timaeus" (Mark 10:46). This is curious because the name Bartimaeus (*Bar Timaeus*) actually means "son of Timaeus." So, in effect, Mark tells us that the beggar's name was "Son of Timaeus, the son of Timaeus."[4] What was probably originally intended was something like this: "He was known as Bartimaeus, which by interpretation means 'the son of Timaeus.'"

The title "Son of David," as employed by the blind beggars toward Jesus, was a messianic title with a nationalistic connotation. It implied that the Messiah would be a son of King David and one of the nation of Israel, and it had strong ties to Old Testament theology (see Jeremiah 23:5–6; Ezekiel 34:23–24).

SYMBOLIC ELEMENTS

Blindness is often a symbol of moral and spiritual decay—or even apostasy.[5] However, it can also be a symbol of ignorance, as in this miracle. The blind men in this narrative are a wonderful representation of "the soul of humanity struggling for the Light,"[6] and Jesus is that light, the Light of the World (John 8:12) to all those who are in "darkness" (D&C 38:8). Bartimaeus and his unnamed companion are symbolic reminders of the fact that we all sit in darkness. But they are also good representations of how one gets out of the darkness. They noticed something was subtlety different (the crowd was passing by), and so they inquired as to what it was they were experiencing. Then they aggressively pursued the Light by forcefully calling out to Christ and by ultimately making their way to Him. This exemplifies our path. With subtlety, the Spirit will give us promptings, a gentle nudging here and there. If we stop and observe those promptings, and inquire of the Lord as to what these mean, we will learn their intent. Then if we follow those aggressively (as did our blind friends), we, like them, will reap the blessings that come from personal revelation.

APPLICATION AND ALLEGORIZATION

In Luke's version of the miracle, Jesus doesn't say, "Your faith has made you *whole*" but "Thy faith hath *saved* you," or as it is often translated, "Your faith has brought you salvation!"[7] The obvious implication is that the miracle of spiritual healing is much more important than the miracle of physical healing. When we discover we are sick, we get treatment and do all we can to regain our health or cling to mortal life. However, when we're spiritually sick, we stress much less about seeking a cure. The mortal experience is not about this life; it is about the next one. We should be a thousand times more concerned about our spiritual health than we are about our physical health. And if we are prone to get help for the one, how can we not feel a need to do so for the other? Rather than clinging to mortality, what we need to do is cling to immortality.

One commentator highlighted the behavior of the blind beggars when they realized a crowd was passing by:

> Ordinarily, as a beggar, Bartimaeus would have sought to make capital out of the crowd. More passers-by meant more money in his box. But as sight was more important to him than money, he deliberately sacrificed financial advantage for eyesight. He would have been a fool had he acted otherwise. Would that many today who are too busy making money to think about their soul's salvation would realize what a treasure they are sacrificing.[8]

The world calls so loudly to us. It is enticing in so many ways. Like the beggars in this miracle story, we must make sure that opportunities for spiritual development always trump monetary or social ventures. Too many in the Church use their tithing to buy things instead of blessings. Too many exchange Sabbath worship for "family time." Let us remember that if we replace our "Sabbath worship time" with "family fun time," it will guarantee the loss of *all* "family time" in the eternities.

The fact that at least one of the beggars "cast away" his cloak to come to Jesus seems potentially symbolically significant. Jesus counseled those who would follow Him, "If thy right eye offend thee, pluck it out, and cast it from thee: for it is profitable for thee that one of thy members should perish, and not that thy whole body should be cast into hell. And if thy right hand offend thee, cut it off, and cast it from thee: for it is profitable for thee that one of thy members should perish, and not that thy whole body should be cast into hell" (Matthew 5:29–30).

> Bartimaeus, leaping up, flung off his outer garments used for protection from the weather, and with an instinct of faith as sure as sight, came to Jesus. . . . Multitudes today need to cast away the garments of self-righteousness they are wrapped in, if they would find themselves at Jesus' feet (Romans 16:32). Those whom He calls must lay aside every weight and besetting sin (Matthew 13:44–46; Philippians 3:7; Hebrews 12:1–3).[9]

What sins are we covering with a cloak of piety or false humility? What worldly things do we wrap ourselves in, seeking protection and shelter from that which truly has no power? What is there in our lives that we need to "cast away" in order to come unto Christ?

When the two men were healed by Christ of their blindness, they then too "followed Him." When God gives us the gift of spiritual insight—as He does for all those who, like these men, cry out to Him—we then can lead others to Him. We can become guides to the Light. And one of the ways we can most effectively do that is to "glorify God" in our daily walk. If we live our lives as we should, the blind will notice something is different about us. That will bring many unto Christ. That will bring many out of darkness and into the Light.

NOTES

1. See Matthews (1969), 67; Lockyer (1965), 232–33.
2. See Mann (1986), 421–22.
3. Matthews (1969), 67.

4. The name appears to be a conflation of the Greek with the Aramaic (see Albright and Mann (1971), 248; Mann (1986), 421).

5. Howick (2003), 182.

6. Lockyer (1965), 235.

7. See, for example, Fitzmyer (1985), 1211, 1216. See also Kistemaker (2006), 176.

8. Lockyer (1965), 233. Kistemaker similarly pointed out, "Bartimaeus left his cloak and possibly some collected coins behind. He was not worried about a potential loss of his few possessions; he believed that regaining his sight was a gift that transcended all earthly goods" ([2006], 176).

9. Lockyer (1965), 234. See also Trench (1962), 272.

JESUS CURSES *a* BARREN FIG TREE

MATTHEW 21:18–21
MARK 11:12–21

THE MIRACLE

Jesus and the Apostles were traveling from Bethany to Jerusalem when they came upon a lone fig tree. Jesus was hungry and so they approached the tree, which had leaves—implying it might also have fruit.[1] But when they got to the tree, it was void of any produce since it was not yet the season for the fruit to appear on the trees. Jesus cursed the tree, saying, "Let no fruit grow on this tree ever again, and no man eat from it again." After the tree was cursed, it withered away, drying up all the way down to its roots.

BACKGROUND

This is the only miracle of Jesus that is a "miracle of judgment" rather than a "miracle of mercy." In this regard it stands out. It is prophetic in its nature, and the fact that it warns of pending doom for a people who reject Him may actually make it a "miracle of mercy."

In both versions of this miracle, it is associated with the narrative of Jesus cleansing the temple. Matthew has the cleansing before the tree cursing, and Mark places it after. In the Matthew account, the tree withers the minute Jesus curses it. In Mark's account, however, the tree does not immediately appear to be affected, but the next day as they pass by it, the Apostles notice that it has withered and completely died.

There is no way to tell which of the two versions is the more accurate.

Jesus's comment regarding the importance of having faith sufficient to move mountains (a comment that only appears in Matthew's account, verse 21) has been connected by commentators to the general message of the cursing of the tree. The religion of Judaism was dead and largely because its leaders had not this kind of faith. Jesus would shortly be crucified, and His Apostles would be expected to take up the reins. They would *need* this kind of faith. They would *need* to move mountains. They would *need* to be void of doubt.[2]

SYMBOLIC ELEMENTS

Fruit generally represents works of righteousness and personal holiness. Foliage can represent outward signs of piety. The latter of these two is not bad if it accompanies the former of the two. Barrenness typically symbolizes the antitheses of fruit and productivity.

Regardless of whether the withering of the tree took place before or after the cleansing of the temple, there is a symbolic message that can be drawn. The tree is often seen as a symbol for covenant Israel or the Jewish religion of Jesus's day.[3] The cursing and withering of the tree, therefore, can imply that that Judaism had become fruitless and would shrivel up and fade away. Jesus warned the Apostles, "Abide in me, and I in you. As the branch cannot bear fruit of itself, except it abide in the vine; no more can ye, except ye abide in me. I am the vine, ye are the branches: He that abideth in me, and I in him, the same bringeth forth much fruit: for without me ye can do nothing" (John 15:4–5). The Jewish leadership of Jesus's day did not get this. They did not attach themselves to the Messiah. Thus, they were fruitless. And as Jesus warned, "If a man abide not in me, he is cast forth as a branch, and is withered; and men gather them, and cast them into the fire, and they are burned" (John 15:6).

Withering represents judgment, loss of blessings, and ultimately death. If fruit is not found at the time of judgment, curses are the inheritance.

APPLICATION AND ALLEGORIZATION

An obvious application of this miracle has to do with living fruitful lives. If we are truly Christian, our lives must evidence that by the good we do and the fruit our works yield. These works will be manifest in our own lives but also in the lives of those for whom we have stewardship or to whom we minister.

> Does not the cursing of the fig tree have a message for Christendom today? . . . The Christendom of today is as unreal and as unfruitful for God as Israel of the past. There are plenty of leaves of religious activities and performances, but so little of the fruit redounding to God's glory. The Lord still comes down to earth looking for practical fruits, even the fruit of the Spirit (Galatians 5:22). Nothing else will satisfy His hunger.
>
> For our individual hearts the solemn message is that the failure to improve privilege entails the removal of the privilege itself. If the branch fails to bear fruit, it is taken away (John 15:2–6). The lamp which fails to shine is taken out of its place (Revelation 2:5). Trees that do not bear fruit are hew down and burned (Matthew 7:19). What the Lord of the harvest desires is performance as well as profession—fruit as well as leaves.[4]

As Israel of old, so also with Christianity today: the fruits we should be bearing are much less frequently found than the Lord would like. The best way to change that is to start with ourselves.

Mark says that the entire tree was "dried up from the roots." Nothing was left. All of it had died. This note brings to mind the prophetic words of Malachi: "For, behold, the day cometh, that shall burn as an oven; and all the proud, yea, and all that do wickedly, shall be stubble: and the day that cometh shall burn them up, saith the Lord of hosts, that *it shall leave them neither root nor branch*" (Malachi 4:1; italics added). Could "roots" represent ancestors, and "branches" symbolize descendants? Though not specifically applicable to the Jews, if you and I are barren of fruit, we shall be left without "roots" or "branches" in the eternal world.

A fig tree would not normally have foliage or fruit in March or April. Thus, this particular tree having leaves at that time of the year has been seen as a symbol for pretension and the attempt to be something we're not. It can represent hypocrisy.[5] The Jews were showing foliage by giving external worship at the temple, but they had not spiritual growth, or fruit. Foliage (or outward appearances) is not enough.[6] We must have a true conversion, a true change of heart, and true and meaningful works.

Mark tells us that "the time of figs was not yet," meaning it was not yet fig season. However, Jesus cursed the tree for not having fruit when one would not naturally expect it. This has been seen as a symbol for the truth that you and I are expected to be fruitful in all "seasons" of our lives.[7] Hence the Apostle Paul said, "Preach the Word; be prepared in season and out of season" (2 Timothy 4:2, New International Version). It may not be our "season" to be bishop or Relief Society president, the elders quorum president or the Primary president, but we must produce fruit anyway. I've known folks who have said, "When I'm called, I'll step it up!" Really? I think you *were* "called" when you sustained the plan in the premortal world. I think you *were* called when you made covenants on the day of your baptism. I think you *were* called when you entered into the oath and covenant of the priesthood or made solemn covenants in the holy temple. From the day we are endowed, we are under covenant to live the law of consecration. As Nibley astutely asked, "What is there to stop me from observing and keeping the law of consecration at this very day as I have already covenanted and promised to do without reservation?"[8] The thing that keeps us from living it, and from pleasing God through blessing others, is our unwillingness to produce fruit out of "season."

NOTES

1. The Joseph Smith Translation suggests that the approach of the tree was not because Jesus was hungry, but that He might teach His disciples (who had merely assumed He was approaching the tree for food) (see Matthews [1969], 69. See also Nicoll [1983], 1:417; Trench [1962], 276).

2. See Kistemaker (2006), 45. John Chrysostom said that this miracle (and the discourse on faith following it) was given "for their sakes, that they might not be afraid and tremble at plots against them" ("Gospel of Matthew, Homily 67:2," in Simonetti [2002], 133).

3. See Mann (1986), 438–39; Nicoll (1983), 1:264; Howick (2003), 124.

4. Lockyer (1965), 238.

5. See Matthews (1969), 68; Locker (1965), 236–37; Trench (1962), 277–78; Howick (2003), 124.

6. See Matthews (1969), 68.

7. See Matthews (1969), 68.

8. Nibley (1989), 173.

Ear *of* Malchus *Is* Reattached *after* Peter Cuts It Off

MATTHEW 26:51–52
MARK 14:47
LUKE 22:50–51
JOHN 18:10–11

THE MIRACLE

Jesus was praying in the Garden of Gethsemane. He had begun the process of atoning for the sins of mankind. He had experienced the visitation of an unnamed angel, and He had begun to experience each of our lives, sins, sufferings, pains, infirmities, and even deaths.

Suddenly, all of this was interrupted. Guards approached. Judas betrayed. Peter reacted. The chief Apostle drew his sword and swung wildly it at the head of one of those who had come for Jesus. Peter's target was a man names Malchus, a slave of the high priest. Malchus's right ear was severed by Peter's wild blow.

Jesus immediately turned to Peter, chastising him and saying, "Peter, put away your sword. Shall I not drink the cup the Father has given me?" (see John 18:11). And then the He added, "All they that take the sword shall perish with the sword" (Matthew 26:52).

Jesus then reached over and placed His hand upon the side of Malchus's head, and the man was instantly healed.

BACKGROUND

While the King James Version calls Malchus a "servant" of the high priest, the Greek clearly implies he was a "slave."[1]

The Greek is unclear as to whether Malchus lost his entire ear or just the lobe of his ear, and commentators seem divided on the question.[2]

SYMBOLIC ELEMENTS

In the Bible, the ear is typically associated with harkening or obeying. Thus we say, someone "inclines" his ear, or in other words, he is prone to obey. To have deaf or uncircumcised ears means one is prone to reject truth, commandments, or wisdom's ways.[3]

APPLICATION AND ALLEGORIZATION

Jesus healed Malchus's ear, though the high priest's slave had not requested it, had not manifest faith in the Master, and was actually technically an enemy of Christ who had come to participate in His arrest. Yet, is there not a type in even this?

> This aspect . . . must not be lost sight of. Jesus had come to lay down His life for sinners, and in the art of healing the wound of Malchus, He embodied His own precept about loving our enemies. This . . . miracle [performed shortly] before He died was wrought upon an enemy. What amazing grace! Truly, there is no limit to it. An open antagonist healed and blessed! Is this not the essence of the gospel, which Paul loved to preach (Colossians 1:21; 1 Timothy 1:12–15)?[4]

The Atonement of Jesus Christ was wrought for all mankind, and all of us desperately need it. One might perceive Malchus as a lost soul, one who had rejected the Messiah and therefore was not likely to inherit the kingdom of God. If so, surely his healing is a moot point. But no! Christ loves all, even those with rebellious, unkind, or disbelieving hearts. And He died to save *all*—even Malchus. Jesus did not withhold His grace from the man with a severed ear. And if Malchus turned to Christ before it was "everlastingly too late" (Helaman 13:38), more of God's grace would be forthcoming. *I stand all amazed!*

Jesus's reprimand of Peter—"Put away your sword! All they that take the sword shall perish with the sword"—offers an important message to us of the war-torn latter days. There certainly are times when we *must* "take up the sword" in defense of "our God, our religion, and freedom, and our peace, our wives, and our children" (Alma 46:12). However, aggression in the name of religion is ever wrong. "Love your enemies, . . . do good to them that hate you" (Matthew 5:44). The ideal society, the millennial society, will be one in which we will beat our swords into plowshares and our spears into pruning hooks (Isaiah 2:4; Micah 4:3). Christians seek to propagate peace, not engage in crusades against the infidel.

At the removal of Malchus's ear, Jesus said to Peter, "Shall I not drink the cup the Father has given me?" Though Peter's intent was to do God's will by protecting God's Son, in reality he was thwarting God's will by seeking to prevent God's plan. Jesus *had* to die. Christ knew that. Peter failed to grasp it. Thus, though his intent was good, it was not in accordance with the mind and will of God. Symbolically speaking, there is a parallel in this as it relates to prayer. Too often we thoughtlessly ask of God things that would thwart His will. For instance, we say in our prayers things like, "Bless us to be good today"—as though God can rob us of choice and thereby destroy the very thing the war in heaven was fought over: agency! Just as Peter's innocent misguided act ran contrary to God's will, you and I must align our prayers with the Father's will so that we do not act contrary to His plan. As you are attentive to the words you speak, you just may find you are praying for that which God cannot do!

The symbolism of the ear was highlighted more than once in the ancient Church. For example, Origen of Alexandria (AD 200–254) believed that Malchus—being a servant of the high priest—was a symbol for the Jewish people and more particularly their leadership, which could not hear Christ. For Origen, the fact that it was the right ear that was removed was symbolic. Right typically represents covenant (or covenant status), and the ear is our ability to hear, understand, harken, and obey. Said Origen, "The right ear of the Jewish people had to be cut off because of their malice toward Jesus."[5] It was, he said, a fulfillment of the Lord's prophecy: "Make their ears heavy, and shut their eyes; lest they see with their eyes, and hear with their ears, and . . . convert, and be healed" (Isaiah 6:10). Hilary of Poitiers (circa AD 315–367) similarly taught, "What was . . . incapable of hearing the truth is now cut off."[6] If they would not listen, they would lose their covenant status, including the right to hear God's voice and to be guided by Him as a people and religion. Such is the promise to all—even those of us living in the latter days.

NOTES

1. See Albright and Mann (1971), 328; Mann (1986), 594.
2. See Brown, Anchor Bible, 805, 812; Mann (1986), 597; Fitzmyer (1985), 1451; Lockyer (1965), 240.
3. See Ryken, Wilhoit, and Longman (1998), 223; Conner (1992), 139; Todeschi (1995), 95.
4. Lockyer (1965), 240. See also Kistemaker (2006), 96.
5. Origen, "Commentary on Matthew 101," in Simonetti (2002), 261.
6. Hilary, "On Matthew 32:2," in Simonetti (2002), 261.

GREAT HAUL *of* FISHES

JOHN 21:1–14

THE MIRACLE

Jesus was dead and His disciples were distraught and confused. Peter, perhaps to get his mind off of the recent events, decided to go fishing late that night. He invited several of the brethren who had been with him earlier that evening, and they agreed to go. And so Peter, Thomas, Nathanael, James, John, and two other unnamed disciples hopped into a boat on the Sea of Tiberias in hopes of some distraction from the painful events that occupied their minds and hearts.[1]

They fished all night but were entirely unsuccessful. There was nothing in their nets. "Those knowledgeable in Palestinian customs assert that on the Lake of Galilee night fishing is usually better than day fishing; and fish caught at night could be sold fresh in the morning."[2] Such was not to be the case on this particular occasion.

At dawn, they were only a hundred yards or so from the shoreline when they heard a man call out to them, "Do you have any fish to eat?" They did not initially recognize Him; perhaps they didn't give an attentive look to see who it was. They simply shouted back, "No! We have nothing." To which Jesus responded, "Drag your nets along the right side of your boat and you'll find fish there."

When the disciples dragged their nets as Jesus had counseled them, the catch of fish was such that it was too large to pull into the boat. The unrealistic nature of the haul caused John to take pause and wonder. Suddenly he realized this could only be the work of one man. "It is the

Lord!" he blurted out, pointing to the shore. Peter, realizing the likelihood of what John had determined, quickly girded himself with his fisher's coat and jumped into the water, swimming to the shore with all of his might. The others in the boat held onto the filled net and rowed their way to the beach.

When they each arrived, they found that Jesus already had coals glowing, fish frying, and bread ready to eat. He told them to bring in to shore the fish they had secured. There were 153 caught in their net. Jesus then invited them to "come and dine" (verse 12). And He took the bread and fish and broke them and distributed them among His disciples. None of them dare ask Him if it was really He.

BACKGROUND

Elder McConkie suggested that they turned to their nets because they had temporal needs that had to be met.[3] W. Robertson Nicoll similarly states, "As the disciples stand together and see boat after boat put off, Simon Peter can stand it no longer but suddenly exclaims, . . . 'I am off to fish'. This is a relief to all and finds a ready response. . . . At once they embark, and as we watch that boat's crew putting off with their whole soul in their fishing, we see in how precarious a position the future of Christianity hung. They were only sure of one thing—that they must live."[4]

Their inability to recognize Jesus could be explained in a number of ways. Perhaps, as on the road to Emmaus or when He appeared to Mary the morning of the Resurrection, Jesus somehow obscured His appearance. Or perhaps since they were tired, they simply didn't look closely. Possibly the rising sun was in their eyes. Or perhaps Jesus had the customary shawl over His head in such a way as to obscure His face. The text is unclear.[5]

It has been suggested that they may not initially have thought much about His suggestion that they drop their net on the right side of the boat. They may have assumed that the unknown man on the shore could see a large school of fish there.[6]

Was Peter naked as the King James Translation suggests? Not likely. That would have been offensive to Jewish sensibilities.[7] He may have been gird in a loincloth or he may have simply tucked or tied his garments in with a belt or cincture so that he could have freedom of movement as he worked.[8]

The meal of fish and bread that Jesus provided in this miracle would potentially bring to the minds of the Apostles a flood of memories. It likely reminded them of the miracle of multiplying the fish and loaves, or of the sermon on the Bread of Life, or of the first post-resurrection meal that He shared with them (consisting of fish), or of His breaking of bread when He introduced the sacrament.[9] One source notes, "It is not too great an exaggeration to say that the catch of fish is the dramatic equivalent of the command given in the Matthean account of the Galilean appearance: 'Go therefore and make disciples of all nations.' "[10]

SYMBOLIC ELEMENTS

Since night fishing was traditionally seen as more productive than day fishing, their success *after* the sun had risen suggests that Jesus not only performed a miracle but did so when it would have been hardest to perform.

We have previously mentioned that fish are frequently used as symbols for those who come into the gospel.[11] Just as Jesus's disciples, through His direction, were able to find the elusive fish they were seeking, so also His "fishers of men" (Matthew 4:19; Jeremiah 16:16) today can find them through His direction.

Jesus has them bring their haul of fish in and count them, though they don't need the fish since Jesus has already provided food. The obvious question is why does John highlight for us the number of fish caught in this miracle? A number of theories have been purposed, each suggesting that the fish had symbolic significance in the miracle:

- Naturalists of the first century were said to have believed there were exactly 153 species of fish. Thus, the number would be highlighted to symbolize the universality of the gospel.[12] Hence, one commentator wrote, "Exegetes agree that it is symbolic of the apostolic ministry, which is to be 'fishers of men,' and that it represents, therefore, the success of the Christian mission to the world."[13]

- Modern commentators often see the number 153 as important only in making the point that there were sufficient fish to have broken the net yet it remained intact. Thus, the miraculous nature of the miracle is found not just in making the fish appear next to the boat and on the shore, but also in making the net stronger than normal.[14]

- Some perceived the number 153 as an example of early Christian gematria, where words have numeric values and numbers are often seen as representing a word or phrase.[15] Thus in the minds of some commentators, the number 153 here is Hebrew gematria for the phrase "the children of God," and it is a symbolic reference to all converts to Christ.[16]

Many commentators feel that the number is symbolic, but which of these theories, if any, is intended by John, we can only conjecture. The number 153 is not a standard symbolic number in antiquity. By highlighting the number, John may have intended nothing more than to say that this was a really significant miracle.[17] After all, an abundant catch of fish was seen anciently as a sign of God's favor.[18]

The net is a fitting symbol for the Church, into which those who have become converted are to be gathered.

Nakedness can be seen as a sign of innocence, but it is also often a symbol of being exposed. Water frequently represents cleansing. Thus, one commentator wrote, "Peter's nakedness in the boat symbolizes his spiritual state after his denial of Jesus; his putting on clothes has been interpreted as his conversion, and his plunging into the water as his purification."[19]

One sixth-century source spoke of the potential symbolism in the sea and the shore referenced in this miracle. He noted,

The question . . . arises as to why, after his resurrection, the Lord stood on the shore while his disciples were laboring in the sea, when before his resurrection he walked on the waves of the sea in his disciples' sight. What does the sea indicate but this present age, which is tossed about by the uproar of circumstances and the waves of this corruptible life? What does the solidity of the shore signify but the uninterrupted continuity of eternal peace? Therefore since the disciples were still held in the waves of this mortal life, they were laboring on the sea. But since our Redeemer had already passed beyond this perishable body, after his resurrection he stood on the shore.[20]

APPLICATION AND ALLEGORIZATION

Jesus appears at sunrise. John likely wishes us to make a connection between the rising of the sun and the raising of the Son. The Apostles worked in the dark and caught nothing. When the light broke and day dawned, they found success. John likely wishes us to make a connection, realizing that their success was because they were being directed by the Light. It is not enough to do the Lord's work. One must work under the direction of Christ.

One author questioned whether their lack of success fishing was really an accident. Might there have been some divine influence behind the failure, which preceded the massive haul?

> "Was it chance? No, it was a providence; it was carefully arranged, disappointing and vexing though it was, by One who was too wise to err, too good to be unkind, and who was preparing to teach them a lesson which should enrich them and the whole Church forever."
>
> The failure put an arrest on their temporal pursuits. Had they been successful that night, it would have been very much harder for them to renounce the craft forever; but their non-success made them more willing to give it up and to turn their thoughts to the evangelization of the world.[21]

Whether it is true that God arranged the lack of success for the Apostles, symbolically speaking, it is certainly true that there will be times when we will not see success; things will go differently than we had planned. Sometimes it seems we are being thwarted and not blessed. Yet this miracle reminds us that God has a plan for each of our lives—a plan that may at times require God to maneuver us to where He needs us. He may need to preempt *our* plans and purposes in order to bring about *His*. Thus, failure is not always truly failure. At times it may simply be evidence that God is working in and through us to get us where He needs us to be.

The unbroken nature of the net—something that surprised Jesus's disciples—has been seen as a symbol for the reality that the Christian community would bring in many of diverse personalities, gifts, and talents. But this would not "rend" the Church. Rather, it would be a blessing to it. For the Church would have the capacity to make a place for all, regardless of their uniqueness.[22] And so it has. As the Church goes into all the world, it brings in converts from diverse backgrounds and traditions. But there *is* room for all. And the diversity of each convert is welcomed because it makes the Church rich and vibrant. As Paul reminded us, all members of a body are needed for the functionality of the body (1 Corinthians 12:12–26). And so, all coverts have their place also.

From the coast, Jesus asked them if they had meat. However, when they got to the shore, they discovered that He already had the coal glowing, fish on the fire, and bread ready to eat. This can serve as a subtle reminder to each of us that Jesus is the source of all, even that which *we* personally produce. He doesn't need what we give, as He can produce all of what He needs in His own miraculous manner; nevertheless, we need to give so as to become like Him. But we see in this miracle a beautiful reminder that Christ is the source of all. Our offerings are merely token gifts of our love and service. But if we succeed in our work in the Church, it will be because He blessed our labors, and not because of what we brought to the proverbial table.[23]

While not part of the miracle proper, John records the following discussion, which ensued after the disciples made their way to shore:

> So when they had dined, Jesus saith to Simon Peter, Simon, son of Jonas, lovest thou me more than these? He saith unto him, Yea, Lord; thou knowest that I love thee. He saith unto him, Feed my lambs.
>
> He saith to him again the second time, Simon, son of Jonas, lovest thou me? He saith unto him, Yea, Lord; thou knowest that I love thee. He saith unto him, Feed my sheep.
>
> He saith unto him the third time, Simon, son of Jonas, lovest thou me? Peter was grieved because he said unto him the third time, Lovest thou me? And he said unto him, Lord, thou knowest all things; thou knowest that I love thee. Jesus saith unto him, Feed my sheep.
>
> Verily, verily, I say unto thee, When thou wast young, thou girdedst thyself, and walkedst whither thou wouldest: but when thou shalt be old, thou shalt stretch forth thy hands, and another shall gird thee, and carry thee whither thou wouldest not.
>
> This spake he, signifying by what death he should glorify God. And when he had spoken this, he saith unto him, Follow me. (John 21:15–19)

What seems significant about this is that Peter had been a fisherman by profession. And now shortly after the death of Christ, he had returned to his boat and nets. Here the Lord asks Peter and, by implication, all who profess to be Christ's disciples, "Do you love me more than you love these fish you have caught?" By interpretation: Do you love me more than the things of this world? More than accolades or achievements? More than money or possessions? More that popularity or ease of life? This is what Christ asks each of us. And this is what we must ask ourselves. And if we *do* love Him more, then our focus must be on feeding His sheep, tending to their needs. That commission is not solely to Apostles. Each of us has a call to minister, to reach out to those around us.

NOTES

1. See Lockyer (1965), 248; McQuade (2008), 162; Howick (2003), 105.
2. Brown (1970), 1069.
3. See McConkie (1987–88), 1:862. See also Kistemaker (2006), 52.
4. Nicoll (1983), 1:867.
5. Brown (1970), 1070; Lockyer (1965), 249.
6. See Nicoll (1983), 1:868.
7. See Brown (1970), 1072.
8. See Nicoll (1983), 1:868; Hendriksen (1953), 482; Brown (1970), 1072. When it says he "girt his fisher's coat unto him . . . and did cast himself into the sea," that is understood to mean that he grabbed the coat, threw it on, cinched the belt around his waist, and then jumped in—as though he did not want to appear before the Lord scantily clad. (See, for example, Tenney, in Gaebelein [1976–92], 2:200; Brown [1970], 1072.)
9. See Lockyer (1965), 250. Raymond E. Brown wrote, "Certainly in primitive iconography, meals of bread and fish (rather than of bread and wine) were the standard pictorial symbols of the Eucharist" ([1970], 1100).
10. Brown (1970), 1098.
11. See Brown (1970), 1097.
12. See Nicoll (1983), 1:896; Brown (1970), 1074; Lockyer (1965), 250.
13. Ellis (1984), 301.
14. See Nicoll (1983), 1:869.
15. In most ancient societies, letters and numbers were used interchangeably. Each letter of an alphabet had a numerical value. For example, A=1, B=2, C=3, and so on. The first nine letters of an alphabet were typically associated with the numbers 1–9. The second nine letters were typically associated with the tens places (J=10, K=20, L=30, and so on). The remaining letters in an alphabet were usually connected to the hundreds places (S=100, T=200, U=300) Technically speaking, gematria is a mode of interpretation in which the numerical value is substituted for each letter in a word. By so doing, a word's numerical value could be determined and compared for potential relationships with other words possessing the same numerical value (see Gaskill [2003], 111–12, 139–48).

16. See Romeo, "Gematria," 263–64. See also Nicoll (1983), 1:869, who also speaks of the gematria connection. See also Brown (1970), 1075; Lockyer (1965), 250.

17. See Brown (1970), 1076.

18. Ibid., 1096.

19. Ibid.

20. Gregory, "Forty Gospel Homilies," 382. See also Augustine, "Tactates on the Gospel of John," 122.6, in Elowsky (2007), 382.

21. Lockyer (1965), 248–49. Lockyer is in part quoting from another commentator on the miracle.

22. See Brown (1970), 1097.

23. One text suggests, "Their return to their former occupation has been a complete failure. They had failed to reckon sufficiently with God's plan for their lives. It is as if he were saying, 'You have caught nothing at all, now have you? Without me you can do nothing. . . . Now I will show you where you should cast the net in order to catch fish'" (Hendriksen [1953], 480). Elsewhere we read, "The writer may well have intended an ironical hint that Jesus knew the helplessness of the disciples when left on their own. It is notable that in the Gospels the disciples never catch a fish without Jesus' help" (Brown [1970], 1070–71). As the Lord Himself reminded us, "Without me ye can do nothing" (John 15:5).

PETER and JOHN HEAL the LAME MAN at the BEAUTIFUL GATE

ACTS 3:1–11

THE MIRACLE

Peter and John were engaged in the post-ascension ministry. They were headed to the temple for the three o'clock hour of prayer when they encountered a man lame from his mother's womb.[1] This Jew, who now was some forty years old, was carried each day by his friends to the temple, where he sat at one of its gates begging for the support he needed to provide his daily bread.

On this particular day as Peter and John passed by, the man called out for an alm. Peter said to the man, "Look at us," and the man did so, expecting a contribution. But as Peter "fastened his eyes upon him," he said to the lame beggar, "Silver and gold have I none; but such as I have, I give to thee" (verse 6). Then, in the sacred name of Jesus Christ, Peter commanded the man to "rise up and walk."

At the instant that Peter uttered his blessing (given in the form of a command), this man who had never walked in his life gained strength in his feet and ankles. Peter took him by the right hand and lifted him up, and the beggar begged no more. Rather, he leaped and walked and praised God. And, Luke informs us, he entered the temple through the "Beautiful" Gate (verse 10) alongside Peter and John, now a convert to Christ.

Many who saw the three in the temple recognized the boisterous man as he whom they had passed time and again at the Beautiful Gate. As he walked about clutching the arms of Peter and John, the onlookers were themselves amazed and in excitement, rushed over see him and inquire as to his healing.

BACKGROUND

Peter and John are depicted here as being devout, attending prayer at the customary hour in the temple each day. This would of course limit the effectiveness of any claims against them for supposedly "breaking the law of Moses." Like Christ, they were found doing as good, practicing Jews of their day did.[2]

Luke refers to the entrance to the temple at which Peter and John found this lame beggar as the "Beautiful Gate." However, there is no mention of that gate in Jewish descriptions of the temple. Scholars conjecture that it may be one of three gates: *The Shushan Gate* (in the eastern wall of the temple, which gave access to the court of the Gentiles from outside), likely located approximately where the modern Golden Gate is; *The Nicanor Gate* (which gave access on the east from the court of the Gentiles to the court of the women), sometimes referred to as the Corinthian Gate or the Bronze Gate; or an additional gate also sometimes called *The Nicanor Gate* (which lead to the court of men). These are the most likely theories regarding the gate to which Luke makes reference. However, scholars are not in agreement as to which the author has in mind.[3]

Scholars have suggested that the reason Peter and John had no money to share with this beggar was because the early Church had consecrated their goods and held "all things in common" (somewhat like the early Latter-day Saints did when they lived the united order). Consequently, they would have had no resources that were *theirs* to give to this beggar.[4]

SYMBOLIC ELEMENTS

This is the first of Peter's miracles recorded in the post-ascension ministry of the Twelve Apostles. For Luke, who records this event, it may signify to the reader that the mantle has now fully fallen upon the shoulders of Peter as the presiding Apostle. That being said, the miracle is wrought in the name of Christ, signifying from whence Peter has authority and also who actually is responsible for this miracle. Peter is the voice, but Jesus is the source.[5]

The silver and gold—of which Peter has none—are placed in contrast with the healing power of the Lord Jesus Christ.[6] This dichotomy can symbolize the reality that the world's treasures are not God's treasures.

One late seventh- to early eighth-century source suggested that this lame man was a symbol for the covenant people and their tendency toward apostasy in Hebrew Bible times. He wrote, "Because the people of Israel were found rebellious not only after the Lord's incarnation but even from the earliest times when the law was given, they were as if lame from their mother's womb."[7]

Generally speaking, the man's disability is offered as a potential symbol for the spiritual and physical disabilities each of us have during mortality. Just as Peter healed this man "lame from birth," God can take away from each of our lives the inabilities we have that keep us from serving and working in the kingdom.

The reference to the "Beautiful" Gate may be entirely symbolic, meaning Luke may have employed that unknown name for a gate of the temple as a symbol for what took place there. A man whose entire life had been hampered by his disability would now receive a new life through this miraculous healing. Could there be anything more "beautiful" than this?

In the spirit of the book of Hebrews, which speaks of the veil of the temple as the flesh of Christ (Hebrews 10:20), Bede the Venerable wrote, "The beautiful gate of the temple is the Lord. Whoever enters through him will be saved."[8] Just as we must pass through the veil to reenter the Father's presence, so also it is through Christ that we gain access to God.

The taking of the man by the hand and lifting him up—while commanding him to "rise up"—has been seen as an "unmistakable" reference to the resurrection, when each of us will also be called forth from the grave and allowed to toss aside our imperfect (and even decomposed) bodies, to be truly whole and perfect, and to enter into God's abode (represented in this miracle by the temple).[9]

The man is found lying *outside* of the gate of the temple, but once healed, he enters into the temple by the gate. Symbolically, if we are not healed (spiritually), we cannot enter into God's presence, symbolized by the temple.

APPLICATION AND ALLEGORIZATION

I am intrigued by the language of Luke, who tells us (in the Greek of Acts 3:11) that the healed man "held fast to" or "clung to" Peter and John.[10] In one sense, this may simply imply his conversion to Christianity and his intention to follow its leadership. But it may also be a general message to the reader about our need to "hold fast to" or "cling to" the prophets and apostles of our dispensation. In the temple drama (in which all participants are actors), the women play the role of the Church (or bride of Christ), and the men perform the part of the Lord and His prophets. At one point, the women veil their faces to symbolize how the bride of Christ (male and female) does not see clearly, and thus she must cling to the Lord and His prophets (symbolized by the men). So also in this miracle, he who was healed "clings" to God's authorized messengers. Why? Because he has discovered what Amos knew long ago: "Surely the Lord God will do nothing, but he revealeth his secret unto his servants the prophets" (Amos 3:7). As one of the Primary songs states,

> Now we have a world where people are confused.
> If you don't believe it, go and watch the news.
> We can get direction all along our way,
> If we heed the prophets—follow what they say.[11]

We must not simply follow but "cling" to their words and counsel. There is safety and peace in following what they teach. There is danger in setting aside their admonitions.

Under the law of Moses, a lamb that was lame or "imperfect" could not be used in the temple as a sacrifice because it was to typify the perfect Christ (see Deuteronomy 15:21; Malachi 1:8, 13). Similarly, according to the book of Leviticus, a man with physical deformities (such as those this brother possessed) was restricted as to his service in the temple and priesthood, and for the same reasons.

> And the Lord spake unto Moses, saying,
> Speak unto Aaron, saying, Whosoever he be of thy seed in their

generations that hath any blemish, let him not approach to offer the bread of his God.

For whatsoever man he be that hath a blemish, he shall not approach: a blind man, or a lame, or he that hath a flat nose, or any thing superfluous,

Or a man that is brokenfooted, or brokenhanded,

Or crookbackt, or a dwarf, or that hath a blemish in his eye, or be scurvy, or scabbed, or hath his stones broken;

No man that hath a blemish of the seed of Aaron the priest shall come nigh to offer the offerings of the Lord made by fire: he hath a blemish; he shall not come nigh to offer the bread of his God.

He shall eat the bread of his God, both of the most holy, and of the holy.

Only he shall not go in unto the veil, nor come nigh unto the altar, because he hath a blemish; that he profane not my sanctuaries: for I the Lord do sanctify them.

And Moses told it unto Aaron, and to his sons, and unto all the children of Israel. (Leviticus 21:16–24)

Of course, today we do not exclude men from service because of a bodily deformity. Nevertheless, the symbolism is instructive. Men who serve in the priesthood or in the temple must be clean. It is not important that they be free from bodily imperfections, but if they are spiritually marred, they must seek healing before they act in the name of the Lord and as a symbol for the Lord.[12] And like the "lame man" in this narrative, the best place for those who are spiritually "ill" to be found is at the house of prayer. Proximity to God always brings blessings.

The brother healed in this miracle had been lame for forty long years. And yet once healed, he suffered no residual effects from his previous malady. While this *can* be true of any physical healing, it is *always* true of a spiritual healing if repentance is sincere and full. The Lord has promised, "Behold, he who has repented of his sins, the same is forgiven, and I, the Lord, remember them no more" (D&C 58:42). One of the most beautiful messages of the gospel of Jesus Christ is that all wrongs can be righted. Jesus can make us completely whole, removing all mistakes and sins from our past. We can be "clean every whit" (John 13:10).

One text on the miracles pointed out, "It is a noteworthy fact that again and again Peter emphasized that the cure had not been effected by any power he had, but only by that of Jesus Christ ([Acts] 3:6, 12,

16; 4:9–12. See 9:34). 'In the name of Jesus of Nazareth rise up and walk.'"[13] Let this be an example to each of us. Peter had learned the lesson of the war in heaven: take not honor to yourself but give *all* honor and glory to God. Doctrine and Covenants 59:21 reminds us, "And in nothing doth man offend God, or against none is his wrath kindled, save those who confess not his hand in all things." Whatever miracles God allows us to be instruments in, may our pride never deceive us into thinking we are the source or that we deserve the praise. Like Peter, we must emphatically give all glory to God.

NOTES

1. The Greek is unclear as to whether the man is actually being carried to the gate when Peter and John see him or whether he was simply carried there each day but was already in his place when Peter and John approached. (See Nicoll [1983], 2:103.)
2. See Nicoll (1983), 2:102.
3. See Fitzmyer, *Anchor Bible*, 277–78; See Johnson (1992), 65.
4. See Fitzmyer (1998), 278; Johnson (1992), 65; Nicoll (1983), 2:103. See also Acts 2:44; 4:32.
5. One non-LDS commentator, speaking of this miracle and its implications for the Church today, noted that we have many in the world and in the Church today crippled by immorality, disabled through their own sins or the sins of others. "Alas! however, so few of these cripples are healed. The great mass of impotent men and women remain impotent. Why? The Church has her . . . preachers and priests; . . . but she is sadly destitute of power to say to a world crippled by sin, unrest, and dread of war, 'In the name of Jesus of Nazareth rise up and walk.' Would that a mighty revival could bring her back to her power in the Acts, when she was to be dreaded as 'an army with banners'" (Lockyer [1965], 262).
6. See Fitzmyer (1998), 276.
7. Bede, "Commentary on the Acts," 39.
8. Ibid.
9. See Johnson (1992), 66.
10. See Fitzmyer (1998), 275, 279; Nicoll (1993), 2:107.
11. Hiatt, "Follow the Prophet," *Children's Songbook* (1991), 110–11.
12. See Johnson, (1992), 65; Lockyer (1965), 261.
13. Lockyer (1965), 262.

DEATH *of* ANANIAS *and* SAPPHIRA

ACTS 4:36–5:11

THE MIRACLE

In the years following the death of Jesus, the Church had begun to live having "all things in common" (the united order). By covenant, participants agreed to consecrate all that they had to the Church. Joseph Barnabas (a Levite convert of Cypriot decent) owned a farm, and so he sold it and gave the proceeds to the Apostles to use in the building up of the kingdom. Two other converts to the faith, Ananias and Sapphira, had also made a covenant to live this higher law but were not as faithful as was Joseph Barnabas in honestly giving all they had to the Church.[1]

Like Barnabas, Ananias and Sapphira also had a piece of property that they sold. But instead of turning *all* of the proceeds over to the presiding brethren, Ananias (with the knowledge of his wife) held back a portion of the profits and lied to Peter and the brethren about how much he had sold the property for. Peter discerned the lie and confronted Ananias about it. Yet Ananias continued in his deception.

Peter said to Ananias, "Why have you let Satan so fill your heart that you would lie to God and steal from Him? Was the property not yours before you sold it? Did you not have the power to decide yourself what you would do with the proceeds once you sold it? What made you do such a thing? You have not lied to men but to God."

When Ananias heard Peter's words convicting him of his sin, he dropped dead. Then, as the word spread of this miraculous occurrence, "great fear came on all them that heard." Peter had Ananias's body taken out and buried.

Three hours later, Ananias's wife returned, unaware of what had happened to her husband. Peter asked her if she had sold the property for a certain amount of money—the amount she and her husband had fraudulently claimed they had. Sapphira confirmed that they indeed had, once again perpetuating their fraud against the Lord and His prophets. Peter then confronted her as he had her husband, saying, "What made you agree to test the Lord's Spirit in this way? Listen; the footsteps of those who have buried your husband are at the door, and they will carry you to your grave also." Immediately Sapphira fell dead at Peter's feet, and she too was carried out and buried.

Great fear came upon the entire Church and upon all those who heard about these miraculous occurrences.

BACKGROUND

One commentary on the passage notes, "The placement of the story of Ananias and Sapphira in Acts 5 is no accident—it comes immediately after the enumeration of the principle features of the law of consecration, in Acts 4:32–35. It is meant to show what happens when certain higher laws of God's economy and social order are deliberately transgressed."[2] Ananias and Sapphira were apparently wealthy. They likely enjoyed the reputation of being two who were generous to the Church by selling properties they owned and contributing the proceeds to the burgeoning Christian community. Yes, they liked the reputation for being generous but apparently did not like the sacrifices required to be worthy of such an accolade. Thus, they pretended they were giving the entirety of their proceeds to the Church when in reality they had been holding back a portion.[3]

Upon hearing Peter's words, Ananias died. However, this should not be understood to mean that Peter cursed Ananias and thereby caused his death. No such pronouncement is said to have been uttered. Ananias died because God took his life. But Peter is not to be seen as responsible for the death of this man. No such suggestion is ever made in the text. And it is God who strikes down the guilty, not His prophets.[4] The same must be said of Sapphira, though in her case, Peter prophesies her demise, which he had not done with Ananias. One source notes,

Peter did not consciously will such a fatal death. He was not the deliberate agent of judgment, even though his exposure of hypocrisy was the occasion of it. . . . [The] sentence of death was immediately executed by God in whose hands are life and death. "The visitation of God" was the cause of death. Peter was only the instrument of justice.[5]

The penalty upon Ananias and Sapphira—issued by God, *not* by Peter—was not intended as cruelty toward them but as a warning to each of us.[6]

It is commonly pointed out by commentators that Ananias and Sapphira were not forced to make the covenant of consecration that they had entered into. Peter even suggested that it was their place to decide what they would do with the land and then with the proceeds after they had sold the land.[7] One source notes, it is "not ownership of property [that] is the fault [of their deaths], but conspiracy [to deceive the prophet] which shatters the unity of the church and threatens the prophetic authority of the Twelve."[8]

SYMBOLIC ELEMENTS

Barnabas serves well here as a symbol of those who make and faithfully keep covenants. He is blessed by his covenants and becomes a blessing to others because he faithfully fulfills them. Ananias and Sapphira, on the other hand, can typify all who enter into covenants but think they can live them halfway with no significant consequences. This unfaithful husband and wife remind us of the dangers of making covenants when we are not completely committed to what we are covenanting to do.

Ananias and Sapphira fell dead at the feet of Peter. Luke Timothy Johnson highlighted the significance of this: "The irony of Sapphira's unintended obeisance to the apostle is surely deliberate. They falsified the gesture of genuine submission when they laid only a portion of their possessions 'at the feet of the apostles,' and now the conspirators fall 'at the feet' of the apostles whose authority they had challenged."[9] They lied to the prophet, which is certainly not an act of submission, but instead an act of rebellion. And they weren't willing to put the money they had made a covenant to consecrate at the feet of the Apostles, so God put their lives there instead.

APPLICATION AND ALLEGORIZATION

One of the poignant messages that can be drawn from this miracle story is that prophets of God are more than mere men. They are indeed humans, but they have gifts beyond their own. They see what humans would not typically see. Peter received revelation from God that allowed him to discern the hearts, actions, and even words of Ananias and Sapphira. And so it is with prophets in our dispensation. They represent God and thus, when necessary, can know the mind and will of God. Consequently, in this miracle we are reminded that they are God's representatives. To lie to them is to lie to God Himself. And there will always be consequences for such choices.

While this miracle teaches us about much more than the law of consecration and the united order, nevertheless, it *does* highlight (in symbolic ways) the consequences of entering into a covenant to live those higher laws and then reneging on our covenants. Ananias and Sapphira died because they sought to keep their covenants in dishonest ways. You and I will die spiritually if we are dishonest in our approach to our covenants. So to lie to the bishop claiming we are a full-tithe payer when we know we are not will surely bring spiritual consequences. To lie to get a recommend to the temple when we know we are not worthy to be there would also surely hinder us spiritually. To take upon us the name of Christ but then to live in an unchristian way would hamper the Spirit in our lives. If we make covenants to God but then are not faithful to those covenants, we die spiritually. In some cases, that may happen instantaneously, as with Ananias and Sapphira. But in most cases, it is a slower process, which develops over time. Regardless, spiritual death is the result. If we are not willing to submit ourselves to God, He will make us submit to the penalties of our rebelliousness.

Doing good for praise or gain is sinful. Ananias is an example of this. He seems fixated on being acknowledged as a significant contributor to the early Christian Church, but he seems hesitant to make the sacrifices of those who have truly consecrated themselves to the kingdom.

> Disciples having lands or houses sold them, and the money secured by their sale was put into one common treasury and used as needed. Barnabas is singled out as having sold all his possessions and surrendering

the money received to the common fund. Because of this self-chosen poverty, Barnabas afterwards worked, as Paul did, for his livelihood (1 Corinthians 9:6). Evidently Barnabas gained praise and prestige by his self-sacrifice, and Ananias had an idea that he could get the same result more cheaply. But the generous, sincere, and spontaneous gift of Barnabas and the others sets forth in dark relief the calculated deceit of Ananias and Sapphira. "The brighter the light, the darker the shadow."

Ananias . . . desired to gain as high a name as Barnabas by seeming to have surrendered to the common treasury all he had gained by the sale of his possessions. . . . His terrible sin consisted in professing to have given all into the common fund, when knowingly he kept part of the price. Satan entered his heart and suggested a compromise between love of Christian praise and worldliness.[10]

Ananias's motivations for giving are potentially skewed. Doing that which is holy for unholy reasons does not bring us joy. In the case of Ananias and his wife, it ultimately brought death.

In all of this, we should not lose the obvious message about dishonestly in any of its forms. Ananias and Sapphira did not *have to* give of their substance and thus really did not *have to* lie. They had made a covenant to give, but it was not an obligatory covenant. They had every right to simply not consecrate their wealth to the Church. That being said, you and I are confronted almost daily with opportunities to be less than fully honest. We must remember the death of these two and its symbolic message to us. They lied, and their spirits departed their bodies as a result. If we are dishonest, the Spirit of God will withdraw from us, and we will be left spiritually dead. That is an eternal verity.

There is an additional potential message in this miracle regarding the dangers of covetousness. Jerome (circa AD 347–420) pointed out that "believers sold their possessions and brought the prices of them and laid them down at the apostles' feet: a symbolic act designed to show that people must trample on covetousness."[11] The reason Ananias and Sapphira lied to the prophet, and thus to God, was because they loved the things of the world more than the things of God. This is an easy trap for any of us to fall into. The world and its baubles glisten. They readily catch our attention. And yet, as Elder Neal A. Maxwell reminded us, "Large bank accounts cannot fill the empty vault of the soul."[12] Money is not in and of itself evil (1 Timothy 6:10). But if it becomes our focus, it can push what really matters into our peripheral vision, and that which is in the periphery is always distorted, because it is never in focus.

NOTES

1. Ogden and Skinner state that "Ananias and Sapphira had covenanted to live the law of consecration as described in Acts 4:32–35. In fact, the higher covenant they had entered into was the same as that practiced by the people of Enoch and the Book of Mormon society described in 4 Nephi, in which the people were of one heart and one mind, dwelt in righteousness, and had all things in common" (*Verse by Verse*, 42).
2. See Ogden and Skinner (1998), 43. See also Nicoll (1983), 2:140.
3. See Fitzmyer (1998), 316.
4. See Johnson (1992), 88; Fitzmyer (1998), 323–24 Nicoll (1983), 2:143.
5. Lockyer (1965), 264.
6. See Nicoll (1983), 2:143. See also Jerome, "Letter 130.14," in Martin (2006), 60.
7. See Fitzmyer (1998), 323; Johnson (1992), 88; Lockyer (1965), 263; Nicoll (1983), 2:138, 141–42.
8. Johnson (1992), 88.
9. Johnson (1992), 89. See also Fitzmyer (1998), 325.
10. Lockyer (1965), 263. See also Nicoll (1983), 2:143.
11. Jerome, "Letter 71.4," in Martin (2006), 58.
12. Maxwell (1997), 360.

APOSTLES GROW *the* CHURCH, HEAL *the* SICK, *and* *Are* DELIVERED *from* PRISON

ACTS 5:12–20

THE MIRACLE

Peter and the other Apostles continued to work many mighty miracles among the people, and they were held in high esteem by those who knew of them. The Church grew greatly during this period, in part because of the work of the leadership of the Church and the lives of its members. When word spread that Peter was visiting a certain location, people from the surrounding regions would carry their sick to the place where Peter was expected, and they would place them in the streets with the hope that Peter would heal them or, at very least, that his shadow would fall upon them (as they believed that even it had the power to heal). Peter and the Apostles were able to cure all kinds of sickness and cast out unclean spirits.

The notoriety of leaders of the Church filled the high priest and the Sadducees with jealously. So they had the Apostles arrested and put them in jail. But during the night, the angel of the Lord appeared to them, opened the gates of the prison, and said to them, "Go, take your place in the temple where you are normally found and teach the people about Christ's life and its effect upon their salvation."[1] So the Apostles entered the temple at dawn and continued to teach as they had before their arrest.

BACKGROUND

Whereas Peter performed the first post-resurrection apostolic miracle, here we begin to see the entire Quorum of the Twelve as centers of miraculous activity. Peter is not the only one healing and blessing. Now each of the Apostles is becoming known for their charismatic gifts, for their endowments of the Spirit.

Regarding the "angel of the Lord" who freed the Apostles from jail, one commentator pointed out, *"Angelos Kyriou* is the Greek translation of the standard Hebrew expression *mal'ak Yhwh,* used in older [Old Testament] books as a theophanic element to express the presence of God to his people or to bring them messages."[2] Similarly, another wrote, "The 'angel of the Lord' (*angelos kyriou*) . . . denotes God himself in his dealings with men ([Exodus] 3:2, 4, 7; passim[3]). While the Greek *angelos,* like the Hebrew *mal'ak,* may simply mean 'messenger,' here it denotes the presence or agency of God himself."[4] The aforementioned interpretations accurately represent how many scholars read this phrase. And while acknowledging that the "angel of the Lord" here *could be* Jehovah, Latter-day Saints are aware that God often sends angels in His name to speak (by divine investiture of authority) on His behalf. It is quite possible that such is happening here, though the text does not indicate.

We tend to see Gamaliel (flourished AD 25–50) in a fairly positive light.[5] We almost picture him as a supporter of Christians because of his suggestion that the Sanhedrin "back off" and let Christianity excel or collapse on its own merits. But note the following:

> This was not Gamaliel's first encounter with the apostles, or even (we should think) with Jesus. Luke specifically identifies him as a Pharisaic member of the Sanhedrin ([Luke] 5:34), and the authority carried by his speech as well as his prestige among the people suggest he is one of its leaders. He had, therefore, been part of the condemnation of Jesus (Luke 22:66–73). Furthermore, he had confronted the apostles Peter and John and had seen the man healed by them standing before him; he saw their *parrēsia* [boldness or confidence] and knew it had to come from Jesus. He had just now heard Peter declare again that the Jesus they had killed was powerfully alive at God's right hand. What does he do? He sent the apostles from the room, and with his colleagues formulates a plan of action based on historical prudence! Fundamentally, he advises a "wait and see" attitude.[6]

Thus while Christians typically like his counsel to the members of the Sanhedrin, we should not be misled into thinking this means he was a supporter of the Christian cause. There is evidence that he may have been quite a thorn in the side of the Church.

SYMBOLIC ELEMENTS

One's shadow is often seen as a symbol of the person (or the soul of the person) to whom it belongs.[7] One text notes, "In the heat of Palestine, shadows are preeminently an image for protection or refuge, especially that which Yahweh provides. . . . The [New Testament] uses the image of 'overshadowing' to depict not so much divine protection as divine presence or power."[8] Another source notes, "The shadow is understood as something more than merely the spot where the sunlight cannot fall. Because it reflects the shape of the person, it is regarded in some primitive thinking [people] as powerful, a vital part of a person."[9]

Luke's language of people being brought into the streets to be healed by Peter is reminiscent of other scenes where people did the same in order to have Jesus heal them (see Luke 4:40; 5:19; 6:18–19).[10] Symbolically, Peter is being depicted as Jesus's successor—the new head of the Church. Jesus's persona—or better put, power—is being transferred onto Peter.

APPLICATION AND ALLEGORIZATION

One commentator wrote, "The faith and good example of the apostles and other Christians have moved people to esteem them highly and put trust in them. Such traits manifest the Christians as a caring community."[11] The number of missionaries we send out will not determine the rate of the growth of the Church in the latter days. Having more missionaries is certainly wonderful and good! However, the faithfulness of the members and the holiness of their lives and demeanor will do more to help the Church grow than will a multiplication of full-time missionaries. How does your life reflect the goodness of the gospel and its standards for personal righteousness? Are people drawn to the Church because of you and how you live your faith?

The Sanhedrin were furious with Peter and the other Apostles for their continued public miracles—blessing, healing, and teaching the good news. In our own lives, we will find that there will be those who will be angry with us as we seek to do good and try to live holy lives. It is the nature of the world. Satan hates holiness. He hates goodness. If we do what's right, we should expect rabid opposition.

Gamaliel is famous for his counsel to the Sanhedrin wherein he recommended that they not get riled up about Christianity and its miracle-performing leaders. Luke records this:

> Then stood there up one in the council, a Pharisee, named Gamaliel, a doctor of the law, had in reputation among all the people, and commanded to put the apostles forth a little space; and said unto them, Ye men of Israel, take heed to yourselves what ye intend to do as touching these men. . . . And now I say unto you, Refrain from these men, and let them alone: for if this counsel or this work be of men, it will come to naught: but if it be of God, ye cannot overthrow it; lest haply ye be found even to fight against God. (Acts 5:34–35, 38–39)

Perhaps there is a lesson in this for us today. As we encounter opposition in our lives, we too should think of the truism articulated here. If the opposition be of man or of the devil, it will come to naught. Thus rather than despair, we should step back and wait to see the hand of the Lord manifest on our behalf.

This miracle reminds us that today's prophets—particularly the First Presidency of the Church—are symbols of Christ. They are His earthly representatives upon the earth today. And like Peter and those who labored with him, where they need to call upon God's power to discern or heal or raise up, they will be given the gifts to so do.

The healing power of Peter's shadow is curious.[12] In a sense it seems quite miraculous and out of the ordinary. Having said that, Jesus frequently healed without contact of any kind, or through materials like spittle or clay. What's important to remember is that it is not the shadow, spit, or clay that holds the healing power. Healing comes by the prayer of faith (James 5:14–15). Symbolically, Peter's shadow reminds us that those who have the gift of healing are relying not on their own power but on the "divine" power, and that power must be resident in them through their faith and faithfulness.

In traditional Christian symbolism, Peter would be a symbol for God, and the First Presidency (Peter, James, and John—or the modern First Presidency) would be a symbol for the Godhead. However, Bede the Venerable (circa AD 672–735) saw another symbolic message in this miracle. He wrote, "Peter is a type of the church, [hence] it is beautifully appropriate that . . . by his accompanying shadow he raised up those who were lying down [diseased or spiritually ill]. So [also] the church, concentrating its mind and love on heavenly things, passes like a shadow on the land . . . renew[ing] . . . with everlasting gifts."[13] The Church has that which is necessary to renew or revitalize those who are spiritually sick. It has healing properties because it is an abode of God's Spirit. If we can get those who are struggling within the shadows of the Church or the temple, God's power can be manifest and their healing can begin.

NOTES

1. The phrase "words of this life" (verse 20) has been interpreted to mean the "words of salvation" or the "words of Jesus who is the author of life" (Johnson [1992], 97).

2. Fitzmyer (1998), 335.

3. "Passim" means something that appears throughout or frequently in a text, here and there, every so often, or commonly.

4. See Longenecker, "Acts of the Apostles," 9:319. See also Johnson (1992), 97. If Luke is suggesting that this "angel of the Lord" is actually God, then he is likely seeking to develop a connection between the earliest Judean community and the beginnings of Christianity. Not all scholars think he is trying to do that, however. Those who argue against the notion that Luke means "angel of the Lord" as God often hold to a position that suggests a stronger Hellenistic influence on the beginnings of the Christian faith.

5. See Fitzmyer (1998), 339 for Gamaliel's lineage and background.

6. Johnson (1992), 102–3.

7. See Cooper (82), 151.

8. Ryken, Wilhoit, and Longman (1998), 779–80.

9. Fitzmyer (1998), 329.

10. Johnson (1992), 95.

11. Fitzmyer (1998), 328.

12. Some have suggested that it only says people "thought" Peter's shadow could heal but that the text never actually says it did heal anyone. However, we agree with W. Robertson Nicoll, who wrote, "Although it is not actually said that a miraculous power went forth from Peter's shadow, it is a question why, if no such power is implied, the words should be introduced at all into a narrative which evidently purports to note the extraordinary powers of the Apostles" ([1983], 2:147).

13. Bede, "Commentary on the Acts of the Apostles," 5.15, in Martin (2006), 62.

STEPHEN DOES GREAT MIRACLES *and* *Is* TRANSFIGURED

ACTS 6:8, 15

THE MIRACLE

As the Church grew in numbers and needs, the members of the Twelve saw that they were spending an inordinate amount of time on temporal matters, including administering goods consecrated to the Church and apparently taking care of the monetary needs of the poor. All this was preventing them from preaching the word. So they felt a need to call assistants who could administer temporal things while they focused on the spiritual matters. Seven men were called: Stephen, Philip, Nicanor, Timon, Parmenas, and Nicolaus.

These seven men were brought to the attention of the Twelve by members of the Church and in response to the request of the Twelve for assistance in identifying some potential assistants. Once it was determined by the Spirit that these were the right men, they were set apart by the Twelve Apostles through the ordinance of the laying on of hands.

Luke does not tell us much about their temporal ministries to which they were specifically called. He does, however, speak of Stephen as serving in a spiritual capacity: preaching and teaching much like the Twelve. The book of Acts informs us that Stephen, as "a man full of faith" (Acts 6:8) and the Holy Spirit, did many wondrous miracles among the people, though Luke does not give us an account of them.

The one thing recorded, evidencing Stephen's extraordinary spiritual endowments, occurred during his arraignment before the Sanhedrin:

> As the result of [his miracles] the rage of the Devil was aroused, and Stephen was arrested on a charge of blasphemy. Witnesses were obtained to testify against Stephen who, as he sat before the council, had a face shining with angelic glory. The wrongly accused was holding such high and holy fellowship with his Lord that nothing could disturb his inner peace, and consequently, his very countenance, like Moses before him, shone with the radiance of heavenly glory. (Exodus 34:28)[1]

As his adversaries were seeking ways to condemn him, Stephen was apparently transfigured before them. "And all that sat in the council, looking steadfastly on him, saw his face as it had been the face of an angel" (Acts 6:15). There was an undeniable luminosity to his countenance, which all present witnessed.

BACKGROUND

Stephen is often described as the first martyr of the post-ascension Church.[2] His stoning "was the signal for a general persecution" of Christians.[3]

Early Christian belief placed Stephen as a member of the original Seventy called by Jesus: "After these things the Lord appointed other seventy also, and sent them two and two before his face into every city and place, whither he himself would come" (Luke 10:1).[4] While the Bible never calls Stephen an Apostle or member of the Seventy, and never implies he is necessarily the equivalent of a General Authority, commentators often puzzle at his spiritual endowments, which seem to suggest he had gifts of the Spirit akin to members of the Twelve. For example, one text states, "Stephen is described as a prophet: he is filled with the Holy Spirit and wisdom ([Acts] 6:6, 10; 7:55), he works 'wonders and signs' with great 'power' (*dynamis*); these are the marks of the prophet (see Acts 2:19, 22, 43; 4:16, 22, 30; 5:12). Equally important is the note that he did his wonders 'among the people' (see [Acts] 2:12, 47; 3:12; 4:1, 10; 5:12)."[5] We cannot say whether Stephen was ever given the equivalent of General Authority status, but we can say that his gifts and spiritual endowments were truly remarkable and were evidences of his great holiness and dedication to the Lord.

SYMBOLIC ELEMENTS

As we have pointed out above, the laying on of hands usually symbolizes that power is being transferred. One who had hands laid upon him was authorized, and the people are expected to obey him as a sanctioned messenger.[6] John Chrysostom (circa AD 344–407) suggested that while a man's hand is laid upon another man's head, symbolically it is the hand of God that is doing the blessing or ordaining. The man performing the ordinance is but a symbol.[7]

Of his glowing face, one commentary suggests that "the change of countenance indicates that Stephen is an authoritative spokesperson for God."[8] Another wrote,

> One's face is one's true self. . . . Literature employs the symbolism of the fact to expose nature and character. Just as the face of Moses showed that he had been with God, so also the company of the divine transfigures the appearance of Jesus. The true character of the martyr Stephen flashes on his visage—a combination of innocence, power and grace that Luke describes as the "face of an angel" (Acts 6:15).[9]

Thus, Stephen's glow suggests he is God's messenger and that his words are those of God, not of man.

As with all prophetic figures, Stephen is a symbol of Christ. His words often parallel those of Christ, as does his arraignment before the Jewish authorities, the trumped up charges, and his ultimate martyrdom.

> That Luke intends the reader to perceive Stephen as a prophet like Jesus is obvious. . . . When we examine the account of Stephen's death, we will see the connections drawn explicitly ([Acts] 7:55–8:2). But even in this opening scene [Acts 6:1–15], Luke has done three things to show the continuity between Jesus and Stephen. First, by making Stephen's wisdom impossible to refute, he shows that he is one of the witnesses prophesied by Jesus, to whom Jesus has given a "mouth and wisdom" that could not be countered ([Acts] 6:10; see Luke 21:15). Second, the succession of events leading to Stephen's speech imitates the sequence of Jesus' passion: the open confrontation, the suborning of spies, the agitation of the populace, the arrest, and the delivery to the council (6:10–12). Third, Luke has shifted to Stephen's "passion" elements that the other Synoptists made part of Jesus' passion: not Jesus but Stephen has "false witnesses" stand against him and accuse him; not Jesus but

Stephen has the charge of "blasphemy" laid against him; not Jesus but Stephen is accused of speaking against the temple. The effect of this overlapping is to insure the reader's perception of Stephen as an authentic witness in continuity with [Jesus]; . . . the same prophetic spirit is at work in him. The pattern of the prophet is enacted in his words and in his deeds, in the division he creates in the people, and in his rejection and suffering.

Finally, as in the hearing before Pilate the charge against Jesus was stated three times with variations (Luke 23:2, 5, 14), so is the charge against Stephen: the false witnesses first accuse him of blasphemous words against "Moses and God" ([Acts] 6:11); then before the council they say that Stephen "speaks against this holy place and the law" ([Acts] 6:13), and finally, this is explicated in [Acts] 6:14 as "Jesus the Nazorean [sic] will destroy this place and change the customs that Moses handed down to us."[10]

Luke wants his reader to see Stephen as a prophetic figure who laid down his life in the image and pattern of the Lord. This narrative reminds us that what Jesus did, His disciples will do too—not for atonement but as testament.

Stephen's name means literally "crown" or "wreath," as in a laurel crown traditionally placed upon the head of the winner of a game or athletic contest.[11] It seems an appropriate name for the martyr Stephen as he was victorious over fear and over the enemies of Christ. He won the great competition that is mortality and is now crowned in the heavens above "to go no more out" (Revelation 3:12).

APPLICATION AND ALLEGORIZATION

Stephen died for the cause of Christ, but he did not live to see the fruits of his sacrifice. He gave the ultimate gift but did not know of his ultimate convert.

Stephen's victorious death was not in vain, for a young man witnessed his death and heard his cry for the forgiveness of his murderers and even though that blood-stained yet angelic face of Stephen only made young Saul's hatred of Christ more intense, such an unforgettable sight left its mark. Stephen's dying message lodged deep in the soul of Saul and paved the way for the Damascus vision. Stephen's martyrdom was the price paid for Saul's soul.[12]

Another commentator pointed out Paul's great work as a missionary to the Gentiles and noted that because of his conversion of Paul, "we might say . . . that Stephen was the precursor of the apostle to the gentiles."[13] Stephen did not know that the way he lived and the way he died would convert one of the greatest missionaries in Christian history. Nor did he know that because of that one convert thousands would be proselyted to Christ. Nor could he realize that his convert would ultimately be the source of the bulk of the Christian New Testament. We can never know the far-reaching effects of our lives, words, or behaviors. As with Stephen, others are watching us. Will the way we live our lives touch hearts and prick consciences the way Stephen's did?

The narrative of this miracle makes it quite clear that Stephen was maligned and misrepresented. He, like Christ, was placed in a circumstance wherein his defense made little difference to those who held earthly power over him. His death was assured regardless of what truths he taught or what support he could garner. Nevertheless, this miracle reminds us that God rectifies falsehoods. While his enemies did not stop their evil pursuits, nevertheless, Luke is quite clear that Stephen's radiating glow let them each know personally that God was with this servant of the Lord. "As if in refutation of the charge made against him, Stephen receives the same mark of divine favor that had been granted to Moses."[14] As we are faithful to our covenants, God too—in His own way and time—will refute our corrupt critics. God vindicates His own. Like Stephen, we must place our trust in Him and know that His hand will be manifest on our behalf here or in the hereafter.

In the narrative of this event, the Twelve asked the general membership for names of capable individuals who might help them administer the Church's temporal needs. One commentary explains, "Acts 6 is a fine example of how delegation operated in the early Church and how inspiration can work both from the bottom up and from the top down. For example, the apostles ask for inspired recommendations (compare Acts 1:23–36) which they then confirm through their own inspiration."[15] While this is true, one important factor in this is the apostolic request for suggestions. In other words, while the provocation of revelation may at times come through a "bottom up" channel, the thing that made such a source of inspiration appropriate was the request of the Twelve for member participation in the process. This narrative is not supporting the laity of the Church writing or counseling the presiding Brethren on *every* or *any* matter that bothers them. If the prophets ask, response is appropriate. But to use this event as support for "counseling" the prophets would be to misread what happened in this story.

NOTES

1. Lockyer (1965), 267.
2. See, for example, Fitzmyer (1998), 344, 350.
3. See Philip Schaff, *History of the Christin Church*, 1:249.
4. See Nicoll (1983), 2:170.
5. Johnson (1992), 108. See also page 110.
6. See Johnson (1992), 107. See also Nicoll (1983), 2:172.
7. See Chrysostom, in Nicoll (1983), 2:167.
8. Johnson (1992), 110.
9. Ryden, Wilhoit, and Longman (1998), 259.
10. Johnson (1992), 112–13.
11. See Fitzmyer (1998), 349–50.
12. Lockyer (1965), 267.
13. M.-É. Boismard, "Stephen," Freedman (1992), 6:210.
14. Nicoll (1983), 2:178; spelling standardized.
15. See Ogden and Skinner (1998), 44.

PHILIP CASTS OUT EVIL SPIRITS *and* HEALS *the* LAME

ACTS 8:5–7, 13

THE MIRACLE

Like Stephen, Philip had been called as one of the seven men who would relieve some of the temporal burdens that had landed on the shoulders of the Twelve Apostles. Luke describes that, also like Stephen's work, Philip's work as more spiritual than temporal.

Philip had traveled to a town of Samaria where he preached to the people about Christ. He also performed a number of miracles while there, including casting out evil spirits and healing those who were lame or had the palsy. His success was great and many believed and were converted to Jesus and His Church.

There was at that time in Samaria a sorcerer by the name of Simon, who "bewitched the people" into thinking he had the power of God with him. He had preached among the people there for some time and many believed in him because of his sorceries. However, like many others in Samaria, when Simon heard Philip's testimony and saw his miracles, he found himself in awe of the man of God, and thus the sorcerer was converted and baptized and thereafter followed Philip.

BACKGROUND

The text says Philip went "down" to Samaria. However, Samaria is north of Jerusalem. Going "down" here is probably simply a reference to the fact that Jerusalem was over eight hundred meters above sea level—a "high" city indeed.[1]

Samaria was originally the name of a city but later became the name of a district in Israel. Thus, Luke could mean that Philip went to the region of Samaria, or he may simply mean that Philip was preaching in a town in Samaria.[2]

The miracles Philip performed were not for the purpose of converting people to the gospel. Signs are never the foundation of a good or solid testimony. It appears that Philip's miracles in this narrative were for the purpose of counteracting the adverse influences and corrupt "wonders" of the magician Simon.[3] It is claimed by early Christians that the sorcerer of this story had bewitched his followers with his tricks and demonic powers, such as flying through the air and "miraculously" appearing out of a cloud of dust.[4] Surely the type of miracles Philip performed, along with the fact that he performed them in the name of Christ (instead of calling *himself* "the great power of God" as Simon had) and with the accompaniment of the Spirit, enabled the crowd to clarify for themselves who was of God and who was operating under the power of the evil one.

SYMBOLIC ELEMENTS

Simon is depicted as a magician whereas Philip is represented as a true priesthood holder. One holds a fictional authority and the other the actual power of God. It has been suggested that Philip's healing of the diseased and his casting out of demonic spirits "represent the kingdom of God's battle against the demonic realm."[5] Lucifer has his false "priesthoods" and Christ's servants their true and living authority.

> Simon is one of a series of characters within the narrative who represent the powers opposed to the kingdom of God, and who by resisting the prophets provide the occasion for a confrontation and decisive demonstration of God's power over Satan and the demonic realm. In the Gospel, Judas provided the paradigm for such characters. His betrayal of Jesus was motivated by Satan entering his heart (Luke 22:3), and his rejection was symbolized by his use of possessions (Acts 1:17–25). In the Jerusalem Church, Ananias and Sapphira also allow Satan to enter their hearts, and their conspiracy against the Holy Spirit is symbolized by their holding back of possessions (Acts 5:2).

Now, in this new territory being claimed for God, the demonic powers in Samaria find their representative in the magician Simon. It is not much of a battle: the wonderworker whose deeds earlier had made crowds gasp and gather around him (8:10) is himself stunned by the thaumaturgic [or "miraculous"] power of Philip. He believes, is baptized, [and] follows Philip around like a devotee (8:13).[6]

Thus, Simon and Philip can represent the two opposite forces in the world: light and dark, good and evil, God and the devil.

APPLICATION AND ALLEGORIZATION

The most obvious application of this miracle has to do with the battle between light and dark or good and evil, which rages in the world around us. In the book of Revelation, we learn that in the last days, Satan's emissary will deceive those that dwell upon the earth "by the means of those miracles which he had power to do" (Revelation 13:14). God has all power and does great things in the Church and in the world He has created. However, Satan—whose power is so very limited—seeks to imitate God's power in an effort to deceive us. There will always be those who seek to draw us off the path, as Simon did those in Samaria. If we are spiritually astute we will be enabled to distinguish between God's messengers and the devil's. There is a distinctly different feeling attending that which is of God and that which is of the devil. The people of Samaria learned this, as must we if we wish to be protected from Satan's servants.

NOTES

1. See Fitzmyer (1998), 402.
2. According to Fitzmyer, the latter interpretation is the most likely. See Fitzmyer (1998), 402. See also Johnson (1992), 145.
3. See Lockyer (1965), 267.
4. See, for example, the late second-century "The Acts of Peter," which expounds on the Lucian account, giving some likely apocryphal details about the figure, Simon. "The Acts of Peter," 2:4, in Schneemelcher (2003), 2:290. See also Johnson (1992), 146.
5. Johnson (1992), 146.
6. Ibid.

Philip *Is* Caught Away *by the* Spirit *That* He *Is* Seen No More

ACTS 8:26–39

THE MIRACLE

The Spirit had guided Philip to Gaza where he found an Ethiopian court official of great authority sitting in his chariot and reading Isaiah chapter 53 while his driver moved the chariot along. The Spirit told Philip to run up to the man's chariot and talk to him. And so Philip did, asking the official if he understood what he was reading. His reply was simply this: "How can I, except someone should guide me?" The man invited Philip into his chariot and the disciple of Christ explained to the Ethiopian that the person Isaiah was speaking about was the Messiah. Philip then "preached unto him Jesus."

As the two traveled together, reading and talking, the Ethiopian saw a body of water and asked Philip to baptize him. Philip said, "If you believe with all of your heart, you may be baptized."[1] The court official declared, "I believe that Jesus Christ is the Son of God." For Philip, this was enough. He and his proselyte entered into the water and the man was baptized.

When they came up out of the water, "the Spirit of the Lord caught away Philip" that the official "saw him no more." He was gone. And so this Ethiopian convert "went on his way rejoicing," and Philip was found at Azotus, preaching in all of the cities.

BACKGROUND

There are two options for interpreting this passage. One is to say that after the soldier was baptized, there was no reason for Philip to remain in Gaza and so, under the influence of the Spirit, he quickly departed to Azotus to preach there.[2] The other possible reading is that Philip was somehow miraculously transported to another location to continue his work there. Elder McConkie explained, "The Spirit of the Lord caught away Philip. Nephi the son of Lehi and Nephi the son of Helaman both had this same experience (1 Nephi 11:1; Helaman 10:16–17). Apparently some similar experiences were known in Old Testament times (1 Kings 18:12; 2 Kings 2:16)."[3] Elder McConkie was not alone in reading this passage in terms of the miraculous.[4] And as noted, there seems to be ample scriptural support for the belief that God can instantaneously transport a non-translated being from one point to another. "Some interpreters see in this episode a parallel to the story of Jesus on the road with the two disciples going to Emmaus."[5] In that incident Jesus, after talking to the two disciples for a time, "vanished out of their sight" (Luke 24:31). Again, He was transported instantly to another location.[6] Herbert Lockyer pointed out that at the coming of Christ, the faithful Saints will also be "suddenly caught up from earth to heaven" (in a manner akin to how Philip was) so that they might descend with Him.[7]

Lucian commentator Joseph Fitzmyer suggests that the "angel of the Lord" in this miracle may well be God Himself "to make clear that this mission of Philip is God-inspired."[8]

The text refers to the Ethiopian as a "eunuch." In the ancient Near East, men who had been physically castrated often served as keepers of the royal harem and sometimes became high-ranking officials in the royal court. However, the Greek and Hebrew biblical words typically translated as "eunuch" do not always mean one who has been castrated.[9] Sometimes the term *eunuch* is used synonymously with words like *soldier* or *official*. With what little is given in this narrative, it is impossible to tell which Luke intends.

Azotus, to where Philip was transported, refers to one of the five ancient Philistine towns due west of Jerusalem.[10]

While the Bible tells us nothing regarding this Ethiopian's life after conversion, Eusebius (circa AD 260–340) claims that this "prince of the Ethiopians" became a missionary, "returning to his country, to proclaim the knowledge of God and the salutary abode of our Savior among men."[11]

SYMBOLIC ELEMENTS

Luke draws unspoken and yet hard-to-miss parallels between the inspired New Testament missionary Philip and the Old Testament prophet Elijah. For example, both receive visitations from the "angel of the Lord" (2 Kings 1:15; Acts 8:26), both are carried by the Spirit from place to place (1 Kings 18:12; Acts 8:39), and both are described as running down the road after the chariot of a powerful official (1 Kings 18:45–46; Acts 8:28–30).[12] Luke's intent in drawing these parallels may be nothing more than to let the reader know that he perceives Philip as being on par with Elijah in power, authority, and spiritual endowments.

Similarly, Luke—as he recounts this story—makes subtle connections between Philip and Jesus. For example, just as Jesus on the road to Emmaus opened the meaning of the scriptures so that His hearers could see Christ in the Old Testament passages being read (Luke 24:25–27, 32), so also Philip does this for his Ethiopian friend who knew not Christ (Acts 8:30–35). Again, Luke appears to be highlighting for his readers the fact that Philip was a man of God sent to do God's will, being endowed with God's wisdom and power.

APPLICATION AND ALLEGORIZATION

As with this official of Ethiopia, God sends to the sincere in heart His authorized messengers. There is no evidence that this man was praying for someone to be sent to him, only that he was studying God's word and trying to figure out both what it meant and how it applied to his personal life. In the process, the Father inspired one of His receptive souls to seek out this son of God and present to him the heavenly truths, which change lives and save souls. The history of the Church is replete with such "chance" encounters—which are not chance at all. At some point in your own personal or family history, the sincerity of one soul opened the windows of heaven, and God poured out His truth, which lead to *you* having the gospel today. That may have happened to one of your familial predecessors, or you may have been the cause of this conversion, but it is the process by which each of us eventually gains access to the restored gospel. We may say that our experience is not dramatic or miraculous like the Ethiopian official's was, but that is only because we are not able (as mortals) to see all of the strings God has pulled to give us this most precious gift. The promptings Philip felt and his miraculous departure at the end all attest to the fact that God is in the details of our conversions, in ways we cannot comprehend.

NOTES

1. Verse 37—wherein Philip asks the Ethiopian if he believes, and the official responds in the affirmative—is missing from many ancient manuscripts (see Johnson [1992], 157; Fitzmyer [1998], 414).
2. See Clarke (1846), 5:746 who leans toward this interpretation.
3. McConkie (1987-1988), 2:88.
4. See, for example, Pratt, *Journal of Discourses* 15:107, 21:307; Marshal, *Tyndale New Testament Commentaries*, 165; Lockyer (1965), 268 Nicoll (1983), 2:226–227.
5. Fitzmyer (1998), 410–411.
6. Of course, at that point in time Jesus would have been a resurrected being, not a mortal.
7. Lockyer (1965), 268.
8. See Fitzmyer (1998), 411, 335. For an examination of differing views on this, see our treatment of the phrase "angel of the Lord" in our discussion of Acts 5:12–20 on page 280.
9. See Fitzmyer (1998), 412; Johnson (1992), 155.
10. See Fitzmyer (1998), 415.
11. See Eusebius, Book 2, Chapter 1, Verse 13 in Cruse (1998), 37.
12. See Johnson (1992), 158.

SAUL *Is* HEALED *from* HIS BLINDNESS *by* ANANIAS

ACTS 9:17–18

THE MIRACLE

Saul of Tarsus loathed Christians and had been stridently perse-cuting them and seeking their death for a number of years. But during a trip to Damascus where he planned to engage in persecution, he was suddenly confronted with a heavenly light, and from that light he heard a voice that said, "Saul, why persecutest thou me?" Saul queried who it was that spoke to him, and he received the response, "I am Jesus whom thou persecutest."

This encounter with the resurrected Lord left Saul blind and affrighted, and so his traveling companions (who had seen the light but not heard the Lord's voice) led Saul by the hand to the city of Damascus where this zealous Pharisee threw himself into extended fasting and prayer.

There in Damascus was a faithful convert to Christianity by the name of Ananias. In a vision, the Lord appeared to him and com-manded him to go to a street called "Straight" and find the house of Judas. There Ananias would find Saul praying and seeking interven-tion and direction. Ananias was told that Saul would be expecting him, as God had given Saul a vision of Ananias coming to heal him of his blindness.

Knowing of the evils Saul had perpetrated against Christians, and believing that Saul had authority given him from the chief priests to arrest him because he was a Christian, Ananias was hesitant. But the Lord assured him that this was His will, for said He, Saul "is a chosen vessel unto me, to bear my name before the Gentiles, and kings, and the children of Israel."

So Ananias did as the Lord commanded and found Saul. He laid hands on him, saying, "Brother Saul, the Lord hath sent me, that thou mightest receive thy sight, and be filled with the Holy Ghost." Saul immediately received his eyesight again and rose up and requested baptism at the hands of Ananias. "And straightway he preached Christ in the synagogues, that he is the Son of God" (Acts 9:20).

BACKGROUND

The significance of this story is evidenced by the fact that Luke tells it three separate times in the book of Acts (see 9:1–20; 22:1–16; 26:9–18). Paul also speaks of it frequently (Galatians 1:11–16; 1 Corinthians 9:1c; 15:8–10; Philippians 3:6–8). "The turning of a Pharisaic persecutor into the apostle of the Gentiles is a paradox so profound that it requires multiple retellings."[1]

While the King James Version has the phrase "it is hard for thee to kick against the pricks" (Acts 9:5), this line does not appear in the best Greek manuscripts and was most likely added later because of a similar line in Acts 26:14.[2]

SYMBOLIC ELEMENTS

Saul is an archetype. He is the quintessential persecutor of God's Church and people. "The archpersecutor of Christians was transformed by the call of Christ into the 'apostle of the Gentiles' (Romans 11:13). The Lucian story of that call and transformation proclaims the power of the risen Christ in the life of a human being. 'Man proposes, but God disposes!' so runs the proverb."[3] Saul is a good reminder to the reader of God's power to change anyone, no matter their path and regardless of their past.

Blindness is often a symbol of misperception or misunderstanding. Sometimes that misapprehension comes because one is genuinely uninformed or deceived. At other times it is the result of one not wanting to know the truth. In the case of Saul, the "scales" on his eyes are metaphorical. They imply that he did not understand. Whether blinded by others or by his own obstinacy, he could not see the truth. "The Light that blinded him paradoxically relieved him of his spiritual blindness."[4] Saul's blindness wasn't really a punishment from God. Rather, it was a consequence of God's power manifest to one unworthy to endure it, and as "an indication of the helplessness of the one who was formerly a powerful opponent."[5] In other words, Saul's blindness reminds us of Christ's power in confronting our own rebelliousness and also the devil's. Saul's blindness and then subsequent sight qualify him as an Apostle—an "eye witness" of the resurrected Lord.[6]

The light Saul faced was itself a divine and important symbol in this narrative. Saul's cessation of maltreatment of Christians came because of the blinding light he encountered on the way to Damascus. "In all visible manifestation of deity recorded in the Old Testament— the burning at Horeb, the pillar of fire in the wilderness, the Holy of Holies—*light* was the magnificent symbol selected for the awful purpose, and most appropriate of Him who dwells in light unapproachable."[7] Light is a traditional symbol for the presence of God.[8]

Saul's fasting is a symbol, "an expression of penitential sorrow and contrition for his perversity."[9] It was a sign of his acknowledgment of his nothingness and his utter dependence upon God. One commentator explained, "Paul places himself in a position to receive further guidance from the Lord."[10] The three days of fasting Paul chose to endure was evidence of his changing heart and also of his desire to submit to the Being he now knew was his God.

Luke's note that Saul fasted—not just for a day but for three days— has been seen as potentially significant. "The explicit mention of 'three days' is provocative, especially since Luke is concerned to conform Paul to the image of Jesus, and Jesus declares such a fast for himself before his death and resurrection (Luke 22:16, 30)."[11] Elsewhere we read,

> As [Jesus's body] had lain three days in the darkness of the grave, Paul was blinded for three days in order to learn the full meaning of death itself and the law and all in which he trusted. During this period of seclusion, he was cut off from the visible world, conditions of outward life were suspended, and he became dependent on others to lead him around. Such blindness was not only the natural result of the vision of supernatural glory; it was divinely arranged and doubtless held for Paul a spiritual significance. It was emblematic of the light into which he was now to be brought. He had boasted of his light and of the fact that

he was a "guide of the blind" (Romans 2:19). Now, with his temporary blindness, there came outward light. Shining upon him an inward light. In spite of his knowledge of Scripture as a Jew, he was blind to their glorious truths. Now, the eyes of his understanding were to be opened. Although he never saw the sun for a season, Paul saw the Son of Righteousness and became His devoted slave.[12]

Bede (circa AD 672–735) wrote, "Since he had not believed that the Lord had conquered death by rising on the third day, [Saul] was now taught by his own experience of the replacement of three days of darkness by the return of the light."[13] Jesus is the light (D&C 88:6–13). Saul had struggled with this truth. He had fought against it. He had rejected the Atonement of Christ and had placed his trust for salvation elsewhere. Now three days into darkness, the light burst upon him again when a man, acting in the name of Christ, placed his hands upon Saul's head and using "the Holy Priesthood after the Order of the Son of God" (D&C 107:3) blessed Saul with the gift of sight—because Christ had specifically commanded this blessing be given. Could any man ask for a more deliberate receipt of Jesus's atoning gift in his personal life?

The name Ananias means "whom Jehovah has graciously given." For Saul, Ananias's visit, healing blessing, and subsequent baptism of him are each acts of "grace," which Jehovah "graciously gave" the former archpersecutor. We each have our Ananias from time to time, reminding us through intervention of God's gracious gifts to us.

APPLICATION AND ALLEGORIZATION

Gamaliel, Saul's tutor, had declared that the Jews should leave the Christians alone. Said he, if they are not of God, they will dwindle away and cease to have any influence upon the world. If, on the other hand, they *are* of God, then anyone who seeks to fight them will ultimately find himself fighting God. Wise counsel! The significance of this advice and its relationship to Saul's preconversion campaign against Christians is explained by one commentator who wrote,

Saul's conversion . . . is the paradigmatic expression of the ironic truth spoken by Gamaliel ([Acts] 5:38–39): no one worked harder to extirpate [or completely destroy] the messianic movement than this agent (as Luke has it) of the chief priest; his failure to stop it and his being transformed into its boldest advocate stands for Luke and his readers as the surest sign that the crucified Messiah was indeed Lord, that their movement "was from God."[14]

Perhaps there is a message in Saul's experience that relates to our own lives. I have known many who are "cause driven." Standing up for a good cause is noble, and at times it can be a good thing. However, as this zealous Pharisee learned, there is danger in being driven by causes if we are not certain they are indeed good. No doubt Saul was quite shocked to learn that his "cause" against Christians was of the devil. We should exhibit caution lest we learn this same lesson.

One commentator on the miracles wrote, "Paul had listened to Stephen's dying words, 'I see the heavens opened, and the Son of Man standing at the right hand of God;' now the persecutor himself sees Him and experiences the transforming power of a personal vision of Christ."[15] Imperfect as we are—and nearly none being as rebellious as was Saul—we nevertheless will each hear the witness of those who *know*: living prophets and apostles. Will we allow those words to take root in our hearts so as to change us? Or will we ignore them, as Saul did with Stephen's testimony? Saul did not heed the glow of Stephen's face or his witness of Christ. If, like Saul, we chart our own path and reject the words and warnings of God's messengers, that may eventually lead us to the feet of God wherein we could hear His voice asking us why we did *not* heed the words of His anointed ones. For certainly the goad will prick more sharply if we struggle against it![16]

Jesus informed Saul that to persecute the members of His Church is equivalent to persecuting Him. Bede the Venerable (circa AD 672–735) wrote, "He did not say, 'Why do you persecute my members?' but 'Why did you persecute me?' . . . He declared that kindness bestowed upon his members are also done to him when he said, 'I was hungry and you gave me to eat,' and he added in explanation, 'So long as you did it to one of the least of mine, you did it to me.'"[17] When we treat others in an unkind or non-Christlike way, we are acting like the preconversion Saul. We can never be unkind to one of God's children and secure the favor of the Father. He loves all of us, and for any of us to be abusive, intentionally hurtful, or unchristian is to ensure His displeasure.

On a related note, Ananias addressed a man whom he believed

to be one of the worst of people as "Brother Saul." What comfort this must have brought to Saul's trembling heart. "The *blasphemer* is now a brother. The stranger is now one of the family."[18] Trusting in the Lord's words and request, Ananias forgave a man entirely undeserving of his clemency. Would you and I have that much compassion? Would we so readily bless, heal, and serve someone who had sought to murder, destroy, and defame our faith and family? Ananias's Christianity is evident for all to see. May we be so forgiving, so Christlike toward our enemies!

One text reminds us, "When we speak of conversions, we often think of Saul's dramatic experience. . . . But other Christians have a quiet or slowly increasing conviction. . . . However we come to Jesus, He transforms our lives if we are willing to make them a mission for Him. Whether we fall down on the road to Damascus or simply feel the still, small voice that leads us into faith, we will never be the same."[19] All who truly live the gospel know this is true. We cannot be faithful and yet miss the power of Jesus's influence in our lives. Christ changes us! He lifts us! He transforms us! While the events leading up to our gaining a testimony may seem very different from Saul's, nonetheless, the impact of Christ in our lives can be as significant. He can make us a powerful witness of Him, an engaged missionary, and a recipient of the gifts of the Spirit—or anything else He needs us to be. If our conversion is real, then the change will be significant.

NOTES

1. Johnson (1992), 166.
2. See Johnson (1992), 163; Fitzmyer (1998), 425.
3. Fitzmyer (1998), 422.
4. Johnson (1992), 165.
5. Fitzmyer (1998), 426.
6. Regarding apostles being "special witnesses" of Christ, see Smith, *History of the Church*, 2:195–96; Smith, *Gospel Doctrine*, 178; Smith, "The Twelve Apostles," *An Address to Seminary and Institute Faculty*, 6, cited in Roy W. Doxey, *Latter-day Prophets and the Doctrine and Covenants*, 4:28; Bruce R. McConkie, *Mormon Doctrine*, 46–47, s.v., "Apostle"; Boyd K. Packer, *Conference Report*, April 1971, 122–25.
7. Locker (1965), 271.
8. See Johnson (1992), 162.
9. Nicoll (1983), 2:234.
10. Johnson (1992), 164.

11. Johnson (1992), 164.

12. Locker (1965), 272.

13. Bede the Venerable, "Commentary on the Acts of the Apostles," 9.9, in Martin (2006), 105.

14. Johnson (1992), 166.

15. Locker (1965), 272.

16. See Locker (1965), 272.

17. Bede the Venerable, "Commentary on the Acts of the Apostles," 9.4, in Martin (2006), 103–104. See also Basil the Great, "Letter 8," in Martin (2006), 104.

18. Locker (1965), 272.

19. McQuade (2008), 172.

PETER HEALS *a* MAN
BEDRIDDEN *for* EIGHT YEARS

ACTS 9:33–34

THE MIRACLE

Peter was visiting members of the Church in Lydda (near the plain of Sharon). While there, he met a man with the palsy who had been bedridden for some eight years. Peter said to him, "Aeneas, Jesus Christ maketh thee whole: arise, and make thy bed." Immediately the man rose up, and many turned to the Lord because of his healing.

BACKGROUND

Lydda was an old town known as Lōd in Old Testament times (see Ezra 2:33; 1 Chronicles 8:12). It is northwest of Jerusalem and sits on the crossroad from Jerusalem to Joppa. By the third century, it was heavily Christian, though its name had been changed to Diospolis (the "city of Zeus").[1]

Sharon was a plain that stretched "along the coast of Palestine northwest of Lydda from Joppa to Caesarea Maritima."[2]

Once healed, Peter commanded Aeneas to "make his bed." Commentators have typically seen this as representative of his complete and instantaneous healing. Thus, one commentator rendered the meaning of the charge as follows: "Now and at once make thy bed for thyself—an act which hitherto others have done for thee."[3]

As Aeneas is a Greek name, most commentators assume he was a convert to Christianity. His conversion would likely have taken place prior to Peter's arrival, making him someone who knew of and believed in the name of Christ (through which Peter healed him). The text, however, does not state this and so we are left to conjecture.

As for Aeneas's bed, we read, "The word used here for the bed of the paralytic is that used of the couches or pallets of the lower class and 'suggests the thought that poverty also was added to his sufferings.'"[4] Thus, his physical trial had brought temporal trials with it, as is so often the case.

SYMBOLIC ELEMENTS

The number eight is traditionally associated with the concepts of resurrection,[5] new beginnings,[6] rebirth,[7] and baptism.[8] Because of its association with resurrection, it is sometimes also seen as the number of Christ. One expert on the symbolism of numbers wrote, "Christ rose from the dead on 'the first day of the week,' that was of necessity the eighth day."[9] Since for all those born in the covenant baptism is to be performed at the age of eight (D&C 68:27), the connection between the symbols of baptism, resurrection, Christ, and the number eight are natural and appropriate. Indeed, the reason the number eight is utilized as a symbol for Christ, resurrection, baptism, and new beginnings is because they are all intricately related ideas.

Aeneas symbolizes all who are spiritually sick—as all humankind is. In the eighth century, Bede the Venerable (circa AD 672–735) described what he perceived Aeneas as symbolizing. Bede wrote,

> This Æneas signifies the ailing human race, at first weakened by [pursuing] pleasure but healed by the work and words of the apostles. . . . Anyone who embraces the unstable joys of the present is as though flattened upon his bed, devoid of energy for twice times four years. For the bed is that sluggishness in which the sick and weak soul takes its rest in the delights of the body, that is, and in all worldly pleasures.[10]

APPLICATION AND ALLEGORIZATION

Peter emphasized that Christ was the one that made Aeneas whole. His eight years of sickness seems related to this truth. As we noted above, the number eight was an ancient symbol of Christ and rebirth. And it is Christ, and Christ alone, who can change us from fallen and broken humans into healed and happy followers of the Lord. It is He alone who can make us Christian in our love and lives. He changes hearts and thereby changes our whole being.

This miracle's wording reminds us of Christ's concern for and attention to "the one." It is reminiscent of Christ's council to "leave the ninety and nine in the wilderness, and go after that which is lost" (Luke 15:4). Thus, Peter said to the man with palsy, "Aeneas, Jesus Christ maketh *thee* whole" (Acts 9:34; italics added).

> **Thee**. That personal pronoun would remind [Aeneas] that although he was a suffering saint, through the years of his physical disability the Lord has not forgotten him. He knew all about the condition of Æneas and the stance where his bed could be found, and He directed Peter to it. *Thee*. Do we not bless Him for the personal address and singular number? He separates *you* from all around you. He knows all about *you*. "The Son of God who loveth *me*," Paul could write (Galatians 2:20). So He knows *your* need and can complete *your* cure. He has a care for *you* in the separateness of *your* temperament, in the plague of *your* heart, in the possibilities of *your* life.[11]

What a beautiful truth! Christ knows *me*! He knows *you*! There is something personal about His concern and love for every one of His Father in Heaven's children—His own spirit brothers and sisters. And in our most difficult hours, we—like Aeneas—can believe that Jesus will send us the help we need to endure or overcome the trial of the moment. As the Lord Himself declared, "With God all things are possible" (Matthew 19:26).

After healing him, Peter commanded Aeneas, "Make up thy bed." One church father suggested a measure of symbolism in this command: "Spiritually this informs us that whoever has received into his heart the firm foundation of faith will not only shake off the torpor in which he has been lying idle but will also produce the good works in which he will be able to rest after his [mortal] toil."[12] If we are truly converted, we will get to work blessing others. For, "it becometh every man who hath been warned to warn his neighbor" (D&C 88:81).

One text on the miracle asks an important question about this healing and its implications in our personal lives as followers of Christ. The healing of Aeneas caused a significant number of people to "turn to the Lord." Is the impact of what Christ has done for us in our personal lives such that it is producing a similar effect upon those who know us? Are others more interested in Christ, the Church, or personal faithfulness because they see in our life and demeanor the power of Christ-centered living? Do we exhibit the Savior in "character and conduct"? These are important questions for each of us to ask ourselves. The answers can be potentially painful. But therein is our invitation for change.[13]

NOTES

1. See Fitzmyer (1998), 444. See also Johnson (1992), 177.
2. Fitzmyer (1998), 445. See also Johnson (1992), 177.
3. Nicoll (1983), 2:246. See also Lockyer (1965), 274.
4. Lockyer (1965), 273.
5. See Cooper (1995), 118; Johnston (1990), 75; Julien (1996), 135 Bullinger (1967), 200; Davis (1968), 122.
6. See Johnston (1990), 75; Cirlot (1971), 233; Julien (1996), 135; Bullinger (1967), 196, 200.
7. See Julien (1996), 135.
8. Cirlot (1971), 233; McConkie and Parry (1990), 46. "According to Clement of Alexandria, Christ placed those whom he gave a second life under the sign of eight" (Julien [1996], 135).
9. Bullinger (1967), 200.
10. Bede, "Commentary on the Acts of the Apostles," 9.33, in Martin (2006), 115.
11. Lockyer (1965), 274; bolding added, but italics in the original.
12. Bede, "Commentary on the Acts of the Apostles," 9.34, in Martin (2006), 115.
13. See Locker (1965), 274. See also McQuade (2008), 173.

TABITHA *Is* RAISED *from the* DEAD *by* PETER

ACTS 9:36-42

THE MIRACLE

While Peter was yet in Lydda where he had recently healed Aeneas, a female member of the Church passed away in neighboring Joppa. Tabitha was a good woman who blessed many lives through her charity.

After her passing, and after her body had been washed and prepared for burial, the members of the Church in Joppa—realizing that the senior Apostle was yet nearby—sent two men to request Peter come as soon as he was able. When Peter received word of the appeal, he went without delay.

Peter found Tabitha's body in seeming repose in an upper room in Joppa. Widows who were mourning her passing surrounded her. In their inconsolable state, they gushed to the Apostle about all Tabitha had done for them in life and of the many garments she had made them over the years. Indeed, many of the mourners were actually wearing clothing the deceased had provided them.

Peter cleared the room of the weeping women and knelt down next to the body of Tabitha. He began praying and then turned to this departed sister and said, "Tabitha, arise" (verse 40). She immediately opened her eyes and when she saw Peter, she sat up. The prophet gave Tabitha his hand, helped her to her feet, and "presented her alive" to those without the room (verse 41). And many in Joppa believed in the Lord because of this miracle.

BACKGROUND

The name Tabitha is the Aramaic version of the Greek appellation Dorcas, both of which mean "gazelle."[1] One commentator suggested, "It was the custom at this period for Jews to have two names, one Hebrew and the other Greek or Latin. As Joppa was both a Gentile and Jewish town, it was usual for people to have two names."[2]

At the time of Tabitha's death, Peter was staying with members in Lydda, which was less than ten miles from Joppa.[3] Thus, presumably he could have arrived by Tabitha's side on the day he was sent for and no later than the day after. One commentary on the Greek pointed out, "Outside Jerusalem three days might elapse between the death and burial, but in Jerusalem no corpse lay over night [*sic*]."[4] It is therefore assumed that Peter, whose place of residency was the holy city, likely rushed to Tabitha's side when he learned of her passing.

Tabitha is said to have sewn "coats and garments" for the widows who were mourning her death. The Greek word translated as "coats" is said to mean literally "an undergarment, usually worn next to the skin."[5] Commentators suggest that these undergarments were "close fitting."[6] If they had any ritual or ceremonial meaning, the text is unclear, but the language is curious.

SYMBOLIC ELEMENTS

Two men were sent on behalf of Tabitha's well-being. One commentator suggested, "The sending of two men may reflect the command of Jesus (Luke 10:1) and community practice in early Christianity (Acts 3:1; 8:14; 13:2; 22:23)."[7] If the sending of these two is more than coincidental, then it symbolically reminds us that God sends forth those who have the healing message "two by two." As Jesus, Paul, and Moses all acknowledged, "In the mouth of two or three witnesses shall every word be established" (Matthew 18:16; 2 Corinthians 13:1; Deuteronomy 17:6). In this case, the "two" were sent to get the agent of healing, Peter. But the act is nonetheless the same; their mission was a saving one.

Peter's foray into the coastal city of Joppa and away from Jerusalem seems to anticipate the act of taking the gospel to the Gentiles, a boundary that will be crossed when Cornelius is converted and when the council at Jerusalem is held.

Notice that Peter tells both Æneas and Tabitha to "rise up" (*anastēthi*), using the [Greek] word associated so frequently with the resurrection of Jesus. The reader is given an early signal that the conversion of the Gentiles that Luke will now relate is to be understood similarly as coming from . . . the power of the resurrected one, and also as itself an extension of the "resurrection/rebuilding" of Israel (Acts 15:16–17).[8]

Thus, symbolically, one sees the expansion of the Church as potentially foreshadowed by Peter's trip to perform healings in regions outside of where the Church was firmly established.[9]

Peter here is taking the role of Christ. He is acting in His stead and name—as all priesthood holders do in any ordinance or priesthood blessing. And Luke seems to be painting a picture for the reader that is designed to remind us that Peter now has the mantle and priesthood keys Christ placed upon him. "There is considerable resemblance between this account and the raising of [Jairus's] little girl by Jesus (Luke 8:49–56): the use of messengers, the weeping bystanders, the exclusion of the outsiders from the room, the call to rise ('Little girl, rise up,' Luke 8:54), the taking by the hand."[10] This same source adds this: "It is fairly obvious that the healing of a paralytic and the resuscitation of the widow are meant to echo the similar accounts told about Jesus (Luke 5:17–26; 7:11–16), and the still earlier prototypes provided by Elijah and Elisha (1 Kings 17:17–24; 2 Kings 4:32–37). Peter is validated once more as an authentic representative of the line of prophets who 'work signs and wonders among the people.'"[11] Luke is calculating to remind his readers (through this Petrine miracle) that the prophets speak and act on behalf of Christ, and He works and acts through them.[12]

APPLICATION AND ALLEGORIZATION

We learn that Tabitha was a philanthropist, per se. While the King James Version is less clear than the Greek on this point, nevertheless, it is clear that she used her gifts to bless the poor and that this was her common or continual practice.

Of the use she made of her substance and time we are fully informed. She employed herself in administering to the necessities of the poor, who were continually before her eyes. How she emulated the example of her Master who "went about doing good" as she diffused good will all around her! She not only did good *works*, but was full of *cheer* and made her exercise of benevolence her habitual practice, as the real force of the Greek implies.[13]

Tabitha was the epitome of what the faithful sisters of the Relief Society do today. As the motto of the Society states, "Charity never faileth." And Tabitha lived that truth. Do we? In a time when fast offerings—if they had been given—would have been given "in kind," Tabitha was generous with her excess, showering those less fortunate with what God had freely given her. Again, it's a clear invitation to you and me.

Related to this is a point made by several of the Church fathers, namely that "Luke would not have provided the meaning of the name" Tabitha or Dorcas "if he had not known there was strong symbolism in it."[14] The fathers saw the meaning of the name ("gazelle") as representative of Tabitha's character: "active and wakeful as a gazelle."[15] She is a symbol for all those who are "anxiously engaged in a good cause, and" who "do many things of their own free will, and bring to pass much righteousness" (D&C 58:27). Are we like Tabitha? Or do we need to be coaxed and encouraged to consecrate ourselves to the cause of the kingdom?

Peter dismissed everyone from the room of Tabitha before he knelt and requested the Lord's blessing, and before he acted as instrument in God's miraculous workings. As we contemplate ordinances within the Church, we may find a subtle lesson in this regarding how the sacred is not for "general consumption." For the Spirit to work its wonders, the audience often needs to be small. And while that is not always the case, it seems true to say that more often than not the most miraculous occurrences in our lives—the most sacred and spiritual experiences—will not come while in a large and noisy group, but rather in a quiet and set-apart time and place wherein the Lord's Spirit can be felt in an unrestrained manner.

The recipients of Tabitha's goodness and generosity praised her after she was gone and held up the tokens of her life of service and holiness—in this case, the garments she had made them. We must never do good so as to be noticed, for this was the sin of Ananias and Sapphira; nevertheless, this miracle story does make one ask: What is the legacy I have left for my posterity? A journal? Family history?

Service in the kingdom? Family traditions? A record of my testimony and spiritual experiences? What have I left that my posterity would be able to hold up as evidence that "this our parents knew, loved, and served the Lord"?

NOTES

1. See Johnson (1992), 177; Fitzmyer (1998), 445; Lockyer (1965), 275; McQuade (2008), 174.
2. Lockyer (1965), 275.
3. See Fitzmyer (1998), 445; Nicoll (1983), 2:247.
4. Nicoll (1983), 2:247.
5. See Thayer (1999), 669, s.v. #5509.
6. Nicoll (1983), 2:248.
7. Johnson (1992), 178.
8. Ibid., 180.
9. See Johnson (1992), 179.
10. Johnson (1992), 178.
11. Ibid., 180.
12. See Johnson (1992), 179. See also Fitzmyer (1998), 445; Nicoll (1983), 2:248–49.
13. Lockyer (1965), 275.
14. Bede, "Commentary on the Acts of the Apostles," 9.36, in Martin (2006), 115–16.
15. Chrysostom, "Homilies on the Acts of the Apostles," 21, in Martin (2006), 115. See also Bede, "Commentary on the Acts of the Apostles," 9.36, in Martin (2006), 115–16.

PETER *Is* DELIVERED *from* PRISON

ACTS 12:7–11

THE MIRACLE

Herod had been harassing the followers of Christ. He had put James, the brother of John, to death by the sword, and he had arrested Peter because he knew that it pleased the Jews.

It was Passover and the senior Apostle was languishing in jail. He had four squads of soldiers guarding him and was kept secured in double irons. It was the intention of Herod to bring Peter before his adversaries after the Passover had concluded. The members of the Church, aware of these happenings, prayed fervently for their prophet.

The night preceding the day that Herod had planned on dragging Peter before the angry crowds, Peter was asleep between two soldiers. Outside of his cell were stationed sentries. Peter was securely chained and thoroughly guarded so as to make his escape impossible.

Suddenly Peter felt someone tapping him on his side. When the Apostle awoke, he discovered that it was the angel of the Lord that had awakened him and Peter noticed that the cell was filled with light. Miraculously, the chains fell from Peter's wrists as the angel commanded him, "Hurry! Get up! Put on your belt, sandals, and cloak, and follow me." Peter followed the angel, though in a state of bewilderment as he did so. The prophet was unsure if this was actually happening or if he was seeing a vision.

The angel led Peter past the first sentinel and then by a second one. They arrived at the heavy iron gate, which led to the city, and suddenly it opened by itself, allowing them to pass. As they moved along one of the streets, the angel abruptly departed, leaving Peter by himself. Suddenly the Lord's prophet realized this was no dream and certainly not just a vision. Peter thought to himself, "I know of a surety that the Lord hath sent his angel, and hath delivered me out of the hand of Herod," and out of the hands of those Jews who were anxiously expecting his arraignment.

BACKGROUND

The "King Herod" mentioned here is Herod Agrippa I (10 BC–AD 44), the grandson of Herod the Great (who had sought the death of Jesus).[1]

The James who is said to have been slain in this story is James the son of Zebedee, once a counselor in the First Presidency of the Church. He is also sometimes called "James the Great," so as to distinguish him from a number of other men by the same name: "James the Less" (Mark 15:40), James the son of Alphaeus (Acts 1:13), and James the brother of the Lord (Galatians 1:19).[2] Eusebius (circa AD 260–340) shares a tradition about the death of James, which he attributes to Clement of Alexandria (circa AD 150–215) and the early Church, namely that "the [guard] who led James to the judgment seat, moved by the way James bore his testimony to the faith, confessed himself to be a Christian. Both therefore . . . were led away to die. On their way, [his jailer] entreated James to be forgiven of him, and James considering a little, replied, 'Peace be to thee,' and kissed him. Then both were beheaded at the same time."[3]

Luke informs us that it was Herod's intention (after the Passover and Feast of the Unleavened Bread were over) to bring Peter before "the people." The book of Acts does not expound on what exactly this means, but it is assumed by scholars that Herod was planning a public trial of some kind, at which the crowds would be in attendance as was the case with Jesus some years before (Luke 23:1–5).[4] Likely, Herod thought this would stir up more anti-Christian sentiment if he sentenced him "openly to death before the people."[5]

Regarding the "angel of the Lord" who freed Peter from jail, as we have noted previously, the phrase (in the Greek) is equivalent to a standard Hebrew phrase that suggests the presence of God. It implies that God Himself is dealing with humankind.[6] Peter ascribes his deliverance to "the Lord" (when he recounts the miracle to others), stating that "the Lord had brought him out of the prison" (Acts 12:17) rather than an angel. Perhaps Peter believed this angel was the Lord, or perhaps he simply assumed that it was a messenger of the Lord acting by divine investiture of authority.[7] The text is unclear, though many scholars perceive it as the former rather than the latter.[8]

SYMBOLIC ELEMENTS

Peter is said to be guarded by "four squads." As noted before, four is the standard scriptural number for "geographic fullness or totality."[9] Though the use of the number here is likely intended literally, the symbolic meaning of the number would be representative of the idea that Peter was "totally" or "fully" guarded. Herod had left nothing to chance. Every precaution had been taken to guarantee that this coveted prisoner did not escape.

Herod can symbolically remind us of the enemy who fights outwardly against God—and even seems successful for a time—but is ultimately destroyed. Just as Herod met a terrible death (Acts 12:23), Lucifer, the "enemy to all righteousness" (Alma 34:23), will also meet a terrible end. Our responsibility is to trust in that promise as foreshadowed in this miracle.

As we might expect, chains are common symbols for "bondage" or "slavery."[10] They can represent "that which ties, restrains . . . or enslaves."[11] One text notes that they often represent "vice personified." "In Renaissance allegory a shackled or otherwise bound figure symbolizes man enslaved by his baser, earthly desires."[12] While this latter meaning has nothing to do with the historical event, it seems germane to the application of the miracle.

Sleep is sometimes a sign of spiritual health.[13] One author suggested that it is a symbol for "a clear conscience and the assurance that God is with you."[14] Thus the Psalmist wrote, "I will . . . lay me down in peace, and sleep: for thou, Lord, only makest me dwell in safety" (Psalm 4:8). "Peter slept, undisturbed by the fear of coming martyrdom. Here we have a picture of clam repose as of one to whom God had given the sleep of His beloved (Psalm 127:2)."[15]

APPLICATION AND ALLEGORIZATION

James was slain, but Peter was preserved. We cannot say what God's purposes are and why He preserved one Apostle but allowed another to be taken. What we can draw from this episode, however, is the truth that righteousness does not bring the promise of physical protection. God has a plan and purpose for each of us. And though we may hope for physical preservation from our enemies, as James and Peter learned, that is not what the Lord has in mind for all of us. Both men died as martyrs: James beheaded, and Peter crucified. We will each have trials and, in the omniscient mind of God, some will be spared the worst while others will be required to take up the cross. It is not our place to ask why, only to embrace the perfect and just will of the Lord. As one commentator put it, "That God delivered Peter proves His power to have delivered James. That He did not deliver James proves that the death of James was within the compass of His will, and we know that in the great unveiling all will be seen to have been right."[16]

The chains with which Peter was bound are a good representation of those things that bind each of us during our mortal experience. And just as God was able to free Peter from a seemingly impossible scenario, He can free each of us from that which binds us—through our faith in Him and through the faith of others who pray on our behalf (just as others prayed for Peter). And as God moved the heavy iron gates without the assistance of human hands, He can also move out of our way those large obstacles that seemingly prevent us from doing His will. All we must do is faithfully follow the Spirit as Peter faithfully followed the angel.

As Peter enjoyed peace and even rest in the most trying of circumstances, God can bring you and me that same peace in our weaknesses and challenges. Peter's life was right with the Lord and that enabled him to have the security that comes through the Comforter. As we align our wills and our lives with God's, we have the promise that His peace will be with us, including during the difficult times. The Lord has promised, "Peace I leave with you, my peace I give unto you: not as the world giveth, give I unto you. Let not your heart be troubled, neither let it be afraid" (John 14:27).

Peter became aware of the light in the prison cell and the angel that was the source of that light. However, the guards who lay chained to him were oblivious to the illumination and the angel that stood before them. One of those in the prison that night was personally prepared to receive the heaven-sent message, and the others were not even though they each lay in close proximity to each other. Are you living your life in accord with the Spirit so that you are receptive to the divinely sent messages? Or are you simply in close proximity to those who are receiving the witness of the Spirit while you lay spiritually asleep and unaware?

NOTES

1. See Fitzmyer (1998), 486; Ogden and Skinner (1998), 61; Johnson (1992), 210.
2. See Fitzmyer (1998), 487; Ogden and Skinner (1998), 61. Another James is mentioned in Acts 12:17. This one is believed to be either the half-brother of Jesus or the son of Alphaeus. See Ogden and Skinner (1998), 63.
3. Eusebius, Book 2, Chapter 9, Verses 2–3, in Cruse (1998), 44. See also Fitzmyer (1998), 211; Nicoll (1983), 2:272–73.
4. See Fitzmyer (1998), 487.
5. Nicoll (1983), 2:273. Chrysostom said Herod "wanted to make a spectacle of the slaughter" of Peter ("Homiles on the Acts of the Apostles," 26, in Martin [2006], 152).
6. See Fitzmyer (1998), 335; Longenecker, in Gaebelein (1976–92), 9:319; Johnson (1992), 97.
7. See McConkie (1987–88), 2:117.
8. For an examination of differing views on this see our treatment of the phrase "angel of the Lord" in our discussion of Acts 5:12–20.
9. Gaskill (2003), 119–20.
10. Cooper (1982), 32.
11. Todeschi (1995), 61.
12. Hall (1974), 121.
13. See Ryken, Wilhoit, and Longman (1998), 799.
14. Madsen (1989), 30.
15. Lockyer (1965), 278. See also Chrysostom, "Catena on the Acts of the Apostles," 12.6–7, in Martin (2006), 153.
16. Lockyer (1965), 278. Lockyer is citing a commentator by the name of Campbell Morgan.

HEROD *Is* SMITTEN

ACTS 12:23

THE MIRACLE

Herod, still baffled and upset over the miraculous prison escape of Peter, made a trip to Caesarea, where his life would end in dramatic fashion. He had come before the people, arrayed in his royal robes and seated upon his throne, that he might address them. As he discoursed to them, clothed in all of his regal splendor, the crowd shouted out that Herod "spoke with the voice of God, not of a human being!" Because Herod did not ascribe honor to God but rather to himself, he was struck dead by "the angel of the Lord"—eaten alive by worms.

BACKGROUND

As to the nature of Herod's death, one ancient Christian text states, "Now Herod died by the worst form of death."[1] Luke informs us here that "he was eaten of worms, and gave up the ghost." Similarly, Josephus and Eusebius each record that Herod contracted some unknown disease, the symptoms of which were as follows: a constant burning fever; an insatiable appetite and thirst that could not be satisfied, no matter how much he ate or drank; an inflammation of the intestines; pain in the colon; a swelling in his feet and belly combined with some sort of clear discharge from those same parts; worms in the lower part of his abdomen; great difficulty breathing; a highly offensive stench associated with his breath; convulsions; itching all over his body; a persistent cough; a tendency for his eyes to roll back into his head; and an uncommonly strong contagiousness.[2] How much of this is hyperbole or legend and how much historical fact, we cannot tell. But what seems clear is this: God struck Herod dead. And his death was not as Doctrine and Covenants 42:46 describes the death of a righteous man or woman: "And it shall come to pass that those that die in me shall not taste of death, for it shall be sweet unto them."

The "angel of the Lord" that freed Peter from prison is now said to have struck Herod dead. If this angel is not Jehovah Himself, he is certainly His emissary, carrying out His will by divine investiture of authority. Notably, "the 'smiting' here has its usual connotation of divine retribution. It recalls especially the killing of the hundred and eighty-five thousand Assyrians in one night by the angel of the Lord (2 Kings 19:35)."[3]

SYMBOLIC ELEMENTS

The worm is a consistently negative symbol in the Bible. It often represents things like "disease" and "decay," but also "death," "dissolution," and the "torture" or "dehumanizing" of a person.[4] One commentator suggested that the worm is a symbol of "that which is despised" and also of God's "judgment."[5]

APPLICATION AND ALLEGORIZATION

Herod reaped the rewards of his own behaviors. He selfishly persecuted Christians because he saw political benefit in it. He put to death certain apostles while seeking the death of others. And he embraced accolades that proclaimed him a god, if not actually placing him *above* God. Such seems heinous enough to justify his demise. His death by worms, therefore, was potentially a symbolic message about the divine judgment he had received. That being said, perhaps we are at times somewhat like Herod. We each have been guilty at some point in our lives of tearing down others in order to make ourselves look good in the eyes of a friend, colleague, or boss. Each of us has sought the harm of another because we perceived that person as an enemy or threat. And so often we fail to give God the credit for things we cannot rightly take credit for—whether that be our attainments, our intellect, our looks, our success, or our spirituality. No, we are not as evil as was Herod! But each of us is guilty of behaviors that bring us a measure of spiritual "death" or "decay." At times we each "dehumanize" others and in so doing, dehumanize ourselves. Let us remember the words of Abinadi:

> Even this mortal shall put on immortality, and this corruption shall put on incorruption, and shall be brought to stand before the bar of God, to be judged of him according to their works whether they be good or whether they be evil—
>
> If they be good, to the resurrection of endless life and happiness; and if they be evil, to the resurrection of endless damnation, being delivered up to the devil, who hath subjected them, which is damnation—
>
> Having gone according to their own carnal wills and desires; having never called upon the Lord while the arms of mercy were extended towards them; for the arms of mercy were extended towards them, and they would not; they being warned of their iniquities and yet they would not depart from them; and they were commanded to repent and yet they would not repent.
>
> And now, ought ye not to tremble and repent of your sins, and remember that only in and through Christ ye can be saved? (Mosiah 16:10–13)

It is curious that immediately after telling of the death of "King Herod," Luke records these words: "But the word of God grew and multiplied." What a contrast! He who would be worshiped as a god suddenly finds that the world moves on without him. God's work and will cannot be thwarted. Man's can and will. If we choose sin and self-aggrandizement over compliance and compassion, we too will bring upon ourselves accountability. Unlike Herod, may we ever remember the Lord's words: "In nothing doth man offend God, or against none is his wrath kindled, save those who confess not his hand in all things" (D&C 59:21). For surely "pride goeth before destruction, and an haughty spirit before a fall" (Proverbs 16:18).

NOTES

1. "The History of Joseph the Carpenter" V. 9, in Roberts and Donaldson (1994), 8:389. This document, traditionally dated to somewhere around the third to fifth century AD, fancifully claims within its pages that it was originally orally dictated by Jesus to His Apostles, who then drafted the record and deposited it in a library in Jerusalem. See Roberts and Donaldson (1994), 8:352, 388.
2. Josephus, "Antiquities of the Jews" Book 17, Chapter 6, Verse 5, 365. See also Eusebius, Book 1, Chapter 8, Verses 5–9, 11, 14 in *Eusebius' Ecclesiastical History*, 23–24; Farrar, *Life of Christ*, 62, 64–65.

3. Johnson (1992), 215. For an examination of differing views on who the "angel of the Lord" might be, see our treatment of the phrase in our discussion of Acts 5:12–20.

4. See Ryken, Wilhoit, and Longman (1998), 969; Cooper (1982), 195; Cirlot (1971), 379.

5. See Connor (1992), 182.

PAUL SMITES ELYMAS
with BLINDNESS

ACTS 13:4–13

THE MIRACLE

Paul and Barnabas were proclaiming the word of God to Jews and Gentiles in Salamis, Paphos, and throughout the island of Cyprus. In the process, they encountered a Jewish man who was a sorcerer and who falsely professed to be a prophet. This man was in the service of the Roman proconsul, Sergius Paulus, who himself was a sincere and intelligent man interested in the message Paul and Barnabas were preaching.

Concerned that Sergius might convert to Christianity, this sorcerer—whose name was Bar-Jesus but who was often called Elymas—opposed Paul and Barnabas. However Paul, being filled with the Spirit, looked Elymas in the eye and said, "You deceitful fraud and enemy of all righteousness—you child of the devil! Will you ever stop twisting the ways of the Lord, making that which is straight crooked?" And then Paul uttered the following punishment upon Elymas: "And now, behold, the hand of the Lord is upon thee, and thou shalt be blind, not seeing the sun for a season" (verse 11). As Paul pronounced, so it came to pass. The sorcerer was immediately struck blind and he went about gropingly, looking for someone to lead him by the hand.

When the proconsul, Sergius Paulus, saw what had happened to Elymas, he was astonished and believed the teachings of Christianity.

BACKGROUND

In Paul's day, Salamis was a port town on the east coast of the Mediterranean island Cyprus and the chief city on the island. Paphos—which was about 108 miles from Salamis on the western end of the island—was (under the Romans) the seat of the governor of Cyprus.[1]

From AD 46 until AD 48, Sergius Paulus was the proconsul, or governor, of a senatorial province, which gives us a sense of when this miracle took place.[2]

In the Greek, Luke calls the sorcerer and false prophet *magos*, which is traditionally interpreted (in this passage) as meaning he was a magician of sorts.[3] Wycliffe translated the word as "witch."[4] However, the actual meaning of the name Elymas is somewhat difficult to interpret. Luke's comment "for so is his name by interpretation" is confusing. Does he mean that the name or title Elymas means "Bar-Jesus," or does he intend the reader to understand that *magos* (or "magician") translates to Elymas. The text is simply unclear.[5] Regardless, the original meaning of the name is unknown. Some commentators think it is Arabic for "wise man." Others hold that it is Aramaic for "dreamer." One suggested that it might be the Greek for "ready." But none of these can be established as fact.[6]

The name Bar-Jesus (which was Elymas's given name) means literally he who is the "son of Jesus" or the "son of Joshua."[7] "The idea of a 'false prophet' who is termed 'son of Jesus' and who opposed Paul is provocative."[8]

There aren't a lot of punitive miracles in the New Testament. However, this one seems like a companion to the one Peter performed that brought the death of Ananias and Sapphira (Acts 5:1–11).

One commentator wrote, "Luke insists that the reason for the conversion of Sergius Paulus is not the blinding of the magician Bar-Jesus but the 'teaching of the Lord' being given by Paul and Barnabas, which caused him no little astonishment."[9] Perhaps. Certainly Sergius proactively requested that the two missionaries teach him. Nevertheless, it is hard to ignore the fact that the proconsul witnessed a rather dramatic miracle and then was baptized thereafter.

SYMBOLIC ELEMENTS

The magician, sorcerer, and false prophet of this miracle stands as an apropos symbol for all emissaries of Satan. The adversary employs those who are willing to live his lie and who are eager to deceive others for the sake of power and gain.

As with other miracles we have discussed previously, so also in this miracle: physical blindness is a fitting symbol for spiritual blindness. And the receipt of blindness after one was able to see can imply God's judgment and also a withdrawal of God's Spirit.

APPLICATION AND ALLEGORIZATION

There is undoubtedly some parallelism being crafted by Luke in his narrative of this miracle. Paul and Elymas seem not simply historic opponents, but symbolic ones also.

> Readers cannot help but pause over the puzzling set of doublings and reversals Luke has here brought together. Are they purposeful? . . . Here we can ask whether Luke has deliberately invited a second and more subtle reading of the story.
>
> What are some of the signals he provides? There is the puzzling matter of names: why is the false-prophet/magician named twice, and so oddly? And is there a connection between this double name and the fact that Luke choses this moment to denominate Saul "as also Paul?" Then there are the parallels: Saul had been an opponent of "The Way" who was blinded by the light and had to be led into Damascus by the hand. Now there is a Jewish opponent who "twists the straight ways of the Lord" and who is blinded by Paul and who needs to have people guide him by the hand. Finally, there are the reversals: the one named "son of Jesus" (*bariēsou*) is called by Paul "son of the devil." Paul is identified as a prophet by being "filled with the Holy Spirit," whereas the "false prophet" is "full of deception and fraud." . . .
>
> Perhaps we are to see Saul, at the moment he takes on his new and proper identity as Paul the Apostle, fighting the final battle with the "Jewish false prophet" within him, blinding the hostile magician that is his former self at the moment he assumes his role as "light to the Gentiles" (see [Acts] 13:47). . . .
>
> Perhaps a better sense of the complex interconnections in this passage may be given by appreciating . . . the equally ambiguous battle between spiritual forces and symbols. At this level the reader can with some confidence assert that it is Paul as "Light of the Gentiles" (as we shall soon be told he is, [Acts] 13:47) who blinds the master of the dark arts Elymas; and it is the Holy Spirit that fills the prophet Paul who casts into confusion the "false prophet" Bar-Jesus.[10]

The parallels in this miracle seem more than coincidental. One can hardly miss how calling Elymas the "son of the devil" (as Paul does) creates a tension with the name Bar-Jesus or "son of Jesus." Whatever else Luke intended, symbolically, the entire episode is a reminder of the conflict that exists between the kingdom of God and the counterfeit kingdom of the devil. It highlights the distinction that must be made between "magic" and divine priesthood, between "twisted/crooked" paths and those that are "straight."[11]

As already noted, physical blindness is ever a symbol for spiritual blindness. "Such blindness remained a terrible emblem of the blindness of [the] soul."[12] And in this miracle, it is a reminder that those who seek to bring to pass wickedness will be blinded from the truth. Their lies become their reality. As Nephi learned, "the mists of darkness . . . blindeth the eyes, and hardeneth the hearts of the children of men, and leadeth them away into broad roads, that they perish and are lost" (1 Nephi 12:17). Jesus put it this way: "For judgment I am come into this world, that they . . . which see might be made blind" (John 9:39). Harkening to Satan's spirit brings a loss of what was once had; light and truth are taken and darkness is all that remains (see D&C 93:39).

John Chrysostom (circa AD 344–407) made an interesting point about the blindness that was brought upon Elymas. He explained, " 'And now, behold, the hand of the Lord is upon you, and you shall be blind.' It was the sign by which Paul was himself converted, and by this he wished to convert this man. And the words 'for a season' were spoken by one who seeks not to punish but to convert. For if he had wanted to punish, he would have made him blind forever."[13] Surely this is the case when God seeks to correct our errant behaviors. He is not punitive in nature, though He is corrective for our benefit and for the sake of our salvation.

NOTES

1. See Fitzmyer (1990), 500, 501; Johnson (1992), 221–222.
2. See Fitzmyer (1990), 501. See also Johnson (1992), 222.
3. See Fitzmyer (1990), 501.
4. See Nicoll (1983), 2:285.
5. See Johnson (1992), 223.
6. See Fitzmyer (1990), 502; Johnson (1992), 223.
7. See Fitzmyer (1990), 501; Johnson (1992), 222.
8. Johnson (1992), 222.

9. Fitzmyer (1990), 504.

10. Johnson (1992), 227.

11. See Johnson (1992), 224. For an interesting conversation about this distinction, see Abraham Kaplan, "The Meaning of Ritual: Comparisons," in *Reflections on Mormonism*, 41–43.

12. Lockyer (1965), 282.

13. Chrysostom, "Homilies on the Acts of the Apostles," 28, in Martin (2006), 161. See also Isidore of Pelusium, "Catena on the Acts of the Apostles," 13.10, in Martin (2006), 161.

Paul Heals *a* Crippled Man *at* Lystra

Acts 14:8–20

The Miracle

Paul left Iconium and headed to Lystra where he and Barnabas continued to preach about Jesus and His salvific mission. While Paul was teaching, there was a man in the crowd who could not use his feet. He had been lame from his mother's womb, having never taken a step. When the man's gaze caught Paul's attention, the Apostle looked intently at him and, sensing this Gentile had the faith to be healed, Paul commanded him, "Stand up upon your feet!" The man instantly jumped up and began to walk around.

So shocked were the Gentile onlookers by Paul's power that they assumed he and Barnabas were gods in human form and they began to worship them. When Paul and Barnabas insisted that they were but men and should not be worshiped, the people were offended and stoned Paul, leaving him for dead.

Background

Paul's discourse (in the verses that follow this miracle) was an effort to keep the people from worshiping him and also an attempt to focus their attention on the true God, whom they *should* worship.

Of the geography described by Luke in his account of this miracle, *The Anchor Bible Dictionary* explains that Lystra is a sight located at Zoldera near Hatun Saray and lying about 24 miles [south] of Konya [also known as Iconium]; . . . it was a moderately important, if somewhat rustic, market town in the relatively backward region of Lycaonia in south-central Turkey. In antiquity, Lycaonia was bounded on the [west] by Phrygia, by Galatia on the [north], Cappadocia to the [east], and the Taurus mountains on the [south]. The most important city in the area, then as now, is Iconium (Konya).[1]

In the Greek, Luke records that Paul ascertained (by discernment through his gaze) that the man lame from birth had the "faith to be saved" rather than the "faith to be healed" (as the King James Translation renders the phrase). The Greek verb *sozo* can imply to "make well" or to "heal," but most translators render the verb "to be saved" instead.

SYMBOLIC ELEMENTS

In what regard is the lame man an archetype or symbol for the reader? He is a familiar icon for our weakness aside from Christ and His intervention.

> Why is this a lame man, and why is he healed? He is lame for the same reason that the characters in Jesus' and Peter's healings were lame: the incapacity to move, the powerlessness to walk, the weakness and the helplessness, all signify the condition of humans with respect to salvation. He is "saved/healed" because he "has faith" (14:9): he perceives in Paul's word the power of god's visitation and is open to its power.[2]

As we have stressed over and over again, without Christ we are each powerless. Our actions, no matter what they are, remain fruitless. We are lame, as it were—immobile. We need Him to heal us, and He has sent His apostolic witnesses with the keys and knowledge to know how to do so.

Bede the Venerable (circa AD 672–735), noting how the Jews were rejecting Paul but the Gentiles were (in many cases) embracing him, suggested that "this sick Lycaonian prefigured the people of the Gentiles, who were for a long time remote from the religion of the law and the temple."[3] In other words, just as Paul healed this man "lame from his mother's womb," he also brought the gospel to the Gentiles apostate from their mother's womb. And just as the Jews rejected Paul's message, many were rejecting Jesus as the Messiah. Thus, Paul became the Apostle to the Gentiles and brought Christ's healing influence to thousands.

APPLICATION AND ALLEGORIZATION

One obvious message that can be drawn from this miracle has to do with the impropriety of deifying one's leaders. Paul was clearly a man of God and had the power of God with him. The Gentiles of Lystra saw this but misattributed the powers to Paul and Barnabas. Perhaps we are occasionally guilty of this ourselves. While we do not worship our leaders, we sometimes wish to hold them to an unfair standard of perfection—and then, if we see any element of humanity or weakness in them, we want to stone them (metaphorically) much as the Gentiles did Paul after this miracle. The Prophet Joseph once said, "I told them I was but a man, and they must not expect me to be perfect; if they expected perfection from me, I should expect it from them; but if they would bear with my infirmities and the infirmities of the brethren, I would likewise bear with their infirmities."[4] We must be careful to not extrapolate from the mantle or keys of the Apostles (or of stake presidents or bishops, for that matter) an expectation of perfection. We must not deify them—not only because (like Paul) it would be contrary to their desire, but also because it would be contrary to the will of God. I have seen some who so deify the presiding Brethren that they refuse to allow them to be humans also. As soon as they then hear or see something that bothers them in one of the talks or lives of a General Authority, they unfairly reject them for their humanity and verbally stone them—all the while dismantling their personal testimony of the Restoration. In the words of the Lord, "Let he who is without sin cast the first stone" (see John 8:7).

The language of the miracle is familiar. It reminds the reader of healings performed by Peter and Jesus. One commentator pointed out, "The description of the man as 'lame from his mother's womb' resembles that of the man healed by Peter in Acts 3:1–10. The resemblance is probably less accidental than a deliberate literary signal. Paul will do the same deeds as Peter and Jesus (compare Luke 5:17–26)."[5] Symbolically, the miracle serves to remind us of the apostolic mantle that falls upon those who are called to that high and holy office. The transformation of Brigham Young's voice and person at the 1844 succession crisis let those who observed it know that Brigham Young was the man the Lord had chosen to succeed the Prophet Joseph. Similarly, there is an account in the life of President Heber J. Grant that seems applicable. Historian Ronald W. Walker wrote,

> From the announcement of his apostolic call, there were whispers and innuendoes about his selection. While his closest associates welcomed his appointment, Elder Grant was painfully aware that it had taken President Taylor's written revelation to convince others that he was apostolic timber. No one doubted his integrity—only his preparation for the calling and what some saw as his preoccupation with business.
>
> Heber himself was probably his toughest critic. . . .
>
> Less than a week [after President Joseph F. Smith died], President Grant was set apart as the Church's seventh prophet, seer, and revelator. . . .
>
> Some doubters received an immediate reassurance. Reminiscent of one of the Church's most cherished traditions surrounding President Brigham Young's succession to leadership, many Saints testified that as they first saw President Grant address them, his face seemed to be transformed into President Joseph F. Smith's visage. Others claimed that they viewed President Smith's figure standing next to their new president.[6]

Like Brigham, Heber J. Grant was momentarily transformed (in the eyes of his viewers) to appear like his predecessor, that those who doubted his call might know that it was indeed of God. Paul was a controversial figure, and some would struggle to accept this former antagonist as a friend of the Church and as an Apostle on par with Peter, let alone with Christ. Thus, though Paul was not visually transformed, he was "seen" in the image of Jesus and Peter by performing almost the identical miracles they had done. This was for his detractors a testament that he *was* an Apostle and that God *was* with him. As one commentator explained, "The usefulness of the story in securing Paul's identity as an authentic prophet in the tradition of Jesus, who healed a lame man (Luke 5:17–26), and of Peter who healed a lame man (Acts 3:1–6) is obvious."[7]

In a general sense, this miracle reminds us of the dangers of worshiping false gods. We should only worship the Father, in the name of the Son and by the power of the Holy Spirit. But to make anything *other than God* the object of our worship is to sin, and it will ultimately lead us to reject the truth He sends through His authorized messengers.

As did Paul and Barnabas, so must we: anytime we find others giving us credit for that which God has done through us, we must deflect all glory back to God. Remember the Book of Mormon's caution against priestcraft and the tendency of some to "set themselves up for a light unto the world, that they may get gain and praise of the world" (2 Nephi 26:29). We may do good, and we may be Spirit-directed, but God is the source of all that is good and holy. You and I are but instruments in His hands. On our own, we are as the paralyzed man in this miracle. Through His power and intervention, we can be as Paul and Barnabas.

NOTES

1. David S. Potter, "Lystra," in Freedman (1992), 4:426.
2. Johnson (1992), 251.
3. Bede, "Commentary on the Acts of the Apostles," 14.8, in Martin (2006), 175.
4. Smith (1976), 268.
5. Johnson (1992), 247.
6. Walker, "Heber J. Grant," 232, 242–243.
7. Johnson (1992), 251.

Paul Casts Out *an* Evil Spirit *and* Then He *and* Silas *Are* Delivered *from* Prison

Acts 16:18, 26

The Miracle

Paul and Silas had gone to Philippi to preach the word. As they traveled to a place where they could pray on the Sabbath, a slave girl approached them. She was a clairvoyant, and her owners made a considerable amount of money showcasing her strange pseudo-spiritual gifts. For several days, this girl followed Paul and his entourage, shouting, "These men are slaves of the Most High God; they are proclaiming to you a way of salvation."[1] Eventually Paul became weary of her strange and disruptive behavior, and so he rebuked the spirit within her, saying, "In the name of Jesus Christ I command you to come out!" The spirit obeyed Paul's command and immediately left the girl.

The owners of the formerly clairvoyant slave realized that because Paul had exorcised the demon in the girl, she no longer had the ability to make them money, and thus they were angry with him. So they laid hold on him, dragged him to the main square, and presented him before the authorities with a complaint that he was "disturbing the peace and advocating practices unlawful for Romans to adopt or observe." The authorities had Paul and Silas stripped and flogged and then thrown in prison where they were securely locked in the innermost cell of the jail, their feet secured in shackles.

At about midnight, these two servants of the Lord were praying and singing hymns as their fellow prisoners listened. Suddenly, a severe earthquake struck, shaking the prison and causing its doors to fly open and the chains to fall from Paul and Silas. When the warden awoke and saw that the doors were opened, he feared that the prisoners had escaped, and he thus prepared to take his own life. But Paul, discerning what his jailer was about to do, called out to him, saying, "Don't harm yourself. We are still here." The warden fell trembling at their feet and asked, "What must I do to be saved?" Paul's answer was simply, "Believe in the Lord Jesus Christ and you will be saved—you and your entire household." The warden believed and took Paul and Silas to his home where he cleansed their wounds (from the flogging), and then he and his entire household were baptized.

BACKGROUND

It was on this trip to Philippi that Paul apparently established the Christian community that would receive the letter known as his Epistle to the Philippians, which he would later write.[2]

As to the geography of Philippi, "the Roman province of Macedonia was divided into four districts (*merides*), and *Philippoi* was a city in eastern Macedonia, situated east of Mt. Pangaeus on the Via Egnatia, which led from Byzantium to Dyrrhachium on the Adriatic [Sea]. Founded . . . by Philip of Macedonia in 356 B.C., it was a gold-mining center in the area. In 167 B.C. . . . . Philippi came under Roman control and was heavily populated by Romans."[3]

As for the crime for which they were incarcerated, one text suggests, "A Roman could not adopt Judaism without liability according to Roman penal code. . . . Paul and Silas, however, have not been proselytizing for Judaism, but the magistrates in Philippi at that time would scarcely have known the difference between Judaism and Christianity."[4] Indeed, it is commonly pointed out that few in the early years distinguished Christianity as a new religion but instead tended to look upon it as a denomination of Judaism.

The Greek is unclear as to whether Paul and Silas were seeking out a synagogue in the area or just looking for somewhere to pray.[5] Whether the former or the latter doesn't seem to matter to the miracle and its application.

SYMBOLIC ELEMENTS

The possessed female has been seen as a symbol for the conquest of true religion over false. One commentator explained, "The exorcism of the possessed slave girl is used by Luke to depict the triumph of Christianity over pagan Greco-Roman practices [and beliefs]. A pagan religious practice is made to acknowledge that salvation comes from the Most High God of Christianity."[6] True religion not only trumps false religion, but the devils must actually acknowledge Jesus to be the true and living God and the means of salvation for all. In a very real sense, this will actually happen when the judgment arrives and all things are weighed in the balance. When we read that "every knee shall bow, and every tongue confess" that Jesus is the Christ (Mosiah 27:31), this includes the devils of hell who will also bow and confess the very One they sought to destroy.

As in so many other passages, the earthquake described here is an appropriate symbol of divine intervention. It can represent God's unmatched power to bring to pass His will.[7]

The warden's act of prostration before the feet of Paul and Silas is a common symbol of submission and likely foreshadowed his ultimate submission to Christ (which he would shortly manifest by baptism).[8]

APPLICATION AND ALLEGORIZATION

Paul's failure to find a synagogue led him to the river's side to pray and, consequently, led to the conversion of Lydia and her entire household. Similarly, Paul's unjust imprisonment led to the conversion of his jailer and the baptism of him and his entire family. In each case, that which appeared to be a misfortune or disappointment was really a blessing in disguise, which enabled Paul and his companion to preach the gospel and to bless others. The establishment of the Church at Philippi came through a series of seeming flukes—but really came through God's workings behind the scenes. As one commentator put it, "Each of these occasions for [the] proclamation [of the gospel] and witness [of its divinity] was unplanned, spontaneous, even accidental, unless one perceives, as Luke surely did, that God's visitation is enabled by just such human experiences."[9] God can also give us experiences in our lives that seem accidental or even frustrating, which may be His means of getting us to where we need to be and to do what He needs us to do. Like Paul and Silas, our challenge is to use those opportunities to the benefit of God's work and for the building of His kingdom.

Conversion comes in many ways. Lydia, we are told, listened to Paul and felt the Spirit of what he taught and was converted. She needed no sign, no great or obvious miracle. Only the sweet whisperings of the Spirit were necessary for her faith to blossom. The clairvoyant girl, on the other hand, required something more dramatic, more forceful. It would take the equivalent of a priesthood blessing to bring her to Christ. Like the slave girl's release from Satan, the jailer's conversion experience was rather dramatic also. An earthquake was required to raise him from his physical *and* spiritual sleep. God speaks to each of us in different ways. Conversion comes in a variety of packages. Hence the need to be Spirit-directed as we share the gospel.

The earthquake that freed Paul and Silas was a miracle that evidenced God's awareness of their plight and also His power to bring to pass His will even against seemingly insurmountable odds. Thus, like Paul and Silas (who prayed and sang hymns as they sat in jail), we must place our trust in "him who is mighty to save" (2 Nephi 31:19). "Earthquakes remind men and women then as well as now that the only fixed ground is God himself. Not even the earth is ultimately stable. They also point to the fact that one day God will shake down all human kingdoms with the appearing of Christ in Glory."[10] We must place our trust in the Lord, and in nothing else. And we must believe that in His own time, He will intervene on our behalf in powerful ways.

An additional symbolic application can be drawn from the earthquake that freed Paul and Silas. William Booth, founder of the Salvation Army, once said of this miracle, "God was so well-pleased with the prayers and praises of Paul and Silas, that He said *Amen*! With a mighty earthquake."[11] God also answers our sincere prayers with earthquakes. Tragically, too often we don't notice the shaking effect of His work on our behalf. He does great things for us, but how many of those great things are missed by us because we are not grateful or because we feel so entitled that we downplay the significance of His frequent intervention?

Because of his acceptance of Christ, there is a change in the life of the jailer. One commentator pointed out,

Before the earthquake, he was so brutal that he could lash prisoners and never turn a hair as he watched their back oozing with blood. Now, as soon as he was saved, he takes water and washes the very stripes he had inflicted. He himself had been cleansed from wounds worse and more perilous than those he had inflicted by his rods. The least he could do was to wash the blood stripes of the prisoners.[12]

The gospel changes lives. Christ changes people! He can dramatically change us *if* we will but let Him!

NOTES

1. Though the King James Version translates this "the way of salvation," most render the Greek "a way of salvation." As to why the evil spirit in this girl would testify of God's authorized messengers, Elder Bruce R. McConkie explained,

> The testimony of the devil-led damsel was true. Paul and Silas were prophets; they had the words and power of salvation. But true testimony from Satan's servants does not lead to salvation. In effect the damsel was saying: 'Go ahead and believe in Paul and Silas and this Jesus whom they preach. I agree they and their Master are of God; and since we are now united on that point, you can also continue to follow me and enjoy the fruits of my divination.' And how many other practitioners of false religions there are who give lip service to Jesus and his doctrines so that people will the more readily follow them and their special brand of 'saving' grace. (McConkie [1987–88], 2:149)

2. See Fitzmyer (1998), 582.
3. Fitzmyer (1998), 584. See also Nicole (1983), 2:343–44.
4. Fitzmyer (1998), 587. See also Nicole (1983), 2:349.
5. See Johnson (1992), 292; Fitzmyer (1998), 585; Nicole (1983), 2:344–45.
6. Fitzmyer (1998), 583.
7. See Ryken, Wilhoit, and Longman (1998), 225. See also Fitzmyer (1998), 588; Johnson (1992), 300; Nicole (1983), 2:350.
8. See Ryken, Wilhoit, and Longman (1998), 522.
9. Johnson (1992), 303.
10. Ryken, Wilhoit, and Longman (1998), 225.
11. See Lockyer (1965), 286.
12. Lockyer (1965), 286.

PAUL HEALS *through* HANDKERCHIEFS *and* APRONS

ACTS 19:11–12

THE MIRACLE

For an extended period in Ephesus, Paul testified boldly of the gospel and of Christ. Day after day he would teach the inhabitants of the Roman province of Asia—Jews and Gentiles alike. Many of the Jews rejected his message and subjected him to public ridicule. This persecution caused Paul to withdraw from the synagogue and to focus instead on Greeks in the region.

During this time, and in spite of the public reviling, God worked many extraordinary miracles through the Apostle. Handkerchiefs and aprons that he had touched were then applied to the sick, and their diseases were healed or, in the case of those possessed by the devil, the touch of these items forced Satan's influence to be withdrawn.

BACKGROUND

Paul initially began his preaching in Ephesus in the synagogue and to those of his former faith. However, when many of the Jews rejected his message, he took his converts and began to preach in the lecture hall of Tyrannus. Thus, Paul's focus shifted from Jews to Gentiles.

Tyrannus is an unknown figure in history. He may have been a teacher in Ephesus or perhaps he simply owned the lecture hall in which Paul preached. But we know nothing of him or whether he personally embraced Paul's message.[1]

While handkerchiefs and aprons are highlighted in this miracle, the text makes it quite clear that it is God—not amulets or Paul—that is the source of the healing.[2] One commentary reports,

> There was no virtue whatever in the handkerchiefs and short aprons Paul gave to the diseased and demon-possessed, even though the cured may have retained them as precious relics. They were only the *media* of the supernatural gift of healing Paul exercised at that time. Ellicott says that "The efficacy of such *media* stands obviously on the same footing as that of the hem of our Lord's garment (Matthew 9:20, 21), and the shadow of Peter (Acts 5:15), and of the clay in the healing of the blind" (John 9:6). *Media* were not imperative, for God, through His Son and the apostles, wrought miracles with and without means.[3]

Similarly, Elder Bruce R. McConkie wrote,

> Healings come by the power of faith; there is no healing virtue or power in any item of clothing, or other object, whether owned by Paul or Jesus or anyone. But rites and objects may be used to help increase faith. . . .
>
> Thus Jesus used spittle and clay to anoint the eyes of a blind man, not that there was any healing power in the mud paste spread on the sightless eyes, but the physical act aided the mental labor out of which faith grew. The same principle is seen in the healing of the woman who touched Jesus' garments, in the dead being raised by touching the bones of Elisha (2 Kings 13:20–21), and in the very ordinance of administering to the sick through the formalities of anointing with oil and laying on of hands.[4]

These physical items may have simply served to bolster the faith of the one seeking God's intervention. However, they were not of themselves capable of bringing to pass the miraculous.

SYMBOLIC ELEMENTS

The handkerchiefs and aprons in this miracle are fitting symbols for those things we can rightly place our faith in: God, Christ, the priesthood. They can represent heaven-sent blessings available to those who put their trust in deity and live worthy of divine intervention.

APPLICATION AND ALLEGORIZATION

As we noted when we discussed the healing of the woman with an issue of blood, the belief that a physical object could be the source of power or healing was common in the first century. Hence Paul's miraculous healings through "handkerchiefs or aprons" here.[5] In other words, in the early Christian Church "things" belonging to Paul and likely other apostles were used in the act of healing individuals who were some distance from the Brethren but who, nevertheless, had faith in their priesthood power. Such miracles were not isolated to the first-century Church, but have happened in this last dispensation also. Wilford Woodruff recorded an experience that is akin to the Apostle Paul's:

> A man of the world [not a Latter-day Saint], knowing of the miracles which had been performed, came to [the Prophet Joseph] and asked him if he would not go and heal two twin children of his, about five months old, who were both lying sick nigh unto death.
>
> They were some two miles from Montrose.
>
> The Prophet said he could not go; but, after pausing some time, he said he would send someone to heal them; and he turned to me and said: "You go with the man and heal his children."
>
> He took a red silk handkerchief out of his pocket and gave it to me, and told me to wipe their faces with the handkerchief when I administered to them, and they should be healed. He also said unto me: "As long as you will keep that handkerchief, it shall remain a league between you and me."
>
> I went with the man, and did as the Prophet commanded me, and the children were healed.
>
> I have possession of the handkerchief unto this day.[6]

As mortals, our faith is naturally weak. Anointing with oil, laying on of hands, speaking aloud when giving a priesthood blessing, and many other such acts help us to place faith in God, Christ, the Spirit, and the holy priesthood. It is always the Godhead who heals, but such physical items and actions can help you and me to trust in the power of the Divine. In this, such actions and items serve as a blessing to us naturally doubting souls.

One commentator pointed out that while Paul healed many in Ephesus—including not only the demonically possessed but those who were physically ill—nevertheless, he was apparently unable to heal his friend and missionary companion, Trophimus, whom he left behind at Miletum with some sort of sickness (see 2 Timothy 4:20). "In His sovereign will, God bestows or withholds supernatural gifts."[7] One is healed while another is not. Our finite minds cannot comprehend all the workings of a just God—but the answer to the question "why him but not me?" is *not* always "because he had faith and you did not." God has a plan, which is much bigger than any of us can comprehend, and in many cases, the one who is *not* healed has great faith, but God has more important work for him to do on the other side of the veil.

Jesus promised, "He that believeth on me, the works that I do shall he do also; and greater works than these shall he do" (John 14:12). The healing of others through one's shadow (as Peter did in Acts 5:15) or by one's handkerchief (as Paul did in this miracle) would be prime examples of this. Jesus did miraculous things, but He did not reserve the power to do so for Himself. Indeed, He desires all who are His true followers to develop their faith to such a degree that He can perform through them whatever miracle He needs done.

The "special miracles . . . God wrought . . . by the hands of Paul"[8] are important because of his life prior to being called as an Apostle. As Saul, he had been a misguided man who hurt many. Now he had a calling in the presiding counsels of the Church. One commentator pointed out that "these miracles authenticate Paul's preaching."[9] Another suggested these miracles are evidence of his "prophetic powers" in this new stage of his life.[10] In a sense, these miracles tell us God is with the Apostle regardless of his human weaknesses—past or present. In a way, this story invites us to accept those called to positions of leadership in the Church—on a general or local level—even though they most certainly have not lived perfect lives, and even though they may still manifest their humanity from time to time. If we are willing to let them serve and are willing to sustain them as they do, the Lord will manifest to our hearts the miracles He is accomplishing through them.

NOTES

1. See Fitzmyer (1998), 648; Johnson (1992), 339.
2. See Nicoll (1983), 2:406.
3. Lockyer (1965), 288.
4. McConkie (1987–88), 2:169.

5. As we noted before, one commentator explained this verse as follows: "We are to picture small bits of cloth, pressed to Paul's skin, and then applied to the sick" (Johnson [1992], 340).

6. Wilford Woodruff, *Leaves from My Journal*, 65. Lorenzo Snow had a similar power. He was promised in his patriarchal blessing that "the diseased shall send to thee their aprons and handkerchiefs, and by thy touch their owners shall be made whole." He experienced this gift and some availed themselves of it. See Snow, *Biography and Family Record of Lorenzo Snow*, 264–65.

7. Locker (1965), 288.

8. See Fitzmyer (1998), 648.

9. Ibid.

10. See Johnson (1992), 343.

PAUL BRINGS EUTYCHUS
BACK *to* LIFE

ACTS 20:7–12

THE MIRACLE

Paul was preaching at Troas and was intending to depart from that region the next day. It was Sunday and the last Sabbath he would spend with the members there, so the Apostle spoke longer than he would typically.

Around midnight, Eutychus, a young man who had come to hear Paul speak, fell asleep while listening to the talk. Throughout the meeting, the youth had been sitting on the window sill. When he dozed off, he fell out of the third-story window and, landing on the ground below, died.

Seeing what had happened, Paul hurried downstairs and wrapped his arms around the deceased boy. Pausing momentarily, Paul said to those gathered, "Don't be alarmed. There is still life in him." The boy revived and he with Paul and the others went back upstairs where they partook of the sacrament. They then ate a meal and chatted until dawn.[1] All present were relieved because of the miracle.

BACKGROUND

The name Eutychus is Greek and means literally "fortunate" or "lucky" one,[2] and appropriately so, as this boy was as lucky as one can be.

Paul's commission for those gathered to *be not alarmed because there was still life in the boy* did not mean that the boy had survived the fall. Rather, Luke intends us to understand that the boy had indeed died but that Paul had brought him back to life. Thus, they were not to worry because Paul had the power to bring the dead back to life.[3]

SYMBOLIC ELEMENTS

As Paul is said to have "fallen upon" the deceased boy before he brought him back to life, we can hardly miss the connections between this miracle of raising the dead and those of Elijah (1 Kings 17:17–24) and Elisha (2 Kings 4:20–37), wherein they treated the deceased in a similar way.[4]

Much of the story seems to parallel Jesus's first appearance to His Apostles after His Resurrection.

> Is it by accident that the story takes place on the first day of the week (Luke 24:1), or that it occurs in an "upper room" (Luke 22:12; Acts 1:13), or that the disciples are gathered to "break bread" (Luke 24:30–35)? All of these are clear verbal pointers back to the resurrection of Jesus and the experience of his risen presence by the first disciples. . . . The small details . . . noted clearly indicate the message Luke wants the reader to derive from the tale: the power of . . . Jesus is at work in the Apostle Paul.[5]

As we have already noted, sleep is often a euphemism for death (see 1 Corinthians 15:6, 18; 1 Thessalonians 4:14; 5:10; D&C 86:3),[6] but it can also be a symbol for indolence or inattentiveness, which brings sin or causes the loss of blessings.[7]

The timing of Eutychus's healing seems symbolic. He is restored to life during the sacrament. Symbolically, this can be seen as highlighting the life-giving nature of that sacred ordinance.[8]

APPLICATION AND ALLEGORIZATION

One application of this miracle has to do with the dangers of "falling asleep" to the things of God. If we allow ourselves to become inattentive to God's word and His Spirit's voice, we (like Eutychus) place ourselves in danger of spiritual death. We must be vigilant daily in doing the "small things" so that we will be awake to the demonic dangers around us. God offers protection, but only to those who are spiritually "awake."

Similarly, there seems to be a metaphor in the fact that Eutychus placed himself on the window's edge. Too many people wish to be "in" the Church while keeping themselves as close to the edge of the "world" as possible. As Eutychus demonstrated for us, we can only stay "in" the Church for so long if we are always sitting on the "edge" of orthodoxy or faithfulness. It is so easy to assume we are safe on the perimeter so long as we're "in" the "building," per se. However, just as Eutychus was lulled unawares to sleep, Satan seeks to get each of us "out" of the Church, and one of the easiest ways to do that is to keep us lingering near one of the exits.

Significantly, as soon as Eutychus was brought back to life, he received of the sacrament of the Lord's Supper. So also when you and I are revived spiritually—after our battles with sin—it is the sacrament that can restore us to full spiritual health and vigor.[9] Indeed, without that salvific ordinance, we are incapable of "reviving" spiritually no matter how insignificant our personal sins seem.

NOTES

1. Some have assumed Paul went back to his sermon and preached it until sunrise. That is quite possible, though the Greek is not clear on that, and some scholars and translations lean toward the idea that Paul and those gathered "chatted" or "conversed" until dawn—perhaps in part about the miracle that had taken place. See, for example, Fitzmyer (1998), 669; Nicoll (1993), 3:426; Thayer (1999), 444. One commentator put it this way, "Paul did not now go on in a continued discourse, as before, but he and his friends fell into a free conversation. They did not know when they should have Paul's company again, and therefore made the best use they could of it when they had it, and reckoned a night's sleep well lost for that purpose" (Church, *NIV Matthew Henry Commentary*, 526.
2. See Fitzmyer (1998), 667, 669; Johnson (1992), 356.
3. See Fitzmyer (1998), 669.
4. See Fitzmyer (1998), 668; Johnson (1992), 356; Lockyer (1965), 289.
5. Johnson (1992), 358.
6. See Marcus (2000), 362, 371; Albright and Mann (1971), 111.
7. See Conner (1992), 169.
8. See Fitzmyer (1998), 668.
9. Ibid.

PAUL *Is* BITTEN *by a* VIPER *but* SUSTAINS NO HARM

ACTS 28:1–6

THE MIRACLE

Along with some two hundred and seventy-five others, Paul was caught in a storm on the Adriatic. The tempest raged constantly for two weeks and all hope of survival was lost by those onboard. On the fourteenth day, they sought to run the ship ashore onto an island, but the ship was destroyed in the process. Passengers swam for the coast or clung to any debris they could lay hold on.

Once ashore, they learned that the island was Malta. Luke informs us that the natives were kind and helped comfort the nearly three hundred people who had swam or drifted ashore with Paul.

A fire was started to warm the cold and weary survivors of the shipwreck. Seeking to help, Paul went out and gathered brushwood to stoke the fire. As he began to place the timber on the fire, the heat of the flames provoked a viper hiding in the wood and it fastened itself onto Paul's hand.

The natives of the island were shocked and said, "This man must be a murderer. Though he survived the sea, Justice will not allow him to go on living—thus She has sent a snake to do what the sea failed to do." They all expected Paul to swell up and drop dead, but he shook off the viper, letting it fall into the fire, and nothing of note happened to him because of the snakebite. The islanders were surprised and conjectured that perhaps Paul was a god.

BACKGROUND

It is believed the Paul and his traveling companions most likely landed on the Mediterranean island of Malta, which is just south of Sicily.[1]

When the Maltese refer to "Justice," they are referring to the goddess of revenge whom some in antiquity believed pursued people for their conduct, executing justice or judgment upon them.[2]

SYMBOLIC ELEMENTS

"The sea," *The New Jerome Biblical Commentary* informs us, is "a common symbol for chaos and death."[3] Joseph Fitzmyer noted that "it can denote the abode of the dead or the final prison of Satan and the demons. It is used often in the LXX [as] the symbol of chaos and disorder."[4]

Viperous serpents are common symbols of the adversary. They often represent Satan and his influence in our lives, including his attempts to destroy us.[5] "From beginning (Genesis 3:1) to end (Revelation 20:2) Scripture portrays the devil in the guise of a serpent."[6] The snake's sudden and unexpected attack is likely also symbolic. "Snakes often struck from [their place of] hiding, biting without warning (Genesis 49:17). This ever-present danger serves as metaphor of sudden judgment (Isaiah 14:29; Amos 5:19)."[7] The fact that the bite does not harm Paul suggests he was judged and found worthy before God. Finally, in this miracle the falling of the snake into the fire well symbolizes the ultimate end of Lucifer and all evil that follows him or is inspired by him.

APPLICATION AND ALLEGORIZATION

Jesus promised His faithful and believing followers, "Behold, I give unto you power to tread on serpents and scorpions, and over all the power of the enemy: and nothing shall by any means hurt you" (Luke 10:19. See also Mark 16:17–18). If God is with us, Satan's power will be limited. Thus, one commentator noted, "The expectation of power over serpents and poison symbolized for believers the waning influence of the evil one and [the] anticipation of the age of the Christus Victor (Mark 16:18)."[8] Satan will surely be bound and eventually destroyed. However, before that millennial day dawns, Christ can intervene in our lives now, causing the evil one to lose power over us. Just as the serpent's bite had no harmful effect on the Apostle Paul, the devil can lose his power to spiritually slay us through our faith in and obedience to Christ and His law.

On a related note, one commentator interpreted the message of the miracle as this: "The lesson for our hearts is that although we are not to expect visible and miraculous interpositions on our behalf in time of need, yet . . . we have the assurance that He will take care of us."[9] In other words, while Paul's dual recovery (first from the shipwreck and then from the viper's bite) might be less than common, God is nevertheless with us and *does* intervene in our lives in seemingly subtle yet no less miraculous ways. If we are worthy of His aid, we should expect it in whatever form He deems best to send it. As Theodoret of Cyr (circa AD 393–466) wrote, "And so also the viper, which drove its teeth into the apostle's hand, since it did not find [in Paul] any entry of sin in him, immediately released him and threw itself into the fire by inflicting on itself a punishment, because it had made an attack against an impenetrable body. Therefore let us fear the beasts, *if* we do not possess the full armor of virtue" as Paul did.[10]

NOTES

1. See Johnson (1992), 461; Nicoll (1983), 2:537.
2. See Fitzmyer (1998), 783; Johnson (1992), 462.
3. Kselman and Barré, in Brown, Fitzmyer, and Murphy (1990), 541.
4. Fitzmyer (1970), 739n31. See also C. S. Mann, who suggested that the sea is sometimes seen as a symbol of the "place of final punishment for demons" (Mann [1986], 278–79). Edwin Firmage indicated that the sea was a symbol for the "repository of impurity" (Firmage, "Zoology," 6:1132).
5. See Cooper (1982), 149.
6. Ryken, Wilhoit, and Longman (1998), 773.
7. Ibid.
8. Ibid.
9. Lockyer (1965), 291.
10. Theodoret, "Catena on the Acts," 312; emphasis added.

THE FATHER *of* PUBLIUS
Is HEALED *by* PAUL

ACTS 28:7–9

THE MIRACLE

In the same vicinity of where Paul was bitten on the hand by a viper, there lived a prominent man of Malta whose name was Publius. This respected citizen took Paul and others into his home for some three days.

While Paul was staying with Publius he learned that his host's father was sick with dysentery and a chronic fever. So Paul went in and gave the man a blessing and he was healed.

When word spread throughout the island of Paul's power to cure, others who were sick came to him requesting to be healed, and the Apostle blessed and cured them.

BACKGROUND

The name Publius means literally "the first of the island" or "the chief of the island," perhaps suggesting the man's prominence in Malta or in that particular part of the island.[1] One source suggests that he was "the chief authority in the island under the Roman praetor of Sicily."[2] While we cannot be certain of this, it would surely explain his prominence on the island and his personal affluence. The very fact that the text appears to say that Publius took in all 276 people who were stranded in the shipwreck seems to confirm his position of prominence and his access to wealth.[3]

Publius's father is said to have had dysentery, which is a type of gastroenteritis wherein the sufferer has a fever, abdominal pain, and severe diarrhea containing blood and mucus in the stools. While dysentery is not mentioned anywhere else in the Bible, we might expect such a diagnoses from Luke, who was a physician.[4]

SYMBOLIC ELEMENTS

We have already pointed out that the laying on of hands, accompanied by the verbal word, is a standard symbol for the authorized conveyance of power or blessings. John Chrysostom (circa AD 344–407) suggested that while a man's hand is laid upon another man's head, symbolically it is the hand of God that is doing the blessing. The man performing the ordinance is but a symbol.[5] In this case, Paul is acting in the stead and place of God, but it is the Father who heals—not Paul.

Often in the scriptures illness is seen as representative of God's disfavor. Health and the receipt of a healing miracle, on the other hand, are typically seen as signs of God's blessings upon the receiver.[6] When someone is healed, God has smiled upon that person. Symbolically, physical healings point us to the spiritual healings, which Christ seeks to effect in each of our lives.

APPLICATION AND ALLEGORIZATION

In this miracle, Paul healed Publius's father and many others. But here and elsewhere, Paul preached the gospel and brought thousands unto Christ. So which was the greater miracle? The healings, or the conversions? One source wisely notes,

> In referring to His own miracles, Jesus said, "Greater works than these shall ye do, because I go to My Father" (John 14:12). Greater works than *miracles*! What could be more supernatural than a miracle? The spiritual conquests of the Church are these "greater works." The majority of the miracles [recorded in the holy scriptures] were local, temporary, and temporal: "greater works" are spiritual miracles, and universal and eternal. The physically dead who were raised, died again. The spiritually dead, quickened by the Spirit, live forevermore.
>
> There are diseases, worse and deeper than bodily diseases—stings of conscience, deadness of heart, blindness to divine truth, paralysis of energy to serve God, hideous inner leprosy. Do those of us who are the Lord's [servants] not need supernatural power if we are to lay hands

on the sin-sick and bring recovery to them? Through us His restoring efficacy can still flow to the needy. He waits and longs to do His *greater works* through our lives, and *signs* are bound to follow faith in His power to bless. . . .

While God is still the same wonderworking God in His own universe, this is the age of spiritual miracles and all things are possible to him that believeth.[7]

As with Paul, we may have opportunities to participate in the temporary physical healing of another. But the greatest gift we can give—the greatest miracle we can perform—is to heal a broken heart or soul. If we can bring another unto Christ, that will change eternity. What greater work could any of us do in our lives?

NOTES

1. See Fitzmyer (1998), 783. See also Lockyer (1965), 291.
2. Nicoll (1983), 2:540.
3. See Fitzmyer (1998), 783.
4. See Johnson (1992), 463; Lockyer (1965), 291.
5. See Chrysostom, in Nicoll (1983), 2:167.
6. See Ryken, Wilhoit, and Longman (1998), 209.
7. Lockyer (1965), 291–92.

EPILOGUE

It seems that miracles have ever been a part of revealed religion. The prophets of the Old Testament were miracle workers. Jesus was unquestionably a miracle worker. And Christ's disciples, who succeeded Him in the leadership of the New Testament Church, also had the gift of working miracles. Yet, in almost a spirit of resignation, one modern commentator on the miracles of the Bible penned this: "It is safe to say that the miracles that occurred in the days of Jesus and the apostles no longer happen today. No human being has the power to . . . give sight to someone . . . blind, make the deaf to hear, . . . or command both storm and wind to cease."[1] I can only say I disagree. God is a god of miracles. He lives, and because He lives, miracles still happen! One of the signs of the Restoration was the reopening of the heavens, outpourings of revelation, and a return of miracles, including those performed through restored priesthood power. All of this is true! And it is a precious component of the Restoration—particularly in the lives of those who have experienced firsthand such miracles (as many of us have).

Jesus promised those who place their trust in Him, "Verily I say unto you, If ye have faith as a grain of mustard seed, ye shall say unto this mountain, Remove hence to yonder place; and it shall remove; and nothing shall be impossible unto you" (Matthew 17:20). The Lord promises miracles in the lives of those who have faith in God. Of course most, I would suspect, would ask, "Under what circumstance would I need to literally move a mountain?" For the majority, this promise is metaphorical; it is symbolic. It reminds us that mortality is filled with obstacles, mountains we must climb or remove. These may be weaknesses, or they may consist of some trial of faith, finance, or family. But they are, nevertheless, seemingly insurmountable when we are confronted with them. They seem impossible to bear and crushing in their weight. And yet Jesus promised us, if we will exercise faith in Him, He will give us the strength to make it over the mountain or to remove the mountain altogether. He is a God of miracles, and we—through our faith—can expect miracles in our lives.

That being said, as wonderful as the miracle of walking on water was and as amazing as the act of feeding five thousand people with nothing but a few scraps of food seemed, the miracles you and I need in our lives today may be different from those. What we need today might be more personal and more practical. We may or may not need to be healed from physical blindness, but each of us needs to be healed from our spiritual blindness, from our inability to "see things as they really are" (Jacob 4:13). Elder Neal A. Maxwell was once asked "Where is the joy in this rigorous living," which is required of Latter-day Saints? To which he responded,

> Seeing a prodigal return . . . is a marvelous thing. To see someone, in the words of Scripture, who comes to himself and resolves that "I will go to my Father" is a marvelous journey for someone to make. The joy comes in seeing someone who has been crusty and difficult to deal with become more meek, or to see a family really come to love and appreciate each other. Those are the real miracles. The multitude were fed five thousand loaves and fishes, yet they were hungry again the next day. But Jesus is the Bread of Life, and if we partake thereof then we will never be hungry again. The most lasting miracles are the miracles of transformation in people's lives. These give one much joy, and while we can't cause these to happen, the Lord lets us, at times, be instruments in that process. This brings great joy.[2]

Our review of the miracles of the New Testament has been filled with such "transformations." We have examined many miracles—historical events—that testify not only of Christ's power *over* life and the elements of nature, but that (through application) have also reminded us of the more important power He has *in* our lives. While He literally walked on water, what seems to matter more to me today is that I can reach up to Him (when I'm spiritually or emotionally drowning), knowing that He will take my hand and lift me out of the very thing that threatens to destroy me. *That* is the great miracle of the gospel; *that* is the great promise of Christ.

In the dozens of miracles we have examined, I have offered applications and allegories that various authors have drawn—all with the intent of making the events of the past applicable to the needs and trials of the present. I have sought to follow Nephi's council and "did liken all scriptures unto us, that it might be for our profit and learning" (1 Nephi 19:23). While fully believing in the value of the intended message of the original author of the text, I've sought to emphasize the additional value of looking for personal applications beyond the original meaning of the story, to look for ways to find personal meaning in the events of scripture that originally had nothing to do with you or I or the day in which we live. It is my hope that through this little study you have felt the Spirit speak to you regarding the miracles Christ has performed in your personal life. But it is also my hope that you have sensed the timelessness of scripture, its ability to speak to you and me today about the trials we face, and Christ's ability to lift our burdens, heal our spiritual sicknesses, and save our sin-stained souls.

NOTES

1. Kistemaker (2006), 254.
2. "Conversation With Elder Neal Maxwell," 143.

BRIEF BIOGRAPHICAL SKETCHES
OF ANCIENT AND MODERN NON-LDS SOURCES CITED

ANCIENT SOURCES

- Ambrose of Milan—Circa AD 333–97—Bishop of Milan and teacher of Augustine.
- Augustine of Hippo—AD 354–430—Bishop of Hippo and one of the most influential voices in Christianity.
- Athanasius of Alexandria—Circa AD 295–373—Bishop of Alexandria and influential figure at the Council of Nicaea.
- Bede the Venerable—Circa AD 672–735—British father who was responsible for the practice of dating events from the birth of Christ by using the designation AD, or *anno Domini* (in the year of the Lord).
- Caesarius of Arles—Circa AD 470–543—A popular sixth-century preacher and bishop of Arles.
- Chromatius—Flourished AD 400—Bishop of Aquileia and friend of St. Jerome.
- Cyril of Alexandria—AD 375–444—The patriarch of Alexandria and the driving force behind the declaration of the Council of Ephesus (AD 431) that the Virgin Mary is the Theotoks or "Mother of God."
- Ephrem the Syrian—Circa AD 306–73—A Syrian Christian commentator and composer of hymns.
- Gregory the Great—Circa AD 540–604—Influential pope, unifying source in Western Christianity, and source for the style of chant known as "Gregorian."
- Hilary of Arles—Circa AD 401–449—Archbishop of Arles and leader of the Semi-Pelagain party.
- Hilary of Poitiers—Circa AD 315–367—Bishop of Poitiers and known as the "Athanasius of the West" because of his position on the Trinity.
- Jerome—Circa AD 347–420—Translator of the Latin Vulgate Bible, and staunch defender of the dogma of the perpetual virginity of Mary.
- John Chrysostom—Circa AD 344–407—Bishop of Alexandria. Famous for his orthodoxy and his attacks on Christian laxity.
- Maximus of Turin—Died circa AD 423—Bishop of Turin, Italy.
- Origen—Circa AD 185–254—An influential expositor and theologian in Alexandria. Believed in the preexistence of the soul—a belief for which he was eventually condemned.
- Peter Chrysologus—Circa AD 380–450—Latin archbishop of Ravenna who emphasized the relationship between grace and Christian living.

- Tertullian—Circa AD 160–225—Born in Carthage, he was the church's first Latin father. Wrote of his discomfort with the laxity of some Christians.
- Theodore of Heraclea—Died circa AD 355—Pre-Nicene bishop of Thrace who sought reconciliation between Eastern and Western Christianity.
- Theodore of Mopsuestia—Circa AD 350–428—Bishop of Mopsuestia and founder of the Antiochene school of exegesis (which emphasized a literal interpretation of the scriptures).

MODERN SOURCES
- Achtemeier, Paul J.—Episcopal biblical scholar and theologian.
- Albright, William F.—Evangelical Methodist archaeologist, biblical scholar, and philologist.
- Barclay, William—Church of Scotland biblical scholar.
- Barré, Michael L.—Catholic clergyman and biblical scholar.
- Boismard, Claude (Marie-Émile)—Roman Catholic biblical scholar.
- Bowden, John—Anglian theologian.
- Brown, Raymond E.—Catholic biblical scholar and theologian.
- Browning, W. R. F.—Anglican exegete.
- Bruce, F. F.—Open Brethren biblical scholar.
- Bullinger, Ethelbert William—Anglican biblical scholar.
- Carson, D. A.—Reformed Evangelical theologian.
- Church, Leslie F.—Methodist theologian and commentator.
- Cirlot, Juan E.—Catholic hermeneutist and symbologist.
- Clarke, Adam—Methodist biblical scholar and theologian.
- Cole, R. Alan—Evangelical biblical scholar and exegete.
- Conner, Kevin J.—Leader and author in the charismatic movement of the Pentecostal faith.
- Cooper, Jean C.—Scholar of comparative religion and symbolism.
- Corbo, Virgilio C.—Catholic archaeologist.
- Craddock, Fred B.—Disciples of Christ biblical scholar.
- Cross, Frank Leslie—Anglican patristic scholar.
- Cruse, C. F.—Episcopal clergyman and translator.
- Davis, John J.—Evangelical biblical scholar.
- Donaldson, James—Scottish Episcopal patristic scholar and theologian.
- Drinkard, Joel F., Jr.—Baptist biblical scholar and theologian.
- Edwards, Douglas R.—Archeologist and biblical scholar.
- Ellis, Peter F.—Catholic biblical scholar and exegete.
- Elowsky, Joel C.—Lutheran theologian and patristic scholar.
- Farbridge, Maurice—Symbologist and scholar of Judaism.
- Farrar, Frederic—Anglican author and theologian.
- Ferguson, Everett—Church of Christ patristic scholar.

- Fitzmyer, Joseph A.—Catholic biblical scholar and theologian.
- Fontana, David—Psychologist and author.
- Ford, J. Massyngberde—Catholic biblical scholar and theologian.
- France, Richard Thomas—Anglican biblical scholar.
- Freedman, David Noel—Biblical scholar and Hebraist.
- Friedrich, Gerhard—New Testament scholar and linguist.
- Fuller, Thomas—Anglican clergyman and historian.
- Gaebelein, Frank E.—Evangelical biblical scholar and theologian.
- Habershon, Ada R.—Baptist symbologist and hymnist.
- Hall, Christopher A.—Episcopalian theologian and patristics scholar.
- Hall, James—Art historian.
- Hare, Douglas R. A.—Christian biblical scholar and church historian.
- Harrington, Daniel J.—Catholic biblical scholar.
- Harris, R. Laird—Presbyterian clergyman and biblical scholar.
- Hendriksen, William—Christian Reformed Church clergyman and biblical scholar.
- Hewitt, Hugh—Presbyterian lawyer, academic, author, and talk show host.
- Hone, William—Anglican author, publisher, and satirist.
- Hunter, Archibald Macbride—Presbyrteiran clergyman, biblical scholar and theologian.
- Jeremias, Joachim—Lutheran New Testament scholar and theologian.
- Johnson, Luke Timothy—Catholic biblical exegete and historian of Christianity.
- Johnson, Sherman E.—Episcopalian theologian and exegete.
- Johnston, Robert D.—An Assemblies of Brethren teacher and author.
- Livingstone, Elizabeth A.—Anglican scholar and theologian.
- Julien, Nadia—Author of several texts on myths and symbols.
- Just, Arthur A., Jr.—Lutheran clergyman and scholar of exegetical theology.
- Kaplan, Abraham—Jewish philosopher and scholar of Hassidic Judaism.
- Kistemaker, Simon J.—Evangelical New Testament scholar.
- Koch, Klaus—Lutheran clergyman and Old Testament scholar.
- Kselman, John S.—Catholic clergyman and biblical scholar.
- L'Engle, Madeleine—Episcopalian author of young adult fiction.
- Liefeld, Walter L.—Evangelical biblical scholar.
- Lockyer, Herbert—Evangelical biblical scholar and clergyman.
- Longenecker, Richard N.—Protestant scholar and exegete.
- Longman, Tremper—Protestant biblical scholar and symbologist.
- Mann, C. S.—Catholic biblical scholar and theologian.
- Marcus, Joel—Catholic biblical scholar and theologian.
- Martin, Francis—Catholic clergyman, exegete and patristic scholar.
- McKenzie, John L.—Catholic theologian and commentator.

- McQuade, Pamela—Christian author of popular religious texts.
- Morris, Leon—Evangelical biblical scholar and theologian.
- Murphy, Roland E.—Catholic biblical scholar and theologian.
- Nicoll, W. Robertson—Scottish Free Church author, Greek scholar and churchman.
- Fredrick W. Norris—Protestant biblical scholar and church historian.
- Oden, Thomas C.—Methodist theologian and ethicist.
- Potter, David S.—Scholar of Greek and Roman history and classics.
- Peake, Arthor S.—Methodist exegete and commentator.
- Rabinowicz, Tzvi M.—Jewish scholar of the Hassidic movement.
- Rest, Friedrich—Protestant churchman and symbologist.
- Roberts, Alexander—Presbyterian churchman and patristic scholar.
- Romeo, Joseph A.—Lutheran theologian and scholar.
- Ryken, Leland—Evangelical theologian and symbologist.
- Schaff, Philip—Protestant theologian and church historian.
- Schneemelcher, Wilhelm—Pastor in German Confessing Church and scholar of New Testament Apocrypha.
- Senior, Donald—Catholic churchman and biblical scholar.
- Simonetti, Manlio—Catholic patristic scholar.
- Sloyan, Gerard S.—Catholic theologian and commentator.
- Spurgeon, Charles H.—Particular Baptist churchman and author.
- Strange, James F.—Biblical scholar and archeologist.
- Tasker, R. V. G.—Evangelical theologian and exegete.
- Thayer, Joseph H.—Protestant churchman, theologian and exegete.
- Todeschi, Kevin J.—Lecturer and author on symbolism.
- Trench, Richard C.—Anglican churchman and theologian.
- Tresidder, Jack—Journalist and symbologist.
- Trigg, Joseph W.—Episcopal churchman and scholar.
- Tuckett, Christopher M.—Anglican churchman and biblical scholar.
- Vine, William E—Plymouth Brethren churchman, biblical scholar and theologian.
- Wessel, Walter W.—Evangelical biblical scholar and commentator.
- Whiston, William—Anglican theologian and promoter of primitive Christianity.
- Williamson, Lamar, Jr.—Presbyterian biblical scholar and theologian.
- Wilson, Walter L.—Nondenominational Christian physician who founded a theological seminary and authored a number of conservative theological texts.
- Wood, Herbert G.—Quaker theologian and biblical scholar.
- Woodward, Kenneth L.—Catholic journalist and *Newsweek Magazine* religion editor.

BIBLIOGRAPHY

Achtemeier, Paul J., ed. *Harper's Bible Dictionary*. San Francisco: Harper San Francisco, 1985.

Albright, William F., and C. S. Mann. *The Anchor Bible: Matthew*. New York: Doubleday, 1971.

Arrington, Leonard J., ed. *The Presidents of the Church*. Salt Lake City, UT: Deseret Book, 1986.

Asay, Carlos E. "Be Men!" *Ensign*, May 1992, 40–42.

Barclay, William. *The Gospel of Mathew*. Revised ed. 2 vols. Louisville, KY: Westminster John Knox, 1975.

Bednar, David A. "Converted Unto the Lord." *Ensign*, November 2012, 106–9.

Boismard, M. -É. "Stephen." Edited by David Noel Freedman. *The Anchor Bible Dictionary*. 6 vols. New York: Doubleday, 1992, 6:207–210.

Bowden, John, ed. *Encyclopedia of Christianity*. New York: Oxford University Press, 2005.

Brown, Matthew B., and Paul Thomas Smith. *Symbols in Stone: Symbolism on the Early Temples of the Restoration*. American Fork, UT: Covenant Communications, 1997.

Brown, Raymond E. *The Anchor Bible: The Gospel According to John I-XII*. New York: Doubleday, 1966.

———. *The Anchor Bible: The Gospel According to John XIII-XXI*. New York: Doubleday, 1970.

Brown, Raymond E., Joseph A. Fitzmyer, and Roland E. Murphy, eds. *The New Jerome Biblical Commentary*. Englewood Cliffs, New Jersey: Prentice Hall, 1990.

Browning, W. R. F. *The Gospel According to Saint Luke*. Norwich, England: SMC Press, 1979.

Bruce, F. F. *The Gospel of John*. Grand Rapids, MI: Eerdmans, 1994.

Bullinger, E. W. *Number in Scripture: Its Supernatural Design and Spiritual Significance*. Grand Rapids, MI: Kregel Publications, 1967.

Carson, D. A. "Matthew." Edited by Frank E. Gaebelein. *The Expositor's Bible Commentary*. 12 vols. Grand Rapids, MI: Zondervan, 1976–92, 8:1–599.

Church, Leslie F., ed. *The NIV Matthew Henry Commentary in One Volume*. Grand Rapids, MI: Zondervan, 1992.

Cirlot, J. E. *A Dictionary of Symbols*. London: Routledge & Kegan Paul Ltd., 1962.

Clarke, Adam. *The Holy Bible Containing the Old and New Testaments . . . with a Commentary and Critical Notes.* 6 vols. New York: Methodist Book Concern, 1846.

Cole, R. Alan. *Tyndale New Testament Commentaries: Mark.* Revised ed. Grand Rapids, MI: Eerdmans, 1997.

Conner, Kevin J. *Interpreting the Symbols and Types.* Revised and expanded ed. Portland, OR: City Bible Publishing, 1992.

Cooper, J. C. *An Illustrated Encyclopaedia of Traditional Symbols.* London: Thames and Hudson, 1982.

Corbo, Virgilio C. "Capernaum." Edited by David Noel Freedman. *The Anchor Bible Dictionary.* 6 vols. New York: Doubleday, 1992, 1:866–69.

Craddock, Fred B. *Interpretation—A Bible Commentary for Teaching and Preaching: Luke.* Louisville, Kentucky: John Knox Press, 1990.

Cross, Frank Leslie, and Elizabeth A. Livinstone, eds. *The Oxford Dictionary of the Christian Church.* 2d ed. New York: Oxford University Press, 1990.

Cruse, C. F., trans. *Eusebius' Ecclesiastical History.* Complete and Unabridged New Updated Edition. Peabody, MA: Hendrickson Publishers, 1998.

Davis, John J. *Biblical Numerology.* Grand Rapids, MI: Baker Book House, 2000.

Doxey, Roy W. *Latter-day Prophets and the Doctrine and Covenants.* 4 vols. Salt Lake City, UT: Deseret Book, 1978.

Draper, Richard D. *Opening the Seven Seals.* Salt Lake City, UT: Deseret Book Company, 1991.

Drinkard, Joel F. "Numbers." Edited by Paul J. Achtemeier. *Harper's Bible Dictionary.* San Francisco: Harper San Francisco, 1985, 711–12.

Edwards, Douglas R. "Gennesaret." Edited by David Noel Freedman. *The Anchor Bible Dictionary.* New York: Doubleday, 1992, 2:963.

Ellis, Peter F. *The Genius of John: A Composition-Critical Commentary on the Fourth Gospel.* Collegeville, MN: The Liturgical Press, 1984.

Elowsky, Joel C., ed. *Ancient Christian Commentary on Scripture: John 11–21.* Downers Grove, IL: InterVarsity Press, 2007.

———. *Ancient Christian Commentary on Scripture: John 1–10.* Downers Grove, IL: InterVarsity Press, 2006.

Farbridge, Maurice. *Studies in Biblical and Semitic Symbolism.* London: Kegan Paul, Trench, Trubner, & Co., 1923.

Farrar, Frederic. *Life of Christ.* Portland, OR: Fountain Publications, 1964.

Ferguson, Everett, ed. *Encyclopedia of Early Christianity*. New York: Garland Publishing, 1990.

Firmage, Edwin. "Zoology." Edited by David Noel Freedman. *The Anchor Bible Dictionary*. New York: Doubleday, 1992, 6:1109–67.

Fitzmyer, Joseph. *The Anchor Bible: The Acts of the Apostles*. New York: Doubleday, 1989.

———. *The Anchor Bible: The Gospel According to Luke X–XXIV*. New York: Doubleday, 1985.

———. *The Anchor Bible: The Gospel According to Luke I–IX*. New York: Doubleday, 1970.

Fontana, David. *The Secret Language of Symbols*. San Francisco, CA: Chronicle Books, 1994.

Ford, J. Massyngberde. *The Anchor Bible: Revelation*. New York: Doubleday, 1975.

France, R. T. *Tyndale New Testament Commentaries: Matthew*. Grand Rapids, MI: Eerdmans, 1997.

Freedman, David Noel, ed. *The Anchor Bible Dictionary*. 6 vols. New York: Doubleday, 1992.

Friedrich, Gerhard, ed. *Theological Dictionary of the New Testament*. 10 vols. Grand Rapids, MI: Eerdmans, 1983.

Fuller, Thomas. *Pisgah Sight of Palestine*. London: William Tegg, 1869.

Gaebelein, Frank E., ed. *The Expositor's Bible Commentary*. 12 vols. Grand Rapids, MI: Zondervan, 1976–92.

Gaskill, Alonzo L. *The Lost Language of Symbolism: An Essential Guide for Recognizing and Interpreting Symbols of the Gospel*. Salt Lake City, UT: Deseret Book, 2003.

Givens, Terryl L., *When Souls Had Wings: Pre-Mortal Existence in Western Thought*. New York: Oxford University Press, 2010.

Habershon, Ada R. *Study of the Miracles*. Grand Rapids, MI: Kregel Publications, 1975.

———. *Study of the Types*. Grand Rapids, MI: Kregel Publications, 1974.

Hall, James. *Dictionary of Subjects and Symbols in Art*. New York: Harper & Row, 1974.

Hare, Douglas R. A. *Interpretation—A Bible Commentary for Teaching and Preaching: Matthew*. Louisvillem, KY: John Knox Press, 1993.

Harrington, Daniel J. "The Gospel According to Mark." Edited by Raymond E. Brown, Joseph A. Fitzmyer, and Roland E. Murphy. *The New Jerome Biblical Commentary*. Englewood Cliffs, New Jersey: Prentice Hall, 1990, 596–629.

Harris, R. Laird. "Leviticus." Edited by Frank E. Gaebelein. *The Expositor's Bible Commentary.* 12 vols. Grand Rapids, MI: Zondervan, 1976–92, 2:499–654.

Hendricksen, William. *New Testament Commentary: Exposition of the Gospel According to John.* Grand Rapids, MI: Baker Books House, 1953.

Hewitt, Hugh. *Searching for God in America.* Dallas, TX: Word Publishing, 1996.

Hiatt, Duane E. "Follow the Prophet." *Children's Songbook.* Salt Lake City, UT: Deseret Book, 1991.

Hinckley, Gordon B. *Teachings of Gordon B. Hinckley.* Salt Lake City, UT: Deseret Book, 1997.

Holland, Jeffrey R. *Broken Things to Mend.* Salt Lake City, UT: Deseret Book, 2008.

Holland, Patricia T. "Walking on Water." BYU Devotional, January 31, 1984. *BYU Speeches of the Year.* Provo, UT: Brigham Young University, 1985, 1–3.

Holzapfel, Richard Neitzel, and Kent P. Jackson, eds. Provo, UT: Brigham Young University Religious Studies Center and Deseret Book, 2011.

Hone, William, comp. *The Lost Books of the Bible: Being all the Gospels, Epistles, and Other Pieces Now Extant Attributed in the First Four Centuries.* New York: Bell Publishing, 1979.

Howick, E. Keith. *The Miracles of Jesus the Messiah.* St. George, UT: Wind River Publishing, 2003.

Hunter, A. M. *The Gospel According to Saint Mark: A Commentary.* New York: Collier Books, 1962.

Hunter, Howard W. "The Beacon in the Harbor of Peace." *Ensign,* November 1992, 18–19.

———. "Master, the Tempest is Raging." *Ensign,* November 1984, 32–35.

———. "Reading the Scriptures." *Ensign,* November 1979, 64–66.

Hyde, Orson. "The Marriage Relations." *Journal of Discourses,* 2:75–87.

———. "Man the Head of Woman, etc." *Journal of Discourses.* 2:257–63.

Jensen, Andrew. *LDS Biographical Encyclopedia.* 4 vols. Salt Lake City, UT: Andrew Jensen Memorial Association, 1901–36.

Jeremias, Joachim. *Jerusalem in the Time of Jesus.* Philadelphia, PA: Fortress Press, 1969.

Johnson, Luke Timothy. *Sacra Pagina: The Acts of the Apostles.* Collegeville, MN: The Liturgical Press, 1992.

————. *Sacra Pagina: The Gospel According to Luke.* Collegeville, MN: The Liturgical Press, 1991.

Johnson, Sherman E. *A Commentary on the Gospel According to St. Mark.* New York: Harper & Brothers, 1960.

Johnston, Robert D. *Numbers in the Bible: God's Design in Biblical Numerology.* Grand Rapids, MI: Kregel Publications, 1990.

Julien, Nadia. *The Mammoth Dictionary of Symbols.* New York: Carroll & Graf Publishers, 1996.

Just, Arthur A. Jr., ed. *Ancient Christian Commentary on Scripture: Luke.* Thomas C. Oden, general editor. Downers Grove, IL: InterVarsity Press, 2003.

Kaplan, Abraham. "The Meaning of Ritual: Comparisons." In Truman G. Madsen. *Reflections on Mormonism: Judaeo-Christian Parallels.* Provo, UT: Brigham Young University Religious Studies Center, 1978, 37–56.

Kimball, Spencer W. *The Teachings of Spencer W. Kimball.* Salt Lake City, UT: Bookcraft, 1998.

————. *The Church News.* "Conference Issues" 1970–87, 12.

Kistemaker, Simon J. *The Miracles: Exploring the Mystery of Jesus's Divine Works.* Grand Rapids, MI: Baker Books, 2006.

Koch, Klaus. *The Rediscovery of Apocalyptic: A Polemical Work on a Neglected Area of Biblical Studies and its Damaging Effects on Theology and Philosophy.* Translated by Margaret Kohl. Naperville, IL: Alec R. Allenson, 1972.

Kselman, John S., and Michael L. Barré. "Psalms," R. Brown, J. Fitzmyer, and R. Murphy, eds. *The New Jerome Biblical Commentary.* New Jersey: Prentice Hall, 1990, 523–52.

LDS Bible Dictionary. Salt Lake City, UT: Intellectual Reserve, 1979.

L'Engle, Madeleine. *Walking on Water.* New York: Bantam Books, 1992.

Liefeld, Walter L. "Luke." Frank E. Gaebelein, ed. *The Expositor's Bible Commentary.* 12 vols. Grand Rapids, MI: Zondervan, 1976–92, 8:795–1059.

Lockyer, Herbert. *All The Miracles of the Bible.* Grand Rapids, MI: Zondervan, 1965.

Longenecker, Richard N. "The Acts of the Apostles." Frank E. Gaebelein, ed. *The Expositor's Bible Commentary.* 12 vols. Grand Rapids, MI: Zondervan, 1976–92, 9:205–573.

Ludlow, Daniel H., ed. *Encyclopedia of Mormonism.* 4 vols. New York: Macmillian, 1992, 4:1447–50.

Madsen, Truman G. *Joseph Smith the Prophet*. Salt Lake City, UT: Bookcraft, 1989.

———. *Reflections on Mormonism: Judaeo-Christian Parallels*. Provo, UT: Brigham Young University Religious Studies Center, 1978.

Mann, C. S. *The Anchor Bible; Mark*. New York: Doubleday, 1986.

Marcus, Joel. *The Anchor Bible: Mark 1–8*. New York: Doubleday, 2000.

Martin, Francis. *Ancient Christian Commentary on Scripture: Acts*. Downers Grove, IL: InterVarsity Press, 2006.

Matthews, Robert J. *The Miracles of Jesus*. Provo, UT: Brigham Young University, 1969.

Maxwell, Neal A. "Plow in Hope." *Ensign*, May 2001, 59–61.

———. "A Conversation With Elder Neal Maxwell." In Hugh Hewitt. *Searching for God in America*. Dallas, TX: Word Publishing, 1996, 119–44.

———. *The Neal A. Maxwell Quote Book*. Cory H. Maxwell, comp. Salt Lake City, UT: Bookcraft, 1992.

McConkie, Bruce R. *Doctrinal New Testament Commentary*. 3 vols. Salt Lake City, UT: Bookcraft, 1987–88.

———. *A New Witness for the Articles of Faith*. Salt Lake City, UT: Deseret Book, 1985.

———. *The Mortal Messiah*. 4 vols. Salt Lake City, UT: Deseret Book, 1980–81.

———. *The Millennial Messiah*. Salt Lake City, UT: Deseret Book, 1982.

———. *Mormon Doctrine*. 2d ed. Salt Lake City, UT: Bookcraft, 1979.

McConkie, Joseph Fielding. *Gospel Symbolism*. Salt Lake City, UT: Bookcraft, 1985.

McConkie, Joseph Fielding, and Donald W. Parry. *A Guide to Scriptural Symbols*. Salt Lake City, UT: Bookcraft, 1990.

McKenzie, John L. *Dictionary of the Bible*. Milwaukee, WI: The Bruce Publishing Company, 1965.

McQuade, Pamela. *The Top 100 Miracles of the Bible*. Uhrichsville, OH: Barbour Publishing, 2008.

Moore, Richard G. "Teaching and Being Taught." *Ensign*, June 2007, 36–37.

Morris, Leon. *Reflections on the Gospel of John*. Peabody, MA: Hendrickson Publisher, 2000.

———. *Tyndale New Testament Commentaries: Luke*. Revised ed. Grand Rapids, MI: Eerdmans, 1999.

———. *The New International Commentary on the New Testament: The Gospel According to John*. Revised ed. Grand Rapids, MI: Eerdmans, 1995.

Nibley, Hugh. *Temple and Cosmos: Beyond this Ignorant Present.* Provo, UT: Foundation for Ancient Research and Mormon Studies, 1992.

———. *Approaching Zion.* Provo, UT: Foundation for Ancient Research and Mormon Studies, 1989.

Nicoll, W. Robertson. *The Expositor's Greek Testament.* 5 vols. Grand Rapids, MI: Eerdmans, 1983.

Norris, Fredrick W. "Antioch." Edited by Everett Ferguson. *Encyclopedia of Early Christianity.* New York: Garland Publishing, 1990, 52–54.

Oaks, Dallin H. "Healing the Sick." *Ensign,* May 2010, 47–50.

———. "Scripture Reading and Revelation." *Ensign,* January 1995, 7–9.

Oden, Thomas C., and Christopher A. Hall. *Ancient Christian Commentary on Scripture: Mark.* Downers Grove, IL: InterVarsity Press, 1998.

Ogden, D. Kelly, and Andrew W. Skinner. *Verse by Verse: The Four Gospels.* Salt Lake City, UT: Deseret Book, 2006.

———. *Verse by Verse: Acts Through Revelation.* Salt Lake City, UT: Deseret Book, 1998.

Packer, Boyd K. *Mine Errand From the Lord: Selections from the Sermons and Writings of Boyd K. Packer.* Compiled by Clyde J. Williams. Salt Lake City, UT: Deseret Book, 2008.

———. *Conference Report,* April 1971, 122–25.

Parry, Jay, and Donald Parry. *Understanding the Book of Revelation.* Salt Lake City, UT: Deseret Book, 1889.

Potter, David S. "Lystra." Edited by David Noel Freedman. *The Anchor Bible Dictionary.* 6 vols. New York: Doubleday, 1992, 4:426–27.

Pratt, Orson. "Revelation from Heaven." *Journal of Discourses,* 15:99–110.

———. "A Double Birthday." *Journal of Discourses,* 21:303–16.

Peake, Arthur S., ed. *A Commentary on the Bible.* New York: Thomas Nelson and Sons, 1919.

Rabinowicz, Tzvi M. *The Encyclopedia of Hasidism.* Maryland: Jason Aronson Publishers, 1977.

Rest, Friedrich. *Our Christian Symbols.* New York: The Pilgrims Press, 1987.

Roberts, Alexander, and James Donaldson, eds. *Ante-Nicene Fathers.* 10 vols. Peabody, MA: Hendrickson Publishers, 1994.

Roberts, B. H., ed. *History of the Church of Jesus Christ of Latter-day Saints.* 7 vols. Salt Lake City, UT: Deseret Book Company, 1978.

Romeo, Joseph A. "Gematria and John 21:11—The Children of God." *Journal of Biblical Literature,* 97, 1978, 263–64.

Ryken, Leland, James C. Wilhoit, and Tremper Longman III, eds. *Dictionary of Biblical Imagery*. Downers Grove, IL: InterVarsity Press, 1998.

Schaff, Philip. *Nicene and Post-Nicene Fathers—First Series*. 14 vols. Peabody, Massachusetts: Hendrickson Publishers, 2004.

———. *History of the Christin Church*. 8 vols. Peabody, MA: Hendrickson Publishers, 1996.

Schaff, Philip, and Henry Wace, eds. *Nicene and Post-Nicene Fathers—Second Series*. 14 vols. Peabody, MA: Hendrickson Publishers, 2004.

Schneemelcher, Wilhelm, ed. *New Testament Apocrypha*. Revised ed. 2 vols. Louisville, KY: Westminster John Knox, 2003.

Senior, Donald. *Abingdon New Testament Commentaries: Matthew*. Nashville, TN: Abingdon Press, 1998.

Simonetti, Manlio. *Ancient Christian Commentary on Scripture: Matthew 14–28*. Downers Grove, IL: InterVarsity Press, 2002.

———. *Ancient Christian Commentary on Scripture: Matthew 1–13*. Downers Grove, IL: InterVarsity Press, 2001.

Sloyan, Gerard S. *Interpretation—A Bible Commentary for Teaching and Preaching: John*. Atlanta, GA: John Knox Press, 1988.

Smith, Joseph. *History of the Church of Jesus Christ of Latter-day Saints*. 7 vols. Salt Lake City, UT: Deseret Book, 1978.

Smith, Joseph F. *Gospel Doctrine*. Salt Lake City, UT: Bookcraft, 1998.

Smith, Joseph Fielding Jr., comp. *Teachings of the Prophet Joseph Smith*. Salt Lake City, UT: Deseret Book, 1976.

———. "The Twelve Apostles," *An Address to Seminary and Institute Faculty*. Salt Lake City, UT: 1958. Cited in Roy W. Doxey. *Latter-day Prophets and the Doctrine and Covenants*. 4 vols. Salt Lake City, UT: Deseret Book, 1978, 4:28.

Smith, Mick. *The Book of Revelation: Plain, Pure, and Simple*. Salt Lake City, UT: Bookcraft, 1998.

Snow, Eliza R. *Biography of Lorenzo Snow*. Salt Lake City: Deseret News, 1884.

Spurgeon, Charles Haddon. *Spurgeon's Sermons*. 10 vols in 5 books. Grand Rapids, MI: Baker Book House, 2007.

Strange, James F. "Cana of Galilee." Edited by David Noel Freedman. *The Anchor Bible Dictionary*. 6 vols. New York: Doubleday, 1992, 1:827.

Swift, Charles L. "Three Stories." *My Redeemer Lives*. Edited by Richard Neitzel Holzapfel and Kent P. Jackson. Provo, UT: Brigham Young University Religious Studies Center and Deseret Book, 2011, 125–46.

———. Doctoral Dissertation. *"I Have Dreamed a Dream": Typological Images of Teaching and Learning in the Vision of the Tree of Life.* Provo, UT: Brigham Young University, 2003.

Talmage, James E. *Jesus the Christ.* Salt Lake City, UT: The Church of Jesus Christ of Latter-day Saints, 1981.

Tasker, R. V. G. *Tyndale New Testament Commentaries: John.* Grand Rapids, MI: Eerdmans, 1997.

Taylor, Jeremy. In Richard C. Trench. *Notes on the Miracles of the Lord.* Grand Rapids, MI: Eerdmans, 1962.

Tenney, Merrill C. "The Gospel of John." Edited by Frank E. Gaebelein. *The Expositor's Bible Commentary.* 12 vols. Grand Rapids, MI: Zondervan, 1976–92, 9:1–203.

Thayer, Joseph H. *Thayer's Greek-English Lexicon of the New Testament.* Peabody, MA: Hendrickson Publishers, 1999.

Todeschi, Kevin J. *The Encyclopedia of Symbolism.* New York: The Berkley Publishing Group, 1995.

Trench, Richard C. *Notes on the Miracles of the Lord.* Grand Rapids, MI: Eerdmans, 1962.

Tresidder, Jack. *Symbols and Their Meanings.* London: Duncan Baird Publishers, 2000.

Trigg, Joseph W. "Allegory." Edited by Everett Ferguson. *Encyclopedia of Early Christianity.* New York: Garland Publishing, 1990, 23–26.

Tuckett, Chriostopher M. "Q (Gospel Source)." Edited by David Noel Freedman. *The Anchor Bible Dictionary.* 6 vols. New York: Doubleday, 1992, 5:567–72.

Vine, William E. *An Expository Dictionary of the New Testament.* Westwood, New Jersey: Fleming H. Revell, 1966.

Walker, Ronald W. "Heber J. Grant." Edited by Leonard J. Arrington. *The Presidents of the Church.* Salt Lake City, UT: Deseret Book, 1986, 211–48.

Wessel, Walter W. "Mark." Edited by Frank E. Gaebelein. *The Expositor's Bible Commentary.* 12 vols. Grand Rapids, MI: Zondervan, 1976–92, 8:601–793.

Wheelock, Cyrus H., and Thomas H. Bayly. "Ye Elders of Israel." *Hymns of the Church of Jesus Christ of Latter-day Saints.* Revised ed. Salt Lake City, UT: Intellectual Reserve, 1998, no. 319.

Whiston, William, trans. *The Complete Works of Josephus.* Grand Rapids, MI: Kregel Publications, 1981.

Williamson, Lamar Jr. *Interpretation—A Bible Commentary for Teaching and Preaching: Mark.* Atlanta, GA: John Knox Press, 1983.

Wilson, Walter L. *A Dictionary of Bible Types*. Peabody, MA: Hendrickson Publishers, 1999.

Wood, H. G. "Mark." Edited by Arthur S. Peake. *A Commentary on the Bible*. New York: Thomas Nelson and Sons, 1919, 681–99.

Woodruff, Wilford. *Wilford Woodruff Journal*. Edited by Scott G. Kenney. 9 vols. Salt Lake City, UT: Signature Book, 1985.

———. *Leaves of my Journal: Third Book of the Faith-Promoting Series*. Salt Lake City, UT: Juvenile Instructor Office, 1881.

Woodward, Kenneth L. *The Book of Miracles: The Meaning of the Miracle Stories in Christianity, Judaism, Buddhism, Hinduism, Islam*. New York: Simon and Schuster, 2000.

Young, Brigham. *Discourses of Brigham Young*. Edited by John A. Widtsoe. Salt Lake City, UT: Bookcraft, 1998.

Young, Brigham. "Increase of Saints . . ." *Journal of Discourses*, 15:135–39.

INDEX

ABOUT the AUTHOR

Alonzo L. Gaskill is a professor of Church history and doctrine at Brigham Young University. He holds a bachelor's degree in philosophy, a master's in theology, and a PhD in biblical studies. Brother Gaskill has taught at BYU since 2003. Prior to coming to BYU, he served in a variety of assignments within the Church Educational System—most recently as the director of the LDS Institute of Religion at Stanford University (1995–2003).